SOCIETY FOR NEW TESTAMENT STUDIES
MONOGRAPH SERIES

GENERAL EDITOR
MATTHEW BLACK, D.D., F.B.A.

ASSOCIATE EDITOR
R. McL. WILSON

28

JESUS AND THE LAW
IN THE SYNOPTIC TRADITION

JESUS AND THE LAW
IN THE SYNOPTIC TRADITION

ROBERT BANKS

Lecturer in History
School of History, Philosophy and Politics
Macquarie University

CAMBRIDGE UNIVERSITY PRESS

CAMBRIDGE

LONDON, NEW YORK AND MELBOURNE

Published by the Syndics of the Cambridge University Press
The Pitt Building, Trumpington Street, Cambridge CB2 1RP
Bentley House, 200 Euston Road, London NW1 2DB
32 East 57th Street, New York, NY 10022, USA
296 Beaconsfield Parade, Middle Park, Melbourne 3206, Australia

© Cambridge University Press 1975

Library of Congress Cataloging in Publication Data
Banks, Robert J.
Jesus and the Law in the Synoptic Tradition
(Monograph series – Society for New Testament Studies; 28)
A revision of the author's thesis, Cambridge, 1969
Bibliography: p. 264
Includes indexes
1 Jesus Christ – Attitude towards Jewish law
2 Law (Theology) – Biblical teaching
3 Jewish law
I Title
II Series: Studiorum Novi Testamenti Societas. Monograph series; 28
BT590.J34B36 1975 241'.2 75-7215
ISBN 0 521 20789 4

Printed in Great Britain by
Western Printing Services Ltd
Bristol

CONTENTS

v

CONTENTS

PREFACE

This book has its basis in a doctoral dissertation accepted by the University of Cambridge early in 1969. In its revision for publication, which was carried out in 1971, I endeavoured to take full account of literature written on the subject since the thesis had been submitted. Due to an unavoidable delay in publishing, I was later able to include reference to the bulk of the relevant material that appeared up until the beginning of 1973, though in this case only in the footnotes.

But for the encouragement of Dr Leon Morris of Ridley College, Melbourne, the way to pursuing research in England would have been considerably more difficult and it was Dr D. B. Knox of Moore College, Sydney, who suggested the idea of Liberty in the New Testament as a fruitful area of study. Financially, I received considerable help from the Tyndale Fellowship for Biblical Research and also appreciated the fine facilities provided for work of this nature at Tyndale House, Cambridge. Assistance was also received from various funds in the University of Cambridge enabling me to spend two extremely profitable terms at the Universities of Basle and Zürich towards the end of my research period. The Anglican Diocese of Sydney, the Inter-Varsity Fellowship of Australia and Moore Theological College also made helpful contributions.

Personally, I am especially grateful to Professor Eduard Schweizer for the stimulation of his seminar in Zürich. Methodologically this was of great benefit. Various comments of Professor J. D. M. Derrett of London University, who was kind enough to recommend the book for publication, prevented me from committing some errors in my treatment of the Jewish background to the gospel material. Above all, however, I am indebted to Professor G. W. H. Lampe for his general guidance throughout the initial course of research. Naturally he cannot be held responsible for the finished product. I would also like to record my appreciation of the typing assistance given by my mother, Mrs E. M. Banks, and by Miss W. Gordon during various stages of the book's preparation and revision. And then the customary, but absolutely necessary, word of thanks to my wife and children who have lived for so many years in the shadow of this book and have given every encouragement throughout.

To the editors of the *Expository Times* and the *Journal of Biblical Literature* and to the managing director of the Paternoster Press I record my indebtedness for their permission to incorporate in this volume material that has been previously published by them, viz. 'Jesus and Custom', *Expository Times*, 84 (1973), 265–9; 'Matthew's Understanding of the Law: Authenticity and Interpretation in Matthew 5:17–20', *Journal of Biblical Literature*, 93 (1974), 226–42; 'The Eschatological Role of Law in Pre- and Part-Christian Jewish Thought', *Reconciliation and Hope: New Testament Essays on Atonement and Eschatology presented to L. L. Morris on his 60th Birthday* (Paternoster and Eerdmans, 1974), pp. 173–85.

ROBERT BANKS

ABBREVIATIONS

REFERENCE WORKS:

A/G — W. F. Arndt and F. W. Gingrich, *A Greek–English Lexicon of the New Testament* (Cambridge, ET 1957)

Bill. — P. Billerbeck and H. L. Strack, *Kommentar zum Neuen Testament aus Talmud und Midrasch* (Munich, 1922–8)

DB — ed. J. Hastings, *Dictionary of the Bible* (Edinburgh, 1909)

Funk — F. Blass, ed. A. Debrunner (trans. R. W. Funk), *A Greek Grammar of the New Testament* (Cambridge, 1961)

HDB — ed. J. Hastings, *Hastings' Dictionary of the Bible* (Edinburgh, 1900)

IDB — *Interpreters' Dictionary of the Bible* (New York, 1962)

JE — *The Jewish Encyclopaedia* (New York, 1901–6)

L/S — H. G. Liddell and R. Scott, *A Greek–English Lexicon*, rev. H. S. Jones and R. McKenzie (Oxford, 1948)

Moulton — J. H. Moulton, W. F. Howard and N. Turner, *Grammar of New Testament Greek* (Edinburgh, 1908, 1929, 1963)

M/M — J. H. Moulton and G. Milligan, *The Vocabulary of the Greek Testament* (London, 1914–29)

PCB — ed. M. Black and H. H. Rowley, *Peake's Commentary on the Bible* (London, 1962)

RGG — *Die Religion in Geschichte und Gegenwart* (Tübingen, 1957³)

TDNT — *Theological Dictionary of the New Testament* (Grand Rapids, 1964–), ET of following

TWNT — *Theologisches Wörterbuch zum Neuen Testament* (Stuttgart, 1933–)

PERIODICALS:

AJT — *American Journal of Theology*

Ang. — *Angelos*

ASTI — *Annual of the Swedish Theological Institute*

ATR — *Anglican Theological Review*

BA — *Biblical Archaeologist*

Bib. — *Biblica*

Bib.Tr. — *Bible Translator*

BJRL — *Bulletin of the John Rylands Library*

BS — *Bibliotheca Sacra*

BVC — *Bible et Vie Chrétienne*

BW — *Biblical World*

BZ — *Biblische Zeitschrift*

CBQ — *Catholic Biblical Quarterly*

EQ — *Evangelical Quarterly*

ET — *Expository Times*

Exp. — *Expositor*

Ev. Th.	*Evangelische Theologie*
HTR	*Harvard Theological Review*
HUCA	*Hebrew Union College Annual*
IEJ	*Israel Exploration Journal*
Int.	*Interpretation*
JBL	*Journal of Biblical Literature*
JJS	*Journal of Jewish Studies*
JJSoc.	*Jewish Journal of Sociology*
JQR	*Jewish Quarterly Review*
JR	*Journal of Religion*
JTS	*Journal of Theological Studies*
JTVI	*Journal of the Transactions of the Victoria Institute*
Jud.	*Judaica*
KD	*Kerugma und Dogma*
MGWJ	*Monatschrift für die Geschichte und Wissenschaft des Judentums*
NKZ	*Neue kirchliche Zeitschrift*
NRT	*Nouvelle Revue Théologique*
NT	*Novum Testamentum*
NTS	*New Testament Studies*
Or. Sy.	*L'Orient Syrien*
RB	*Revue Biblique*
Rech. SR	*Recherches de Science Religieuse*
RHPR	*Revue d'Histoire et de Philosophie Religieuses*
RQ	*Revue de Qumran*
RTP	*Revue de Théologie et de Philosophie*
Scr.	*Scripture*
SJT	*Scottish Journal of Theology*
St. Ev.	*Studia Evangelica*
St. Th.	*Studia Theologica*
Th.	*Theology*
TL	*Theologische Literaturzeitung*
TSK	*Theologische Studien und Kritiken*
Tyn. B.	*Tyndale Bulletin*
TS	*Theologische Studien*
TZ	*Theologische Zeitschrift*
VT	*Vetus Testamentum*
WTJ	*Westminster Theological Journal*
ZAW	*Zeitschrift für die alttestamentliche Wissenschaft*
ZEE	*Zeitschrift für evangelische Ethik*
ZNW	*Zeitschrift für die neuetestamentliche Wissenschaft*
ZTK	*Zeitschrift für Theologie und Kirche*

INTRODUCTION

The struggle between law and liberty forms one of the major threads of human history and, paradoxically enough in view of the victories the latter is supposed to have won, it is a conflict that is particularly characteristic of our own age. At present, the ideal of personal independence and the vision of the free society are again exercising the minds of men, so much so that in some circles the reality of advances already made has been openly challenged. Hand in hand with this call for individual and social self-determination has gone a denunciation of all that would bind and restrict human freedom. Authoritarianism and regimentation, institutionalism and bureaucracy, law and custom, all have come under criticism and judgment. In other quarters, however, a discernible reaction to such a view has begun to assert itself on the ethical scene, with the result that 'law and order' has become one of the central issues of the day.

Christian thinkers have by no means been exempt from the ideas and tendencies that surround them and, though initially lagging behind the mood of the age, have recently begun to apply themselves to the issues it raises. Thus the New Theology has brought with it a New Morality keenly attuned to the ears of the time, in which such conceptions as law and love, structure and freedom, are often as radically polarised as in much secular literature. At the same time, this challenge to traditional patterns of personal and social behaviour has led other christian thinkers to appeal for the maintenance of those long-standing ethical norms and rules that have formed the basis of christian attitudes and christian morality in the past.

From all this, a study of Jesus' attitude to the Law may well seem far removed. Yet this is hardly the case, for both sides in the current christian debate invoke his example in support of their views. Whether they are contending for the 'new' morality or the 'old', for the relaxation of traditional christian prescriptions or their preservation, the activity of Jesus is presented as the paradigm for the one course or the other. This appeal to Christ is well-founded. In his day, contemporary interpretations

I

of the Jewish Law provided the main context within which his teaching was formulated and he was frequently constrained to define his position in relation to them. The gospels contain ample evidence of the struggle that ensued throughout his ministry, ultimately resulting in its termination.

Although many of the specific questions agitating the modern mind differ significantly from those that confronted him in the course of his ministry, a study of Jesus' attitude to the particular moral and legal concerns of his time does supply us with the fundamental principles from which an understanding of contemporary issues can begin. To neglect this material, or to be content with merely superficial interpretations of it, as has frequently been the case on both sides of the dispute, would be a considerable mistake. This examination of Jesus' attitude to the Jewish Law, then, is partly intended as a preliminary contribution to this wider discussion. However, as its title indicates, it is primarily concerned with the specialised investigation of the question that is the province of biblical exegesis, and it is to that aspect of the matter that we must now turn.

The issue of Jesus' attitude to the Jewish Law has, of course, long been a subject of fascination to New Testament scholars. At present their interest shows little sign of abating, though the way in which the evidence is handled, and the perspective from which the matter is approached, has over the years undergone considerable alteration. There have been three distinct stages of the enquiry which, not surprisingly, correspond to the different phases through which the quest for the historical Jesus has passed. In each case, they have been accompanied by a significant revolution in exegetical method.[1]

---

[1] A full survey of the considerable body of material that has grown up around the subject and a detailed account of the course which the debate has taken has yet to be attempted. In the meantime, however, a beginning has recently been made by K. Berger, 'Die Gesetzesauslegung Jesu' (Diss., 1968), pp. 5–83, now summarised in K. Berger, *Die Gesetzesauslegung Jesu. Teil I: Markus und Parallelen* (1972), pp. 3–11, while W. E. Keller, 'The Authority of Jesus as reflected in Mark 2.1 – 3.6' (Diss., 1968), provides a selective history of interpretation of this aspect of the question. For a good summary of the Jewish discussion up till the beginning of the postwar period, only introduced in the following discussion where it has moved into the centre of the New Testament debate, see J. Jocz, *The Jewish People and Jesus Christ* (1949), pp. 15–42, 286–90. A

In the century following the rise of historico-critical investigation, concentration on an historical Jesus stripped of supernatural and eschatological characteristics brought with it great interest in his relationship to the Law. It was probably the most discussed aspect of his ministry. Whereas preceding orthodox theology had viewed his teaching as an 'exposition' of Mosaic commands,[1] the new liberal enquiry, while continuing to affirm that no abrogation of the Law had occurred, spoke rather in terms of Jesus' penetrating behind the letter of the Law to its inner moral and spiritual principles.[2] Later in the century both a distinction between his private and public teaching and his development from a more to a less conservative position were advocated as solutions to the problem raised by the detection of apparent discrepancies in his sayings concerned with the Law.[3] Meanwhile, others began to argue that, in isolated sayings at least, an abrogation of the Law was involved.[4] An attempt was also made to reconcile elements of continuity and

serious Islamic critique has now also been supplied by Isma'il Ragi A. al Fariqui, *Christian Ethics: A Historical and Systematic Analysis of its Dominant Ideas* (1967), pp. 50–136.

[1] On the earliest discussions of the Church Fathers see now G. Bourgeault, *Décalogue et morale chrétienne: Enquête Patristique sur l'utilisation et l'interpretation chrétienne du décalogue de c. 60 à c. 220* (1971). A convenient outline of later Catholic and Protestant attitudes, and of the difficulties inherent in their position, is to be found in H. K. McArthur, *Understanding the Sermon on the Mount* (1961), pp. 26ff. The views of the Puritans are especially treated by E. F. Kevan, *The Grace of Law* (1964). For an attempt at a comprehensive survey see now B. Reike, *Die Zehn Worte in Geschichte und Gegenwart* (1972).

[2] Among the first to speak in this manner were H. S. Reimarus, *Von dem Zwecke Jesu und seiner Jünger* (1778); D. F. Strauss, *Das Leben Jesu* (1837); A. Ritschl, *Die Entstehung der altkatholischen Kirche* (1850); and F. C. Baur, *Vorlesungen über neutestamentliche Theologie* (1864). Later see especially R. Mackintosh, *Christ and the Jewish Law* (1886) and A. Harnack, 'Hat Jesus das alttestamentliche Gesetz abgeschafft?', *Aus Wissenschaft und Leben*, II, 227–36. The most forceful restatement of the traditional Protestant view during this period came from P. Fairbairn, *The Revelation of Law in Scripture* (1869).

[3] The first was suggested by J. Ph. Glock, *Die Gesetzesfrage im Leben Jesu* (1885), and the latter by E. Jacob, *Jesu Stellung zum mosaischen Gesetz* (1892); H. J. Holtzmann, *Lehrbuch der neutestamentlichen Theologie* (1896) and E. Klostermann, *Jesu Stellung zum Alten Testament* (1904).

[4] So especially A. J. Meinhold, *Jesus und das Alte Testament* (1896) and M. Kähler, *Jesus und das Alte Testament* (1896). Later K. Benz, *Die Stellung*

discontinuity between Jesus' teaching and the Law through use of the conception of 'fulfilment'.[1] At the end of the period, with the introduction of comparative religious and eschatological ideas into the discussion, a new emphasis on the sovereignty of Jesus over the Law began to make itself felt.[2]

A new approach to the issue was adopted through the serious application of form-critical criteria to the synoptic texts, for this led to a new interest in the rôle of the earliest christian communities in preserving and transmitting the original message. The first result of this procedure was to offer a different solution to the presence of discrepancies in the records, for these could now be attributed to divergences in outlook among the different churches. The residue of genuine sayings was then variously interpreted. The earlier liberal formulation of the question was again advanced, now usually accompanied by an admission of Jesus' subordination or occasional abrogation of at least the ritual commands.[3] Others, in comparison with Pharisaic and Qumran teaching, spoke instead of a 'radicalisation' of the Law which involved an occasional setting aside of its less significant commands.[4] Some conservative scholars, insisting that the teaching of Jesus did not contradict the intent of the Old Testament demands, nevertheless agreed that it went beyond

---

Jesu zum alttestamentlichen Gesetz (1914) and J. Hänel, *Der Schriftbegriff Jesu* (1919) went further and claimed that Jesus expressed a consistently hostile attitude towards the Law throughout his ministry.

[1] M. S. Terrey, 'The Old Testament and the Christ', *AJT*, 10 (1906), 233–50 and F. Barth, *Die Hauptprobleme des Lebens Jesu* (1911).

[2] This was particularly emphasised by E. Schürer, *Das messianische Selbstbewusstsein Jesu Christi* (1903) and A. Schlatter, *Die Theologie des Neuen Testaments* (1909–10). On the other hand G. Kittel, *Jesus und die Rabbinen* (1914²), drew a distinction between the teaching of Jesus, to which his contemporaries offered parallels, and the uniqueness of his person.

[3] Most comprehensively by B. H. Branscomb, *Jesus and the Law of Moses* (1930) but also by T. W. Manson, 'Jesus, Paul and the Law', *Judaism and Christianity* (ed. E. I. J. Rosenthal, 1938), III, 125–41 and in his subsequent writings; A. Wilder, *Eschatology and Ethics in the Teaching of Jesus* (1950²); and, most recently, R. Schnackenburg, *The Moral Teaching of the New Testament* (ET 1965). Many others could be cited.

[4] Thus, for example, W. Grundmann, *Jesus der Galiläer und das Judentum* (1940); V. E. Hasler, 'Gesetz und Evangelium in der alten Kirche bis Origenes' (Diss., 1953); R. Bultmann, *Theology of the New Testament* (ET 1952), I, 11ff.; H. Braun, *Spätjüdisch-Häretischer und frühchristlicher Radikalismus*, I, II (1957); G. Bornkamm, *Jesus of Nazareth* (ET 1960).

their natural implications and therefore that it contained something quite new.[1] Against these three, a more radical evaluation
dropped the Mosaic Law as a starting-point of explanation and
instead related Jesus' injunctions to the immediate Will of God
against which all the Old Testament commandments were to be
tested.[2] It was further suggested that all positive sayings over
the Law were to be regarded as later additions so that his original teaching consisted in an explicit abrogation of the Law.[3]
The interpretation of the authentic logia over the Law thus
covered the whole range of possibilities from conservative
acceptance to radical rejection. In the meantime others,
frequently refusing to relegate apparently contradictory sayings
to variations in *Gemeindetheologie*, suggested that the so-called
inconsistencies resulted from the overlapping of the old age and
the new in Jesus' ministry while, in some quarters, the search
for a single integrating principle with which to combine the
various facets of Christ's teaching on the Law developed, in
different ways, the over-arching concept of 'fulfilment'.[4]

During this period closer attention was, of course, given to
the different tendencies evident in the synoptic presentations.
Matthew was generally regarded as a 'catholic' gospel containing both stricter and laxer attitudes to the Law, though occasionally it was interpreted as possessing either a purely nomistic

---

[1] So E. Percy, *Die Botschaft Jesu* (1953) and P. Verweijs, *Evangelium und neues Gesetz in der ältesten Christenheit bis auf Marcion* (1960).

[2] Particularly in W. G. Kümmel, 'Jesus und der jüdische Traditions-gedanke', *Heilsgeschehen und Geschichte* (1965), pp. 15–35; H. J. Schoeps, 'Jesus und das jüdische Gesetz', *Aus Frühchristlicher Zeit* (1950), pp. 212–20, and K. Niederwimmer, *Der Begriff die Freiheit im Neuen Testament* (1966).

[3] As earlier J. Leipoldt, *Jesu Verhältnis zu Griechen und Juden* (1941) but more importantly by E. Stauffer, 'Neue Wege der Jesusforschung', *Gottes ist der Orient* (1959), pp. 182ff.

[4] For the former see N. B. Stonehouse, *The Witness of Matthew and Mark to Christ* (1944) and now W. D. Davies, 'Mt. 5.17, 18', *Christian Origins and Judaism* (1962), pp. 30–66; for the latter H. J. L. Ljungmann, *Das Gesetz Erfüllen: Matth. 5.17ff. und 3.15 Untersucht* (1954) and G. F. Knight, *Law and Grace* (1962). It should perhaps be noted that some conservative critics have bypassed the form-critical development of the discussion altogether and continued to explain Jesus' teaching as merely an 'exposition' of the Mosaic commands, e.g. J. Wenham, *Our Lord's View of the Old Testament* (1953); C. F. H. Henry, *Christian Personal Ethics* (1957) and J. Murray, *Principles of Conduct* (1957).

or emancipated view of the Mosaic legislation.[1] Mark was usually conceived as abrogating both oral tradition and written law, and either as approximating to the position of Peter, or reflecting a Gentile Christianity which formed the presupposition of Pauline theology.[2] Luke, on the other hand, was not considered to be especially interested in the question, and attempts to document his understanding more closely varied between nomistic and liberal evaluations of his attitude.[3]

In the most recent phase of synoptic criticism, interest in the communities from which the gospels emerged has largely given way to a study of the theological tendencies of the evangelists themselves. As a result of this investigation it has been suggested that Matthew, while differing from the rabbinic understanding of the Law through the hermeneutical primacy he attaches to the 'love-commandment', nevertheless exhibits distinct Jewish-christian tendencies in his affirmation of parts of the oral tradition and in his creation of a christian halakhic tradition with which other parts of it have been replaced.[4] However, calling

---

[1] A prime exponent of the 'catholic' nature of the First Gospel was B. H. Streeter, *The Four Gospels* (1936[6]), pp. 500ff., but more recently see G. Hebert, 'The Problem of the Gospel According to Matthew', *SJT*, 14 (1961), 403–13. A nomistic understanding was adopted by E. von Dobschutz, 'Matthäus als Rabbi und Katechet', *ZNW*, 27 (1928), 338–48 and G. D. Kilpatrick, *The Origins of the Gospel According to St. Matthew* (1946). On the other hand B. W. Bacon, *Studies in Matthew* (1930) and B. H. Branscomb, *Jesus and the Law of Moses*, sought for the milieu of the gospel in a Petrine and Hellenistic Christianity respectively.

[2] For the first see J. C. Fenton, 'Paul and Mark', *Studies in the Gospels*, ed. D. E. Nineham (1955), pp. 89–112; for the second, M. Werner, *Der Einfluss paulinischer Theologie im Markusevangelium* (1923) and H. G. Wood, 'Mark's Gospel and Paulinism', *ET*, 51 (1939–40), 327–33. A 'Pauline' tendency in Mark had earlier been suggested by Holtzmann, Weiss, Harnack and others.

[3] Contrast, for example, the judgments of T. E. Blieben, 'The Gospel of Luke and the Gospel of Paul', *JTS*, 45 (1944), 134–40 and B. H. Branscomb, *Jesus and the Law of Moses*. De Wette and Overbeck had previously noted Luke's apparent unconcern with the issue of the Law.

[4] This interpretation of Matthew has been fully developed by G. Bornkamm, 'End-expectation and Church in Matthew' and especially G. Barth, 'Matthew's Understanding of the Law', both in *Tradition and Interpretation in Matthew* (ET 1963). In addition, attention has been drawn to Matthew's christian halakhic activity particularly by R. Hummel, *Die Auseinandersetzung zwischen Kirche und Judentum im Matthäusevangelium* (1963); W. D.

upon the results of previous source- and form-critical studies, other commentators have linked the more rigorously conservative legal sayings to a Jewish-christian element in Matthew's tradition, arguing that these were no longer characteristic of his own Hellenistic-Jewish christian or Gentile-christian understanding as his redactional activity demonstrates.[1] Mark is generally viewed as upholding a radical Gentile-christian approach to the Law, though it has been recently suggested that his abrogation of the Law may have been less comprehensive than that in Matthew, and that in some respects his ethical understanding may be considered a precursor of *Frühkatholizismus*.[2] Luke, it has been claimed, portrays Jesus as a conservative upholder of the Mosaic legislation who nevertheless, according to the *Gesetzesverständnis* of late Judaism, comparatively neglects the cultic and ceremonial commandments.[3] As for the attitude of Jesus himself, little has been attempted from a *redaktionsgeschichtliche* standpoint. Concentration on the creative tendencies of individual evangelists has, in fact, pushed this fundamental question quite into the background.[4]

Recent interest in the question is probably due to the

Davies, *The Setting of the Sermon on the Mount* (1964) following an earlier lead given by E. Schweizer, 'Matth. 5.17–20 – Anmerkungen zum Gesetzesverständnis des Matthäus', *TL*, 77 (1952), 479–84, now in *Neotestamentica* (1963), pp. 399–406.

[1] See G. Strecker, *Der Weg der Gerechtigkeit* (1962); W. Trilling, *Das wahre Israel* (1964); R. Walker, *Die Heilsgeschichte im ersten Evangelium* (1967) and R. Guelich, 'Not to Annul the Law rather to Fulfil the Law and the Prophets' (Diss., 1967). For a contrary view see H. T. Wrege, *Die Überlieferungsgeschichte der Bergpredigt* (1968).

[2] The usual interpretation is clearly stated in S. Schulz, *Die Stunde der Botschaft* (1967), and the two modifications may be found in R. Walker, *Die Heilsgeschichte*, and A. Suhl, *Die Funktion der alttestamentlichen Zitate und Anspielungen im Markusevangelium* (1965). The similarity between Marcan and Pauline themes has been re-asserted by Q. Quesnell, *The Mind of Mark* (1969), p. 226.

[3] This is the view of H. Conzelmann, *The Theology of St. Luke* (ET 1960). An even stricter interpretation of Luke's attitude has recently been advanced by H. J. Jervell, 'The Law in Luke-Acts', *HTR*, 64 (1971), 21–36.

[4] We have, in recent studies of the Fourth Gospel, almost the reverse process taking place. Since the renewed interest in the historical basis of the material also affects those passages in which the question of law comes into focus, the time has certainly come for a reconsideration of John in this connection.

emphasis laid upon Jesus' view of the Law in the literature of the so-called 'New Morality'. Despite constant reference to the subject, however, it nowhere contains a detailed analysis of the relevant biblical material. Assuming a polarity between law and love, Jesus' teaching and behaviour is depicted as always being grounded in the latter, circumstances themselves suggesting the content or application which love should have in any particular situation. A radical negation of the Law, indeed of any law, is therefore implied.[1] In two instances, however, subtler exegetical caveats have entered into and qualified this estimate. It has been suggested that Jesus' non-prescriptive love ethic could issue in obedience to the Law in circumstances where love demanded it and that, even where it did not have this consequence, fulfilment not abrogation of the Law's requirements is involved.[2] However, all such treatments are sketchy and selective in character, frequently presuming upon earlier examinations of Jesus' attitude which, in the light of recent gospel criticism, are now in need of considerable revision.

Indeed, even prior to the serious employment of *redaktionsgeschichtliche* methods and the emergence of the New Morality, little attention of a comprehensive nature was paid to Jesus' attitude to the Law, and more than four decades have passed since the last full-scale treatment of the subject appeared.[3] In

---

[1] Cf. D. Rhymes, *No New Morality* (1964); J. Fletcher, *Situation Ethics: The New Morality* (1966); H. A. Williams, 'Theology and Self-Awareness', *Soundings: Essays Concerning Christian Understanding* (Cambridge, 1966), pp. 67–102; W. Pittenger, *Love is the Clue* (1967). See further, H. Cox, *The Situation Ethics Debate* (1968).

[2] So respectively, O. S. Barr, *The Christian New Morality: A Biblical Study of Situation Ethics* (1969) and J. A. T. Robinson, *Christian Morals Today* (1964) now reprinted in *Christian Freedom in a Permissive Society* (1969).

[3] I refer, of course, to B. H. Branscomb, *Jesus and the Law of Moses* (1930). Unfortunately, only part of the comprehensive dissertation of B. Lanwer, 'Jesu Stellung zum Gesetz' (1933), is accessible, while the detailed treatment of H. Ljungmann, *Das Gesetz Erfüllen* (1954), only deals with a portion of the synoptic evidence. The only other sizeable contribution to this quest is that of K. Berger, *Die Gesetzesauslegung Jesu* (1972), which, as its title suggests, does not deal with all the passages that are relevant to an investigation of Jesus' attitude to the Law but only with those in which he is represented as making some direct comment on it. Some clarification of the relationship of this study to Berger's work may at this point be helpful. His original dissertation first came to my attention in the final stages of

view of the exegetical and hermeneutical advances that have been made since that time, therefore, a new investigation is long overdue. Furthermore, in the same period it is not too much to say that a revolution has occurred in the understanding of the Law in the Old Testament, one that has important implications for New Testament enquiry. In addition, the comparative materials yielded by the finds at Qumran, whose relevance for the question of Law in the New Testament has already received considerable attention, also need to be integrated into the overall study of the problem.

We commence, then, at the foundation point of our discussion, the granting of the Law itself at the beginning of Israel's history. From there we will seek to trace through the various interpretations that were placed upon it in the Old Testament, inter-testamental and later Jewish writings. Only so do we construct a sufficiently clear and detailed background against which the teaching of Jesus, and that of the communities and evangelists who preserved and interpreted it, can be properly understood.

preparation of the thesis on which this study is based. Unfortunately the 1968 Rotaprint version of Berger's dissertation had been quite severely condensed, indeed a number of his major conclusions had to be omitted, and it was only possible to use his material with great care. The first half of his full text, which was published in 1972, only came into my hands after the revised version of my thesis had been accepted for publication. For this reason, and in view of its incomplete character – his section on the historical Jesus, for example, has not yet appeared – I was again forced to refer to it sparingly. Taking into account the independent character of our work on this question, some of the similarities in our approach as well as the considerable differences in our conclusions are all the more interesting.

PART ONE
LAW IN THE OLD TESTAMENT
INTER-TESTAMENTARY
AND LATER JEWISH
LITERATURE

Three aspects of Law in the Old Testament and Judaism have particular relevance for our investigation:

a. the basis of Law. Is it to be viewed as a means of winning Yahweh's favour, or as a response of gratitude to the favour he has already shown?

b. the character of Law. Is it an embodiment of timeless norms embracing the whole of life, or does it consist of regulations that are historically conditioned, capable of modification and applicable to some, but not all, spheres of human behaviour?

c. the permanence of Law. Is it an immutable and eternal order that will persist into the Age to Come, or does it possess only provisional and this-worldly significance?

The study of these various aspects is complicated by the fact that in the Old Testament one simply cannot point to such a unified concept as the inclusive term 'Law' suggests. In the Old Testament it is viewed from several different perspectives, while even within single traditions diverse tendencies can be detected. It is important that these various stances *vis-à-vis* the Law be carefully delineated, and also that enquiry be made into the factors at work which gave rise to such different approaches. For whereas an examination of the three aspects of Law throughout the traditions of Israel will provide comparative data for the treatment of Law by Jesus himself, investigation of the latter may well shed considerable light on the source of his attitude and teaching.

Before embarking on this investigation, however, it would be helpful to clarify what is meant by several of the key terms around which it revolves *viz.*, law, custom, casuistry, legalism and Law.

In biblical thought and practice, the term *law* (whose connotations must not automatically be interpreted in terms of the present meaning of the word) always contains a strong element of authority and is expressive of an authoritative, in the biblical case divinely authoritative, order. This does not necessarily mean that it is to be distinguished from other expressions of social solidarity or order by its coercive character nor that it has received any systematic codification. Quite apart from these it has an authority which other norms in society, however venerated and however subject to differing degrees of negative and positive sanction, do not inherently possess. So, for example, in any society there are a large number of more or less overt practices which stem from traditionally observed and currently approved patterns of behaviour. Such are unofficial *customs* and from them laws in the more technical sense often develop. The more public sentiment attaches to a custom, and the more institutionalised it becomes, the more likely it is eventually to gain legal recognition. To do so, however, it has to be overtly reinstated at a second and higher level: it has to have a 'justiciable' form, i.e., it must become a rule that is capable of authoritative determination and reinterpretation by one of the recognised legal representatives or institutions of society. Though customs may be regarded, then, as incipient, or better potential, law, it is necessary for a distinction to be maintained between them and law as such.

Since through their reinterpretation laws are capable of being not only applied to new and changing circumstances but of being elaborated and multiplied to deal with areas of life, or details of behaviour, never considered under the original legislation, a quite extensive *casuistry* may be built up around the basic legal norms. In itself, such a procedure is a quite valid, because generally necessary, affair. It can happen, however, that the provisions enacted become so detailed and numerous that rather than furthering they can actually hinder the development of proper social, or religious, relations. Even submission to an extensive casuistry, however, may lead only to what may be termed a nomistic attitude to life. While in this legal regulations play a pronounced part in human interaction they do not as yet dominate individual motivation and purpose. Thus they are valued not in and for themselves but for the light they throw on the way in which life should be conducted and are recognised as gifts of God to be received and utilised in grateful response for all that he has done. Any elaborate casuistry, however, because of the preponderance and predominance of regulations, strengthens the possibility of a development towards a *legalistic* attitude to social and religious life. In this, there is a concentration on obedience to rules increasingly for their own sake, one that tends to be external in character rather than the expression of a genuine attempt to relate responsibly to God and to others. There is also an increasing conviction that observance of them is an achievement that, as cause is to effect, actually determines what God's attitude is to be in return. Since such an attitude is rarely, if ever, found in its pure form, use of this term generally refers to tendencies within religious writings and movements rather than to actual states.

Apart from these terms, it only remains to mention that whenever the word *Law* appears, capitalised and with or without a qualifying adjective, it is a basic part, or all, of the legal order i.e., the Law as a body of rules or 'system', that is in view.

A THE LAW – ACHIEVEMENT OR RESPONSE?

I OLD TESTAMENT

There has been a widespread, though not unanimous, agreement in Old Testament research in recent years, as to the fundamental importance of the covenant for Israel's religion. In particular, this fact is stressed again and again as of primary significance for a proper understanding of Israelite Law.[1] Though the historical circumstances accompanying the making of the

---

[1] Testimony to this is so widespread that documentation is really superfluous. One need only consult the recent histories of M. Noth and J. Bright; theologies of E. Jacob, Th. C. Vriezen, G. A. F. Knight and G. von Rad; ethics of J. L'Hour and H. van Oyen, as well as more specialised books and articles, some reference to which will be made in the following pages. It must be noted, however, that some recent studies, especially those of L. Perlitt, *Bundestheologie im Alten Testament* (1969), and E. Zenger, *Die Sinaitheophanie: Untersuchungen zum jahwistischen und elohistischen Geschichtswerk* (1972), have insisted that the covenant idea is a Deuteronomic creation. A valuable critique of this view has been provided by D. J. McCarthy, 'berît in Old Testament and Theology', *Bib.*, 53 (1972), 110–21.

covenant have in the past been strongly disputed, substantial
form-critical reasons have recently been adduced for supposing
that the tradition of the Exodus belongs essentially to that of the
covenant at Sinai.[1] Support for this conclusion has been drawn
from a consideration of the comparative material supplied by
the Hittite treaties of the fourteenth and thirteenth centuries,
for the inclusion in the structure of both treaties and Sinai
traditions of, *inter alia*, an historical prologue and a list of
stipulations, is held to strengthen the view that the historical
basis of the covenant lay in the Exodus, and that a list of stipulations was an integral part of its character.[2]

a Historical material

In the JE account the covenant idea also occurs in the narratives dealing with the patriarchal period. Whereas the understanding of God revealed through the Exodus and Sinai events
has clearly influenced the portrayal of his relationship with the
fathers, the basic assumptions for such an interpretation are
already present in the earlier material itself. While it has been
customary to view this covenant as unconditional in character,
this overlooks the demands expressed in Gen. 18.17–19 and
26.2–5 which are closely associated with it.[3] It is also important

---

[1] Especially by W. Beyerlin, *Origins and History of the oldest Sinai Traditions*
(ET 1965), who, against the reconstructions of such figures as M. Noth and
G. von Rad, endorses and extends the criticisms of A. Weiser, J. Bright,
M. Newman and others. More recently the link between the two events
has been affirmed by E. W. Nicholson, *Deuteronomy and Tradition* (1967),
pp. 41ff., and, in a qualified way, by H. Gese, 'Bemerkungen zur Sinai-
tradition', *ZAW*, 79 (1967), 137–54 and J. M. Schmidt, 'Erwägungen
zum Verhaltnis von Auszugs- und Sinaitradition', *ZAW*, 82 (1970), 1–30.

[2] Cf. R. E. Clements, *Prophecy and Covenant* (1965), p. 54. The best survey of
the extensive literature on the treaties is that of D. J. McCarthy, *Der
Gottesbund im alten Testament* (1967[2]). Hesitations as to the validity of these
comparisons have been expressed by K. Baltzer, *Das Bundesformular* (1960),
pp. 37–40, and R. Smend, *Die Bundesformel* (1963), p. 34, n.16, and these
have since been more strongly advanced by D. J. McCarthy, *Treaty and
Covenant* (1963), pp. 161–6; E. Gerstenberger, 'Covenant and Commandment', *JBL*, 84 (1965), 38–51; and, especially, F. Nötscher, 'Bundesformular und "Amtshimmel"', *BZ*, 9 (1965), 181–214.

[3] The conditional character of this covenant is stressed by G. Östborn, *Tora
in the Old Testament* (1945), p. 104, and M. E. Kline, 'Law and Covenant',
WTJ, 27 (1964), 3ff., against J. Begrich, 'Berit', *ZAW*, 60 (1944), 1–11;
A. Jepsen, 'Berit', *Verbannung und Heimkehr* (1961), 161–80 and D. N.

to note that in the JE history, the covenant with Abraham occupies a position of considerable significance even, it has been argued, of pre-eminence over that concluded at Sinai.

So far as the Sinai covenant itself is concerned, there are strong grounds for arguing that the Decalogue, at least in its original form, from the beginning formed an integral part of it.[1] Over against attempts to trace the origins of these laws to the cult and, more recently, wisdom circles, or to press too strongly the parallels provided by the Hittite treaties, it is probable that the basic form of the Decalogue had its source in a 'prophetic' word of Yahweh to Israel setting forth the basic norms of community life. It is more preferable to regard it in these terms than to speak of its being a cultic response, wisdom code or legislative decree.[2] It is only through the giving of this 'Law' that the covenant comes to full expression and that Israel's appropriation is made complete. Thus it is no more possible to subtract the commandments from the covenant and be left with a residuum of pure grace than subtract grace from

---

Freedman, 'Divine Commitment and Human Obligation', *Int.*, 18 (1964)' 420ff. Its priority is emphasised by G. E. Mendenhall, 'Covenant Forms in Israelite Tradition', *BA*, 17 (1954), 72, and F. C. Fensham, 'Covenant, Promise and Expectation', *TZ*, 23 (1967), 310.

[1] See the survey of R. J. Thompson, *Moses and the Law in a Century of Criticism since Graf* (1970), and the bibliography in H. H. Rowley, 'Moses and the Decalogue', *Men of God* (1963), p. 2 n.2.

[2] Cf. recently A. Jepsen, 'Beitrage zur Auslegung und Geschichte des Dekalogs', *ZAW*, 79 (1967), esp. 300–3. For the cultic approach see H. Reventlow, 'Kultisches Recht im Alten Testament', *ZTK*, 60 (1963), 267–304. An origin in wisdom circles is advocated by G. Föhrer, 'Das sogennante apodiktisch formulierte Recht und der Dekalog', *KD*, 11 (1965), 49–74; J. J. Stamm and M. E. Andrew, *The Ten Commandments in Recent Research* (1967), pp. 57ff.; E. Nielsen, *The Ten Commandments in New Perspective* (1968), pp. 33ff., and especially E. Gerstenberger, *Wesen und Herkunft des 'apodiktischen Rechts'* (1965), pp. 83ff. However, A. Phillips, *Ancient Israel's Criminal Law* (1970), has argued that the Decalogue was the basis for Israel's criminal code; as such it was distinguished from all other legal enactments and was decisive for the maintenance of the covenant relationship, at least until after the exile with the appearance of P. All these dissent from the original thesis of A. Alt, *Die Ursprünge des israelitischen Rechts* (1934), that the apodictic formulation is unique to Israel. The most recent detailed investigation of such formulations will be found in G. Loedke, *Gestalt und Bezeichnung alttestamentlicher Rechtssätze. Eine form-geschichtlich-terminologische Studie* (1971).

the commandment, for the covenant does not so much precede Law as incorporate it.[1]

The commandments, then, have the character of gift as well as obligation and can be regarded both as a practical outline of the way of life that is pleasing to Yahweh as well as an expression of the way in which Israel is to demonstrate its loyalty to him.[2] However, granted that obedience to the commandments is not in the first place the means by which favour with Yahweh is created, is it not yet the decisive factor in the maintenance of that favour? And if this is the case, is it not in the nature of both response and achievement? Traditional theology has always denied that this is the case, for it was the impossibility of fulfilling the Law that was regarded as the Law's most characteristic feature. If this is so, the Law brings not only gift and obligation, but judgment as well.

The legitimacy of this way of understanding the Law has been brusquely challenged by von Rad who asserts that 'such demands as we have in these "tables" were regarded as capable of fulfilment, and that easily', and that 'Israel only encountered the law in its function as judge and destroyer at the time of the preaching of the prophets.' However, the force and earnestness with which the stipulations were impressed upon the people, together with the punishment suffered by those who transgressed them (Ex. 32.31ff., Num. 11.1ff., 14.11ff.), indicate that from the beginning the possibility of judgment was latent within the demand.[3] Since the Law is not viewed as necessarily

---

[1] Nevertheless, to define 'covenant' in terms of 'reciprocal obligation' rather than relationship including obligation, as E. Kutsch, 'Gesetz und Gnade', *ZAW*, 79 (1967), 18–35, does not quite put the emphasis in the right place.

[2] For the first: H. J. Kraus, 'Freude an Gottes Gesetz', *Ev.Th.*, 10 (1950–1), 338ff.; and second: E. Würthwein, 'Der Sinn des Gesetzes im Alten Testament', *ZTK*, 55 (1958), 266ff.

[3] So W. Zimmerli, *The Law and the Prophets* (1965), p. 60 and in 'Das Gesetz im Alten Testament', *Gottes Offenbarung* (1963), pp. 270ff., against G. von Rad, *Old Testament Theology* (ET 1961–5), I, 195–6. As well as in traditional theological formulations, over-emphasis on the condemnatory function of the Law takes place in E. Hirsch, *Das Alten Testament und die Predigt des Evangeliums* (1936) and R. Bultmann, 'Prophecy and Fulfilment', *Essays Philosophical and Theological* (1955), pp. 182ff.

resulting in it, however, the first part of von Rad's claim must be allowed to stand. Is it then a question of achievement on Israel's part if through obedience the covenant is maintained? On the contrary, it is Yahweh who is viewed as maintaining the covenant, not only later in Israel's history when it is clear that the nation has departed from it, but from the very beginning of her existence as she repeatedly despises its obligations.[1] To talk in terms of an achievement on Israel's part would therefore be erroneous.

Although the original provenance of the so-called Covenant Code (Ex. 20.22 – 23.33) remains in dispute, its covenant basis continues to be strongly affirmed.[2] The principle on which the laws have been arranged has also been subject to continuing enquiry, but whatever the pattern on which they have been ordered, there are good grounds for suggesting that its provisions were intended to provide the basis for the emerging Israelite state.[3] This increase in 'legislation' was a necessary consequence of Israel's transition from a semi-nomadic to a more settled state and should not be interpreted as indicative of a new strictness in the way in which Yahweh's will was conceived which introduced an alteration in Israel's situation *vis-à-vis* its God.[4]

In Deuteronomy, the Exodus-redemption motif is clearly

---

[1] W. Eichrodt, *Theology of the Old Testament* (ET 1961–5), I, 457–67, has here drawn a valuable distinction. In the early period, though the expectation of judgment was very real, Israel looked on the whole for 'individual divine acts of punishment' through which the covenant would be maintained by the removal of rebellious elements. Only in the later period did the expectation arise of 'corporate national guilt', judgment upon which would result in the abrogation of the covenant.

[2] For a discussion of its date, provenance and purpose, see most recently, S. M. Paul, *Studies in the Book of the Covenant in the Light of Cuneiform and Biblical Law* (1970), pp. 104ff.

[3] Differing, though not entirely unrelated, views of the purpose of the Code have been suggested by E. Robertson, 'The Riddle of the Torah', *BJRL*, 27 (1943), 377 (cf. A. E. Guilding, 'Notes on the Hebrew Law Codes', *JTS*, 49 [1948], 43ff.) and A. Phillips, *Law*, pp. 159ff., both of whom relate it more closely to the Decalogue stipulations.

[4] Cf. C. M. Carmichael, 'A Singular Method of Codification of Law in the Mishpatim', *ZAW*, 84 (1972), 19–25 who argues from its form that it contains not so much a developed legal code as broad principles of religious, moral, and social behaviour.

fundamental (Deut. 5.6; 6.20ff.; 10.12ff.; 26.5ff.), while the covenant concept is the most impressive image through which the reality of God's relationship with Israel is conveyed.[1] It generally refers to the covenant established at Sinai (5.2–3; 29.1, 25) but also signifies the covenant with the fathers (4.31; 7.12ff.; 8.1ff.) and that renewed in Moab (29.1ff.). One can also discern a slight shift in the concept of the covenant in these writings, for it occasionally carries the sense of a constantly enduring relationship (7.9; 17.2; 31.16ff.) and can even be used of the obligations of that relationship themselves (4.13; 9.9ff.; 10.8). The stress upon its permanent character, while militating against tendencies to base the relationship with God upon the principle of works, does open up the possibility of its being taken more and more for granted even when obedience is lacking. On the other hand, the equation with obligation brings into prominence the legal basis of the covenant and makes it easier for this element to be isolated from its context in redemption and covenant. However, the presence of both elements in Deuteronomy, held in tension as they are so carefully, prevents the possibility of any misunderstanding with respect to its own position.[2] While obedience is an integral aspect of the covenant relationship, it cannot be regarded as the creative factor in that relationship. Nor can it be so considered with reference to the maintenance of the covenant. It is true that promises of blessing and threats of judgment are constantly encountered in the context of demands for obedience. This is particularly clear in 11.26–8 and 28.1–68 where the way of Blessing and way of Curse are set as clear alternatives before the people.[3] Nevertheless, in view of the perspective outlined in 9.6–29, it is clear that Israel has failed to fulfil its covenant responsibilities and that it is in fact Yahweh who has

[1] For comparisons and contrasts with the Treaty-Covenants see especially M. Weinfeld, 'Deuteronomy – The Present State of the Inquiry', *JBL*, 86 (1967), 253–5 and now *Deuteronomy and the Deuteronomic School* (1972), pp. 59–157.

[2] See further S. Hermann, 'Die konstruktive Restauration. Das Deuteronium als Mitte biblischer Theologie', *Probleme biblischer Theologie*, ed. H. W. Wolff (1971), pp. 155–70 esp. pp. 162–4.

[3] See especially D. R. Hillers, *Treaty-Curses and the Old Testament Prophets* (1964), pp. 30–40 where these passages are particularly considered in the light of parallels in the Treaty documents.

graciously determined to uphold the covenant and ensure that it remains in force.[1]

In comparison with the traditions so far examined, the priestly writings exhibit a strange ambivalence. Thus while they contain no explicit reference to the covenant at Sinai, the idea of the covenant becomes their fundamental theological and religious datum.[2] Since particular stress is laid upon the covenants concluded with Noah and Abraham (Gen. 9.8–17; 17.1–27), this means that the divine covenant which is decisive for Israel is established before the giving of the Law and that reference to the proceedings at Sinai is not central to it. While the connection between covenant and Law is weakened, however, the bond still remains and in P (Gen. 17.9–14) as earlier in JE (Gen. 18.17–19), obligations are also associated with the Abrahamic covenant. Indeed the priority given to this covenant is merely a further development of the position it holds in the JE narrative itself. Moreover, in Lev. 26.5 there could even be a reference to the Sinaitic covenant and it is by no means impossible that an original account of it in P was omitted when it was joined to JE.[3]

The character of the Law as gift i.e., as offer followed by acceptance, is prominent throughout, and while the threat of judgment may have fallen into the background, the increase in the number of sacrifices and the stress upon the necessity of

---

[1] M. Noth, 'The Laws in the Pentateuch: Their Assumptions and Meaning', *The Laws in the Pentateuch and Other Essays* (ET 1966), p. 101 agrees that in the main the initiative lies in his hands but claims that 'God's blessing as a reward earned by fulfilling the law appears first in secondary passages in Deuteronomy'.

[2] Cf. E. Jacob, *Theology of the Old Testament* (1958), p. 215, and Th. C. Vriezen, *An Outline of Old Testament Theology* (ET 1958), p. 142. On the character of P generally, see R. Rendtorff, *Die Gesetze in der Priesterschrift* (1954) and K. Koch, *Die Priesterschrift von Exod. 25 bis Lev. 16* (1959). W. Brueggmann, 'The Kerygma of the Priestly Writers', *ZAW*, 84 (1972), 397–414, has also drawn attention to the centrality of the theme of re-entry into the promised land, and subsequent blessing, throughout the work.

[3] According to C. Barth, 'Theophanie, Bundschliessung und neuer Anfang am dritten Tag', *Ev.Th.*, 28 (1968), 521–33, however, the main themes of P in the Sinai narrative are the revelation of Yahweh and the introduction of valid worship rather than the covenant. He suggests that the present compilation reflects later developments, particularly in its depiction of the establishment of the covenant as a covenant renewal.

atonement for sin, is indicative that this aspect was also taken seriously. In addition, the covenantal foundation of the sacrificial legislation is strongly emphasised: the cult exists in order that communion between man and God may be maintained, not so that it may be achieved.[1] It is worth noting here that the Holiness Code in Lev. 17 – 26 appears to be an interesting combination of both Deuteronomic and priestly elements, and is clearly older than P itself.[2]

A further shift in the understanding of the covenant takes place in the later historical works – Chronicles, Ezra and Nehemiah. In view of the interest in the election of individuals rather than the election of Israel, and concentration upon the Davidic and Levitic covenants rather than that concluded with Abraham or at Sinai (of which there is no mention), what is to be made of the Chronicler's interpretation of Israel's legal traditions? Are the Sinai, and Exodus, events regarded merely as provisional steps towards the full covenant later established with David or are the Davidic, and Levitic, covenants themselves illustrative of a more basic covenant concept which has been removed from the historical sphere?[3] Isolated references to the saving events of the past can, however, be found (1 Chron. 16.12; 17.21–2; 2 Chron. 6.54; 7.22; 22.10), while in the covenant renewals of Ezra and Nehemiah we again catch a glimpse of that historical basis of the covenant which Chronicles appears to lack (Neh. 9; Ez. 9.5ff.). In particular the prayer of Ezra at the time of the covenant renewal is a stirring

---

[1] The covenant basis of the sacrificial legislation has been strongly affirmed by R. J. Thompson, *Penitence and Sacrifice in Early Israel* (1963), p. 9. This is reinforced by the fact that sacrifice could only be offered for certain specific sins and that for the rest the offender was obliged to cast himself upon the mercy of God. For a different approach to these writings see M. Noth, *Laws*, pp. 92–3, who considers that the idea of the covenant survives merely as a decorative feature of the narrative so that the Law now takes on an absolute character; and W. Eichrodt, *Theology*, I, 57; W. Zimmerli, *Prophets*, p. 91, and E. Jacob, *Theology*, p. 216, who argue that the covenant relationship is so anchored in the Abrahamic history that the idea of its involving a mutual responsibility is quite done away.

[2] Cf. recently P. Ackroyd, *Exile and Restoration* (1968), p. 90 and, more fully, W. Thiel, 'Erwägungen zum Alter des Heiligkeitsgesetzes', *ZAW*, 81 (1969), 40–73.

[3] So, respectively, D. J. McCarthy, 'Covenant in the Old Testament', *CBQ*, 27 (1965), 239, and W. Eichrodt, *Theology*, I, 64.

recital of all the great saving events of Israel's history. Moreover while the eternal character of the Davidic covenant is frequently stressed and its centrality for the Chronicler is clear (1 Chron. 17.11ff.; 22.9; 28.4ff.; 2 Chron. 21.7), there is both mention of the Abrahamic covenant (1 Chron. 16.14ff.; 2 Chron. 30.6) and the strong suggestion of a conditional character attaching to the covenant with David, indicating that Yahweh's blessing was not regarded as being automatically guaranteed (1 Chron. 22.11ff.; 28.7ff.; 2 Chron. 6.16ff.; 7.17ff.; 33.7ff.).[1]

It cannot be denied that in all these works the Law has moved into a position of prominence which it had not occupied before. This is particularly clear in the central place given it in the life of the community, and in the Chronicler's understanding of history as largely a series of examples of obedience to it.[2] This new zeal for the Law has been regarded as 'not less than a reversal of the older order: whereas the Law was formerly the expression of the covenant, it now becomes the condition of its restoration'.[3] As such it has been viewed as responsible for the legalistic development of later Jewish thought and life. Tendencies leading in this direction are undoubtedly present in these writings, but they are still held in check by the covenant idea and have not become sufficiently independent to dominate it. Indeed the emphasis upon the Law was due to a determination to take Yahweh's demands seriously so that the covenant relationship might remain unimpaired and not be terminated by him again (2 Chron. 33.8; Neh. 10.8; 13.8). Thus 'to begin with this did not involve a change in the theoretical position of the Law. The duty of keeping the Law was still, indeed in a renewed sense, the result, not the basis, of their election.'[4]

---

[1] Cf. G. Widengren, 'King and Covenant', *JJS*, 2 (1957), 24, and Z. W. Falk, *Hebrew Law in Biblical Times* (1964), p. 46. This is in accord with a similar emphasis in the earlier Deuteronomic history (2 Sam. 23.5; 1 Kings 2.3) and the Psalms (89.30ff.; 132.12). It is therefore incorrect to regard the Davidic covenant as of a purely promissory character and as quite independent of its Sinaitic predecessor. Cf. A. H. J. Gunneweg, 'Sinaibund und Davidsbund', *VT*, 10 (1960), 335ff.; M. L. Newman, *The People of the Covenant* (1962), pp. 149ff.; R. E. Clements, *Abraham and David* (1967), pp. 62-5.

[2] See further G. von Rad, *Das Geschichtsbild des chronistischen Werks* (1930).

[3] So E. Jacob, *Theology*, p. 274.

[4] W. Gutbrod, art. νόμος, *TDNT*, IV 1045.

b Prophetic writings

Recent assessments of the prophets have largely rejected the view that they were the originators of all that was distinctive in the religion of Israel and argued instead for their dependence upon earlier tradition. It has been frequently noted, for example, how central is the idea of Israel's redemption by Yahweh in the Exodus.[1] It is strange, therefore, to discover explicit reference to the covenant at Sinai only in Hos. 8.1 and Jer. 11.4; 34.13ff., though there is also mention of that concluded with Noah (Isa. 24.5; 2 Isa. 54.10) and with David (Jer. 33.20ff.; Ezek. 16.8, 59; 2 Isa. 55.3) as well as references of a general nature (Hos. 6.7; Ezek. 17.19; Jer. 14.21; 22.9; 3 Isa. 56.4, 6). However, absence of the technical term in passages dealing with the events of the Exodus and Israel's desert origin does not necessarily imply absence of the idea. There are good grounds for thinking that, until the time of Jeremiah, the prophets deliberately avoided a term which all too easily could become a slogan for the national security they were so strongly condemning. This means that most probably 'the prophetic appeal to the election of Israel was an appeal to the covenant'.[2]

The prophetic understanding of the Law is to be considered

[1] Cf. Hos. 2.14–15; 11.1ff.; 12.9ff.; 13.4ff.; Amos 2.10; 3.1–2; 9.7; Mic. 6.4ff.; Isa. 4.2; 10.24–6; 11.11–16; Jer. 2.5–7; 7.21ff.; 11.3ff.; 16.14f.; 23.7f.; 31.31–4; 34.13; Ezek. 20.1ff.; 2 Isa. *passim*. See further C. R. North, *The Old Testament Interpretation of History* (1946), pp. 44ff.; G. H. Davies, 'The Yahwistic Tradition in the Eighth-Century Prophets', *Studies in Old Testament Prophecy*, ed. H. H. Rowley (1950), pp. 37–51; N. W. Porteous, 'The Prophets and the Problem of Continuity', *Israel's Prophetic Heritage* (1962), pp. 11–25.

[2] R. E. Clements, *Prophecy*, p. 55. Cf. E. Lohmeyer, *Diatheke* (1913), pp. 57ff.; P. van Imschoot, *Théologie de l'Ancien Testament* (1954), pp. 244–55; J. Lindblom, *Prophecy in Ancient Israel* (1962), pp. 329–30. This is much to be preferred to the position of R. Kraetschmar, *Die Bundesvorstellung im Alten Testament* (1896), recently renewed in C. F. Whitley, *The Prophetic Achievement* (1963), pp. 30–1 that the eighth-century prophets did not know at all of the covenant idea. Additional support for prophetic knowledge of the conception has recently been derived from evidence in their writings suggesting a consciousness of their task as 'covenant-mediators'. Here we are especially indebted to H. B. Huffmon, 'The Covenant Lawsuit and the Prophets', *JBL*, 78 (1959) 285–95; J. Harvey, 'Le "rib-pattern" requisitoire prophétique sur la rupture de l'alliance', *Bib.*, 43 (1962),

within this framework. Although direct reference to specific legal formulations (as in Hos. 4.2; Jer. 7.9) is infrequent, there is ample evidence of a concern for the Law in general and for its fundamental principles (e.g., Amos 2.4, 5; Hos. 4.6; 8.1, 12; Mic. 6.6–8; Isa. 33.14ff.; Jer. 2.8; 6.19; 9.13; 16.11; 26.4ff.; 44.10, 23; Ezek. 20.7ff.; 43.12; 2 Isa. 47.17–18; 51.7) and a written Law seems to be presupposed in Hos. 8.12 (unless it alludes to the writing of the Decalogue on tablets of stone as in Ex. 31.18; Deut. 9.10).[1] However, while the grounding of such Law in divine graciousness is constantly affirmed, the accent falls upon the necessity of obedience and, in so far as that has not occurred, upon the inevitability of judgment.[2] In the new situation that had developed as a result

172–96; F. C. Fensham, 'Common Trends in the Curses of the Near Eastern Treaties...', *ZAW*, 75 (1963), 155–75, and D. R. Hillers, *Treaty-Curses, passim*, as well as various studies of this phenomenon in individual prophetic writings.

[1] The earlier influential thesis of J. Wellhausen, *Prologomena to the History of Israel* (ET 1885), that the Law was later than the prophets, is, therefore, inappropriate.

[2] This particularly explains the prophetic attitude to the cult. Earlier views represented the prophets as totally rejecting cultic arrangements, and these have been most recently revived in R. Hentschke, *Die Stellung der vorexilischen Schriftpropheten zum Kultur* (1957), pp. 74ff.; 88ff.; C. F. Whitley, *Prophetic Achievement*, pp. 61–92, and, in a different form, by M. Sekine, 'Der Problem der Kult-polemik bei den Propheten,' *Ev.Th.*, 28 (1968), 605–9. Later investigations tended to associate them more closely with the cult, as A. R. Johnson, *The Cultic Prophet in Ancient Israel* (1962) and, most radically, A. Haldar, *Associations of Cult Prophets among the Ancient Semites* (1945). In the main these have been superseded by a more moderate appraisal of their attitude for which H. H. Rowley, 'The Prophets and the Cult', *Worship in Ancient Israel* (1967), pp. 144–75 provides a detailed bibliography. According to this approach, prophetic attacks upon the cult (e.g., Isa. 1.11–17; Hos. 6.6; Mic. 6.6–8), including the acute condemnations of Amos (4.4ff.; 5.21ff.) and Jeremiah (6.20; 7.9ff. *et al.*) are primarily repudiations of its abuse. Their appeal elsewhere to Mosaic traditions which include the cult, their predictions of the future in which cult is an element (cf. Jer. 33.18), and their use of cultic terminology and forms (see R. Rendtorff, *TL*, 81 [1956], 339–42 and E. Würthwein in *Tradition und Situation* [1963], pp. 115ff.) support this interpretation of their polemic. Cf. more recently, D. E. Gowan, 'Prophets, Deuteronomy and the Syncretistic Cult in Israel', *Transitions in Biblical Scholarship*, ed. J. C. Rylaarsdam (1968), pp. 93–112 and J. G. Williams, 'The Social Location of Israelite Prophecy', *Journal of the American Academy of Religion*, 37 (1969), 153–65.

of Israel's continued unfaithfulness, the threat of Law was interpreted in a more radical way, yet one, as we have seen, that was always latent within the covenant tradition itself.

In the post-exilic prophets there is an intensification of the idea of election as well as a greater interest in both Law and cult. Within this framework both the Exodus (3 Isa. 63.11ff.; Hagg. 2.5; Zech. 10.10) and covenant at Sinai (3 Isa. 56.4; Zech. 9.11; 11.10; Mal. 2.4ff.) are mentioned, but are not particularly stressed. The element of judgment is again strikingly present though, as in the earlier prophets, beyond it lies the glorious future for Israel which Yahweh is to secure. This heightening of emphasis upon election and Law, especially the latter's cultic aspects, brings with it obvious dangers. Yet so long as the Law is associated with judgment, and the initiative in the covenant lies in Yahweh's hands, the dangers are minimised. With certain modifications, therefore, the message of these prophets is in accord with the teaching of their eighth-century predecessors.[1]

c Wisdom literature

There is a growing tendency to date the material contained in the wisdom literature, though not necessarily its collation, in the pre-exilic period and, without denying its obvious affinities with 'international' wisdom, to regard it as possessing an indigenous life within Israel with its own distinctive emphases. This has led to a stronger emphasis upon the links between wisdom, covenant and Law.[2] Evidence for such an association, however, should not be overestimated. At no point do the events of the Exodus come into view, and there is a total silence with respect to the establishment of a covenant or covenants with the nation. The only possible references to the Mosaic Law (Prov. 6.23; 19.16; 28.4ff.; 29.18; Eccles. 12.13; Job 23.12),

---

[1] Cf. J. Lindblom, *Prophecy*, pp. 378–410. This is also true for the late book of Daniel, as even M. Noth, *Laws*, p. 105, is willing to admit.

[2] Cf. especially D. R. Hubbard, 'The Wisdom Movement and Israel's Covenant Faith', *Tyn.B.*, 17 (1966), 20, but see also Th. C. Vriezen, *Theology*, p. 336; G. A. F. Knight, *A Christian Theology of the Old Testament* (1959), p. 259, and F. D. Kidner, *Proverbs* (1964), p. 34. On the relationship between wisdom and the cult see G. von Rad, *Wisdom in Israel* (ET 1972), pp. 186–9. For a discussion of its links with Deuteronomy in particular, see M. Weinfeld, *Deuteronomy*, pp. 158–70 and 244–81.

in view of the identification of Torah with sapiental instruction elsewhere (Prov. 1.8; 3.1; 4.2–3; 6.20; 7.1–2; 10.8; 13.14; 31.26; Eccles. 8.2, 5), are also to be interpreted as relating to instruction in wisdom. Wherever sacrifices are mentioned they are condemned (Prov. 15.8; 21.3; 21.27) though, as with the prophetic polemic, this need not entail complete rejection. It has been argued, however, that this corpus of literature as a whole is set within the traditional religious framework, indeed presupposes it, and that such were its own concerns that elaboration or even allusion to that framework was bound to be infrequent. This is supported by the predominant use of the covenant name Yahweh in references to God, as in the conviction throughout that there exists a stable relationship with him. The covenant basis, then, is to be related more specifically to the larger context within which the wisdom tradition developed than to the actual teaching of the literature itself.[1] The ambiguous position of the Mosaic Law in this teaching, as to a lesser extent in the prophetic writings as well, is a point to which we must return in the following section.[2]

2   LATER JEWISH LITERATURE

Before considering the inter-relationship of Law and covenant in the post-biblical literature, it is instructive to examine the processes at work in the LXX treatment of ברית. It is almost uniformly translated by διαθήκη and consequently the voluntary pact involving mutual obligations becomes more a legal disposition like the testamentary decision familiar to Greek

---

[1] Cf. W. O. E. Oesterley, *The Book of Proverbs* (1929), pp. x–lxi and G. von Rad, *Theology*, 1, 433–5.

[2] Despite the existence in the Psalms of a considerable body of material relevant to our theme, for the purpose of this study it may be left to one side, for the literature does not spring from a homogeneous Sitz-im-Leben. It consists of responses from all the various traditions within Israel, and the latter are not always easy to identify when specific Psalms are under consideration. In so far as it is possible to set isolated Psalms in the context of one of the three main traditions that have been examined, they do not add anything particularly new, serving rather to confirm tendencies already detected. It should be noted, however, that the covenantal context of this literature has been recently stressed by A. Weiser, *The Psalms* (ET 1962), pp. 37ff. This includes the wisdom Psalms as well.

civil law, from which the profane use of the term derives (cf. Gen. 15.18; 17.2; Ex. 2.24; 6.4; 34.10; Lev. 26.45; Num. 25.12–13; Deut. 9.5; 29.12, 14; Josh. 24.25; Neh. 9.8).[1] It also, on occasions, translates such terms as תורה, עדות, דבר and is often used in parallelism with νόμος, ἐντολαί, κρίματα and similar expressions (cf. Gen. 6.18; Ex. 31.16; Lev. 24.8; Deut. 4.23; 3 Kings 8.21). Schoeps therefore maintains that it 'can hardly be translated as *foedus sive pactum*; the meaning seems to fluctuate only between *testamentum* and *statutum* – though it still has the subsidiary meaning *promissio*'.[2]

It has been urged, however, that an echo of the original treaty relationship survives in the linguistic usage ἀνὰ μέσον, μέτα, and that the bilateral character of the covenant is not entirely lacking in the Greek term itself.[3] It should also be recognised that the dual use of the term in the LXX partly stems from the complex content of the word which the translators were seeking to grasp. In the Old Testament itself, as we have seen, ברית is occasionally used of legal regulations and also occurs in contexts where, although it is not altogether lacking, the reciprocal aspect is subordinate. It cannot be denied, however, that the predominance of these two usages in the LXX means that the term does place the emphasis differently from the Hebrew and that it cannot simply be subsumed under the covenant concept.[4]

---

[1] Note, however, that in 3 Kings 11.11 it is translated by ἐντολάς, in part of the MS. tradition of Deut. 9.5 by μαρτύριον, and by συνθήκη in 2 Kings 17.15. See further the investigations of E. Riggenbach, 'Der Begriff der ΔΙΑΘΗΚΗ im Hebräerbrief', *Theologische Studien Theodor Zahn* (1908), pp. 294ff.; E. Lohmeyer, *Diatheke*, pp. 78ff., and J. Behm, art. διαθήκη, *TDNT*, II, 126ff.

[2] H. J. Schoeps, *Paul, The Theology of the Apostle in the Light of Jewish Religious History* (ET 1961), p. 216. Cf. E. Lohmeyer, *Diatheke*, pp. 80, 95–7, who feels that in the LXX the idea of reciprocity has quite ceased to exist.

[3] By J. Behm, *TDNT*, II, 216 and W. Eichrodt, *Theology*, I, 66 respectively.

[4] For the influence of the LXX rendering of covenant in the sense of 'disposition' upon the writings of Philo see especially A. Jaubert, *La Notion d'Alliance dans le Judaïsme* (1963), pp. 375ff. E. Lohmeyer, *Diatheke*, pp. 95–7 agrees that there is no complete transformation of meaning in the LXX, but tends to over-emphasise the element of 'disposition' in the Old Testament term. Meanwhile H. J. Schoeps, *Paul*, p. 216, quite rightly protests against the claim that διαθήκη, because of its stress upon the sovereign will of God, is religiously more valuable than its Old Testament

a Inter-testamentary works

In considering the inter-testamental literature, we turn first to those writings in which the historical and/or legal interest is uppermost.[1] The redemption from Egypt is mentioned in Esther 13.16; Judith 5.10ff.; 1 Macc. 4.9 and 3 Macc. 2.6ff., where it is chiefly regarded as the ground of the past and continuing election of Israel. With the exception of Judith 5.17ff., however, it is not brought into touch with the idea of obligation on Israel's part. Though the reality of punishment for her offences is certainly present (cf. Tobit 13.5; 2 Macc. 6.12–16; 7.31ff.), there is no trace of the prophetic message of national judgment, termination of the old covenant and expectation of the new.[2] In these writings ברית is used with reference to the covenant with the fathers (1 Macc. 2.50ff.; 4.10; 2 Macc. 1.2ff.) as well as to the covenant regulations (1 Macc. 1.15, 63; 2.20–1, 27), the Law as a whole (1 Macc. 1.57) and even the Jewish nation itself (Judith 9.13). Since it is clear from 1 Macc. 2.50ff. and 4.9ff. that the term 'fathers' extends to all the

---

counterpart. In the latter, God's sovereign will is most supremely shown in the condescension to 'covenant' with man in such a way that mutual obligations are binding on both parties.

[1] Classification of the inter-testamentary writings into the categories employed in surveying the Old Testament material becomes increasingly difficult but, since however much traditions may begin to merge during this period they are still able to be distinguished, it is valuable to consider them separately. The division followed here is broadly that of H. Maldwyn Hughes, *The Ethics of the Jewish Apocryphal Literature* (1909). The recent restriction of apocalyptic to 1 Enoch, 2 Esdras and 2 Baruch advocated by D. Rössler, *Gesetz und Geschichte: Untersuchungen zur Theologie der jüdischen Apokalyptik und der pharisäischen Orthodoxie* (1960) is quite indefensible as A. Nissen, 'Tora und Geschichte im Spätjudentum', *NT*, 9 (1967), 246–7, rightly points out. Nevertheless, in that the other writings are not as wholly given over to apocalpytic interests as these three, there is some justification for according them a less central position. The dating of some of these books, especially the Testaments of the Twelve Patriarchs, is a notoriously difficult problem and the possibility of christian interpolations clouds the issue still further. Their inclusion should not be taken to imply the pre-christian origin of all the references cited. A survey of the debate on this issue with respect to the Testaments has been provided by M. de Yonge, 'Recent Studies on the Testaments of the Twelve Patriarchs', *Svensk Exegetisk Arsbok*, 36 (1971), 77–96.

[2] Cf. E. Sjöberg, *Gott und die Sünder im palästinischen Judentum* (1939), p. 204.

faithful leaders of Israel from Abraham to David, this idea of the covenant takes on a permanent character, and it is this which clears the way for the application of the term to Israel herself, an ominous development indeed. Moreover, it is extremely difficult to distinguish the meaning of covenant in these passages from the laws associated with it.[1] It becomes apparent, therefore, that the equation of covenant with divine dispensation and divine statutes does not represent two opposing tendencies, but rather two aspects of one development in which subordinate notes in the Old Testament conception have become the leading themes. Also present is the beginning of a reliance upon works of the Law as the ground of salvation in such passages as Tobit 4.10; 12.9 and 2 Macc. 7.38, though elsewhere Old Testament perspectives continue.

The apocalyptic literature, prophecy's most direct descendant, contains many references to the Exodus from Egypt. In a number of passages it is no more than a passing reference (Ass.Mos. 1.4–5; 2 Bar. 75.7) but elsewhere it is closely bound with the giving of the Law at Sinai (Jub. 1.48–50; Ass.Mos. 3.11ff.; 1 Enoch 89.21ff.; 2 Esd. 5.27; 9.29ff.; 14.3ff.). Indeed, in that the Law is regarded as antedating Sinai both among the Gentiles (2 Esd. 3.33ff.; 2 Bar. 48.38ff.) and Jews (Jub. 24.11; 2 Bar. 57.2) and ultimately as eternal in character (Jub. 3.31; 6.17 et al., Ass.Mos. 1.12ff.; 1 Enoch 92.6; 2 Bar. 59.2; 77.15ff.), there can be little doubt that subordination of election to Law has actually occurred.[2] Nevertheless in Jub. 1.21; 2 Esd. 9.32ff.; 14.29ff. and especially Bar. 1.9ff., 2.11ff., it is linked in a most prophetic way with the disobedience of earlier generations, followed in Jub. 1.21 by a plea for a new heart and a new spirit, and in Bar. 2.30ff. by the expectation of a future everlasting covenant with Israel through which their obedience will be sealed. Closer inspection reveals, however, that this is no more than a re-affirmation of the old covenant

---

[1] See further F. M. Abel, *Les Livres des Maccabees* (1949), p. 37; S. Tedesche, *The First Book of Maccabees* (1950), p. 71 and A. Büchler, *Studies in Sin and Atonement* (1928), pp. 14–16.

[2] The additional references cited by A. Nissen, *NT*, 9 (1967), 259, do not necessarily imply the unhistorical nature of the Law in these writings. See here 1 Enoch 90.8; 99.10; 2 Esd. 8.12; 13.54ff.; 14.40; 2 Bar. 38.2; 48.24; 51.3ff.; 59.7; 77.16.

for it is linked with 'the commandments of life' (Bar. 3.9) and 'the law that endureth forever' (Bar. 4.1) while the outcome of the new heart is the keeping of 'all the commandments' (Jub. 1.24). The expectation therefore differs from the prophetic predictions in Jer. 31.31ff. and Ezek. 36.25ff. with which the two passages are so obviously affiliated.

In these writings the term is used of the covenant with the patriarchs (Jub. 14.20; 15.4ff.; 22.15ff.; Ass.Mos. 1.9; 3.9; 4.2ff.; 11.17; 2 Bar. 84.8), of the rite of circumcision (Jub. 15.13–14, 26, 29; 16.14; 20.3) and, very frequently, the commandments (Jub. 1.5; 21.4; 23.16–19; 24.11; 30.21; 33.19; Ass.Mos. 1.14, cf. 3.12; 2 Esd. 4.23; 5.29; 7.24, 83; 8.27; 2 Bar. 41.3) but not of the covenant at Sinai as involving anything over and above the commandments associated with it.[1] There are also occasional expressions of a doctrine of works, more common in the later literature (cf. Test.Lev. 13.5; Naph. 8.5; 2 Esd. 8.26–30; 2 Bar. 14.7; 24.1; 51.7; 67.6; 84.10), though other passages affirm the priority of grace (Bar. 2.19ff.), or a combination of faith and works (2 Esd. 9.7; 13.23), and the difficulty experienced in observing the Law (2 Esd. 3.22; 9.36).[2] On the whole, despite the presence and development of legalistic tendencies – more pronounced in some writings rather than others and particularly in later works rather than earlier – biblical emphases appear to predominate.

Noteworthy is the intrusion of historical, covenantal and legal themes into the inter-testamentary wisdom literature. The redemption from Egypt is mentioned three times, being subordinated to other motifs in Wisd. 10.18ff. and Ecclus. 45.1ff., only in Wisd. 19.6ff. sharing more in common with Old Testament perspectives. The idea of the covenant is more

---

[1] For its use of the covenant with the patriarchs cf. Ps.Sol. 9.18–19, and of the commandments, Ps.Sol.10.5; 17.7. There is an explicit reference to the covenant with Noah in Jub. 6.10–14 and 14.20 as also in 1 Enoch 60.6. Strangely enough, this is the only reference to the covenant in the latter work.

[2] In 2 Esdras, however, it is the acceptance not observance of the Law by which men will be judged at the Last Day. Cf. G. H. Box, *The Pseudepigrapha of the Old Testament* (1913), II, ed. R. H. Charles, 554–5. E. Sjöberg, *Sünder*, pp. 239–40 further points out that in this literature, as distinct from later rabbinic conceptions, it is by no means certain that the majority of Israelites will be saved.

prominent, references being made to the covenant with the patriarchs (Wisd. 12.21; 18.22; Ecclus. 44.11ff.) as well as with Noah (Ecclus. 44.18), Aaron (Ecclus. 45.7ff.), Phineas (Ecclus. 45.24) and David (Ecclus. 45.25; 47.11). This multiplication of covenants, together with the use of συνθήκη in Wisd. 12.21 and the plural usage elsewhere, clearly indicates that a fragmentation of the notion has taken place. Mostly, however, it is equated with God's statutes both as a whole (Ecclus. 17.12;24.23;28.7;39.8;42.2;45.5) and individually (Wisd. 18.9; Ecclus. 14.12; 14.17; 16.22; 41.19; 44.11; 45.17).[1] The subordination of covenant to Law is particularly clear in those passages in which the Law is represented as being antecedent to it (Ecclus. 24.6; 44.19ff.). As elsewhere in the inter-testamentary literature, then, the Law is no longer an order of life within election and covenant as it is in the Old Testament, but is rather a timeless and intrinsically valid expression of the divine will. Though there are statements to the effect that a man's future position will be decided by the relative amount of his good and evil acts (Ecclus. 3.3, 14, 30; 12.7, 8; 16.14; 18.22; 19.11; 28.1ff.; 34.31; 35.3) notes of divine grace are by no means lacking (Ecclus. 2.17; 9.4; 39.6 et al.), and this doctrine of recompense is after all chiefly related to this present life. Thus despite tendencies in the direction of later rabbinic thinking there is still much in common with certain Old Testament wisdom conceptions.[2]

b   Later Jewish groups

The Qumran material, along with its legal orientation and wisdom inheritance, displays a strong interest in the prophetic literature and in that to which it gave way, apocalyptic. Influenced as it is by each of these traditions it occupies in the Judaism of its day a position similar to that of Deuteronomy in relation to the Old Testament literature, and it is interesting to note that judging from the copies of books preserved at Qumran

---

[1] This is also quite possibly the meaning in Ecclus. 44.20 in which case διαθήκη in this book never refers to the 'covenants' with the fathers. Cf. R. Smend, *Die Weisheit des Jesus Sirach* (1906), p. 423.

[2] Cf. R. H. Charles, *Pseudepigrapha*, II, 411–12; W. O. E. Oesterley, *The Jews and Judaism during the Greek Period* (1941), p. 61; H. Maldwyn Hughes, *Ethics*, p. 45 and E. Sjöberg, *Sünder*, p. 209.

Deuteronomy was the most popular, followed by Isaiah and Psalms. Interest in the Exodus is in terms of its eschatological interpretation rather than the recounting of past events (CDC 3.5ff.; 5.17ff.; 8.14ff.; 1 QM 11.9–10) and no less emphatic is their concern with the covenant.[1] Though election is subordinated to Law (1 QSb II), it is to the covenant, though not that concluded at Sinai, that their election and, despite judgment, preservation, is due (CDC 8.14ff.; 1 QSb V). Appeal is made to the covenant with the fathers (see esp. CDC 1.4; 3.4; 4.9; 6.2; 8.18; 12.11; 1 QM 13.7–8; 14.8; 1 QSb IV), its eternal character being especially noted (cf. CDC 2.16; 3.4, 13; 1 QS 3.12; 4.23; 5.6; 1 QM 17.3). Though, as in the rabbinic literature, perspectives upon this are not completely homogeneous and contrary notes are sometimes present, the emphasis generally falls upon the past gratuitousness of God in granting the covenant and on his present faithfulness in constantly maintaining the covenant with his people.[2] Since it is only within the Qumran community that this renewal of the covenant is held to have taken place, this itself is frequently referred to as 'the covenant' (CDC 2.2; 6.12; 9.2–3; 13.14; 15.5; 1 QH 5.23; 1 QS 1.8, 16, 18; 2.10, 12, 18; 3.11; 5.20; 6.15; 8.17; 10.10; 1 QM 14.4ff.) or 'the new covenant' (CDC 6.19; 8.21; 19.34[B] and, possibly, 20.12[B] and 1 QHab. 2.3). Although the idea contained in the latter expression unmistakably points in the direction of the prophetic ideal in Jer. 31.31ff., it is basically a re-affirmation and renewal of the old covenant that is involved.[3]

[1] See especially the detailed study of O. Betz, 'The Eschatological Interpretation of the Sinai-Tradition in Qumran and the New Testament', *RQ*, 6 (1967), 89–107.

[2] The gracious aspect of the covenant idea at Qumran is heavily stressed by J. G. Harris. 'The Covenant Concept among the Qumran Sectaries', *EQ*, 39 (1967), esp. 86–8. He fails, however, to distinguish sufficiently between the different nuances in the conception and therefore presents too uniform a picture of the way in which it is used in these writings.

[3] Cf. K. Schubert, *The Dead Sea Community* (1959), p. 150; M. Black, *The Scrolls and Christian Origins* (1961), pp. 91, 97; A. R. Leaney, *The Rule of Qumran and its Meaning* (1966), p. 106. A. Jaubert, *Alliance*, p. 223, states that this does not mean that the new is superior to the old, 'mais jamais la loi n'avait été mieux connue et mieux pratiquée par une collectivité en Israël'. On the basis of the passage in Baruch and the testimony in CDC, W. D. Davies, *Setting*, pp. 48–9 (cf. J. Barr, *DB* [1963], p. 184), speaks of

This is confirmed by the possibility of equating these senses of covenant with the precepts entailed in it (1 QH 7.10; 10.30; 15.15; 1 QSa 1), which in turn explains the apparent silence in these writings with respect to anything more being contained in the covenant idea than the giving of the Law.[1] To be clearly noted, however, are the solemn proclamation in 1 QS 1.16–18 of the blessings and curses attaching to obedience or disobedience to the stipulations, very much in terms of Deut. 28; the confessions of sinfulness and inability to keep the Law in such passages as 1 QS 1.21 – 2.1; CDC 20.28–30 which have much in common with Neh. 9; the references to the love of God as the basis of obedience in 1 QH 10.16; 11.18–19; 1 QS 11.2–5; 11.13b–17; and the many celebrations of the grace and righteousness of God as the ground of salvation in 1 QS 7.28–30; 9.14–15; 10.5–9; 14.23–4 and throughout 1 QH. Nevertheless, obedience to the Law of Moses, as interpreted by the Teacher of Righteousness in the regulations of the community, remains of decisive importance. This is the import of the much discussed passage 1 QHab. 8.1–3 which despite its clear testimony to human weakness remains centred upon the Law. The 'faith in the Teacher of Righteousness' that is considered a prerequisite for salvation refers to acceptance of and fidelity to his teaching, and is associated with 'labour' in the Law.[2] We

the hope of a 'new covenant' persisting as a 'dynamic element in Judaism'. In view of the silence elsewhere in the inter-testamentary and later Jewish literature, however, this would seem to be something of an overstatement.

[1] R. L. Déaut, 'Une citation de Lév. 26.45 dans le Doc. de Damas I:4; VI:2', *RQ*, 6 (1967), 289–91, maintains, however, that the reference to Lev. 26.45 along with that of Lev. 26.42 in these verses implies the tradition of a covenant at Sinai, and compares a similar fusion in Codex Neofiti 1.255b–256a.

[2] See especially the detailed discussion in H. Braun, *Qumran und das Neue Testament* (1966), I, 169–71, 209. This is also the emphasis in references to the necessity of knowledge in 1 QH, as M. Mansoor, *The Thanksgiving Hymns* (1961), p. 69, points out. Too Pauline an interpretation is often given to the passage from the Habbakuk Commentary, as in C. T. Fritsch, *The Qumran Community* (1956), pp. 126–7; R. K. Harrison, *The Dead Sea Scrolls* (1961), p. 121, and, to some extent, M. Black, *Scrolls*, pp. 125–8. The teaching it contains is chiefly a continuation of Old Testament ideas modified by legalistic development rather than a near anticipation of New Testament conceptions. See further, more generally, W. D. Davies, 'Flesh and Spirit', *The Scrolls and the New Testament*, pp. 180–1, and W. Brownlee, *The Meaning of the Qumran Scrolls for the Bible* (1964), p. 150.

find here, then, strongly nomistic and charismatic piety inter-twined but on the whole the idea of Law as response rather than achievement clearly prevails.

The chief antecedents of the rabbinic literature appear to be legal and wisdom traditions but, especially in the pre-Destruction period, apocalyptic strands were also present. In both halakhic and haggadic materials D. Daube has found ample illustration of the continuing importance of the Exodus events.[1] Considerable ambiguity exists, however, as to the ground of Israel's election. Sometimes this is ascribed solely to the grace of God (Mek.Ex. 13.4; 19.2; Pesik.K. 47a; Sif.Num. 15.41), though at other times reference is made to the merits of the fathers (Mek.Ex. 13.4; Tos.Sot. 11.10; Ex.R. 1.36) or certain merits associated with Israel herself such as meritorious deeds (Num.R. 3.2), observance of the Sabbath (Mek.Ex. 16.24), and acceptance of Torah (Num.R. 14.10). It would be mis-leading, however, to construe the latter purely in legal terms, for in addition to Israel's merits the element of love in the relationship between God and Israel is present in the rabbinic doctrine. Nevertheless, the impression is often gained of a reciprocal doctrine of election towards which there appears to be an increasing tendency in Jewish thought, for it is rather the older expressions of Jewish piety, especially in liturgical con-texts as the Shema and Eighteen Benedictions bear witness, which preserve the more biblical emphasis.[2] Disagreement also existed as to the indissolubility of the bond between God and Israel, R. Meir, speaking for the overwhelming majority voice in rabbinic Judaism, strongly opposing the view of R. Judah ben Ilai who considered the relationship as conditional upon

---

[1] D. Daube, *The New Testament and Rabbinic Judaism* (1956), pp. 275–82.

[2] K. Emmerich, 'Die Juden', *TS*, 7 (1939), concluded that God did not elect Israel but Israel God, a position that has been rightly, if rather one-sidedly, criticised by H. J. Schoeps, 'Haggadisches zur Auserwählung Israels', *Aus Frühchristlicher Zeit* (1950), pp. 184–200. Cf. also S. Schechter, *Some Aspects of Rabbinic Theology* (1909), pp. 57–64. The love aspect in the relationship between God and Israel is well documented by B. W. Helfgott, *The Doctrine of Election in Tannaitic Literature* (1954), p. 138, and refs. cited. A comprehensive and balanced treatment of the variety of different, even contradictory, perspectives in the literature is to be found in M. Kadushin, 'Aspects of the Rabbinic Concept of Israel', *HUCA*, 19 (1945–1946), esp. 57–71.

good behaviour (Sif.Deut. 14.1; 32.1; 32.5; b.Kid. 36a.) Most probably these two conceptions of the election of Israel would not have been consciously recognised as mutually exclusive. Precisely because they were held together in a contradictory unity, however, prophetic pronouncements to the effect that God remains sovereign in election and reprobation were unable to assert their full influence.[1]

In these writings, perhaps significantly, the theme of the covenant is dealt with less frequently than in the inter-testamentary literature. In Mek.Ex. 23.19 the covenants with Noah, Abraham and Israel are mentioned. Elsewhere, however, the term is used with reference to Torah generally (Sif.Num. 15.22; Sif.Lev. 26.14; Sif.Deut. 17.2), the individual commandments (b.Sot. 37b; j.Sot. 21c), the sabbath (Mek.Ex. 19.5) and, most frequently, circumcision (Mek.Ex. 18.3; Sif.Num. 15.31, cf. Bill., I, 991; II, 627ff., 671). While some precedent is found for these uses in the Old Testament, it is clear that the legal aspect of the conception – a subsidiary motif in the biblical writings – is now uppermost. According to Mek. Ex. 12.6, in fact, 'by בוית is meant nothing other than Torah'. This centrality of Torah in rabbinic thinking no doubt explains the reticence with respect to the covenant in these writings resulting in, at best, an ambiguous and, at worst, a misleading understanding of the original idea.[2] Election is now bound directly with Law rather than being linked together with it through the idea of the covenant in which both are held in a proper perspective. This means that it is no longer the covenant which encompasses the Law, but the Law which antedates and is the ground both for the covenant (Sif.Lev. 11.45; Mek.Ex. 20.3) and election (Sif.Num. 15.41; Sif.Lev. 19.36; 22.33; 25.38; Sif. Deut. 15.15; 16.12).[3] A similar

---

[1] Cf. W. Förster, *Palestinian Judaism and the New Testament* (1964), pp. 191–2; J. Jocz, *A Theology of Election* (1958), p. 64, and the extensive discussion in E. Sjöberg, *Sünder*, pp. 30–71, 95–124.

[2] On the rabbinic silence here see J. Bonsirven, *Le Judaïsme Palestinien* (1934–5), I, 79ff.; K. Schubert, *Die Religion des nachbiblischen Judentums* (1955), p. 30; H. J. Schoeps, *Theologie und Geschichte* (1949), p. 90. The popularity of the idea in christian literature was almost certainly an additional, and fundamental, ground for its omission.

[3] On the relationship between Law and covenant see especially A. Jaubert, *Alliance*, p. 291. A. Nissen, *NT*, 9 (1967), 257–8, on the other hand,

ambiguity occurs in the rabbinic teaching on reward and merit with respect to salvation in the life to come, and in the stress laid upon inward piety as opposed to mere externalism in the obedience demanded by God. In spite of the less legalistic ideas contained in, for example, Ab. 2.8; Num.R. 19.8; Mk. 12.28ff. and elsewhere, such other passages as b.Kid. 40b; Tos.Sanh. 13.3; Makk. 3.16; b.Ber. 28b, not to speak of the overall portrait in the gospels and in Josephus, it would be fair to say that while no uniform doctrine is found, and occasional notes of grace are struck, that the emphasis upon works is the dominant motif.[1]

We have come a long way from the perspective on election, covenant and Law outlined in the earliest accounts. In those narratives a strong emphasis was laid upon Yahweh's initiative in selecting Israel from among the nations, in establishing a secure relationship with her people and in providing the practical basis upon which that relationship could be maintained. Election, covenant and Law, therefore, are at once carefully balanced in respect of each other yet closely interrelated with each other, and all three are grounded in the initial call, bond and set of obligations to which Abraham earlier responded. With the passing of time, new situations arose in which these foundations had to be reiterated and renewed. The growth of various traditions about them, the entrance into a different social context and confrontation by new pressures and circumstances both from within the nation and outside it, lent a distinctive character to each of these re-affirmations. While a variety of tendencies may be detected in the historical writings,

evaluates the rabbinic evidence in too biblical a manner. The relationship between Law and election is sensitively treated by H. Hruby, 'Der Begriff und Funktion des Gottes Volkes in der rabbinischen Tradition', *Jud.*, 21 (1965), 23ff.

[1] Thus neither the overemphasis upon the legalistic orientation of Pharisaism in E. Schürer, *A History of the Jewish People* (1896), II, 91ff., nor its dismissal in reaction by R. T. Herford, *The Pharisees* (1924), pp. 124–5; *Talmud and Apocrypha* (1933), p. 142, is an accurate reflection of the evidence. The presence of contradictory elements, and the inability of either to predominate, is maintained by C. G. Montefiore, 'The Old Testament and Judaism', *Record and Revelation* (1938), ed. H. W. Robinson, p. 438, and J. Parkes, *Jesus, Paul and the Jews* (1936), p. 70. A more realistic appraisal is provided by W. Förster, *Judaism*, p. 223.

there is a general inclination to detach ideas of election, covenant and Law from their historical basis, lay greater stress on Israel's part in preserving the relationship established by them, and centre attention more exclusively on the Law as a whole and the individual commands of which it is constituted. Throughout the Old Testament period this takes place without any serious distortion of the basic orientation of the earliest accounts. This was at least partly due to the influence of the prophetic and wisdom traditions which during this time continually acted as a brake upon these other developments. These two approaches also testified to the possibility of maintaining a stance towards the Law which, while not antagonistic towards it, focussed attention upon wider and narrower moral concerns respectively.

The inter-testamentary literature reflects an intensification of the tendencies that were developing in material relating to election, covenant and Law though, on the whole, biblical emphases retained their pre-eminence. During this period, a reorientation of the prophetic viewpoint away from the present revelation of Yahweh, and a domestication of the wisdom inheritance through its closer association with the Law, resulted in a lessening of their impact upon the mainstream of Jewish thought. Elsewhere the influence of Greek conceptions and terminology was beginning to have a corrosive effect upon the religious understanding of these concerns in Diaspora Judaism. Nevertheless, in the latest period, the underlying presence of certain prophetic and wisdom themes in the convictions of the newer religious groupings helped preserve authentic biblical perspectives in their several viewpoints. This was less evident among the Pharisees than at Qumran, for while the latter were ever in danger of slipping from a casuistic attitude to Yahweh's demands into a legalistic attitude to Yahweh himself, the more ambiguous positions of the former suggest that frequently this particular point had already been passed. It is now time, however, to leave this investigation of the basis of Law and turn to a consideration of the character it possessed in the different traditions within biblical, inter-testamentary and Jewish thought.

B THE LAW – RIGID OR FLEXIBLE?

I OLD TESTAMENT

The most important term for a consideration of the character of Law is תורה which is used some 220 times in the Old Testament. The word occurs only rarely in JE. In the older prophets and the wisdom literature it is found infrequently, but often emphatically. It is the Deuteronomic and priestly authors, as well as the Chronicler, who bring it into more common use. The growth of תורה should not merely be thought of in terms of a movement from oral to written law, as is sometimes supposed, for both forms already existed at an early period. While it is true that there was an increasing emphasis in later times upon its being put into writing, therefore, there was no simple evolution from the one to the other.

In Israel, the main instruments of תורה are the priest, prophet and wise man, and it is important for our purpose to clarify the particular meaning of the term for each.[1] Since, as the basic work of G. Östborn has demonstrated, the etymology of the word remains obscure, it is its usage in the Old Testament which is of greatest significance. Here there now seems to be fairly general agreement that its primary sense is 'instruction'. The word itself, therefore, tells us nothing of the way in which the Law was given, but rather suggests that its general purpose was the guidance of God's people in the various matters to which it relates. This also indicates that the end of the Law lay beyond mere obedience to rules in the knowledge of God and his will.

When the content of these 'instructions' is examined more closely, the presence of two significant factors forbids their being understood as absolute and timeless norms embracing the whole

---

[1] To these G. Östborn, *Tora*, pp. 54–88, and G. Widengren, *JJS*, 2 (1957), 1–32, add the king, but he is rather to be considered as a guardian of the Law than as an imparter of it. Cf. C. R. North, *The Second Isaiah* (1964), p. 110. Though the presence of these three classes from the earliest times is no longer contested, it is unwise to set up too rigid categories in distinguishing them for their functions not infrequently overlap.

of human life, and therefore as possessing a rigid and authoritarian character: (1) inasmuch as the provisions of the Law are related to specific situations, changing historical circumstances result in a corresponding re-interpretation of those provisions so that תורה is *flexible in application*; (2) though its intention is to embrace every sphere of life, it does not set out to cover every possible contingency or every possible area of concern by means of a detailed casuistry, so that תורה is *limited in extent*. These two factors must now be examined in greater detail.

a   Historical material

It is as well to begin with the Decalogue itself, for it is above all the place where the 'eternal moral law' is usually considered to have been embodied. As the previous investigation has shown, however, Israel did not understand the Decalogue as an absolute moral law prescribing ethics. Rather was it recognised as a revelation given at a particular moment in history, through which she was offered the saving gift of life and given assistance in understanding how at that time such a gift was to be appropriated. With the passing of time, this historical revelation was interpreted afresh in the light of new circumstances, added to in the light of new situations, and summarised in a more comprehensive norm of behaviour.

So, firstly, by no means did Israel have in her possession a ready-made, all-inclusive definition of the meaning and scope of the commandments. This is particularly clear with regard to the first and second commandments, for in that the situations in which she had to remain loyal to them were constantly changing there was need for continual re-interpretation, and this the prophets proceeded to do. As for the second table of the commandments, subsequent codes may to a large extent be regarded as extended commentaries upon them. Deuteronomy, in particular, provides a clear example of the way in which older traditions were handled with quite extensive freedom.[1]

Also discernible is the supplementing of older negative commandments, which themselves marked out general boundaries for behaviour rather than prescribed precise paths, with a positive counterpart, as well as the increasing tendency in the

---

[1] See especially G. von Rad, *Studies in Deuteronomy* (ET 1953), pp. 22–4.

later codes to add motive clauses to older stipulations, designed no doubt to increase their meaningfulness and encourage their observance.[1] Furthermore, the differences in these successive codes on related points indicate that just so far as the Law was precisely applicable to one age it ceased to be directly relevant to another. A good example of this is provided by the Deuteronomic legitimation of a single altar at Jerusalem (Deut. 12.1ff.) instead of the plurality of sacrificial locations permitted in the Book of the Covenant (Ex. 20.24). There are also clear examples of new instructions being added which have no discernible basis in any previous legal statutes.[2]

Finally, even the ten commandments are not viewed as the ultimate norm of Israel's conduct. Thus in Deuteronomy all the commandments are considered within the context of the one great command to love Yahweh and him alone (Deut. 6.4ff.). In this connection it is also significant that, Deuteronomy apart (which in any case is rehearsing the original Sinaitic covenant) no single literal doublet of the Decalogue is to be found in the ethical tradition of Israel.[3]

---

[1] This is worked out in detail by B. Gemser, 'The Importance of the Motive Clause in Old Testament Law', *VT* Suppl. 1, 50–66. He gives the following figures for the incidence of such clauses – Book of the Covenant 17 per cent; Deuteronomy 60 per cent; Holiness Code 65 per cent. The interpolation of homiletical material into legal codes, especially evident in Deuteronomy, is an example of a similar tendency on a much larger scale.

[2] Cf. H. W. Robinson, 'Law and Religion in Israel', *Judaism and Christianity* (1938), ed. E. I. J. Rosenthal, III, 61. G. von Rad, *Deuteronomy*, p. 23, suggests that Deut. 20.1–9; 26.1–11 and 29.1–9 all 'make obligatory on the present not any norms of a legal kind, but old cultic usages'. Other examples are provided by J. Weingreen, 'Oral Torah and Written Records', *Holy Book and Holy Tradition* (1968), ed. F. F. Bruce and E. G. Rupp, pp. 61ff., who refers to Num. 27.1–11; 15.32–6 and Lev. 24.11–16 as examples of new legal rulings for which no provision had been made in the Mosaic code and, outside the Pentateuch, to the novel regulations behind 1 Kings 21; Amos 8.5 and Jer. 17.21–2. See further, D. Daube, *Studies in Biblical Law* (1969), pp. 78ff.

[3] See further the remarks of F. E. Vokes, 'The Ten Commandments in the New Testament and in First Century Judaism', *St.Ev.*, V (1968), 146. Some, as e.g., Th. C. Vriezen, *Theology*, p. 336, claim that a shortened form of the Decalogue is to be found in Lev. 19.3ff. and 12ff. This, however, cannot be sustained, for it is artificial to separate the commands parallel to those in the Decalogue from the mass of other laws in the same context. The conjunction of the Decalogue commands with the others in a

These three factors indicate that Yahweh's demands did not stand absolutely above time for Israel, for every generation was summoned anew to listen to them and to interpret and apply them for itself. תורה, then, is flexible in application.

In the next place, as has been mentioned, it is the purpose of תורה to embrace every sphere of life so as to bring it under obedience to Yahweh, and to lay claim to the whole man, his inner attitudes as well as his outward activity. This comprehensive intention can be illustrated from the Decalogue, not only in its conjunction of religious and ethical demands but also, as evident in the last commandment, in its concern for motive as well as outward behaviour. It is significant, however, that no attempt is made in it to build up a casuistic system that would cover every contingency in the realm of conduct and every nuance in the realm of motive. In fact, apart from two exceptions, it confines itself to a few basic negations which act as signposts on the borders of a large area of life to which he who belongs to Yahweh must give heed.

When the detailed enactments in other Old Testament Law collections are examined, it is clear that they are also far from being exhaustive codes covering every aspect of life. Outside them lie large areas of activity which remain completely unregulated. The wisdom literature demonstrates how wide was the scope for further advice and counsel in the field of *personal and social morality*. Civil laws cover only certain aspects of *economic and political life* and leave considerable room for various kinds of additional independent administration.[1] In the realm

rather haphazard fashion indicates just how little the Decalogue prescriptions were regarded as distinctive or absolute norms. K. Berger, *Gesetzesauslegung* (1972), p. 259, has also rightly pointed out that 'Stücke wie Hos. 4.2 und Jer. 7.9...spiegeln sich Reste von Traditionen, die sich auch im Dekalog niedergeschlagen haben, die aber auch ganz ohne den Zusammenhang des Dekalogs überliefert werden konnten.'

[1] This had already been clearly shown by P. Fairbairn, *Law*, pp. 96ff. It is confirmed by the fact that although transmission and codification of the laws was primarily in the hands of the priests, it was within the individual local communities that much of the formation and administration of Israelite Law took place. Good examples of this practice can be seen in such passages as Ruth 4.1ff. and Jer. 26. A discussion of the judicial arrangements that existed in Israel from early monarchical to Deuteronomic times may be found in G. C. Macholz, 'Zur Geschichte der Justizorganization in Juda', *ZAW*, 84 (1972), 314–40.

of both *individual and corporate worship* there was considerably more room for individual initiative than is often realised.[1]

Not only, then, was there freedom to re-interpret and alter the Law as new situations arose, but, due to the limited extent of specific legislation, there was freedom of action in those areas of life upon which those enactments did not intrude. The Law, therefore, was not immutable, nor did it seek to regulate the whole of man's existence in a concrete way. In both respects it possessed a limited and conditional character.

The matter cannot be left there, however, for it is clear from a study of later Judaism that for some time tendencies corroding both these factors had been in operation. At what point did they begin, and how successfully were they resisted throughout the Old Testament period? The first place at which the accusing finger of unnecessary casuistry comes to rest in Israel's history is the promulgation of the Deuteronomic Law.[2] It is regarded as present in the attempt to use case law to compel morality or make it into statutory law, in the inscribing of the Law in a Book (Deut. 17.18–19) and in the tendency to speak of 'the (or this) Law' in the singular as if it had become an absolute entity (Deut. 1.5; 4.8, 44; 17.18–19 *et al.*).

Against this, however, must be set the following factors: (1) though the laws are comprehensive in character they do not have a casuistic stamp – thus noteworthy is the persistence of negative formulations (e.g. Deut. 27.15ff.) as well as the appearance of exhortations and ordinances which have more in common with the counsel of the wise than legal pronouncements (15.7–11; 16.11–14 *et al.*); (2) the ethical demands are placed firmly in the foreground while a relative lack of concern

---

[1] In the realm of private worship there was scarcely any regulation at all. As far as public liturgy is concerned it should be remembered that most of the laws relating to worship were intended as directions for the priest, and that considerable freedom was left to the worshipper within the general liturgical framework. Moreover, many brought voluntary offerings to their shrines or later the Temple since all the circumstances of daily life could provide motivation for them. Even with regard to the priests there seems to have been the possibility of a more prophetic role. The presence of literary homilies in Deuteronomy, Chronicles and certain prophetic passages lends support to this suggestion.

[2] So G. E. Wright, *The Biblical Doctrine of Man in Society* (1954), p. 104.

for absolute correctness is evident in the cultic legislation;[1] (3) the centrality of the motive of love for God is the basis for obedience (Deut. 5.10; 6.5; 7.9; 10.12 *et al.*) while the designation of the fellow-Israelite as 'brother' throughout indicates that the obligation to him is far from being of a merely legal kind; (4) the emphasis upon the unity of the Law is not an innovation since it already occurs in JE (Ex. 13.9; 24.12) and in the prophets (Amos 2.4; Hos. 4.6; 8.1, 12), nor is it the first time the Law has been set in written form (cf. Ex. 24.7, 12; Hos. 8.12);[2] (5) as already demonstrated, there is considerable flexibility in the handling of older legal traditions and a fresh and relevant interpretation of their significance. Behind these factors lay a striking fusion of prophetic and wisdom influences with the legal material. The work which resulted can scarcely be regarded as introducing a casuistic emphasis entailing an increasing strictness in the way in which Yahweh's will was regarded.

Against the priestly legal compilations has been mentioned the objectivity with which the material seems to have been gathered, as well as the renewed interest in ritual legislation. As has already been indicated, however, much of this material is concerned with regulating the technicalities of the cult: as the 'professional priest's handbook' it is not surprising that there is little room for exhortation and interpretation in its rubrics. Further, despite the minor redactions of the post-exilic period, the basic stratum of this law has now been shown to stretch back into pre-exilic times, much of it to the beginning of the nation's history, thus confirming the tradition that an integral aspect of the original covenant at Sinai was the regulation of cultic life. Moreover, cultic material in P stands within the wider revelation of the Mosaic Law which surrounds it i.e., alongside other legal and religious ordinances as well as moral norms.[3]

---

[1] See further H. W. Wolff, 'Das Kerygma des deuteronomistischen Geschichtswerks', *ZAW*, 73 (1961), 183.

[2] Cf. W. Beecher, 'Torah: A Word Study in the Old Testament', *JBL*, 24 (1905), 12–13. On the following point, similarities and differences between the rabbinic and Deuteronomic approaches have been explored by J. Weingreen, 'The Deuteronomic Lawgiver: A Proto-Rabbinic Type', *Transitions*, pp. 76–89.

[3] This is illustrated outside the actual blocks of legislation in the emphasis upon moral conduct in the accounts of the Patriarchs as in the continual

Thus, as in Deuteronomy, we find a central place given to the love-commandment, this time however directed towards the neighbour (Lev. 19.18, 34). The presence of additional 'motive-clauses' in the legislation has already been mentioned. It is also interesting to note once again the continuance of negative formulations of the commandments (Lev. 19.13ff.). Caution must be observed, therefore, in ascribing the source of the legal material in this literature to misplaced casuistic zeal. Here and there evidence of such may be discernible, but it does not dominate the material as a whole.

The centrality of the Law and the prominence of particular, especially cultic, stipulations in the later historical works is certainly marked. It has been claimed that alongside references to 'the Law' in the traditional sense, much more common in this literature is the equation of a recent cultic usage with a canonical ritual provision, and that this is indicative of the ascendancy of casuistry. However, though the prevalence of the second usage is striking, indeed ominous (cf. 1 Chron. 16.40; 2 Chron. 8.13; 23.18; 30.16; 31.3; 35.12; Ezra 3.2, 4 and Neh. 10.28, 29, 34, 36, 44; 13.3 which although resting on older legislation – Ex. 24.12–16; 20.8–11 – go far beyond the directions in those enactments), the evidence does not fully substantiate this claim. Perhaps the theme of the unity of the revelation of Yahweh's will is waning, but it is still the dominant feature in this material (cf. 1 Chron. 6.16; 22.12; 2 Chron. 12.1; 14.4; 17.9; 25.4; 31.21; 33.8; 34.14, 15, 19; 35.26; Ezra 7.6, 10, 12, 14, 21, 26; Neh. 8.1, 2, 3, 7, 8, 13, 18; 9.3, 26, 29, 34). Also still in view is the underlying motive of love for Yahweh (Neh. 1.5), though nowhere as prominent as in Deuteronomy or even the Priestly writings, while an attitude of rejoicing in the Law is everywhere present. Whereas, then, certain tendencies appear in the post-exilic period which have opened up the way towards a casuistic understanding of the Law, it cannot be said that any of these writings have become predominantly formalistic in character.

moral assessments that pervade the historical sections. Within the legal material it is present in such passages as the list of instructions protecting the weaker members of the society from those who might be tempted to exploit them, e.g., women (Lev. 20), small landholders (Lev. 25), etc.

b Prophetic writings

Prophetic concern for the Law has already been demonstrated. There can no longer be any doubt that, alongside other basic Israelite traditions, it formed a basic element in their preaching. But was it the basic element in their moral instruction? The central conception for the prophets seems rather to have been צדקה which is viewed not only as the standard of man's relationship with God but also of his relationship with his neighbour (Amos 5.7, 24; Hos. 10.12; Zeph. 2.3; Isa. 5.7, 23; Jer. 4.2; 9.24; 22.3; Ezek. 3.20; 14.14, 20; 18.22–6; 33.12–18; 2 Isa. 48.1, 18; 51.1; 3 Isa. 56.1; 57.12; 58.2–8; Mal. 3.3).[1] Though it is found only rarely in the historical books, in the prophetic literature it occurs more frequently than the appeal for משפט (with which it is often coupled) or the demand for obedience to תורה (with which it is also occasionally associated). It is certainly far more than a strictly legal or judicial notion.[2] While it has sometimes been defined purely in terms of the demands of relationships which are so varied in character and context that they cannot be reduced to general principles, it is rather to be viewed in terms of a wide universal norm which possesses different applications in different circumstances.[3]

What we find here, then, is a conception of Yahweh's will that is not opposed to the Law, indeed embraces it as a fundamental part of its message, yet proceeds to require more than that which the Law demands. Most striking in this connection is the use of the term תורה not of the demands of the Law but

---

[1] The term is also descriptive of the Servant or his mission in 2 Isa. 41.10; and 45.13. It is predicated of Yahweh himself in Hos. 10.12; Mic. 6.5; Isa. 1.27; 5.16; 11.4, 5; 33.5; 2 Isa. 45.8, 19, 23–4; 51.5ff.; 3 Isa. 63.1. It is, of course, also prominent in eschatological contexts.

[2] So already S. A. Cook in W. Robertson-Smith, *The Religion of the Semites* (1927³), p. 656, in disagreement with W. Robertson-Smith, *The Prophets of Israel* (1919), pp. 71ff.; M. Lazarus, *The Ethics of Judaism* (1900–1), pp. 135–6, and T. H. Robinson, *Prophecy and the Prophets in Ancient Israel* (1957²), p. 164.

[3] Cf. esp. N. Snaith, *The Distinctive Ideas of the Old Testament* (1944), pp. 76–7, and E. Jacob, *Theology*, pp. 94–6. The alternative view has been maintained by E. R. Achtemeier, 'Righteousness', *IDB*, IV, 80 and G. von Rad, *Theology*, I, 371–3.

of the prophet's own message from Yahweh. This is a most significant usage and is attested throughout the pre-exilic and exilic periods (cf. Isa. 1.10; 8.16, 20; 30.9; Jer. 6.9; 26.4ff.; 44.10; 2 Isa. 51.4, 7).[1] It indicates quite clearly where the emphasis lay in the prophetic writings.

The message of Ezekiel has also been regarded as a decisive turning point in the casuistic development of Israelite law.[2] In his prophecy, however, we find again the persistence of negative formulations in the spirit of the Decalogue legislation (e.g., Ezek. 18.16ff.) and the use of תורה in connection with the prophet's own teaching (Ezek. 43.11–12), while the heavily cultic chapters towards the close of the work possess a symbolic and eschatological character and were not intended to be understood in a literal and programmatic manner (Ezek. 40–8). However, it must be admitted that concentration upon cultic matters in these chapters involved the possibility of misinterpretation in a later, more prosaic, age. In the post-exilic period, the prophetic writings are no exception to this new interest in the cult (3 Isa. 56.7; Hagg. 1.8ff.; 2.3ff.; Mal. 1.7ff.; 3.3ff.), in addition to which heightened importance seems to have been placed upon the sabbath (3 Isa. 56.2, 4; 58.13; 66.2, 3). Nevertheless, the unity of Yahweh's will is still stressed (Mal. 4.4ff.), the underlying motive of love for Yahweh does not go unmentioned (3 Isa. 56.6), תורה can still refer to the demands of the prophetic message (Zech. 7.12) and צדקה continues to cover far more than mere obedience to the Mosaic legislation. Even in the late book of Daniel, where the way in which the dietary laws are conceived appears to be quite casuistic, there is to be found the equation of תורה with prophetic instruction (Dan. 9.10) together with a unified conception of the Law which includes far more than the ritual commandments (Dan. 9.11, 13) and is again permeated by the motive of love (Dan. 9.4).

---

[1] For the influence of this usage upon the Deuteronomic literature note, for example, 2 Kings 17.13. Even the Mosaic Law is regarded as the תורה of the greatest of the prophets, that is, Moses (Deut. 4.1; 11.18ff.). On all this G. Östborn, *Tora*, pp. 127ff., should especially be consulted, as also W. J. Beecher, *JBL*, 24 (1905), 1ff.

[2] So L. Köhler, *Old Testament Theology* (ET 1957), pp. 181ff.

c Wisdom literature

I have suggested previously that wherever תורה is mentioned in these works it refers to the instructions of the wise (Prov. 1.8; 3.1; 4.2–4; 6.20; 7.1–2; 10.8; 13.14; 31.26; Eccles. 8.2, 5; Job 6.24; 8.8) so that this is also probably the meaning in the only passages in which a reference to the Mosaic Torah is at all possible (Prov. 6.23; 19.16; 28.4ff.; 29.18; Eccles. 12.13; Job 23.12). In these instructions there is no thought of asking obedience to an extensive casuistry covering every aspect of life. They are rather to be regarded as practical advice for the man who wishes to be faithful to God and neighbour in his general behaviour. This way of approaching the material is confirmed by the nature of Wisdom itself which is viewed, not as a burden laid upon men, but as a gracious gift to be freely appropriated by those seeking obedience to Yahweh.[1] This lines up with the character of the specific teachings themselves which, as the recurring words 'instruction', 'knowledge', 'insight' and 'counsel' indicate, is inextricably linked with the need for understanding and discernment as opposed to naked obedience.[2]

It is further to be noted that both 'love' (Prov. 4.6; 8.17, 21; 9.8; 10.12; 17.9) and 'righteousness' (Prov. 2.9; 8.8, 18, 20; 10.2; 11.4ff.; 12.17, 28; 13.6; 14.34; 15.9; 16.8, 12, 31; 21.21) are key concepts throughout their teaching, though neither figure quite so prominently as in the prophetic literature. However, it is significant that, unlike the prophets, here the official Law does not even form part of the instruction that is laid down. The teaching that is given, while it is in no sense set over against the traditional Law, goes both behind it and considerably beyond it. This particular understanding of the

---

[1] See R. E. Murphy, 'The Kerygma of the Book of Proverbs', *Int.*, 20 (1966), 4, who, defining kerygma as 'the proclamation of a religious message (which need not deal with the points of Heilsgeschichte nor be found in a liturgical context) with the invitation to accept it', contends that 'Proverbs 1–9 is as "kerygmatic" as almost anything the Old Testament has to offer.' Cf. also D. A. Hubbard, *Tyn.B.*, 17 (1966), 20–4 and J. W. Montgomery, 'Wisdom as Gift', *Int.*, 16 (1962), 43–57.

[2] For a fine detailed survey of all that is involved in the word 'counsel' see P. A. H. de Boer, 'The Counsellor', *Wisdom in Israel and in the Ancient Near East* (ed. M. Noth and D. Winton Thomas, 1955), pp. 42–71.

will of Yahweh, independent of Law and prophecy though by
no means uninfluenced by them or conceived without the
framework of ideas and demands contributed by them, provides
an even clearer example than prophecy of a tradition within
Israel in which the Law appears to be a basic but not the central
consideration. If this is an accurate interpretation of both the
wisdom and prophetic traditions then we have unearthed a fact
of considerable importance for the theme of this study.[1]

2 LATER JEWISH LITERATURE

We consider first the Septuagintal usage of the term under
discussion. In the LXX, תורה is normally translated by
νόμος and since, by this stage, the former had come to denote
the traditional Law almost without exception, and the latter in
contemporary Greek usage was chiefly defined in terms of legal
custom, the idea conveyed by νόμος acquired a more standard-
ised and specialised sense than it possessed in the Old Testament. The more natural Greek equivalent of the term, understood in its primary meaning of 'instruction', would have been
something like διδαχή or διδασκαλία.[2] Thus not only does a
more strongly legal element enter into the use of νόμος in the
historical material centring upon Law, but also the prophetic
νόμος and the νόμος of the wise are now subsumed under the
idea of legislation as well.[3] However, a unified understanding

---

[1] Again I do not intend to examine the Psalms from this perspective. It
should perhaps be noted, however, that the so-called 'legalistic' Psalms
(Ps. 1, 19, 119), as M. Noth, *Laws*, pp. 88–90, concedes, need by no means
be illustrative of a formalistic tendency. See further H. W. Wolff, 'Psalm
1', *Ev.Th.* 9 (1949–50), 385–94; H. J. Kraus, *Ev.Th.* 10 (1950–1), 337–51,
and, most recently, B. de Pinto, 'The Torah and the Psalms', *JBL*, 86
(1967), 154–73, who extends this into other Psalms possessing a Torah
vocabulary. It is quite possible, in fact, that תורה in these Psalms does not
refer to the official Law at all, but rather to the instructions of the wise.

[2] Cf. C. H. Dodd, *The Bible and the Greeks* (1935), p. 32. For a most complete
and detailed evaluation of the Greek materials see G. Kleinknecht, art.
νόμος, *TDNT*, IV, 1023–35.

[3] C. H. Dodd, *Bible*, p. 32, claims that only in Prov. 7.2, where תורה is
rendered by λόγος, and Job 22.22, where it is replaced by ἐξηγορία, is a
sense other than the strictly legal expressed in the translation. Both he
and W. Gutbrod, *TDNT*, IV, 1046, point to the lack of a consistent pattern
in some instances of תורה being translated by νόμος and some not,

of the Law is still present: indeed, in several passages there is the replacing of a number of original plurals by the singular. It is also interesting to note that in a number of instances, where it is particularly appropriate, the verbal form תורה is translated by διδάσκειν, and this suggests that the translators were at least aware that 'instruction' was one aspect of the meaning of the term. Moreover, it is most likely that as a result of Greek influence the translators viewed the Law from the standpoint of παιδεία and, whatever dangers such influence may contain, it could hardly but preserve an element of 'instruction' in their understanding of תורה.[1]

a Inter-testamentary works

The Law has, in fact, become the basis of all writings and all parties during this period. In the historical and pseudo-historical books it certainly occupies a pre-eminent place. It is now suggested further, however, that the task of the prophets was merely to apply it (1 Esd. 8.82ff.; 2 Macc. 2.1ff.), and that the Temple ritual is only valid because commanded in it (1 Macc. 4.42ff.).[2] Righteousness becomes increasingly viewed in terms of Law (Tobit 14.9), as also does counsel (Tobit 4.18–19). Indeed, in Tobit (1.3; 2.14; 12.9; 14.11) the former is equated with almsgiving, the beginning of a tendency which was to have wide repercussions in the rabbinic literature. Especially the ritual commandments come in for added emphasis: so the sabbath (Judith 8.6; 1 Macc. 1.39; 2.41; 10.34; 2 Macc. 5.25ff.; 6.6ff.; 12.38; 15.1ff.), festivals

though the latter feels that in a number of cases there is an indication that the Hebrew bears a sense not in accordance with the main post-exilic meaning of νόμος and תורה.

[1] Cf. H. J. Schoeps, *Paul*, p. 31, noting that 'this paedagogic concern is closely interwoven with the anthropocentric humanistic piety of Hellenistic Judaism. The focal point is the pious life of man, the human religious disposition. Here lurk all the dangers of establishing a human claim over against God, and of replacing the Old Testament religion of grace by a human religion of virtuous works.' It should also be noted here that with the translation of צדקה by δικαιοσύνη the LXX tends to formalise 'righteousness' in a similarly juristic manner. See further C. H. Dodd, *Bible*, pp. 42–57.

[2] Direct witness to the cessation of prophecy occurs in 1 Macc. 4.46; 9.27; 14.41. There is a useful discussion of this theme in I. Abrahams, *Studies in Pharisaism and the Gospels* (1924), II, App. XIV, 120–8.

(Judith 8.6; Tobit 1.6; 2.1–3; 1 Macc. 1.39; 10.34; 2 Macc. 6.4–6; 12.31), new feasts (1 Macc. 4.59; 7.49; 2 Macc. 1.9, 18; 10.5–8), sacrifices (Judith 4.14; 16.16, 18; 2 Macc. 1.8; 10.3), tithes (Tobit 1.6; Judith 11.13), dietary laws (Judith 11.12; Tobit 1.10–11), circumcision (1 Macc. 2.46; 2 Macc. 6.10), ablutions (Judith 12.7; 16.8) and avoidance of unlawful marriages (1 Esd. 8.69; Tobit 4.12). While definite references to the teaching of halakha are not found in these writings, the books of Tobit, Judith and 2 Maccabees show tendencies towards the later interpretation of the Law associated with Pharisaism, while 1 Maccabees is inclined in a more Sadducaean direction. In the midst of this encroachment of Law upon other areas of life, emphasis upon ceremonial regulations and a certain rigidity of interpretation, one still finds affirmations of the necessity of love towards God and brethren (e.g., Tobit 4.13).

Despite occasional attempts to prove the contrary, the same concern with the Law is also to be found in the apocalyptic literature (cf. Ass.Mos. 3.11; 9.4ff.; 2 Enoch 31; 2 Bar. 38.4; 44.3, 7; 54.14; 57.2; 2 Esd. 7.45, 72, 94; 13.42).[1] νόμος, in fact, never refers to the writer's message, not even in Baruch for all its prophetic undertones, though, as we shall see, very often a particular way of viewing the Law is present. It is true that a revelation alongside the Law is still alive here, but this is especially associated with the unfolding of apocalyptic secrets and it is significant that these are pseudonymous in character and located in the past. Such an approach to revelation apart from the Law is not so evident in passages dealing with ethical instruction. Further, in some of these writings, especially

---

[1] See Diss. of H. Preisker, 'Die Ethik der Evangelien und die jüdischen Apokalyptik' (1915), p. 35. Thus W. Bousset, *Jesu Predigt*, p. 30 n. 1, rightly protested against the thesis of W. Baldensperger, *Das Selbstbewusstsein Jesu* (1888), pp. 57ff., that there were two poles around which Jewish thought revolved, 'nomism' and 'messianism', apocalyptic concerning itself only with the latter. In this connection see also E. Ehrhardt, *Die Grundcharakter der Ethik Jesu* (1895), pp. 37ff., and C. C. Torrey, *JE*, i, 673. A cleavage between apocalyptic and Pharisaism has been suggested more recently by G. F. Moore, R. T. Herford and D. Rössler. Contrast, however, J. Bloch, *On the Apocalyptic in Judaism* (1952), p. 35, and the discussions in W. D. Davies, *Christian Origins*, pp. 19ff.; D. S. Russell, *Apocalyptic*, pp. 20ff., and A. Nissen, *NT*, 9 (1967), 245ff.

Jubilees, there is an interest in questions of halakha.[1] Also noteworthy is the particular stress laid upon ceremonial commandments in many of these works. References to these are chiefly found in the Testaments, 2 Baruch and again Jubilees as also, less strikingly, in the Assumption of Moses, 2 Enoch and the Psalms of Solomon.

This is not to say, however, that some notable differences of emphasis do not occur when this literature is compared with contemporary and later writings more directly bound with the Law. Thus νόμος is closely linked with various lists of social virtues (Test.Reu. 3.8ff.; Jud. 18.3ff.; Iss. 5.1ff.; Dan 5.1ff.; Gad 3.1ff.; Ash. 5.1ff.; 6.3ff.; Benj. 10.3ff.), and elsewhere with similar compilations of both positive (Jub. 36.3ff.; Sib.Or. 3.237ff.; 3.630ff.; 1 Enoch 91.3ff.; 94.6ff.; 2 Enoch 9.1ff.; 44.4ff.; 45.1ff.; 52.1ff.) and also negative (1 Enoch 94.6ff.; 95.1ff.; 96.4ff.; 98.6ff.; 99.1ff.; 100.7ff.; 2 Enoch 10.4ff.; 34.1ff.) ethical maxims. While in content these often recall the basic moral injunctions of the Decalogue and the prophets (cf. Ex. 20; 33; 34; Hos. 4.2; Jer. 7.3ff. etc.), in form they have more in common with similar lists in the Wisdom literature (e.g., Prov. 6.17ff.) and in Hellenistic paranesis.[2] In a few passages these take the form of instructions in the mouth of the speaker, and here perhaps we have an echo of the independent תורה of the prophets and wise found in the earlier biblical writings. On the other hand, social and ceremonial requirements are occasionally juxtaposed (e.g., Jub. 20.2ff.) and, as we have seen, there is a considerable emphasis upon the ritual laws in a number of these works.

It has been claimed, however, that one finds here a conception of Law which has its essence in monotheistic worship and observance of social commandments, and that the Law here is viewed as a unity, not as a collection of single commandments, sin being defined in terms of apostasy rather than transgression

---

[1] Cf. L. Finkelstein, 'The Book of Jubilees and the Rabbinic Halakha', *HTR*, 16 (1923), 39–61; Ch. Albeck, *Das Buch der Jubiläen und die Halakha* (1930); S. Zeitlin, *The Book of Jubilees: Its Character and Significance* (1939), pp. 1–31, and M. Testuz, *Les Idées Religieuses du Livre des Jubilees* (1960), pp. 101ff.

[2] Note especially the detailed investigation of this phenomenon in the important contribution of S. Wibbing, *Die Tugend- und Lasterkataloge im Neuen Testament* (1959), pp. 24–42.

of individual demands.[1] A. Nissen, however, has pointed to the emphasis on single, and especially ritual, commandments in Ass.Mos. 3.12; 8.5; 9.4, 6; 12.10ff.; Jub. 1.9, 14, 24; 2.33; 3.31; 23.16; 24.11; 32.10; Test.Reu. 3.8; 6.8; Lev. 9.6–7; 14.4ff.; Jud. 13.1; 16.3–4; Zeb. 3.4; Naph. 8.7ff.; Ash. 4.5; 5.4; 6.1, 3; 2 Enoch 59.3ff.; 68.6ff., as to the many references to individual, and particularly ceremonial, regulations in 2 Bar. 5.7; 35.4; 44.3; 48.22; 57.2; 61.6; 66.2ff.; 77.4; 79.2; 82.6; 84.17ff.; 86.2, and the plural forms used in 2 Esd. 3.33ff.; 4.23; 7.11ff.; 9.32; 13.42, though here ritual laws are not mentioned. 1 Enoch appears to be the only exception to this practice, and while single virtues or vices are mentioned in such passages as 1 Enoch 68.4; 94.7; 95.2, 6; 96.5; 97.8; 99.15; 104.9ff., these are all of a social nature and are nowhere correlated with such expressions as 'laws', 'commandments', 'ordinances', 'statutes' and the like. Only here, then, could the Law be considered a unity, and only in this book and in 2 Esdras do social observances exclude reference to ritual commandments.[2] Yet on the whole in these works, there is a marked freedom from casuistry in any highly developed form, and in several there is eloquent testimony to the necessity of inward as well as outward obedience (cf. Test.Gad. 6.1; 1 Enoch 9.4; 2 Enoch 61.4; 2 Bar. 84.10), and the primacy of love (towards God: Test.Benj. 3.1; towards brethren: Reu. 6.9; Sim. 4.7; Gad 6.1ff.; 7.7; Jos. 17.2; towards neighbour: Test.Benj. 3.3ff.; God and neighbour: Test.Iss. 5.2; 7.6; Dan 5.3). In this literature, therefore, despite the centrality of Torah, many prophetic and wisdom influences live on.[3]

In contrast to its Old Testament counterpart, reference to the

---

[1] For the first see K. Berger, *Gesetzesauslegung* (1972), pp. 40–1, and, for the second, D. Rössler, *Gesetz*, pp. 80, 86.

[2] See further A. Nissen, *NT*, 9 (1967), 262ff. For a contrary view of the Book of Enoch see C. Kaplan, 'The Pharisaic Character and the Date of the Book of Enoch', *ATR*, 12 (1929–30), 531–7. C. Larcher, *Études sur le livre de la Sagesse* (1969), ch. 2, however, has recently stressed the affinity of certain sections of the book with the Wisdom movement.

[3] For a devaluation of Wisdom influence upon the rise of apocalyptic see P. von der Osten-Sacken, *Die Apokalyptik in ihrem Verhältnis zu Prophetie und Weisheit* (1969). Though he tends to overstate his case, the contrary view of G. von Rad, *Wisdom* (1972), would still seem to have much to commend it.

Mosaic Law now explicitly occurs in the apocryphal wisdom literature. νόμος (frequently without the article) is used in this way in Wisd. 6.16; 18.4, 9; Ecclus. 2.16; 9.15; 15.1 et al.; Ep.Ar. 30, 171, 313 et al.; 4 Macc. 1.16 et al. The explicit identification of Wisdom and Law is found in Ecclus.Prol., 15.1; 19.20; 21.11; 24.8, 23; 33.3; 34.8; 39.8; Ep.Ar. 139; 4 Macc. 1.16.[1] There is, further, a significant emphasis in Ecclesiasticus, the Epistle to Aristeas and 4 Maccabees on ritual commandments. Other factors are at work, however, to decelerate this drift towards nomism. Thus despite the equation of νόμος with Torah in the Wisdom of Solomon, there are surprisingly few references to the Law in this book. Furthermore, in 2.11–12 and 6.18 it is possible that νόμος is being used in a much wider sense, and this is also probably the case throughout Ecclesiasticus. The same has even been suggested for the reference in 4 Macc. 1.16.

This has again led to the claim that in the Hellenistic-Jewish wisdom literature νόμος is not *de facto* the Old Testament Law but 'lediglich ein Monotheismus, verbunden mit allgemeinen und sozialen Tugenden'.[2] In view of the clear identification of νόμος with the Mosaic Code throughout 4 Maccabees, especially with the ritual provisions of that Law (cf. 1.34; 2.5; 4.23; 5.16ff.; 9.15ff.), this is most unlikely for that work. This is also the case with the Epistle to Aristeas, as is evident from the teaching expressed in 127ff.; 144ff.; and 168ff. It is true, however, that both these books seek to emphasise the ethical character of the commandments.[3] Since in Ecclesiasticus also the ritual laws are accorded considerable importance, and Hellenistic influence is generally absent, it would be more correct to speak of an emphasis upon the social commandments rather than a restriction *lediglich* to them. The latter may be more applicable to the Wisdom of Solomon where the Hellen-

[1] Perhaps also in Wisd. 6.18, as G. Rawlinson, *Commentary on the Apocrypha*, ed. H. Wace (1888), II, 457, suggests but this is arguable, as the following comments indicate.

[2] K. Berger, *Gesetzesauslegung* (1972), p. 39.

[3] Philo, in Eusebius, *Praep. Ev.*, 8.7, also associates νόμος with a catalogue of social virtues, but since he kept the Law punctiliously and denounced Jews who violated its literal import (cf. esp. *De Migrat. Abr.* 260), it would also be incorrect to attribute to him a liberal estimate of the Law.

istic impress is most evident in the use of νόμος (2.11; 6.4; 9.5) and the listing of virtues (8.7) though in this book Old Testament influence is still strong, indeed probably dominant.[1]

Whatever the exact sense of νόμος in these writings, it is clear that it includes far more than a knowledge of the legal commandments. In the Wisdom of Solomon, for example, it embraces knowledge of the elements of the universe (7.17ff.), virtues not drawn directly from the Law (8.7) and divination of present riddles and future happenings (8.8); in Ecclesiasticus, material from the prophets and writings (see the Prologue), wisdom in other nations as well as Israel (24.6) and other general instructions scattered throughout the book. In addition, one notes the absence of definite references to halakha.[2] Also evident is the significant place given to inward motives (cf. Ep.Ar. 168 and the emphasis on love towards God in Ep.Ar. 229; Ecclus. 1.10; 2.15–16; 7.30; 47.8; towards men in Ep.Ar. 207; Ecclus. 13.15; Wisd. 12.19; 4 Macc. 13.24; and of Wisdom in Ecclus. 4.12–14; 40.20; Wisd. 6.12, 18; 7.10 and Righteousness in Wisd. 1.1; 8.7). The strong ethical emphasis placed upon ceremonial commandments (n.b. Ecclus. 34.18ff.; 35.1ff.; Ep.Ar. 170, 234, cf. Philo in *De Spec.Leg.* 1.162ff.) has already been mentioned. Despite the increasingly central place occupied by Law in this literature, therefore, in most cases extensive legal casuistry is absent.

b Later Jewish groups

The dominant religious group within Judaism until the destruction of Jerusalem was the Sadducaean Party. Over against the Pharisees they gave sole authority to the written Scripture,

---

[1] Cf. S. Wibbing, *Kataloge*, pp. 29–30. On the general character of wisdom theology *vis-à-vis* Greek and Jewish thought see now the detailed studies of J. Marböck, *Weisheit im Wandel. Untersuchungen zur Weisheitstheologie bei Ben Sira* (1971); C. Larcher, *Études sur le livre de la Sagesse* (1969), and J. M. Reese, *Hellenistic Influence on the Book of Wisdom and its Consequences* (1970), *passim*.

[2] So R. Marcus, *Law in the Apocrypha* (1927), p. 73. A Sadducaean tendency, modified by a later Pharisaic redaction, is usually argued for Ecclesiasticus. Cf. G. H. Box and W. O. E. Oesterley, *The Apocrypha of the Old Testament* (1913), ed. R. H. Charles, I, 283. According to S. Belkin, *Philo and the Oral Law* (1940), pp. vii–x and *passim*, however, Philo displays an acquaintance with Palestinian halakha.

especially the Pentateuch, and rejected the high position accorded to the oral tradition.[1] In some respects this acted as a counter to the growth of an excessive casuistry, but it also meant that the Law was often applied with literal severity to situations which had never been contemplated in it. In any event, situations arose which necessitated some form of interpretation of it, and from this developed a Sadducaean tradition which tended to be overly conservative and generally incapable of adjusting to new conditions (cf. Bill., iv, 344–52).

A second grouping concerned with the Law were the Am-Ha-Areṣ. The question of their identity is exceedingly complex and, since most of the evidence is culled from the polemical works of those who opposed them, there is considerable room for speculation.[2] Rather than a social cleft separating this class from others, as has frequently been argued, more probably the barrier arose from the attitude taken up by it towards the so-called 'tradition of the elders' which they also regarded as a Pharisaic innovation.[3] There seem to have been two main classes within this grouping, the common people who were well-intentioned but often lax, and the Anawim who were the more devoted. While the latter failed to comply with many Pharisaic traditions, their practice presupposed the binding norm of the Law, and involved the observance of other religious customs of a more ancient origin.[4] It is quite possible that their conserva-

---

[1] The view of the Fathers (Hipp., *Haer.* 9.24; Origen, *Contra Cels.* 1.49), that the Pentateuch alone was regarded by them as canonical, is incorrect. See further J. W. Lightley, *Jewish Sects and Parties* (1925), p. 70.

[2] The various passages have been collated and examined by A. Büchler, *Der galiläische Am-Ha-Areṣ des Zweiten Jahrhunderts* (1906).

[3] Cf. S. Cohon, 'The Place of Jesus in the Religious Life of his Day', *JBL*, 48 (1929), 102 and M. Friedländer, *Die religiösen Bewegungen innerhalb des Judentums im Zeitalter Jesu* (1905), pp. 78–113. For contrasting views see, however, I. Abrahams, *Studies*, ii, 647–99; S. Zeitlin, 'The Am-Ha-Areṣ', *JQR*, 23 (1932–3), 45–61 and, partly, G. F. Moore, 'The Am-Ha-Areṣ and the Haberim', *The Beginnings of Christianity* (ed. F. J. Foakes-Jackson and K. Lake, 1920), i, 439ff.

[4] Details of their peculiarities are set out in L. Finkelstein, *The Pharisees* (1946[3]), i, 43–72; S. E. Johnson, 'Jesus and First Century Galilee', *In Memoriam Ernst Lohmeyer* (1950, ed. W. Schmauch), pp. 73ff. and L. E. Elliott-Binns, *Galileean Christianity* (1956), p. 25. It is probable, therefore, that the first group was not as antinomian as has often been suggested (e.g., W. Bousset, *Die Religion des Judentums im späthellenistischen Zeitalter*

tism was of a religious nature, and that it stemmed from the preservation of a piety more in accord with Old Testament conceptions – similar perhaps to that reflected in some of the inter-testamentary literature.

There seem to have been a number of sectarian groups on the fringe of Israel's religious life, most important of which were the Essene circles. It is clear from the testimony in Josephus (*Ant.* XVIII. 1.5; *War* II. 8–9) and Philo (*Quod Omnis Probus Liber* 12), that these were centred upon Torah and possessed their own authoritative halakha. Even if the community at Qumran is not to be identified with these groups, as a few have suggested, it is clearly related to them. Obedience to the Law, as interpreted by its own traditions, was the rationale of its whole existence and in many ways, especially with respect to laws concerning purity, the sabbath and exclusiveness, it surpassed the casuistry of the Pharisees.

This does not mean, however, that the scrupulous fidelity to the Law characteristic of the sect need be equated with an external, chiefly ritualistic, casuistry. Attention can once again be drawn to the intensely moral lists of social responsibilities in such passages as 1 QS 4.3–8 and 9.14. Though elsewhere social and ritual laws are closely interwoven (e.g., CDC 1.1–7; 6.12ff.; 6.20 – 7.3), it is clearly intended that the moral aspects should penetrate the legal.[1] This is also the case with such casuistic stipulations as those surrounding the sabbath, where obedience is sought not merely in the avoidance of certain actions but in thought and word as well (1 QS 3.4; 5.13ff.). A central position is given to love – both to God (CDC 20.21; 1 QH 14.26; 15.9–10; 16.7, 13) and brethren (CDC

[1926, ed. H. Gressman], p. 187, and J. Klausner, *Jesus of Nazareth* [1925], p. 196), nor the latter the more mystical and less nomistic figures of W. Sattler, 'Die Anawim im Zeitalter Jesu Christi', *Festgabe für Adolph Jülicher* (1927), esp. pp. 9ff., while the more liberal approach to the Law supposed for Galilee (as W. Bauer, 'Jesus der Galiläer', *op. cit.*, pp. 16–34; W. Grundmann, *Jesus*, pp. 77ff.) does not rest on any historical foundation. See M. Goguel, 'Jésus et la tradition religieuse de son peuple', *RHPR*, 17 (1937), 244; L. Goppelt, *Jesus, Paul and Judaism* (ET 1964), p. 46 and W. D. Davies, *Christian Origins*, p. 21.
[1] See again S. Wibbing, *Kataloge*, pp. 43ff., and also J. Baumgartner, 'Sacrifice and Worship among the Qumran Sectaries', *HTR*, 46 (1953), 141–59.

6.21; 1 QS 1.9; 2.24; 4.4–5; 5.25) – as also the imperative to seek righteousness (CDC 20.30ff.; 1 QS 2.24; 4.2; 5.3–4; 8.1–2; 10.26) and knowledge (1 QS 4.3, 22ff.; 1 QH 1.21–3; 7.26; 9.17; 12.3–13). Though in all cases these are primarily interpreted in terms of the regulations of the community, the stress laid upon ethical obligations entails the preservation of many Old Testament prophetic and wisdom emphases.[1] This is nowhere more evident than in the hymns of the community where only a few explicit references to the Law occur (1 QH 4.10; 5.11; 6.10), a clear indication that it did not fill their thought and worship to the exclusion of all else, and that they were able to view it with some sense of perspective.[2]

For the rabbis, Law not only moves into the central position, it becomes almost the sole object of concentration. This has two significant results. In the first place, the whole of Scripture comes to be regarded as Torah because in it all God has revealed his character and ways, as well as what he requires of men in their relations with him and their fellows. Thus תורה can refer to sections of the Pentateuch which do not possess a legal character (Sif.Deut. 1.1; 11.21), or writings outside the Pentateuch altogether (Sif.Deut. 11.26; Mek.Ex. 15.8). Nevertheless, the other Old Testament writings were regarded as subordinate to the Pentateuch, and as merely reaffirming the revelation contained within it, while the decease of the prophets meant that no voice from that quarter is heard again in Israel (Tos.Sot. 13.2).[3] In the second place, all life is comprehended in terms of Law and the conviction arises that every human action must find its correspondence in a divine command. Differences as to the way in which this was to be done gave rise

---

[1] Cf. especially F. Nötscher, *Zur theologischen Terminologie der Qumran-texte* (1956), p. 62, and, on wisdom, see further B. Reicke, 'Traces of Gnosticism in the Dead Sea Scrolls', *NTS*, 1 (1954–5), 138ff.; W. D. Davies, *Christian Origins*, pp. 119–44, and, for 1 QH, M. Mansoor, *Hymns*, pp. 65–74.

[2] According to W. D. Davies, *Christian Origins*, pp. 180–1, the community reveals no sense of an essential incompatibility between life 'under the Law' and life 'in the Spirit', and R. Longenecker, *Paul*, pp. 8off., wishes to describe their position as 'nomistic' but not 'legalistic' in character. Contrary evaluations are documented, though not shared, by H. Braun, *Qumran*, II, 88ff.

[3] The possibility remains that the Bath-Qol may yet sometimes speak directly to Israel, but even this is considered with caution. Cf. Bill., I, 127–8.

to the different schools within Pharisaism which, before A.D. 70, were vying for supremacy. The oral Law that was propounded came to be regarded as on the same level as written Torah, and was considered to have stemmed from Moses (Ab. 1.1; Sif.Deut. 11.22). Great emphasis is laid upon ritual requirements, especially those concerning defilement and the sabbath, and the few Old Testament provisions are multiplied into a complex network of regulations.[1] There is also an increasing regulation of both public and private worship.[2] All legal requirements come to be considered as of equal importance, at least from the viewpoint of obedience. Righteousness becomes defined almost solely in terms of תורה, and although occasionally it is set in contrast with observation of the strict letter of the Law (cf. Gen.R. 49.4), it is frequently equated with almsgiving as the most important fulfilment of that Law (cf. Bill., I, 387).[3]

It cannot be maintained, however, that this necessarily resulted in religious life becoming so formalised that it gave no thought to motives, nor so much a burden that it lacked any sense of freedom or joy.[4] It must be remembered that Torah included haggadah as well as halakha and that here, despite an increasing tendency not to look for reasons behind laws so as to encourage obedience (cf. Pesik. 40a), there were hortatory as well as legal counsels.[5] Moreover, there was an emphasis upon intention as well as upon external actions, and several passages speak of motivation for obedience in terms of love towards God (Ab. 1.2; Sif.Lev. 19.18; Sif.Deut. 6.5–6; Sot. 5.5; b.Sot.

---

[1] P. Bläser, *Das Gesetz bei Paulus* (1941), p. 39, estimates that the 5 Old Testament passages dealing with the sabbath are amplified into 39 articles and 1521 passages in the Mishnah.

[2] See L. Ginzberg, *JE*, I, 210 and, more recently, W. D. Davies, *PCB*, p. 709.

[3] On the idea of righteousness in rabbinism see E. G. Hirsch, *JE*, I, 422–4; G. F. Moore, *Judaism in the First Centuries of the Christian Era*, I, 494–6; II, 170–1; G. Schrenk, *TDNT*, II, 186, 196–8.

[4] This assessment is nowhere more striking than in E. Schürer, *History*, II, 2, 90ff. In view of the advances that have been made in the study of rabbinics since the appearance of his work, it is all the more surprising to find his accusations against Pharisaism virtually unchanged in R. Bultmann, *Theology*, I, 11–12. On the other hand, the more idyllic portrait of rabbinic religion in the works of G. F. Moore, R. T. Herford and others, is just as one-sided in the opposite direction.

[5] See further A. Nissen, *NT*, 9 (1967), 255–6.

31a; b.Shabb. 88b), as something that cannot be regulated or enforced by legislation.[1] In others there is a concern to locate the fundamental principles of the Law (in Ab. 1.2 by Simon the Righteous; b.Shabb. 31a by Hillel; Sif.Lev. 19.18 by Akiba) though, significantly enough, reference is not made in this connection to the Decalogue.[2] Though righteousness is viewed in terms of the Law, it incorporates all these aspects of Torah as well as external obedience to its requirements, and fundamentally is conceived as an imitation of God himself (Sif.Deut. 6.6; 11.22; b.Sot. 14a).[3] It should be noted, however, that the presence of elements within rabbinism stressing intention, motivation and basic principles does not in any way detract from the absolute and independent validity of each commandment and the necessity for obedience to it.

The detailed casuistry of the rabbinic schools was held in check to some extent by two other factors. Despite the high regard in which both oral and written Law were held, and the consequent rigidity this imposed upon ethical action, there was provision not only for amplification of the Law to meet new or changed circumstances but also the relaxing, even annulling, of specific legislation.[4] The principle upon which these alterations

---

[1] Consult R. Sander, *Furcht und Liebe im palästinischen Judentum* (1935), pp. 118ff. Note also the Shema, Eighteen Benedictions, and beginning of the 613 commandments. On the centrality of this motif for Hillel cf. Ab. 1.12; b.Shabb.31a, and for Johanan b. Zakkai cf. Ab.R.N. 1, 4. See further E. Stauffer, *TDNT*, 1, 43.

[2] Though it was later excluded, at this time the Decalogue was cited with the Shema in the synagogue and Temple (cf. Tamid IV, V), and was contained in the phylacteries (cf. Phyl. at Qumran Cave I, 8; Nash Papyrus). However, there does not appear to be any reference to it elsewhere in the rabbinic, or even apocryphal and pseudepigraphal, writings. It is not even included in the lists of tens set out in Ab.5.1ff., though mention is made of it in Philo (*De Decal.*) and Josephus (*Ant.* III.5, 4). According to F. E. Vokes, *St.Ev.*, v, II, 151 it is 'significant that the Decalogue by itself is not picked out as a whole as the summary or crown of divine law', while in the examples of its use that we do possess 'variations in order and text are. . .interesting, not as representing different traditions, but as evidence that the Decalogue was not felt to be sacrosanct'.

[3] Detailed studies of the centrality and significance of this idea have been provided by I. Abrahams, *Studies*, II, 138–82 and H. Kosmala, 'Nachfolge und Nachahmung Gottes', *ASTI*, 3 (1964), 54–110.

[4] On rabbinic 'realism' in interpretation see, *inter alia*, B. Cohen, 'Canons of Interpretation of Jewish Law', in *Law and Tradition in Judaism* (1969),

were validated is exemplified in Ber. 9.5 and in the Prosbol of Hillel, a legal fiction enabling substantial changes in the law to take place (see Sheb. 10.3ff.; Git. 4.3ff.; Sot. 9.9ff.). Furthermore, whereas many areas of life were subjected to extensive casuistic analysis, such virtues as filial piety, philanthropy, charity and so on possessed no rigid standard but, in rabbinical terms, were 'committed to the heart' i.e., left to individual conscience (cf. Pea. 1.1). Pharisaism, then, is a complex phenomenon and these several factors set their seal on the fact that rabbinic Judaism did not completely give way to a casuistic legalism but that in it certain Old Testament wisdom and prophetic impulses continued to have their effect.[1] However, it was not only from these sources that influence was exerted upon the Pharisaic outlook for, despite its antagonistic stance towards Greek ideas and culture, to some extent its legal structure and in some respects its more progressive approach to the written Law, were shaped by the presence of certain Hellenistic tendencies within it.[2]

We have observed that threads of continuity and discontinuity can be traced through the differing attitudes towards the Law that came to expression between the conclusion of the covenant at Sinai and the destruction of Jerusalem in the first

pp. 44–51. According to D. Daube, 'Texts and Interpretation in Roman and Jewish Law', *JJSoc.*, 3 (1961), 3–28, the Pharisees did not initially feel the need to derive their new interpretations from Scripture itself. It was only after the time of Hillel that this became the rule. That it did so was a victory for Sadducaean procedure for it was their continuing insistence upon this principle that forced the Pharisees ultimately to come to terms with it.

[1] The rabbis, of course, consciously regarded themselves as the inheritors of the prophets. The latter were viewed, however, chiefly as the bearers of tradition (Bab.Meg. 3a; Bab.Zeb. 62a) and as the creators of halakhoth (b.Kidd. 43a; b.Pes. 117a; Taan. 4.1–2; Erub. 21.c.15). See further W. D. Davies, 'Reflections on the Tradition: Aboth Revisited', *Christian History and Interpretation: Studies Presented to John Knox* (ed. W. R. Farmer, C. F. D. Moule and R. R. Niebuhr, 1967), pp. 131ff.

[2] The influence of Hellenism upon Pharisaism has been remarked upon by a number of scholars, among them S. Liebermann, D. Daube, M. Smith and W. D. Davies. See, most recently, E. Rivkin, 'Pharisaism and the Crisis of the Individual in the Graeco-Roman World', *JQR*, 61 (1970), 27–53 who considers that it was partly for this reason that Pharisaism was able to respond in a creative fashion in the face of the inadequacy of a literal view of the Pentateuch and the collapse of priestly religion.

century. This is so even within the Old Testament for, as we have seen, during this period there was no unified conception of the Law which received universal acceptance within Israel. In part, this stemmed from the nature of Law itself and, in part, was a consequence of new circumstances that emerged. The prophetic foundation from which it sprang at the beginning of Israel's history, the flexibility that marked its growth and application, and the limits within which it operated opened up the possibility of its varied development. The social and political pressures which it encountered both internally and externally also contributed to the way in which it unfolded. In addition to these two factors, there was the presence of religious groups within Israel involved in applying and transmitting תורה which possessed different areas of responsibility and correspondingly different conceptions as to how their task was to be carried out. Examination of the more historical writings demonstrated the tenacity with which the character of Law as instruction, the significance of basic moral principles within it, and the motivation that should accompany its observance, continued to assert their influence. Nevertheless, tendencies towards its increasing codification, concentration upon ritual commandments and encroachment upon other areas of human activity can also be detected. Throughout the Old Testament period, however, these do not entail any drastic alteration in the way in which Law is conceived. While endorsing the centrality of the official Law, the prophetic tradition also considered itself to be an instrument through which Yahweh issued תורה to Israel. Such instruction was mainly concerned with rather wider ethical norms and it was to these that the prophetic writings chiefly sought to draw Israel's attention. The wise men also regarded themselves as bearers of תורה and this took the character of guidance to individual members of society with respect to their everyday behaviour. Though never referring specifically to the Mosaic legislation, they undoubtedly made their pronouncements within the framework provided by it. Nevertheless, in the prophetic and wisdom traditions we find evidence of an ethical stance in which, in the first case, the traditional Law played only a subordinate role and, in the second, though presupposed it was *de facto* absent altogether, as well as of the fact that תורה itself is a rich and complex phenomenon.

In the inter-testamentary literature we see three factors at work – the survival of Old Testament motifs, the intensifying of tendencies leading towards later Judaism and the introduction of Hellenistic influence. Most striking is the increasing centrality of the official Law, not only in works with an historical and/or legal interest but in the apocalyptic and wisdom literature as well. Associated with this is a growing emphasis on those commandments, frequently ritual in character, which distinguished the Jews from other nations. Less pronounced is the movement towards the incorporation of Greek ethical ideas into Jewish material. Where it does occur this generally results in an underlining of the importance of the social commandments and virtues which accompany them. These two developments bring with them the danger of an evolution into a legalism, on the one hand, and a humanism, on the other. As yet, however, there is no extensive casuistry and though a few works appear to express a legalistic approach in most this is not the case. In material where they arise, anthropocentric tendencies are held in check by a firm grasp of Old Testament conceptions. Indeed in certain of these writings there is even a deepening of several Old Testament ideas. It seems to have been the political and cultural conditions of the second century which gave rise to the later Jewish groupings and so to Judaism proper. To this point the various religious traditions within Israel evolved side by side without much conflict and with a certain degree of interpenetration. After the crisis had passed, however, there was a new alignment of parties. In these Hellenism and assimilation were largely repudiated and brotherhoods were formed to keep the Law in stricter fashion. It is not easy to disentangle the numerous elements in their approach to the Law and even more difficult to weigh up the factors involved and assess the consequences for their general religious outlook. Certainly the latter must have varied greatly according to individual experience. At the risk of over-generalisation, however, it would be reasonable to assume that it was probably among certain groups within the Am-Ha-Areṣ, whose piety may be reflected in the figures depicted in the opening chapters of Luke's Gospel, that Old Testament attitudes most strongly prevail. At Qumran, despite its preoccupation with the legal regulation of even the minutest details of community life, deep chords of prophetic faith were continually struck. Among the Sadducees, on the other hand, a stricter concentration on the letter, and implications, of the Mosaic legislation itself seems frequently to have resulted in a more restrictive, and hence less authentic, response to Yahweh's demands. Between these two, Pharisaism stood in a somewhat ambiguous position, at times expressing sentiments perfectly in keeping with its biblical origins, at others displaying that loss of perspective in religious matters that the Gospel portraits so frequently attest.[1]

[1] The detailed investigation of the understanding of Law in apocalyptic circles and at Qumran by M. Limbeck, *Die Ordnung des Heils. Untersuchungen zum Gesetzesverständnis des Frühjudentums* (1971), unfortunately came to my notice too late to be satisfactorily utilised in this study. He rightly pleads for a more sustained historico-critical approach to the literature and for the recognition of a greater diversity of views even between works within a similar tradition, e.g. CDC and 1 QS. His insistence that in these writings (a) Law is not regarded as the means by which justification with God is achieved, (b) concentration on ritual commandments is not necessarily inconsistent with an affirmation of the broad character of God's salvation, finds general endorsement in my own brief assessment of these texts. It could be, however, that Limbeck himself tends to interpret individual works in too unitary a manner and fails to note the presence of contrary notes within them. His chief contribution lies in his attempt to demonstrate that (a) in these writings, Law must principally be seen in relation to the all-embracing and definitive cosmic will of God, active in creation, history and human affairs, in which men are graciously allowed to participate through their involvement in those earthly institutions such as Law, Cult and Calendar, in which it is embodied or reflected, (b) such a conception of salvation, which is very different from, say, the Pauline approach though not legalistic in character, should not be judged too hastily by alternative interpretations of God's plan for men and the way of life consequent upon it. While the notion of such a cosmic 'Ordnung des Heils' does, as he shows, provide the context within which the understanding of Law in some of these works is elaborated, he tends to play down the contribution of those writings in which the idea is less apparent and perhaps to underestimate in some others the extent to which concentration on the Mosaic Law tends to diminish the loftiness and weaken the significance of this conception. Also, his hesitancy in bringing external criteria to bear on the literature in order to evaluate its character, results in a somewhat uncritical appreciation of its outlook, one that is not sufficiently alert to the religious and moral inadequacies inherent in it. It is unfair, however, to deal with such an extensively researched and extremely suggestive work in a cursory manner.

C THE LAW – ETERNAL OR PROVISIONAL?

The permanent character of Yahweh's covenant with Israel, particularly in its Abrahamic and Davidic forms, is stressed throughout the historical and prophetic literature. Associated with this we find, notably in P though the implication is not absent elsewhere, that individual statutes are described as having been given 'forever', or as 'everlasting'.[1] Though such statements are accompanied by occasional warnings against disobedience, the possibility of a dissolution of the covenant, and with it its legal obligations, does not seem to have been seriously entertained. It was, of course, the prophets who faced up most realistically to the inevitability of just such a dissolution. In so doing they not only predicted the certainty and totality of the coming judgment but went on to present visionary glimpses of what lay beyond it. This eschatological hope was greatly influenced by the Exodus events, the first deliverance from Egypt becoming the prototype of the future redemption (Hos. 2.14–15; Mic. 7.15; Isa. 10.24ff.; 11.15–16; Jer. 16.14–15; 31.31–4; Ezek. 20.33ff.; 2 Isa. 42.13ff.; 49.8ff.).[2] The promise of a new covenant is also prominent in these writings (Jer. 31.31–4; 32.38–40; 50.5; Ezek. 16.60ff.; 34.25; 37.26; 2 Isa. 42.6; 49.8; 54.10; 55.3; 59.21; 61.8; Mal. 3.1).

What part does the Law play in this complex of ideas? In particular, five passages require consideration – Isa. 2.1–5 (cf. Mic. 4.1–5); 2 Isa. 42.1–4; 51.4; Jer. 31.31–4; Ezek. 36.24–8. The equation of תורה with the prophetic message rather than the traditional Law throughout Isaiah inclines one to

---

[1] צולם often means quite simply 'for a long time' but in these passages it should probably be given its strongest connotation. See L. Köhler and W. Baumgartner, *Lexicon in Veteris Testamenti Libros* (1953), pp. 688–9.

[2] See further J. Daniélou, *Sacramentum Futuri* (1950), pp. 131ff.; J. Marsh, *The Fullness of Time* (1952), ch. 4; and U. Mauser, *Christ in the Wilderness* (1963), pp. 15–52. Other election traditions surrounding David and Mt Zion were also prominent (cf. Isa. 2.1ff.; Mic. 4.1ff.; 2 Isa. 55.1ff.; Ezek. 40–8) but the two should probably be viewed as alternative rather than rival typological categories.

interpret the word in a similar sense in 2.3. It would then refer to something far wider than the Law, particularly those fundamental ethical principles reiterated throughout the work, and would be equivalent to the phrase 'the word of the Lord' with which it appears to stand in parallelism.[1] In Isa. 42.1ff. the Servant is described as one who will announce משפט (v.3) and give תורה (v.4). B. Duhm, who first emphasised this aspect of the Servant's mission, defined both activities in terms of the Law and this has been vigorously maintained by W. D. Davies. In accordance with this writer's usage elsewhere, however, משפט would refer generally to concrete expressions of the will of God rather than exclusively to the Mosaic Law, whereas תורה has, in the total setting of the passage, almost the sense of 'revelation'.[2] This is also surely the case in Isa. 51.4–5 where תורה is linked with such conceptions as 'righteousness' and 'salvation'.[3]

Four main interpretations of תורה in Jer. 31.33 have been suggested: a. the written Law; b. the Decalogue; c. instruction or revelation and d. inward principles. As we have seen, תורה is used in Jeremiah with reference to the traditional Law. However, in several contexts it appeared in conjunction with the 'word' of the prophet indicating that it cannot be fulfilled properly unless the prophetic word is also heeded (2.8; 9.12–13; 16.10–12) while in others it was equated with that prophetic word itself (6.19; 26.4–5; 44.18).[4] The same conjunction of ideas occurs in 31.33–4 where the 'law' (v.33) written in the heart is linked with 'knowledge'

---

[1] The commentators do, in fact, generally interpret the word in the general sense of 'instruction'. By dating the passage in the post-exilic age W. D. Davies, *Setting*, pp. 138ff. nevertheless seeks to give this sense a greater legal connotation. According to the detailed investigation of these verses by H. Wildberger, *Jesaja* (1965), pp. 78–80, however, such a dating is unnecessary.

[2] Cf. C. R. North, *Second Isaiah* (1964), pp. 108–9; C. Westerman, *Das Buch Jesaja: Kapitel 40–66* (1966), p. 81, and, on the latter term, J. Skinner, *Isaiah: XL–LXVI* (1927), p. 27, against B. Duhm, *Das Buch Jesaja* (1914), pp. 284ff. (cf. E. J. Kissane, *The Book of Isaiah* [1943], II, 36) and W. D. Davies, *Setting*, pp. 134ff.

[3] So recently J. L. McKenzie, *Second Isaiah* (1968), pp. 36–8. Note also Isa. 59.20–1.

[4] On the close relationship between traditional Law and prophetic word in Jeremiah see further J. Bright, *Jeremiah* (1965), pp. 63–4 (on 8.8).

(v.34) of the Lord. It is clear from Jer. 2.8; 3.15; 5.1–4; 8.7; 11.18; 24.7; 32.8; 44.29 that knowledge of Yahweh embraces much more than obedience to the Law, and this is reinforced in the present passage by the phrase 'they shall teach no more every man his neighbour' (v.34). It seems probable then that תורה in v.33, as in the Isaianic passages, refers primarily to the survival of Yahweh's prophetic instruction beyond the disintegration of the present covenantal framework.[1] At first sight only the Law seems to be in view in Ezek. 36.24–8. In this Yahweh speaks of a 'new spirit' and a 'new heart' which will bring with it obedience to 'my statutes'. It is significant, however, that Ezek. 40–8 contains items which have no parallel in the Mosaic Law, while 43.11–12 and 44.5 explicitly refer to the presence of prophetic תורה. One should be careful, therefore, in reading too literal a meaning into the 'statutes' referred to in 36.27.

In all these passages, the presence of תורה in the new age of Israel's history is affirmed. Such תורה, however, refers primarily to the prophetic instruction. This should not be separated from, indeed it includes, the traditional Law, but it is not that Law which is central in their thinking. It is most strongly in view in the Ezekiel passage and though in Jeremiah the emphasis is principally upon ethical requirements, in view of 33.18 it must have also contained ritual stipulations. This would also certainly be the case in the Isaianic passages as well.

2   LATER JEWISH LITERATURE

In the post-biblical literature a significant shift in attitude can be detected in each of these traditions. It is, however, quite consistent with developments within them that have already been noted, especially the coalescence of each more closely around the Law. In material of an historical or legal character this is simply taking up the tendency in P to insist upon the eternal character of many of the Law's requirements though

---

[1] W. D. Davies, *Setting*, pp. 127ff. places the emphasis here upon the Mosaic Law, citing in support the somewhat similar terminology to Jer. 33.33 in Ps. 37.31; 40.8; Deut. 11.18; 30.14. In light of Jeremiah's use of תורה elsewhere and the tenor of the present passage, I do not find these comparisons compelling.

without acknowledging the conditional element which is present on the boundary of the earlier work. Good examples of this occur in Tobit 1.6 and in the 'Formulary of Blessings' (1 QS6) at Qumran. Though reference to it does not appear as frequently as one might expect, the rabbinic writings clearly presuppose the eternal validity of the Law throughout.[1] Not only of Torah as a whole is the idea expressed (Ex.R. 33.7), but even of the words, the very jots and tittles, that make it up (Ex.R. 6.1; Lev.R. 19.2). Both these emphases represent a stricter and more comprehensive attitude than in P. Closer to the latter is the statement in b.Yom. 5b that the sacrificial laws will be particularly observed in the time to come. An interesting tendency is noticeable in j.Meg. 1.70d where it is only of the Pentateuch that eternity is predicted, the Prophets and Writings having ceased in the Messianic time. No doubt this is based on the view expressed in b.Shab. 104a, Ex.R. 42.8 and elsewhere that the prophets brought nothing additional to the Law but only re-instituted commandments that had originally been uttered by Moses. For most rabbis, however, the other Scriptures also possessed eternal status, however inferior to the Pentateuch they may have been considered. Parallel to this, at the other end of the time-scale, is the affirmation of Torah's pre-existence in such passages as Ab. 3.15; Sif.Deut. 11.10 and Gen.R. 1.1.

A similar attitude to the Law is displayed in the apocalyptic tradition. In the book of Jubilees the eternal character of the Law is ceaselessly reiterated. Its enactments, written on heavenly tablets (3.31; 6.17) and mediated by angels to man

---

[1] Cf. Bill., I, 244–7. In later rabbinic writings a clear distinction is drawn between the 'Messianic Age' and the 'Age to Come'. This is already present in the statement of R. Johanan in b.Ber. 34b (and pars.) and in the discussion centring on the length of the Messianic time (b.Sanh. 99a *et al.*) as in the late apocalyptic writings (2 Bar. 40.3; 2 Esd. 7.28–31 and Rev. 20.4ff.). A rigid separation does not seem to occur in the sayings of the earlier teachers recorded in the Mishnah e.g., those of Eliezer, Hillel and Shammai, nor in the remainder of the apocryphal and pseudepigraphal literature. The period following upon the destruction of Jerusalem is therefore usually considered to be the decisive point from which the distinction became more apparent. See further on this point M. Löwy, 'Messiaszeit und zukünftige Welt', *MGWJ*, 5 (1897), 401 and K. Schubert, *Religion*, p. 49.

(1.27) are considered to be the complete expression of Yahweh's
will. Ritual laws are given special prominence, especially those
dealing with the sabbath (2.26ff.), circumcision (15.26ff.),
festivals (6.17; 16.29), tithing (32.10). To these is ascribed
eternal validity. In the other apocalypses it is rather the Torah
as a whole which is in view (Bar. 4.1; 1 Enoch 99.2, 14;
2 Esd. 9.37; 2 Bar. 77.15, cf. Ps.Sol. 17.37). In all of these,
with the exception of 1 Enoch, the Law is identified with
Wisdom. This is indicated in Bar. 3.9ff.; 2 Bar. 77.16 and
2 Esd. 8.52ff.; 13.54–5. In 1 Enoch, however, the identification is not explicitly made, indeed in 42.1ff. it appears to have
been decisively rejected. It is interesting, therefore, that it is not
Torah but wisdom and righteousness which are associated
chiefly with the activity of the Elect One who is to come
(39.6; 42.1ff.; 43.6; 48.1; 49.1; 53.7; 71.14, 16; 91.10).
Thus here too we have testimony to the persistence of a tradition in which the Law, however highly it may be evaluated, is
not in the Coming Age the only, or even central, factor, while
even in the other apocalypses the content of that Law has been
considerably amplified.[1]

The Old Testament wisdom literature, geared as it is to the
present world and devoid of eschatological conceptions, is silent
as to the duration of its תּוֹרָה. In the apocryphal wisdom
literature, however, the everlasting character of the Law does
find expression in Ecclus. 24.9, 33 and most probably in
Wisd. 18.4. Nevertheless it is implied that wisdom, which

---

[1] The assertion of A. Schweitzer, *The Mysticism of Paul the Apostle* (ET
1956[2]), pp. 191–2 (cf. also H. J. Schoeps, *Paul*, p. 172), that late Jewish
apocalypses while not expressing the idea that Law is of no further
importance in the time to come are so dominated by the idea that they
nowhere assert that Law will be in operation nor describe life in terms of
perfect obedience to it, goes too far beyond the evidence. While it is true
that in the Psalms of Solomon, 2 Baruch and 2 Esdras the term 'Law' is
not emphasised in passages dealing with the messianic period, ideas of
'wisdom' and 'righteousness' which elsewhere in these works are equated
with the Law do appear (cf. Ps.Sol. 14.1–2; 2 Bar. 67.6 and passages
cited above). While, as we have seen, this does not occur in 1 Enoch, there
is mention in this work of the eternal duration of the Law (1 Enoch
99.14). His attempt to bypass this with the statement 'that the Law is
eternal does not mean it is of eternal application', picturing its position in
the Messianic Age as of the same order as its pre-existent state, is not
particularly satisfying.

though equated with the Law is also more comprehensive than it, can be spoken of in similar terms.[1]

Comparison with the Old Testament position, therefore, shows that in each of these traditions there is a heightened though not exclusive emphasis upon the future importance of the Law. We must now turn to those passages which allegedly testify to the occurrence of changes in the Law and/or granting of a new Law in the days to come.[2] In the first place, brief mention may be made of those texts in which certain difficulties and obscurities in the Torah are mentioned as being clarified in the Messianic era. It is above all Elijah who will return at that time to explain the significance of points in the Law that had perplexed the rabbis. However, the solution of difficulties and apparent contradictions that was to take place through his activity only served to highlight the unity and perpetuity of the Law.[3]

[1] On the latter see W. J. Deane, *The Book of Wisdom* (1881), p. 209. Ecclus. 1.15 speaks of wisdom as an 'eternal foundation', a description which at first sight appears to be a direct statement of its everlasting character. The verse, however, is full of difficulties and has been amended by R. Smend, *Weisheit*, p. 11 (cf. G. H. Box and W. O. E. Oesterley, *Apocrypha*, ed. R. H. Charles, I, 319), to read 'established for ever' i.e., from eternity. There is a similar thought in Wisd. 7.26 where wisdom is described as an 'effulgence from everlasting light'. In these verses, therefore, the theme of Wisdom's pre-existence, already affirmed in Prov. 8.1ff., is taken up anew (see further Wisd. 9.1ff.; Ecclus. 1.4ff.; 24.9). The implication is probably present, however, that it is eternal in the other direction as well, and Ecclus. 24.9 illustrates just how closely the two thoughts are bound together. There is a further clear testimony to the eternal character of the Law in Philo, *De Vita Mos.* 11.44.

[2] R. Longenecker, *Paul: Apostle of Liberty* (1964), pp. 128–9, has rightly warned that in taking up such a survey the concepts 'abrogation of the Law' and 'establishment of a new Law' are not, as is commonly assumed, complementary and that they must be treated as quite separate questions. A further clarification is provided by H. M. Teeple, *The Mosaic Eschatological Prophet* (1957), pp. 15ff., who states that there was a considerable variety of opinion concerning the degree of observance of the Law in the time immediately preceding the Messianic period (e.g., Tos.Eduy. 1.1; Cant.R. 2.9) and to what extent the Law should be binding upon Gentiles (e.g., Gen.R. 98.9). None of these discussions, however, were intended to 'involve any change in the Law itself but merely a change in the degree of observance of it'.

[3] Cf. Sh. Spiegel, 'Ezekiel or pseudo-Ezekiel', *HTR*, 24 (1931), 260–1. See also H. Danby, *The Mishnah* (1933), p. 436 n.19, and G. Barth, 'Law', p.

Other passages seem to suggest that there will be an annulment of particular provisions in the Law. So according to
Lev. R. 9. 7, this will be the fate of all sacrifices and prayers but
that of Thanksgiving. Such an attitude probably springs from
the conviction that since in that period sin would not exist these
sacrifices would be unnecessary. However, the passage is late
and cannot be dated before the latter half of the second
century.[1] Yalkut on Prov. 9. 2, probably to be dated earlier in
the second century, speaks of Purim and the Day of Atonement
as the only Festivals which will be celebrated in the Messianic
time. One should reckon with the possibility, however, that
both these passages are more concerned to emphasise the
importance of the activities mentioned than to deny the continuance of others.[2] One of the views expressed in Midrash
Tehillim on Ps. 146. 7 insists on the abrogation of the distinction
between clean and unclean animals in this future period but
this is immediately followed by two contradictory opinions.[3] A
change in Torah also seems to be implied in Sif.Deut. 17. 18.
However, the parallel passage in Tos.Sanh. 4.4ff., which is
most likely earlier, specifically defines the change as concerning
only the script of Torah, not its contents.[4]

A more important passage is b.Shab. 151b in which R.
Simeon b. Eleazar (c. A.D. 165–200) draws a comparison between the state of the dead and the Messianic era. In the latter,
contrary to the present, 'there is neither merit nor guilt' and

---

156 n.4, on Eduy. 8. 7 against M. Löwy, *MGWJ* (1904), p. 324. Many of
these passages are collected in L. Ginzberg, *Eine unbekannte jüdische Sekte*
(1922), pp. 303ff.

[1] So H. Loewe, *A Rabbinic Anthology* (1938), p. 350, though J. Israelstam,
Midrash Rabbah:Leviticus, p. 114, disputes his attributing it to Menahem
of Galilee.

[2] Cf. J. Klausner, *From Jesus to Paul* (ET 1944), p. 321 n.13.

[3] W. D. Davies, *Setting*, p. 164 n.1, makes the suggestion that the greater
strictness of the Law's demands in the future reflected in the second
contradictory opinion testifies to the possibility of a change in the Torah.
However, though the statement does refer to an increased strictness in
marital relations such are not regulated on the whole by statutes in the
Old Testament, and it is God's presence, not Torah, which alters the
situation here. It should be noted that some Jewish scholars are doubtful
about the authenticity of these and related passages in the Midrash (cf.
Davies, *Setting*, p. 164 n.1).

[4] Against J. Bonsirven, *Judaïsme*, I, 453 n.9.

W. D. Davies, comparing this text with the freedom of the dead from the Law mentioned in b.Nid. 61b, suggests this means that 'the Torah no longer holds in the Messianic Age'. H. J. Schoeps interprets b.Shab. 30a and Kil. 9.4 in the same way. Freedom of the dead from the Law, however, need not involve any limitation of its validity. It is merely the case that such are now, by the nature of the case, no longer able to observe it.[1] Similarly, cessation of the יצר הרע in the Messianic time, the conception that appears to underlie the statement in b.Shab. 151b, does not invalidate Torah but merely the possibility of acquiring merit or guilt through it. A prediction of the complete abrogation of Torah has been derived from b.Sanh. 97b and Ab.Zar. 9a: 'The world is to exist six thousand years. In the first two thousand years there was desolation, two thousand years the Torah flourished; and the next two thousand years is the Messianic era. . .' However, such schematisations, which are typically third century in outlook and not relevant for earlier periods, are aimed at fixing the date of the Messiah rather than limiting the validity of Torah.[2] The view that within the framework of a doctrine of the immutability of Torah occasional expectations of its modification and partial abrogation are to be found, exceeds the evidence adduced in its support.

We turn next to those passages in which it has been alleged that a new Torah is explicitly indicated. Just as we commenced the previous set of texts with an examination of the future activity of Elijah and its possible connection with changes in Torah, so it is necessary here to enquire into the hope surrounding the return of Moses, or of a figure like him, and their bearing on the question of a new Torah. There is reference to a return of Moses in several rabbinic passages. These state that his death and burial in the wilderness took place so that in the future he might lead that generation into the promised land. All these, however, are later than the first century A.D. The earliest is

---

[1] Against W. D. Davies, *Setting*, p. 170, and H. J. Schoeps, 'ΧΡΙΣΤΟΣ ΤΕΛΟΣ ΝΟΜΟΥ', *Aus Frühchristlicher Zeit* (1950), p. 223. On b.Nid. 61b see also H. Silver, *A History of Messianic Speculation in Israel* (1927), p. 9; J. Jocz, *Jewish People*, p. 155; R. N. Longenecker, *Paul*, pp. 130–1. W. Bacher, *Die Agada der babylonischen Amoräer* (1967²), p. 105 n.23, however, limited this abrogation to the ceremonial commandments alone.

[2] Cf. E. Bammel, 'Νόμος Χριστοῦ', *St.Ev.*, III (1964), 122, and H. Freedman, *Sanhedrin* (Sonc. trans.), ch. 11, p. 657 n.9.

probably Sif.Deut. 33.21 which is said to come from the school of R. Ishmael (A.D. 120–40) though the Midrash is not dated until the seventh century or later.[1] The return of Moses and Elijah together is mentioned in Deut.R. 3.17. Despite the later redaction of the Midrash it has been suggested that since the tradition is presented by Johanan ben Zakkai it is most probably early. However, this view has been strongly contested.[2] We must conclude that the idea of a reappearance of Moses at the beginning of the Messianic Kingdom is a later innovation.[3] Moreover, in none of these passages is his supposed return associated with any legislative activity.

A further group of passages speak not of a return of Moses but of a figure who possesses Mosaic characteristics. In this connection, references to the prediction in Deut. 18.15, 18 of a 'prophet like Moses' are first to be considered. It is rather surprising to find only three occurrences of this prophecy in the rabbinic literature, each of which relates the promise to one of the past prophets (Pesik. 112a; Sif.Deut. 18.15, 16).[4] In 1 Macc. 4.46 and 14.41 mention is made of the expectation of 'a (faithful) prophet'.[5] Even if Deut. 18.15–18 lies behind the

---

[1] The most comprehensive discussion of these, and other, rabbinic passages is probably that in R. Bloch, 'Die Gestalt des Moses in der rabbinischen Tradition', *Moses in Schrift und Überlieferung* (GT 1963), pp. 95–171.

[2] Thus against I. Abrahams, *Studies*, II, 53; H. J. Schoeps, *Theologie und Geschichte des Judenchristentums* (1949), p. 96; H. M. Teeple, *Prophet*, p. 45 and T. F. Glasson, *Moses in the Fourth Gospel* (1963), p. 27 n.2, see J. Jeremias, *TDNT*, IV, 855 n.96; G. H. Boobyer, 'St. Mark and the Transfiguration', *JTS*, 41 (1940), 130 and J. Giblet, 'Prophétisme et attente d'un messie prophète dans l'Ancien Judaïsme', *L'Attente du Messie* (1954), pp. 102–3.

[3] Cf. P. Volz, *Die Eschatologie der jüdischen Gemeinde* (1966 ed.), p. 195. It is also significant that no account of the assumption of Moses occurs in the apocalyptic work of that name. The earliest references appear to be post-christian (2 Esd. 14.9; 2 Bar. 59.3–4), but rabbinic sources indicate that alongside it the biblical view also prevailed. See the discussion in H. M. Teeple, *Prophet*, pp. 41–3.

[4] Cf. also Philo, *De Spec. Leg.* I, 65. A further parallel in Ass.Mos. 10.15, despite R. H. Charles, *Pseudepigrapha*, II, 412, is uncertain, as J. Jeremias, *TDNT*, IV, 857 n.114 points out. Test.Lev. 8.14ff. cannot credibly be derived from Deut. 18.15, 18 as some have surmised.

[5] The similar reference in Test.Benj. 9.2, sometimes alluded to in this connection, is probably a christian interpolation. Cf. R. H. Charles, *Pseudepigrapha*, II, 358 against R. E. Brown, 'The Messianism of Qumran', *CBQ*, 19 (1957), 59 n.35.

passage, something that is by no means certain due to the general nature of the prediction, it is more likely that it does so only in the sense of prophesying the coming of a figure who, like Moses, will stand as a representative between God and the people, not in terms of any detailed similarity with the actual role of Moses. In fact, his task does not appear to be that of giving new legislation in an eschatological context, but of settling certain disputed points not covered by Torah.[1]

On the basis of CDC 6.8ff., and certain other passages, it has been maintained that the Teacher of Righteousness is also described in terms of Deut. 18.15–18.[2] Whether this is so or not, CDC 1.10–12 suggests that his task is that of setting out instructions for the life of the community rather than making alterations in the Mosaic Law or giving utterance to new Torah. CDC 6.14 implies that these were to be regarded as an interim-ethic, valid only until the dawn of the Messianic era.[3] A fragment of the Testimonies Scroll cites Deut. 18.15–18 in connection with a further figure – the Prophet to come – and from 1 QS 9.9–11 and CDC 6.14 it has been inferred that he also

---

[1] So P. Volz, *Eschatologie*, pp. 193–4; J. Giblet, 'Prophétisme', p. 105, and W. D. Davies, *Setting*, pp. 143–5. A stronger link with Deut. 18.15–18 is insisted upon by W. Brownlee, *The Dead Sea Manual of Discipline* (1951), p. 50; R. Schnackenburg, 'Die Erwartung des "Propheten" nach dem NT und dem Qumran-Texten', *St.Ev.*, I (1959), 631–2 and F. Gils, *Jésus, Prophète d'après les Évangiles Synoptiques* (1957), pp. 30–1. However, if any figure is to be associated with the expectation of the prophet, it is more likely to be Elijah, especially in view of the Torah ministry later connected with his return. Cf. J. Klausner, *Messianic Idea*, p. 260 (though W. Wirgin, *On Charismatic Leadership from Simon Maccabeus until Simon bar Kochba* [1964], has recently argued for Samuel).

[2] See, apart from the writings of Jeremias, Gils, Schoeps and Giblet already mentioned, especially N. Wieder, 'The "Law-Interpreter" of the Sect of the DSS: A Second Moses', *JJS*, 4 (1953), 158–75; G. Vermès, 'Die Gestalt des Moses an der Wende der beiden Testamenten', *Moses in Schrift und Überlieferung* (GT 1963), pp. 85ff.; and O. Betz, *Offenbarung und Schriftforschung in der Qumran-sekte* (1960), pp. 62ff. Other titles and descriptions are applied to both Moses and the Teacher – e.g., 'star', 'vessel', 'craftsman' – but since these were applied to other figures as well they are less relevant here. Cf. J. Morgenstern, *Some Significant Antecedents of Christianity* (1966), pp. 1ff.

[3] In view of this, the translation 'lawgiver' in these passages is better rendered 'searcher of the law' (Ch. Rabin, *The Zadokite Documents* [1958²], p. 22) or 'law-interpreter' (N. Wieder, *JJS*, 4 [1953], 159).

has some legislative activity. Again it must be stressed that it is only the rule of the community, not at all the Mosaic Law, which is involved. It should be noted here that the identification of these two figures, despite some support, is highly questionable, as is the attaching of any messianic significance to their activity.[1] Moreover, despite the appearance of some Mosaic traits in the Teacher, and the reference of the Deuteronomic passage to the prophet, if any one figure is to be associated with either it would again seem to be that of Elijah, especially in view of his dual role as preparer for the Messianic era, and interpreter of uncertain aspects of the Law.

Samaritan expectation, centred around the coming of Ta'eb, appears to have awaited a figure with similarities to Moses. In fact, Deut. 18.15–18 seems to form the basis of their eschatological speculation and was even regarded by them as the tenth commandment.[2] In view of their recognition of the Pentateuch alone this is scarcely surprising and it is precisely this limitation which advises caution in arguing for a corresponding concept in orthodox Jewish thought at the same time, quite apart from the lateness of the sources which refer to this expectation. In any case, it is important to note that the Samaritans did not look for the Ta'eb to bring a new Law or make alterations in the old, but principally to instruct non-Samaritans in the existing Torah.[3]

In the New Testament several passages reflect popular

---

[1] Consult the detailed discussion in H. Braun, *Qumran*, I, 149–50; II, 67–8. The suggestion of W. D. Davies, *Setting*, pp. 149–50, that the future 'making new' in 1 QS 4.18–26 included refashioning of the Law is highly conjectural.

[2] See M. Gaster, *The Samaritans* (1925), p. 91; W. A. Meeks, *The Prophet-King* (1967), pp. 250ff.

[3] It is extremely doubtful whether the term 'Messiah' should be ascribed to the Ta'eb expectation. Against S. Mowinckel, *He That Cometh* (ET 1950), p. 293; J. Jeremias, *TDNT*, IV, 858, and H. M. Teeple, *Prophet*, p. 108, it must be remarked that the term is never applied to him in the Samaritan writings. Since his function is only one of restoration and he possesses no royal lineage, the description is probably inappropriate. Cf. J. MacDonald, *The Theology of the Samaritans* (1964), p. 361. Indeed his inferiority to Moses has been emphasised by J. E. H. Thompson, *The Samaritans* (1919), pp. 194–5, and A. Merx, *Der Messiah oder Ta'eb der Samaritaner* (1909), p. 43. The description in John 4.25, therefore, has its basis in christian terminology. Cf. P. Volz, *Eschatologie*, p. 200.

expectation of a coming prophet (Mark 6.15; 8.28; Matt. 11.9, 14; 17.12; John 1.21, 25; 6.14; 7.40). The variety of figures put forward in these texts shows just how little uniformity there was in the popular hope and it is apparent that even if Deut. 18.15–18 played some part in the expectation, it was by no means the dominant category. The figure of Elijah is once again prominent.[1] It has also been claimed that the revolutionary prophets mentioned in Jos., *Ant.* xx.97–9; 167–72; *War.* II.261 (cf. *Ant.* xx.188; *War.* VII.438; Acts 21.38) held Mosaic and Messianic pretensions. It is more likely, however, that parallels with Elijah and Elisha (for Theudas), and Joshua (for the prophet from Egypt) rather than comparisons with Moses and Messianic connotations lie behind their activities. If Deut. 18.15–18 does, at least in part, lie behind such expectations, it cannot be said to involve any notion of lawgiving.[2]

There remain certain other passages which allegedly depict the Messiah as a second Moses even though there is no reference to Deut. 18. These have as their basis the doctrine that the deliverance from Egypt is a type of Messianic redemption. While the two periods are typologically linked in the Old Testament, Apocrypha and Pseudepigrapha, no reference is made in these works to the later rabbinic principle 'as the first redeemer (Moses), so the final redeemer (Messiah)'. It has been suggested that earlier traces of this idea can be detected in the deliberate echoes of Mosaic times in the Qumran writings (CDC 1.7ff.; 4.3; 6.5; 8.14ff. *et al.*), the desert prophets mentioned by Josephus (above) and certain other passages in the

---

[1] See further E. Fascher, ΠΡΟΦΗΤΗ (1927), p. 208; R. Meyer, *Der Prophet aus Galiläa* (1940), p. 98, and R. E. Brown, *The Gospel According to John* (1966), pp. 234–5, and note on 1.27. For all these passages but John 6.14 it is generally agreed that a Messianic identification of the prophet is out of the question. That this is true for John 6.14 as well see W. Baldensperger, *Selbstbewusstsein*, pp. 114–15; R. Bultmann, *Das Johannesevangelium* (1950[11]), p. 61; J. H. Bernard, *The Gospel According to St. John* (1942), I, 37; H. Strathmann, *Das Evangelium nach Johannes* (1955), p. 114.

[2] Cf. E. Meyer, *Ursprung und Anfänge des Christentums* (1925), II, 402–5, and O. Betz, *Offenbarung*, pp. 99–109 against W. Staerk, *Soter* (1933), I, 66; J. Jeremias, *TDNT*, IV, 859; G. Vermès, 'Moses', p. 85; U. Mauser, *Wilderness*, pp. 56–7. Messianic designations are denied these prophets by F. J. Foakes-Jackson and K. Lake, *Beginnings*, IV, 276; H. A. Guy, *New Testament Prophecy* (1947), p. 26, and R. Schnackenburg, *St.Ev.*, I (1959), 628.

New Testament (Mark 1.4ff.; Matt. 24.23ff.; Acts 21.38). However, the association with the wilderness is based less on the past *appearance* of Moses or the expected appearance of the Mosaic Messiah than on the fulfilment of prophetic pronouncements as to the *place* of the eschatological drama. There is also the strong possibility that quite other considerations, such as secrecy and convenience, played their part in the locations chosen.[1] In addition, it should be noted that the rabbinic examples are not only late but are scarcely representative.[2]

We must conclude, then, that there is no evidence for prechristian speculation on the return of Moses or of a figure fashioned in his likeness and given his functions. Where the expectation of a 'prophet like Moses' does occur the emphasis is laid more on God's action in raising up a prophetic spokesman rather than on any special similarity to the ministry of Moses. This is, in fact, the meaning of both Hebrew and Greek renditions of the passage from Deuteronomy itself, a point that is often overlooked in this whole discussion.[3] It has been too readily assumed that Moses himself is predicting the future appearance of an *alter ego*. In the later references, as we have seen, whatever Mosaic characteristics may be present, the dominant type seems rather to have been Elijah. Certainly

[1] For John the Baptist see C. C. McCown, 'The Scene of John's Ministry', *JBL*, 59 (1940), 130, and for Josephus especially F. J. Foakes-Jackson and K. Lake, *Beginnings*, IV, 277. The contrary view is put by J. Jeremias, *TDNT*, IV, 861–2 and H. M. Teeple, *Prophet*, p. 113.

[2] See Qoh.R. 1.9 in the name of R. Jiçchaq II (*c.* 300). The parallel in Midrash Samuel 14.9 ascribes it to R. Levi (cf. Num.R. 11.2 and Ruth R. 5.6) who is to be dated about the same time. The theme is developed in a number of detailed comparisons between Moses and the Messiah elsewhere. See further R. Bloch, 'Moses', pp. 159–64. The reference in Tanchuma eqeb 7b, ascribed to R. Akiba, which is claimed by Jeremias and Teeple (above) to be the earliest occurrence, is a comparison with Mosaic times not Moses himself, and the scriptural reference is to Job 30.4 not Deut. 8.3 as in the later examples. Moreover, R. Akiba seems to have thought of the Messiah in Davidic rather than Mosaic terms. In any case his view is immediately contradicted. Again it must be emphasised that, in all these examples, reference to a new Law is nowhere in view.

[3] As well as the commentaries on Deuteronomy of S. R. Driver, G. A. Smith, H. Wheeler Robinson and J. Reider *ad loc.*, see also H. J. Cadbury, *Beginnings*, I, 5, 372 n.2, and F. F. Bruce. *The Acts of the Apostles* (1952²). p. 113.

Messianic identifications cannot be sustained for in our period that seems first to have taken place in christian exegesis.[1] In no single instance is any legislative activity *vis-à-vis* the Mosaic Law associated with these expectations. Indeed in Deut.R. 8.6, whether it be a case of anti-christian polemic or not, such activity is expressly prohibited. 'Moses said to them: So that you may not say "another Moses will rise and bring us another Torah from heaven", I have long made known to you: the Torah is not (any longer) in heaven.' The Messiah when he comes will rather be the great teacher of Torah.[2]

Quite apart from the expectation surrounding Moses there are four other places in which the idea of a 'new Law' is said to be present. Tg.Jon. on Isa. 12.3, based on first-century traditions, states that in the Messianic time 'ye shall receive אולפן חדת with joy from the מבחירי עדיקיא'. D. Daube, equating אולפן with תורה, understands from this that Israel will be given a better Law, a new and final revelation. מבחירי עדיקיא must, however, refer to a group rather than a single individual, and in this case it becomes difficult to see how אולפן could refer to new Torah.[3] Qoh.R. 11.8 maintains that 'the תורה which a man learns in this world is vanity with the תורתו של משיח'. The similar, and earlier, saying in Qoh.R. 2.1 (in the name of R. Simon b. Zabdai *c.* A.D. 300) makes it clear, however, that it is not Torah itself which will be subject to change, but man's study and knowledge of it.[4] In Lev.R. 13.3 R. Abin b. Kahana

[1] Even so the emphasis is upon the raising up of a prophetic spokesman as such, not on any particular likeness to Moses. See further F. Hahn, *Christologische Hoheitstitel* (1963), pp. 353–4. Cf. also W. A. Meeks, *Prophet-King*, p. 29, who nevertheless places too much weight on the importance of Moses with respect to the expectation of a prophet, and O. Cullman, *The Christology of the New Testament* (ET 1959), p. 23, who, however, admits the fusion of the two at some points in the New Testament. H. M. Teeple, *Prophet*, pp. 102ff., also recognises the distinction but confuses the issue by referring to a 'Prophet-King Messiah' when the latter is rather to be regarded as a 'Prophet-King' in lieu of the Messiah.

[2] See especially P. Seidelin, 'Der Ebed Jahwe und die Messiasgestalt im Jesajatargum', *ZNW*, 35 (1936), 194ff., and the passages cited by W. Gutbrod, *TDNT*, IV, 1057.

[3] W. D. Davies, *Setting*, p. 174, admits that what is meant by the plural is not clear. But see D. Daube, 'ἐξουσία in Mark 1.22 and 27', *JTS*, 39 (1938), 55.

[4] Cf. A. Cohen, *Midrash Rabbah: Ecclesiastes* (Sonc. trans.), p. 51.

(fourth century A.D.) provides a solution to the problem raised by the illegal procedure involved in the slaying of Behemoth by Leviathan in the Messianic Age by quoting Isa. 51.4 '(new) instruction shall go forth from me' (only some MSS read 'new'). Quite apart from the variation in the manuscripts, it would be more in line with rabbinic processes to think here in terms of a new interpretation of the Law by which the contradiction will be abolished.[1] A more fundamental passage is Yalkut on Isa. 26.2 which states that 'God will sit and expound תורה חדשה which he will, one day, give by the Messiah's hand.' It is, however, grammatically possible to interpret the phrase טעמי תורה חרשה as if it read טעמי תורה חדשים i.e., 'new grounds of Torah'. Moreover, the compilation to which it belongs is extremely late, not earlier than the thirteenth century. It is doubtful, therefore, whether the passage is sufficiently early to warrant serious attention.[2]

In this discussion we have observed the basis for the view that the Law is eternal in the priestly writings of the Old Testament. The prophets also spoke of the permanence of Torah but in different terms, laying greater stress on the presence of prophetic revelation, within which the Mosaic Law was encompassed, in the days to come. With only one exception, however, the intertestamentary writings, including for the first time the Wisdom literature, spoke only of the traditional Law in this fashion and this was further elaborated upon in later rabbinic teaching. On

---

[1] Thus J. Israelstam, *Midrash Rabbah: Leviticus* (Sonc. trans.), p. 167, against K. Köhler, *JE*, v, 216; H. J. Schoeps, *Paul*, p. 172 n.4, and W. D. Davies, *Setting*, p. 167. See also the similar ideas mentioned in the passage Tg.Cant. 5.10. W. Bächer, *Die exegetische Terminologie der jüdischen Traditionsliteratur* (1965), I, 56; II, 64, claims that חרש and חדוש, in both Tannaitic and Amoraean periods, were technical terms for the outlining of a new halakha as a legitimate interpretation of Torah.

[2] On the grammatical point see Gesenius-Kautzsch, p. 492, comparing 1 Sam. 2.4; 1 Kings 1.41; Isa. 2.11 *et al*. That a new Torah is implied here is the view of G. Friedländer, *The Jewish Sources of the Sermon on the Mount* (1911), p. 57; K. Köhler, *JE*, v, 216; H. J. Schoeps, *Zeit*, p. 224 n.4; H. M. Teeple, *Prophet*, p. 26; and W. D. Davies, *Setting*, p. 177. The references in Sib.Or. 3.373-4 and 3.757-8 which do seem to advocate a new Torah owe too much to the Greek ideal of a universal law of nature to be relevant here. The passages in Justin, *Dial.* 11, 19, 21, 34 referring to Isa. 51.4-5 and Jer. 31.31ff. ought not be regarded as evidence for the attitude of contemporary Judaism to the question in the NT.

investigation, no adequate basis was found for the view that within the framework of a doctrine of the immutability of Torah occasional expectations of its modification or partial abrogation were to be found. Such alterations as were to take place only enhanced its authority and indicated that in the future it would be understood more accurately and observed more closely.

It would be unwarranted to infer from the presence of an untypical opinion to the contrary (*viz*. Midr.Tehillim on Ps. 146.7) or from the occasional anti-christian polemical utterance on the subject (e.g. Deut.R. 8.6) that there was a more widely-held minority view on the question within pre-Jamnian Judaism. So far as the first is concerned, the veneration with which the Law was held within all Jewish groups during this period, however differently this may have been expressed, and the centrality it possessed in their outlook and conduct, including their views on the future, makes any such possibility extremely unlikely.[1] With respect to the second, it is highly improbable, despite recent suggestions to the contrary, that the earliest christian writers, notably Matthew, thought in terms of Jesus as the new Lawgiver at all.[2] In addition to these factors, when in the later centuries flexibility was once again allowed to rabbinic eschatological speculations, no such view of Torah re-emerged. Had it done so, the possibility of its temporary suppression due to the ascendancy of rabbinic elements opposed to apocalyptic speculation would carry more weight, but this is not the case.

[1] See G. F. Moore, *Judaism*, I, 273.

[2] See further pp. 229-34. There is, in any case, a difficulty with this line of reasoning reluctantly acknowledged by Davies himself. Having hesitantly agreed with the thesis of J. Klausner, *Messianic Idea*, pp. 466-9, that the New Torah doctrine arose when relations between Church and Synagogue had become less antagonistic and speculation along similar lines less unthinkable, he admits that he is 'not quite sure that he [i.e., Klausner] is correct in thinking that it would be easier for later Judaism to contemplate a New Torah than it would have been for first-century Judaism. The antipathy to Christianity had become greater, not less.' He sidesteps the problem raised by such an admission by proposing that 'the concept of a new Torah might perhaps have been indigenous and not merely the result of Christian influences'. In distinction from Davies, Klausner, of course, argued that it was *only* in the later post-apostolic period that belief in a new Torah arose.

It is for this reason that the very circumstantial case built up by W. D. Davies for the presence of such a belief in the earlier period, relying as it does almost entirely on his interpretation of the later rabbinic speculations, loses most of its plausibility when a different construction is placed upon them. Thus against those who claim that the idea of a new Torah was widely held in rabbinic literature or that there were at least elements in Judaism which thought in such terms, it must be insisted that all such passages belong to a considerably later period than the first century A.D. and that in so far as more is meant than a new interpretation of the old Torah one cannot speak of such an expectation in the later period either.[1]

In this survey of the status, meaning and duration of Law three main religious traditions have been distinguished – legal, prophetic and sapiental. It has been pointed out that this demarcation was not at any stage in Israel's history regarded as absolute. Even in the earliest period a good deal of inter-mingling took place between them. Though this tended to increase with the passing of time, in the inter-testamentary period these three approaches are still discernible. Only at the latest stage of the development does the level of cross-fertilisation lead to a blurring of their distinctive contributions and to the partial eclipse of two of the traditions at the expense of the third. It remains now only to set out briefly the revelatory datum from which these attitudes were derived and the nature of the authority expressed in them.

There are good grounds for thinking that it was to the priests that Israel looked not only for instruction in the contents of their covenant obligations but also for the history of God's promises and saving deeds which underlay those requirements. It was their task, together with their scribes, to mediate these historical and legal traditions to the present. This involved, as we have seen, not merely a recounting of past events and demands but also their application to present circumstances. As a result there developed the writing of further history which was viewed in terms of faithfulness or disobedience to the given revelation, and the issuing of new legal decisions so that older

[1] For a similar judgment see E. Bammel, *St.Ev.*, III (1964), 123. See also G. Barth, 'Law', pp. 154–6, and, partly, J. Klausner, *Messianic Idea*, pp. 466–9.

legislation could be brought into touch with contemporary situations. Thus though their task was primarily a deductive one it is not accurate to say that it lacked a creative element.[1] Nevertheless, so predominant was its orientation to the past that the speaker or narrator rarely seems to acquire any distinctive authority of his own. Even Moses only occasionally speaks in the first person, in terms of 'the statutes and ordinances which *I* teach you' (Deut. 4.1), or in the command 'to lay up these words of *mine* in your heart and in your soul' (Deut. 11.18ff.).[2] Such instances, however, are rare and, significantly enough, occur only in Deuteronomy. Here Moses is presented primarily in prophetic rather than legislative terms and the influence of the wisdom tradition is also quite strong. The historico-legal books of the inter-testamentary period add little to this picture, apart from witnessing to a certain hardening of Torah and a corresponding loss of creativity and development within the tradition.

Though not sitting loose to the historical traditions of Israel the prophets are more concerned with the present demands of Yahweh upon his people. It is this contemporary word of Yahweh, which can include reference to both past acts and future deeds, that is decisive for their message. As evidenced by the constant formula 'Thus saith the Lord' this leaves little room for the intrusion of their own authority. Nevertheless, so possessed can they become by the message entrusted to them that on occasions they appear to make the very words of Yahweh their own. This is dramatically apparent in the sudden changes from the usual third person reference to Yahweh to a first person address to their audience in which they appear to speak as Yahweh.[3] In the inter-testamentary apocalyptic literature a similar concern with the present manifestation of Yahweh's will can be discerned, though this is certainly

[1] Cf. P. J. Budd, 'Priestly Instruction in Pre-exilic Israel', *VT*, 23 (1973), 1–14, who distinguishes between priestly oracles, proclamations, directions and verdicts and says that Torah was particularly linked with the latter two.
[2] Cf. also Deut. 4.40; 5.1ff.; 8.1; 10.12–13; 11.1, 8–9, 13; 12.32; 13.45–7.
[3] See Hos. 4.4ff.; 9.10ff; Isa. 1.11ff., 24ff.; 5.3ff.; 10.5ff.; 29.1ff.; 34.1ff.; Mic. 2.12f.; Jer. 5.7; 12.5ff.; Zech. 10.6ff.; Mal. 3.1ff. Note especially on this question the consideration given to this phenomenon, as to the whole subject we are examining, by R. B. Y. Scott, 'Priesthood, Prophecy, Wisdom and the Knowledge of God', *JBL*, 80 (1961), 8.

restricted by their custom of casting such messages into the mouths of earlier figures and throwing chief emphasis upon events which lie in the future. Nevertheless, perhaps as a result of wisdom influence, there is an increasing tendency to accentuate the authority of the apocalyptic seer. So it is that in a number of works the formula 'I say to you' occurs, usually followed by a pronouncement of some significance.[1] Other strong affirmations are found in Test.Reu. 4.5: 'observe all things that I command you and you shall not sin'; 1 Enoch 94.5: 'hold fast my words in the thoughts of your hearts, and suffer them not be effaced' and 2 Enoch 40.2: 'I know all things...' (cf. also 46.1; 47.1).

The wise men draw their instruction neither from enquiry into the present will of God, nor deduction from his past manifestation in promise, event and demand. Their concern is with the experience of God, man and nature as mediated through common human experience and the observance of natural phenomena. In so doing, wisdom thinks resolutely within the framework of a theology of creation and, in relation to other literature, has a relatively timeless quality about it.[2] In these writings it is Wisdom herself rather than God who addresses Israel (cf. Prov. 1.22ff.; 8.4ff., 32ff., etc.), but far more frequently the wise man speaks in authoritative terms concerning his own message. So, for example, Prov. 4.20–2: 'Be attentive to my words, incline your ears to my sayings. Let them not escape from your sight, keep them within your heart. For they are life to him who finds them, and healing to all his flesh.' Or Job 36.4: 'For truly my words are not false; one who is perfect in knowledge is with you.'[3] In the inter-testamentary period this development is even more marked. Compare Ecclus. 3.1:

---

[1] See especially Jub. 36.11; Test.Reu. 4.5; 6.5; Naph. 4.1; Gad 5.3; 1 Enoch 92.18; 94.1, 3; 102.9; 2 Enoch 2.2. A detailed, though not exhaustive, treatment of the apocalyptic consciousness may be found in D. S. Russell, *Apocalyptic*, pp. 158–77.

[2] See further W. Zimmerli, 'The Place and Limit of Wisdom in the Framework of Old Testament Theology', *SJT*, 17 (1964), 148 (= *Gottes Offenbarung*, pp. 300–13).

[3] Cf. Prov. 2.1–2; 3.1–2; 4.10; 5.1, 7; 7.1–3; 22.17ff.; 23.26; Job 34.2, 16; 36.3f. For a discussion of this phenomenon, which also takes note of the differing evaluations of the sage's authority that have been advanced by Pedersen, Fichtner, Skladny, Kayatz as well as Zimmerli, de Boer and

'Hear me, your father, O my children, and do thereafter that
ye may be saved' and above all the extended soliloquy in
6.23–9: 'Give ear my son and accept my judgment and refuse
not my counsel...Come unto her with all thy soul and keep
her ways with thy whole power...For at the last thou shalt
find her rest; and she shall be turned for thee to gladness....'[1]

With the exception of the Pharisees, little can be said on this
question so far as the parties of the New Testament period are
concerned. Since no documents are available for the Sadducees
and the Am-Ha-Areṣ one can only speculate as to their attitude.
No doubt the former continued the approach of the Old
Testament and especially Apocryphal legal literature. Their
concentration on the written text, particularly the Pentateuch,
would have further reduced the possibility of a creative understanding of the Law and more markedly restricted the authority
of the teacher. The piety of the latter would appear to have had
its roots in the other inter-testamentary traditions and may have
largely preserved the stance towards authority and revelation
exemplified in them. At Qumran, where each of the main
traditions survives in a new form, the documents so far examined do not seem to contain the authoritative mode of address
of apocalyptic and late-wisdom literature.

It is among the rabbis that some evidence exists of this
phenomenon. It is present in a subdued manner when a freer,
new or contradictory halakhic opinion was introduced with the
formula 'I hear it from...but thou must say...'.[2] Here, the
first part refers to a scholarly opinion, frequently of a literal
nature, which, on the basis of relevant texts, the hearers must
reject in favour of an alternative viewpoint. A more ex-

McKane see J. L. Crenshaw, *Prophetic Conflict: Its Effect on Israelite Religion*
(1971), esp. Exc.B. "esa and dabar: The Problem of Authority/Certitude
in Wisdom and Prophetic Literature' (pp. 116–23).

[1] Note also Ecclus. 23.7; 31.22; 33.17; 39.12; 50.27–9; Wisd. 6.22ff;
7.17; 8.10ff. For the address by Wisdom herself in similar terms see
especially Ecclus. 24.19–22, 32ff. A development in the notion of authority
attaching to the wise man in this literature has particularly been insisted
upon by G. von Rad, *Wisdom*, pp. 54–7.

[2] Cf. Mek.Ex. 19.20; 20.13, 14; 21.12. Though mentioned in S. Schechter,
Aspects, pp. 213ff.; I. Abrahams, *Studies*, 1, 16 and B. H. Branscomb, *Law*,
pp. 239–40, this material has been dealt with most fully by D. Daube,
Judaism, pp. 55–62.

plicit claim to authority occurs in the use of the expressions
אומר אני and ואני אומר as formulas prefacing one particular
opinion in contrast to another.[1] However, such affirmations
of personal authority occur within the narrow context of legal
interpretation and innovation which the rabbis circumscribed
for themselves and, as such, can scarcely be placed on the same
level as the previous examples we have noted.

The material gathered in this survey of Law in the Old
Testament and Judaism does have considerable importance for
the examination of Jesus' own attitude to the Law, particularly
in supplying the full and proper context in which his teaching
may be considered, as well as in providing a series of perspectives on the Law which may assist in finding the solution to a
number of difficulties and obscurities that arise in his teaching.
This has been frequently recognised before, but usually within
the limits of too narrow a canvas. Often his teaching has been
set over against that of one particular party and considered in
relation to it – usually, but not always, the Pharisaic – the
attitude of other groups within contemporary Judaism being
left out of view altogether. Where a broader context has been
sought this has usually drawn its boundary around contemporary Jewish movements with an occasional glance at some
aspects of the inter-testamentary literature. Rarely has this
material been considered in detail, not to speak of the rich
cross-current of approaches to the Law reflected in the main
Old Testament traditions, any one of which may have been
revitalised and sharpened in the teaching of Jesus. All this is
even more marked when the grounds from which these attitudes
were derived, and the authority with which they were expressed, are brought into consideration. Here, particularly in
the Old Testament and Apocryphal wisdom literature and in
some of the apocalyptic works of the inter-testamentary period,
lies important comparative material for the study of the basis
and authority of Jesus' words on the Law.

---

[1] Examples of the former may be found in Sif.Lev. 14.21; Tos.Bek. 6.15;
Tos.Pes. 8.18, 21; and of the latter in both halakhic – Tos.Bikk. 1.2;
Tos.Mik. 3.4 – and haggadic – Sif.Num. 11.21–2; Sif.Deut. 6.4 –
passages. For further details see G. Dalman, *Jesus-Jeshua* (ET 1929), p. 73,
and, in greater detail, M. Smith, *Tannaitic Parallels to the Gospels* (1951),
pp. 27–31.

PART TWO
LAW IN THE
SYNOPTIC TRADITION

Any examination of the synoptic gospels must bear in mind three factors at work in the tradition: the original material, its transmission by the christian community, and the final redaction by the evangelists. In establishing the distinctive viewpoints of the latter there would be some advantage in considering each gospel in turn. However, since our concern is essentially with Jesus' own attitude, it will be more appropriate to examine the material in terms of his response to the issues that arose as reported in the different accounts. In approaching the documents this way, three types of passages may be distinguished: incidental sayings and actions alleged to bear on his attitude to the Law; debates and controversies over particular legal issues; teaching on the Law of a more general or extensive nature.

So far as the term νόμος is concerned, it is interesting to note that it occurs only eight times in Matthew, nine times in Luke, while in Mark it is absent altogether. Generally it refers to the Pentateuch, in particular to its legal contents (Matt. 5.17–18; 7.12; 12.5; 22.36, 40; 23.23; Luke 2.22, 23, 24, 27, 39; 10.26; 16.17) though elsewhere, as I shall argue in due course, it denotes the 'prophetic' aspect of these books (Matt. 11.13; Luke 16.16; 24.44). It is nowhere used of the oral Torah, and in one pericope (Matt. 15.2ff.; cf. Mark 7.5ff.) this is described as ἡ παράδοσις τῶν πρεσβυτέρων. It can be seen at once that the incidence of the term in the gospels is extremely slight. This becomes even more apparent when it is realised that two occurrences in each gospel are parallels (Matt. 5.18 = Luke 16.17; Matt. 11.13 = Luke 16.16), possibly also a third (Matt. 22.36 and Luke 10.26). Five in Luke have their context in the infancy narratives (Luke 2.22, 23, 24, 27, 39). Three in Matthew have their authenticity in dispute (Matt. 5.17; 7.12; 22.40). The meagre occurrence of νόμος, however, is no measure of the extent to which the problem of Law arises in the gospels, and so it becomes necessary to refer to other passages in which the term does not occur at all.[1]

[1] So, for example, as H.-W. Kuhn, 'Zum Problem des Verhältnisses der markinischen Redaktion zur israelitisch-jüdischen Tradition', *Tradition*

A INCIDENTAL SAYINGS AND ACTIONS

There are a number of passages in the synoptic gospels where, it has been alleged, reference is made to the Law, but only in an incidental or allusive fashion. Related to these are certain other passages in which the attitude of Jesus towards Jewish customs or the Pharisaic tradition comes into view. It is through consideration of these that an understanding of Jesus' position with regard to the Mosaic Law can best be approached. Before proceeding to that, however, it is advisable to recall what was said earlier about the distinction between customs and laws. It was suggested that whereas both encompassed widely endorsed, and generally traditionally observed, social norms, to which coercive sanctions of varying kinds were attached, that the latter were in addition justifying rules accessible to reinterpretation by recognised legal institutions. It was also acknowledged that customs quite frequently provided the basis from which laws emerged. This is a process we have seen at work in the development of the Mosaic Law in the Old Testament.

In the New Testament period, the Pharisees also adopted certain widely observed customs into their legal tradition. They also created, as we have seen, a large number of additional regulations to which they gave an authoritative status equal to that afforded the written Torah. However, it was the legitimacy of their interpretation of that Torah which gave rise to various disputes in early Judaism as to the validity of the legal rules orally promulgated by them. Custom, then, because of its unofficial, if potentially legal, character and oral tradition because of its controverted, if possibly justifiable, legal status, are distinct, if related, entities, alongside the Law with which Jesus had to come to terms. It is conceivable, of course, that together with many of the Jewish people, particularly those who were favourably inclined to the Pharisees, Jesus could have viewed all three on the same legal plane. As the following

und Glaube. Das frühe Christentum in seiner Umwelt (ed. G. Jeremias, H.-W. Kuhn and H. Stegemann (1971)), p. 301 n.10, comments, 'Aus dem Fehlen des Begriffs "Gesetz" im MkEv können keine sicheren Schlüsse gezogen werden' for 'gerade "Mose" hier haufig in gesetzlichen Zusammenhängen genannt wird'.

examination will show, however, the singular position he accorded to the Mosaic Law led to a differentiation between them and to a distinctive approach to each.

I   ATTITUDE TO CUSTOMS

In the gospels we find several references to Jesus' attendance in the synagogue (Mark 1.21/Luke 4.31; Mark 1.39/Matt. 4.23/Luke 4.44; Mark 6.2/Matt. 13.5/Luke 4.16; Luke 13.10). His repeated practice attested in these passages is generally regarded as indicative of the seriousness with which he viewed the observance of customary obligations. On each of these occasions, however, his attendance is associated with a ministry of healing or, more frequently, teaching. His constant presence in the synagogue, therefore, probably stems more from the opportunities for ministry it provides than from faithfulness to the customs of his fathers.

This is even the case in Luke, despite the fact that it is his gospel alone which inserts an explanation of Jesus' behaviour, in the phrase 'as his custom was' (κατὰ τὸ εἰωθὸς, Luke 4.16). In view of the words 'and he was teaching them in the synagogue' in the previous verse (Luke 4.15), and the use by Luke of κατὰ τὸ εἰωθὸς of Paul's synagogue ministry (Acts 17.2, the only other occurrence of the phrase in the New Testament), there is a strong possibility that it refers to the practice of Jesus within the synagogue rather than to the regularity of his attendance.[1] This would also appear to lie behind Luke's greater interest in Jesus' relationship with the synagogue, for though reference to his attendance at it occurs in all the synoptics it is Luke who records the largest number of such instances. In both these ways, then, Luke is merely pointing up the emphasis in the Marcan tradition (Matthew has no additional references), and there seems little reason to doubt that this tradition itself reflects the original attitude of Jesus.[2] Presumably

[1] Among the commentators, however, only E. E. Ellis, *The Gospel of St Luke* (1966), p. 96, seems to recognise this possibility. A. Plummer, *Commentary on the Gospel according to St Luke* (1905⁴), p. 118, expressly rejects it, but allows that the reading of the lesson may be the practice in view.

[2] W. Rordorf, *Sunday* (ET 1968), pp. 67–8, concurs, though with Jesus' attitude to the sabbath rather than the synagogue especially in mind. Agreeing that 'on every occasion preaching was the purpose of his visit to

Luke's interest in this question stems from his concern to relate the appearance and ministry of Jesus to Judaism as a whole.

While the origins of the Temple-tax are still contested, it now seems probable that its exaction in the time of Jesus did not rest upon any requirement of the Mosaic Law. Though precedent for it has been found in the half-shekel offering to the Tabernacle recorded in Ex. 30.11–16 (cf. j.Shek. 1.46a; b.Meg. 29b; Jos., *Ant.* III.194–6), it would appear to rest upon a halakhah that became binding no earlier than the close of the Hasmonaean period. As the evidence from Philo, Josephus and the Mishnah demonstrates, both in Palestine and the Diaspora the custom became a symbol of national and religious unity. Nevertheless, during the time of Christ there was considerable controversy as to the compulsory nature of the obligation. The Sadducees took exception to it, probably because of its recent origin, while the Qumran covenanters felt bound to pay the levy only once, thus more correctly interpreting its alleged biblical precedent. It is significant that in Matt. 17.24–7 the matter is not raised by the scribes or the Pharisees but simply by those responsible for collecting the tax, and that there is no attempt to bring Jesus into conflict with either the written or oral Law.[1] What is at issue is his willingness or otherwise to observe a custom that is honoured by the majority of his fellow-

the synagogue' he warns that 'this does not mean that Jesus...was very strict about the sabbath commandment'. B. H. Branscomb, *Law*, p. 127, is therefore quite wide of the mark with his claim that by his attendance Jesus sanctioned the oral Law which alone regulated synagogue proceedings.

[1] Here the treatment of J. Liver, 'The Half-Shekel Offering in Biblical and Post-Biblical Literature', *HTR* 56 (1963), esp. pp. 178–91 is to be preferred over the more customary critical opinion represented in H. Montefiore, 'Jesus and the Temple-Tax', *NTS*, 11 (1964–5), 60–71. The former points out that though it is the collection for the Tabernacle in Ex. 25.1ff. which lies behind the similar imposition in the reign of Joash, that there is no evidence in 2 Chron. 24.6 that the tax amounted to half a shekel or that it became an annual levy. Thus the one-third shekel stipulation in Neh. 10.33–4 must be regarded as an innovation and is, in any case, only of temporary duration. This is why no mention of such a levy occurs in the inter-testamentary literature, not even in contexts where it would have been extremely appropriate (e.g., Tobit 1.6ff.). For the Qumran evidence see further J. Liver, pp. 191–8. There is also reason to believe that some rabbis were exempt (cf. E. Klostermann, *Das Matthäusevangelium* [1938³], p. 146, and Bill., 1, 771) and possibly some Galileans (cf. J. Schmid, *Das Evangelium nach Matthäus* [1959¹¹], p. 265) though the latter, like the

countrymen. As a matter of fact, the wording of the question indicates the expectation of an affirmative answer. In parabolic language, Jesus argues that in their position as 'sons' of the 'king' he and his disciples are absolved from any compulsion in this matter. Most probably the analogy is with the natural sons of a king as contrasted with foreigners (2 Chron. 21.17) rather than the situation of Israel *vis-à-vis* non-Jews (Neh. 9.2), since otherwise his statement would imply that the Temple stipulation was unjust. Nevertheless, Jesus continues, though he is not obliged to comply with the tax, he will do so in order to avoid causing unnecessary offence. What we have here, then, is another example of his practice of judging such customary obligations in the light of considerations external to them. In this instance his attitude is derived less from the nature of his mission, as in the synagogue references, than from the character of those to whom it is addressed.

This narrative has frequently been regarded as a later construction. Attention has been drawn to the terminology of the narrative sections, the prominent position accorded to Peter, the more relevant setting in the life of the later Jewish-christian communities, and the unusual character of the appended miracle. While the form in which the story has been transmitted has obviously been affected by such factors, and its point in Matthew probably has to do with the legal tax established after the destruction of Jerusalem to support the council at Jamnia, the possibility of its having possessed an original context in the ministry of Jesus should not be excluded.[1] If so, his acknowledgment of the custom of paying the traditional tax, as contrasted

Sadducees, may have regarded the tax as too recent an innovation. After A.D. 70 the Romans continued to demand payment of the tax for the temple of Jupiter Capitolinus in Rome.

[1] On this tax see H. Graetz, *Geschichte der Juden* (1908), IV, 441ff. The extent to which Matthew has been responsible for the present form of the passage has been demonstrated by W. G. Thompson, *Matthew's Advice to a Divided Community: Mt. 17.22 – 18.35* (1970), pp. 51ff., who finds evidence of Matthaean redaction in all the narrative sections. It is interesting to observe that R. Bultmann, *History of the Synoptic Tradition* (ET 1963), pp. 34–5, and H. Braun, *Radikalismus*, I, 123 n.1, regard the dominical saying, though not its present context, as authentic. This has been extended over a larger part of the narrative by H. Montefiore, *NTS*, 11 (1964–5), 64–71, and J. D. M. Derrett, 'Peter's Penny: Fresh Light on Matthew 17.24–27', *Law in the New Testament* (1970), pp. 250–8, both of whom, however, suggest

with his refusal to observe Pharisaic tradition, must stem from his unwillingness to offend those who were not necessarily antagonistic to his mission as distinguished from his determination to oppose those who, on legalistic grounds, were. While it is possible that the principle enunciated in the narrative may also apply when questions of legal obligation are in view, this can only be tested in passages where these occur and cannot simply be assumed as a matter of course.[1]

In Mark 2.18–22 and pars. the custom of fasting as practised by the followers of both John the Baptist and the Pharisees is contrasted with the conduct of Jesus' disciples. The question is asked in Mark by a section of the crowd, not so much in order to clarify Jesus' attitude to the Law on this point as to probe his disciples' failure to adopt the pious conventions of contemporary religious groups.[2] The reply falls into two parts, the first of which is most probably a proverbial saying referring to the behaviour of the groom and guests at a wedding, without any

rather questionable *Sitze-im-Leben* in the ministry of Jesus. So far as Matthew is concerned, G. Strecker, *Gerechtigkeit*, p. 31 n.1, and S. Schulz, *Botschaft*, p. 161, are certainly incorrect in considering the passage to be uncharacteristic of Matthew's theological perspective. Also mistaken are G. Bornkamm, 'End-Expectation', p. 31 and G. Barth, 'Law', p. 85 n.2, who feel the pericope to be illustrative of Matthew's attitude to the ceremonial Law; R. Hummel, *Auseinandersetzung*, p. 104, who regards it as indicative of his church's attitude to Jewish institutions generally; R. Walker, *Heilsgeschichte*, pp. 101–2, 134, and W. D. Davies, *Setting*, pp. 389–91, who suggest that Roman institutions are in view.

[1] See, however, J. Schniewind, *Das Evangelium nach Matthäus* (1956[8]), p. 196, and W. G. Thompson, *Matthew's Advice*, pp. 58–9, both of whom relate it directly to Jesus' understanding of the Law, and B. H. Branscomb, *Law*, p. 127, who regards it as an example of his compliance with the oral tradition. Jesus' reply also makes it quite clear that his attitude differed from that of the Sadducees, who refused to pay the tax altogether, and from that of the Sectarians, who were guided by a particular understanding of the biblical 'precedent'.

[2] In Matthew, the query originates with the disciples of John and in Luke with an anonymous 'they' (not the scribes and Pharisees of 5.30 since the latter are mentioned in 5.33). The intent of the statement in his account is especially heightened by the addition πυκνὰ καὶ δεήσεις ποιοῦνται. Since the following remarks have reference only to fasting, however, T. Schramm, *Der Markus-Stoff bei Lukas* (1971), pp. 106–7, is probably correct in assuming that the addition stems from Luke's source rather than his own hand.

messianic or eschatological overtones being intended (2.19a).[1] In the second, he replies that it is specifically because of his presence with the disciples that fasting has become unnecessary. (This does not necessarily infer, of course, that he is dispensing them from the one legal fast, the Day of Atonement, or that he is condemning the practice itself.[2]) Three main objections have been urged against the authenticity of the following verse in which Jesus appears to sanction a future discipline of fasting. In contrast to the preceding saying it is regarded as explicitly allegorical and therefore incompatible with it. Elsewhere in his teaching, however, Jesus follows a proverbial saying or scriptural illustration with a more direct reference to his own ministry (cf. Mark 2.17a–17b). It is also suggested that the prophecy of the Passion it contains occurs too early and is best explained as a *vaticinium ex eventu*. On the other hand, since the future reference here, unlike the later predictions, is extremely veiled it is possible, without according Mark chronological precision, that the saying was uttered at a reasonably early stage in the ministry.[3] It is also felt that the injunction to fast in this verse is too much at variance with 2.19a to be appropriate here. However, νηστεύουσιν in v.20 is probably being used metaphorically and so does not refer to the actual practice itself. Indeed, this is even possible for the first part of Jesus' reply as well, in which case Matthew's πενθεῖν in 9.15 has accurately interpreted the sense. Thus it becomes clear that the purpose of the reply is not at all to give a basic pronouncement about fasting. In it Jesus' concern is mainly to contrast future sadness with present joy, and only secondarily to suggest that

---

[1] Ct. J. Jeremias, *TDNT*, IV, 1103, and C. E. B. Cranfield, *The Gospel according to St. Mark* (1959), pp. 108ff. The same is true of the proverb in the previous pericope (2.17a).

[2] Cf. K. H. Rengstorff, *Das Evangelium nach Lukas* (1958⁸), p. 80. Abrogation of the Law here is suggested only by E. Lohmeyer, *Lord of the Temple* (ET 1961), p. 29.

[3] This is preferable to the suggestion of K. Schaefer, 'und dann werden sie fasten am jenem Tage', *Synoptische Studien* (1953), pp. 131ff., and J. G. Cremer, *Die Fastenfrage Jesu* (1965), p. 5, that the phrase is merely the counterpart of μετ' αὐτῶν ἐστιν in 2.19a. Attempts to locate the moment from which Jesus would be absent from them – e.g., arrest, death, resurrection, ascension, etc. – do not sufficiently take into account the veiled nature of the reference.

such joy is incompatible with present fasting also.[1] As with the previous examples, the criterion by which the customary practice is to be considered derives from the ministry of Jesus, though here it is his personal participation in it which is uppermost.

Other customs observed by Jesus include prayer before meals (Mark 6.41; 8.6; 14.22), blessings over the wine at table (Mark 14.23) and the singing of a hymn at the Passover feast (Mark 14.26). Branscomb cites these practices as indicating his approval of much of the oral Law. So, for example, he claims that the blessings over bread and wine correspond to Pharisaic regulations (Tos.Ber. 4.1; Pes. 10.7) and the Passover hymn to the specified recitation of the Hallel (Pes. 10.7). On the contrary all three, however much the Pharisees integrated them into their discipline, have a much older history and it is here far more likely that Jesus is observing pious customs rather than specific rabbinic stipulations. Moreover, in the context in which these occur in the ministry of Jesus, it is significant that a new and particular meaning is given to them, though this does not necessarily follow in every case in which a custom is observed by Jesus. Here one could refer to Jesus' wearing κρασπέδα on his garments as befitted a loyal Jew (Matt. 9.20; 14.36).[2] It could also be noted here that it has occasionally been suggested that Jesus' action in Matt. 21.14 i.e., healing the blind and the lame in the Temple, runs counter to a traditional ordinance excluding their presence from the Temple courts. However, this has been refuted by G. Dalman who maintains that no evidence for such a custom exists.[3]

Matthew and Luke record the request of the disciple who

---

[1] See A. Feuillet, 'La controverse sur la jeûne', *NRT*, 90 (1968), pp. 113–36, 252–77. This accords well with the fact that we have no evidence of the use of this verse among the Fathers as a proof-text to justify the practice of fasting. J. Jeremias, *TDNT*, IV, 1103 n.41, suggests an Aramaic original underlying the double use which means both 'to be sad' and 'to fast' and this is by no means impossible.

[2] Interestingly enough, although this requirement was commanded not only in the tradition but in the Law itself (Num. 15.37ff.; Deut. 24.12), B. H. Branscomb, *Law*, pp. 115–16, allows that Jesus was complying here with custom rather than rabbinic law. For his discussion of the other passages see p. 127.

[3] G. Dalman, *Sacred Sites and Ways* (1935), pp. 291–3.

pleaded time to perform burial rites for his father before committing himself to follow Christ (Matt. 8.21ff.; Luke 9.60). The Lucan form is generally regarded as the more original for in it the call of Jesus precedes the request of the would-be disciple, though the additional command to 'preach the kingdom of God' is a typically Lucan theme.[1] Jesus' reply has been condemned not only for its insensitivity and severity but also for its transgression of hallowed custom, oral tradition and even the fifth commandment.[2] Certainly both the Old Testament (Gen. 25.9) and the Apocrypha (Tobit 4.3; 6.14) bear witness to the importance of this ceremony, while according to the rabbinic literature it took precedence over every religious duty (Ber. 3.1) and was compulsory even upon a priest (Sif.Lev. 21.3 cf. Bill., I, 487ff.; IV, 559ff.). Considerable discussion has centred around the state of the father's condition and the exact meaning of Jesus' response, but it is far more likely that, as in the surrounding pericopes, it is the priority of discipleship over domestic responsibilities that is at stake rather than an issue relating to oral or written Law and that the reply of Jesus is a purely proverbial one with no actual referent(s) in view.[3] Even within the Law itself a similar sacrifice was demanded of those who took Nazirite vows (Lev. 21.1ff.; Num. 6.6–7). The other sayings in the gospels concerning the renunciation of parents in favour of commitment to Christ (Luke 8.19–21 and pars.; 11.27–8; 12.51–3 and pars.; 14.23–7

---

[1] Arguing for Lucan originality are C. G. Montefiore, *The Synoptic Gospels* (1927²), II, 132–3; T. W. Manson, *The Sayings of Jesus* (1954), p. 73, and J. Schmid, *Matthäus*, p. 167. The particular emphasis given by Luke to the passage is described by H. Conzelmann, *Luke*, p. 40, and that by Matthew in G. Bornkamm, 'The Stilling of the Storm in Matthew', *Tradition and Interpretation in Matthew*, p. 54.

[2] On the latter see A. Wilder, *Eschatology*, p. 173; B. H. Branscomb, *Law*, p. 196; A. Schlatter, *Der Evangelist Matthäus* (1959⁵), p. 288, and J. Schniewind, *Matthäus*, p. 114.

[3] On the first point see P. Bonnard, *L'Évangile selon St. Matthieu* (1963), p. 119, against E. Hirsch, *Frühgeschichte des Evangeliums* (1941–51), II, 313, and W. Grundmann, *Das Evangelium nach Lukas* (n.d.), pp. 205ff. On the second point see R. Bultmann, *Tradition*, p. 105 and T. W. Manson, *Sayings*, p. 73. To refer to the man himself, as T. M. Donn, *ET* 61 (1949–50), 384, to those who have not hearkened to Christ, as most commentators, or to substitute an Aramaic correction, as I. Abrahams, *Studies*, II, 183–4, and M. Black, *ET* 61 (1949–50), 219–20, is unnecessary.

and par.; 18.29ff. and pars.) are also to be interpreted in terms of the priority of Christ's call over familial concerns and not as sayings directed particularly at the oral or written Law. This is confirmed by the fact that elsewhere the importance of the fifth commandment is stressed by Jesus (Mark 7.10 and pars.). Recognition of the hyperbolical nature of the terminology in these passages also renders the apparent antithesis much less acute. Once again, parallels can be derived from the Old Testament (Deut. 33.9–10; 1 Kings 19.19–21; Ezra 24.16) as well as from the Pseudepigraphal (Jub. 23.16, 19) and, though it is not characteristic of it, the rabbinic literature (Sot. 9.15; b.Sanh. 97a).

Finally in this connection some reference should be made to the parables concerning the new and old wine and the new and old cloth in Mark 2.21–2 and pars. In their present context they illustrate the point of Jesus' sayings in the fasting narrative which immediately precedes them, but it is almost certain that they were originally spoken on another occasion. Their essential teaching appears to be the discontinuity between the new and the old reality and it is tempting to allegorise them so as to make this more specific. It is extremely doubtful, however, whether it is legitimate to make point by point applications of the details within them. This is especially to be noted against those who wish to interpret these sayings as being directed against Pharisaism or even the Mosaic Law.[1] The question of Law is nowhere in sight and since the original thrust of their application is unknown it would be unwise to regard them as an attack on the disciples of John or a blanket condemnation of Judaism. The Lucan addition in v.36 and the supplementary parable in v.39 merely sharpen the picture in the other two gospels, the first emphasising the importance of the new and the second the significance of the old, without denying the general incompatibility of the two. The additional parable, therefore, is not, as is often suggested, a plea for conservatism that is fully out of harmony with the two that precede it. It does, however, further

---

[1] Against S. Schulz, 'Markus und das Alte Testament', *ZTK*, 58 (1961), 190, and B. Lanwer, 'Gesetz', p. 52, see rather the approach of R. A. Harrisville, 'The Concept of Newness in the New Testament', *JBL*, 74 (1955), 78. Still less are they descriptive of the old world's dissolution with the eschatological arrival of the New Age as some have maintained.

illustrate Luke's special concern for Israel.[1] The parables, then, offer us little more than a general truth, that what is coming with Christ cannot be contained within the dimensions of previous understanding and experience, and that it must to some extent come into conflict with it. As to the way in which that is to take place, and at what points, the parables can give us no help. For that one must turn to such specific encounters with the institutions of the old order as we have been, and will be, examining. So far as customs are concerned, from what we have been able to ascertain Jesus' attitude to them is consistently determined by the claims of his mission in the situation in which they are encountered. This means that his observance or non-observance of them does not arise from his reverence or lack of reverence for the practices themselves. It derives rather from the possibility or otherwise of compliance with them forwarding the ministry in which he and his disciples are at present engaged. It is now appropriate to see whether this approach to customary activities contains a principle relevant to Jesus' attitude to the Law as well.

2 ATTITUDE TO LAW

A number of incidental sayings and actions of Jesus are alleged to illustrate his attitude to the Law, oral and written. Some of these, however, may be dismissed from the outset. B. H. Branscomb refers to Jesus' prohibition against the carrying of vessels through the sacred enclosure after the cleansing of the Temple, an action he compares with the requirement in the

---

[1] On this see particularly the interesting remarks in H. van Goudoever, 'The Place of Israel in St. Luke's Gospel', *NT*, 8 (1966), 122–3. On this general interpretation of the parables see especially H. Flender, *St. Luke, Theologian of Redemptive History* (ET 1967), pp. 20–1, as well as W. Grundmann, *Lucas*, pp. 133ff.; N. Geldenhuys, *Commentary on the Gospel of Luke* (1950), pp. 196–7, and M.-J. Lagrange, *Évangile selon St. Luc* (1948²), p. 73. This is more satisfactory than the alternative explanation of A. Kee, 'The Old Coat and the New Wine', *NT*, 12 (1970), 19, according to which the central point of the parables is the danger of loss rather than the presence of incompatibility. It will also be clear from what has been said that T. Schramm, *Lukas*, pp. 107ff., is unlikely to be correct in regarding 5.36c, 39 as stemming from the tradition rather than from Luke himself.

Mishnah that the Temple-court not be used as a thoroughfare (Mark 11.16 cf. Ber. 9.5). In the following verse, however, Jesus cites Isa. 56.7 ('My house...prayer') as the motivation behind the prohibition and this places the emphasis quite differently from the Jewish teaching on the holiness of the Temple.[1] A. Finkel lists a number of other, no less probable, examples. From Mark 1.21 he deduces that Jesus entered the city boundaries before sunset in order not to transgress the rule of Tehum (Erub. 4.3, 4, 11), an interpretation that has no basis whatever in the text and one which other activity of Jesus on the sabbath would lead us to doubt (cf. Mark 2.23ff.). From Luke 4.40 he infers that Jesus waited until the sabbath was over before proceeding with various undertakings, though in Luke 13.13 Jesus insists that the sabbath is the very day which is appropriate for such matters. From Luke 8.46 and Matt. 15.23 he concludes that Jesus adhered to the Pharisaic code of purity by which a person in an environment of impurity was denied the power of healing (Mek.Ex. 12.1), overlooking the fact that in both instances the women were healed. From Luke 7.36; 11.37 and 14.1 he reasons that in the beginning Jesus only attended those homes where the meal was prepared in a state of cleanliness, whereas the practice of Jesus (Luke 5.27ff.) and attitude to such regulations (Luke 11.37ff.) is shown to lie in a quite different direction.[2] None of his examples, therefore, can be regarded as pertinent to the issue.

Four times in Matthew's gospel, reference is made to the practice of sacrifice. Two of these references (Matt. 9.13; 12.7) occur in the context of controversies over the Law and will come in for consideration at a later stage. In Matt. 5.23–4, within the framework of the first of the Antitheses in the Sermon on the Mount, an allusion to sacrifice forms the basis of an illustration emphasising the necessity of reconciliation. The latter must precede the offering of the sacrificial gift (τὸ δωρόν here, of

---

[1] Cf. E. Lohmeyer, *Das Evangelium des Markus* (1953[12]), p. 236, against B. H. Branscomb, *Law*, p. 127; S. E. Johnson, *A Commentary on the Gospel according to St. Mark* (1960), p. 190, and D. E. Nineham, *The Gospel of St. Mark* (1968), p. 304. Against Lohmeyer, however, the authenticity of the quotation, which occurs in all three gospels, is to be accepted. See on this V. Taylor, *The Gospel according to St. Mark* (1966[2]), p. 436.

[2] A. Finkel, *The Pharisees and the Teacher from Nazareth* (1964), pp. 131–2.

course, refers to a private rather than public sacrifice). In Matt. 23.18–20, within the framework of the speech against the Pharisees, mention of sacrifice occurs in Jesus' criticism of Pharisaic casuistry with respect to oaths. In view of the incidental fashion in which sacrifice is referred to in both these passages, however, it would be improper to attribute to his words anything more than an illustrative purpose. Sacrifice forms part of the scenery, not content, of the instruction. We must conclude, then, that in these verses neither Jesus nor Matthew is expressing his attitude to this aspect of the law of Moses.[1] This will also prove to be the case in Matt. 9.13 and 12.7. Considering the significance of this legislation for other movements in contemporary Judaism, however differently they may have interpreted it, it is the absence of such an interest that is the most striking feature of the gospel narratives.

All the gospels record Jesus' desire to observe the Passover feast during his last week in Jerusalem (Mark 14.12ff.). Although the matter-of-fact nature of the disciple's question in v.12 is usually taken to imply that observance of the Passover meal had been Jesus' regular custom, this is not necessarily the case. Their initiative in asking could just as easily have stemmed from their presence in Jerusalem at this particular time as from his past practice in the matter. There is also some doubt as to the time the meal was held and whether it was in fact the Passover supper. Most probably it was, but in any case the special character with which Jesus invested the meal by associating it with his death lifts it into an altogether different

---

[1] For Jesus cf. especially E. Lohmeyer, *Das Evangelium nach Matthäus* (1962³), pp. 121–2. Thus B. H. Branscomb, *Law*, pp. 126–7, is thoroughly astray in producing these verses as evidence for Jesus' compliance with the tradition of the elders, arguing that 'he approved the sacrificial system, the performance of which. . .was dependent upon the provisions of the oral Law'. For Matthew, G. Bornkamm, 'End-Expectation', p. 31, and G. Barth, 'Law', p. 90, incorrectly argue for an insight here into Matthew's understanding of the ceremonial Law. Not so G. Strecker, *Gerechtigkeit*, p. 31 n.1; G. Eicholz, *Auslegung der Bergpredigt* (1965), p. 75, and S. Schulz, *Botschaft*, pp. 161, 209, though only by relegating these passages to a nomistically-inclined Jewish-christian source which does not represent Matthew's theological viewpoint. However, since the presence of a pro-cultic tendency is the major reason for assigning these verses to such a context. it is possible that they originated with Jesus himself.

category. Here we have an instance of observance of the Law becoming the occasion of testimony to the ministry of Jesus.[1]

An affirmation of the Law has frequently been located in the addition of the words μηδὲ σαββάτῳ in Matthew's version of the flight from Jerusalem in the Last Days (Matt. 24.20). If this is so, the addition reflects the strict observance of the sabbath practised in some Jewish-christian circles and is a clear indication of the Jewish predilections of the evangelist himself.[2] However, since flight on the sabbath in such circumstances may possibly not have been condemned by current rabbinic thinking, it would be strange if either Matthew or his church adopted a stricter viewpoint.[3] It is far more likely that the hindrances posed by the sabbath arise not so much from Jewish-christian principles as from the sabbatarian scruples of the Jews e.g., shutting of gates of the cities, difficulty in procuring provisions, etc.[4] Thus the difficulties to be encountered – child-bearing, weaning of children, hardship of winter, restrictive sabbath laws – all possess the character of physical obstacles to flight and a consistent exegesis can be given to the whole passage. In view of Matthew's additions elsewhere in which he

---

[1] On the Passover background to the meal, and the question of its timing, see J. Jeremias, *The Eucharistic Words of Jesus* (ET 1966), pp. 41–88. At this point it may be asked why consideration is not given to sayings of Jesus concerned with the Temple. This subject, however, is quite clearly a separate field of investigation. While the activities that take place within the Temple are the object of Mosaic legislation, the Temple itself is not.

[2] So, for example, G. D. Kilpatrick, *The Origins of the Gospel according to St. Matthew* (1946), p. 116; E. Lohse, 'Jesu Worte über den Sabbat', *Judentum, Urchristentum und Kirche* (1960, ed. W. Eltester), p. 89 and *TWNT*, VII, 30; K. Niederwimmer, *Freiheit*, p. 162, and many of the commentators. G. Barth, 'Law', p. 92, and C. F. D. Moule, 'St. Matthew's Gospel: Some Neglected Features', *St.Ev.*, II (1964), 96, maintain, however, that though this indicates sabbatarianism, this is not to say that Matthew's gospel was Judaistic.

[3] The Jewish practice in this matter, gathered in Bill., I, 952–3, has been conveniently summarised by G. Barth, 'Law', pp. 91–2.

[4] This interpretation has hardly come in for serious consideration. See, however, the tentative remarks of G. M. Harman, 'The Judaism of the First Gospel', *JBL*, 14 (1895), 123. It was also approached by E. Hirsch, *Frühgeschichte*, II, 313; A. Schlatter, *Matthäus*, p. 706, and R. C. H. Lenski, *Interpretation of St. Matthew's Gospel* (1932), p. 917, who stressed, however, the antagonism of the Jews rather than the physical difficulties.

draws the attention of his readers to the Old Testament law affected by a particular utterance of Christ, a position I shall argue for throughout, the phrase probably stems from the evangelist himself.[1]

Mark 1.40–5 relates the story of the leper healed by Jesus (cf. Matt. 8.1–4; Luke 5.12–14). It closes with the instruction to show himself to the priest in the Temple and to offer for cleansing the things Moses commanded in the Law in such cases. It has frequently been suggested that this instruction demonstrates Jesus' faithfulness to the Law when moral issues were not at stake, the additional words εἰς μαρτύριον αὐτοῖς being held by some expressly to point up this fact.[2] This phrase is in fact decisive for a proper understanding of Jesus' intention. It can scarcely refer simply to the Israelites to whom the original Law was given, as some have suggested, nor to the fact of the cure before the eyes of the priests, as others have contended, for in every instance in which it occurs in the gospels it relates to the mission and message of Christ. It is less easy to decide whether it should be interpreted with Mark 6.11 (cf. esp. Luke 9.5) in terms of a 'testimony against Israel' or in a positive sense (cf. Matt. 10.18 and pars.; 24.14 and pars.) as a 'testimony to Israel'. In view of the Old Testament and post-christian usage (Deut. 31.26; Josh. 24.27; Ign., *Tr.* 12.3; *Phld.* 6.3) it is more likely to be the former, but we cannot be certain.[3] In either case it becomes clear that the instruction was

---

[1] Further slight support for this comes from the incidence of μηδέ in the gospels, since it occurs eleven times in Matthew as opposed to six times in Mark and eight in Luke. See especially Matthew's use in 10.9ff. and 23.10ff. The first evangelist also has a tendency to form pairs with conjunctions (see p. 206 n.3). S. Schulz, *Botschaft*, p. 161, and R. Walker, *Heilsgeschichte*, p. 134, had already disassociated Matthew from any Judaistic emphasis but once again by apportioning the phrase to his source-material rather than his own theological perspective. G. Strecker, *Gerechtigkeit*, p. 18 n.3 (cf. W. Rordorf, *Sunday*, p. 68), following earlier suggestions of Loisy and Weiss, seeks for its source rather in Jewish-apocalyptic tradition which forms the basis of the discourse.

[2] See especially A. Plummer, *Luke*, p. 150, and W. C. Allen, *Commentary on the Gospel according to St. Matthew* (1922³), pp. 75–6.

[3] Note, however, the assurance of H. Strathmann, *TDNT*, IV, 502–3; P. Bonnard, *Matthieu*, p. 114; E. Lohmeyer, *Lord of the Temple* (ET 1961), p. 26, and T. L. Budesheim, 'Jesus and the Disciples in Conflict with Judaism', *ZAW*, 62 (1971), 195–8, though the latter, against Lohmeyer,

given not to highlight Jesus' faithfulness to the Mosaic Law, but that through its observance its adherents might be brought face to face with their own failure and with the corresponding reality of Christ's power. The reverse, however, has especially been insisted upon for Matthew's presentation. It has been suggested that his positioning of the pericope immediately after the Sermon on the Mount is consciously designed to illustrate the truth of Matt. 5.17 ('I came not to destroy...but to fulfil') in practice. But this presumes a conservative understanding of Matt. 5.17 which, as later examination will show, is by no means certain. Further, Matthew's omission of what the healed man does in response to the command of Jesus means that the latter 'must be understood less as a command than in the sense of an attestation of himself'.[1] In this way, Matthew underlines the christological direction of the pericope that is already present in the Marcan account. More recently, a similar intention has been argued for Mark. It has been suggested that the evangelist deliberately placed the pericope before the 'controversy-stories' in Mark 2.1 – 3.6 to show that, despite his apparent disregard of the Law, Jesus was in fact obedient to it.[2] However, in Mark also a christological orientation is far more likely. If the interpretation offered above proves to be acceptable then, as we shall see, the teaching of this pericope is quite consistent with the emphasis of the succeeding passages. It is therefore unnecessary to posit a Jewish-christian origin for this saying because of its ultra-conservative attitude to the Law. Indeed there is every likelihood that the tradition here is primitive.[3]

---

sees it more as a condemnation of the cultic tradition of the priests itself. The outlook expressed in Mark 3.4 would strengthen the above interpretation of μαρτύριον in Mark, whereas Luke's attitude to Judaism would suggest the reverse for his account. On Luke's general understanding of 'witness' see further O. Michel, 'Zeuge und Zeugnis. Zur neutestamentlichen traditionsgeschichte', *Neues Testament und Geschichte: Historisches Geschehen und Deutung im Neuen Testament*, ed. B. Reicke (1972), pp. 23–4.

[1] So H. J. Held, 'Matthew as Interpreter of the Miracle Stories', *Tradition and Interpretation in Matthew*, pp. 256–7.

[2] D. E. Nineham, *Mark*, p. 87.

[3] Against R. Bultmann, *Tradition*, p. 240, and W. E. Bundy, *Jesus and the First Three Gospels* (1955), pp. 127–8, see the careful defence of its authenticity in V. Taylor, *Mark*, pp. 185–6.

From this affirmation of the Law we turn to those occasions on which Jesus appears directly to violate the laws of defilement. Luke 7.14; 8.54 (and pars.) tell of his physical contact with the dead and it has been suggested that by this action Jesus incurs ceremonial uncleanness. In fact the touching of the leper in the incident just examined would also, according to Lev. 5.3; 13.45-6, result in defilement. It is claimed that in such cases Jesus allowed ritual considerations to give way before the higher principle of love.[1] Even if this were the case, the action could scarcely be termed a breaking of the Law, for it would simply have necessitated his fulfilment of the regulations associated with the removal of such defilement, which are provided in the Law itself, to have rectified the situation. It is more likely, however, that circumstances of this kind were not envisaged in the Law and that its provisions did not strictly apply to them.[2] This would seem to be so even in the Old Testament itself, as the dealings of Elijah (1 Kings 17.19ff.) and Elisha (2 Kings 4.34ff.) with the dead, and the contact of the priests (Lev. 13.1ff.) with the leper, indicate.[3]

An indirect attack upon the Mosaic Law has occasionally been inferred from Jesus' condemnation of the priest in the parable of the Good Samaritan (Luke 10.28-37). It has been suggested that his failure to help stemmed from his fear of incurring defilement by the touching of a corpse.[4] This interpretation is open to several difficulties. In the first place, it is difficult to regard the attitude of the Levite as also being governed by ritual considerations. Defilement could only occur for him

[1] So A. Plummer, *Commentary on the Gospel according to St. Matthew* (1915), pp. 142-3; A. H. McNeile, *The Gospel according to St. Matthew* (1935), p. 102; N. Geldenhuys, *Luke*, pp. 185-6; S. Johnson, *Mark*, p. 62; P. Bonnard, *Matthieu*, p. 13; G. B. Caird, *Luke*, p. 92, and also F. Barth, *Hauptprobleme*, p. 90; J. Parkes, *Jesus*, p. 35, and A. Richardson, *The Miracle-Stories of the Gospels* (1941), p. 61. Luke 7.38; 8.44ff. (and pars.) can hardly be considered relevant here since it is the women, not Jesus, who take the initiative.

[2] Cf. R. Mackintosh, *Law*, p. 117; M.-J. Lagrange, *Évangile selon St. Marc* (1947), p. 29; K. H. Rengstorf, *Lucas*, p. 76.

[3] A. Schlatter, *Matthäus*, pp. 269-70, and C. E. B. Cranfield, *Mark*, p. 93, go further and assert that these actions demonstrate Jesus' consciousness of his position above, though not necessarily against, the Law.

[4] Cf. J. Mann, 'Jesus and the Sadducaean Priests', *JQR*, 6 (1915-16), 415-22, and J. D. M. Derrett, *Law*, pp. 208-27.

during the carrying out of his cultic obligations and since Levites attending their courses went up together in bands, not singly, in the parable he is probably returning from Jerusalem rather than heading towards it.[1] As far as the priest himself is concerned, there is no hint in the story that such a motive was the decisive factor in determining his behaviour. It is possible that the priest was governed by the thought of the victim's proximate death, or by doubt as to the possibility of his being dead already. In the first case, justification for helping was granted in rabbinic law itself; in the second, blame attaches not so much to the Law as to the scrupulosity of the priest. It is doubtful, therefore, whether the written or oral Law is at issue in the parable at all.[2]

The results of this examination of incidental material relating to custom and Law are admittedly meagre. A number of passages which have been frequently regarded as bearing on Jesus' attitude to the oral or written Torah – synagogue attendance, payment of the Temple-tax, refusal of fasting, renunciation of familial claims, etc. – were seen to be dealing with conventional modes of Jewish behaviour rather than with Pharisaic traditions or the Mosaic Law. On some occasions these were complied with, on others not, the character and outworking of Christ's mission determining the appropriateness or otherwise of their observance. This also appeared to be the case in the two instances in which observance of certain requirements in the Law was more definitely in view – the keeping of the Passover Festival and compliance with the regulations concerning cleansing from leprosy. In other instances, apparent affirmations and violations of the Law were found to be dealing with issues other than those surrounding the Law e.g., references to sacrifices and the sabbath, parables concerned with fasting and the Good Samaritan, or with situations the Law was not intended to cover for which there was some analogy in the Old

---

[1] See further J. Jeremias, *The Parables of Jesus* (ET 1963³), pp. 203–4, and W. Monselewski, *Der Barmherzige Samariter* (1967), p. 142.

[2] Cf. E. Linneman, *The Parables of Jesus* (ET 1966), p. 53. In substantial agreement here are W. Grundmann, *Lukas*, p. 224; J. Schmid, *Das Evangelium nach Lukas* (1960⁴), p. 192; W. Beilner, *Christus und die Pharisäer* (1959), p. 135; E. E. Ellis, *Luke*, p. 195.

Testament itself, even to some extent in legal material e.g., contact with the unclean and the dead.

The chief impression which these pieces of evidence supply is that of a life neither geared to nor drawn up against the Law, but one that is moved by quite different considerations yet to which observance of the Law can indirectly be made to bear witness. Whether this was carried on largely independently of the claims of the Law or in some more positive or negative relationship to them cannot be judged on the limited evidence that has so far been surveyed. Nevertheless, in view of the concentration upon the Law, particularly the ceremonial legislation, among religious groups in Judaism who were contemporary with Christ the slight incidence of legal material in contexts where reference to it would have been extremely appropriate, is already significant. As far as the evangelists are concerned, Luke's foremost interest appears to be in the character of Jesus' ministry and its general relationship to Judaism rather than with the specific issue of the Law. Matthew, on the other hand, seems especially concerned with the implications of Jesus' attitudes and teaching for Jewish customs and laws, though he is chiefly inclined to lay stress upon, and heighten the significance of, the person of Jesus in such narratives. Mark does not demonstrate as yet any distinctive approach to the subject, although it is interesting to note that also in his account a more indirect christological reference is apparent. For more light on the tendencies present in the writings of the evangelists and on Christ's own outlook, we must turn to the more specific controversies and debates over the Law that are recorded elsewhere in the gospels.

B DEBATES AND CONTROVERSIES

Of the six passages which concern us here, three – those dealing with table-fellowship, the sabbath and laws of purity – are set within the framework of a *Streitgespräch*. Two others – the pericopes concerned with divorce and the Great Commandment – though not strictly in the form of a 'controversy-story' nevertheless do contain a strong polemical note. In only one instance – that of the rich young man who enquires after eternal life – is

Jesus' response concerning the Law set in a non-polemical context. All these passages repay the most careful consideration in the attempt to detect the motivation and substance of his statements relating to the Law, as also the particular colouring given to them in the individual synoptic records.

I TABLE-FELLOWSHIP

On a number of occasions Jesus' table-fellowship with publicans and sinners receives comment from onlookers. It is the subject of disapproval by the crowd in Luke 19.7 and the Pharisees in Luke 15.2, while Jesus himself echoes their accusation in Matt. 11.19 (cf. Luke 7.34). Only once in the gospels is he publicly challenged by the scribes and Pharisees on this issue (Matt. 9.9–13 and pars.). Deep importance was attached to table-fellowship in the OT for it was regarded not only as socially binding men to one another but also as binding them to God. So dominant for the Pharisees was this religious aspect, and so stringently did they interpret it, that they refused to eat with Gentiles and even the bulk of the Jewish population as well. They were convinced that such contact would involve trans-gression of the Law, especially rules concerning defilement and, by implication, the non-payment of tithes.[1]

While the three accounts are in substantial agreement through-out, some typical differences appear in their presentations. In place of Mark's reference to the scribes and the Pharisees, Matthew simply mentions the latter as the opponents of Jesus, a tendency that emerges elsewhere in his gospel. In the closing statement concerning Jesus' mission to sinners, Luke's addition of the words εἰς μετάνοιαν is in accord with his special interest

[1] Cf. Dem. 2.3; j.Shabb. 3c. According to b.Ber. 43b there is the further danger of falling into lawless conduct through observing the example of such people. The 'sinners' mentioned along with the 'publicans' in the pericope probably include not only persons of immoral life (cf. I. Abra-hams, *Studies*, 1, 55 and Bill., 1, 498), but also those of a more respectable character who did not, however, observe the rabbinic regulations (cf. K. H. Rengstorf, *TDNT*, 1, 327). On the significance of table-fellowship in biblical and Jewish thought generally see further O. Hofius, *Jesus Tisch gemeinschaft mit dem Sündern* (1967), pp. 11ff. and, earlier, J. Jeremias, *Jesus als Weltvollender* (1930), pp. 77ff.

in this idea in both the gospel and the Acts.[1] Neither of these alterations, however, elucidates the particular motive behind the Pharisees' question, nor brings Jesus' reply into a more specific association with the oral or written Law. An addition which could assist in this direction is the Matthaean quotation of Hos. 6.6. This is placed between the two elements of Jesus' response to the Pharisaic criticism, that is, his mention of the rôle of the physician to the sick and the reference to his own engagement in a ministry to sinners. The citation of the prophetic passage ('I desire mercy and not sacrifice') would seem to imply that a concern for the Law did lie behind the Pharisees' question. Through its insertion Matthew turns a pronouncement-story highlighting Jesus' ministry to outcasts into a *Streitgespräch* focussing on the opposition such a ministry provoked and the attitude that initiated it. What exactly is the force of the quotation? It has been advanced that with it Matthew is seeking to justify the association of Jesus with sinners by emphasising the priority of the moral over the ceremonial Law. This seems unlikely since it would involve giving the verse a quite different sense to that which it possesses in the Old Testament and in later Jewish writings.[2] In fact the distinction between moral and ceremonial commandments appears to be considerably later than the New Testament period. More on this presently. It has also been suggested that the citation provides an example of *Toraverschärfung* similar to that practised at Qumran though perhaps with more radical implications. Or, in view of the similarity between the introductory words πορευθέντες δὲ μάθετε and the rabbinic

---

[1] See H. Conzelmann, *Luke*, pp. 99–101. Despite his analysis of Luke 5.32 (p. 155 n.1) the redaction is more in the nature of an expansion of the tradition than an alteration in theological perspective.

[2] Against W. C. Allen, *Matthew*, p. 90; J. Hänel, *Schriftbegriff*, p. 170, and, more recently, the interpretation contained in S. Schulz, *Botschaft*, p. 83, as also G. Strecker, *Gerechtigkeit*, p. 32 n.4. The earliest known citation comes from Johanan b. Zakkai who employed it with particular force after the destruction of the Temple. However, no critique of sacrifice is involved; it is merely that for the time being the will of God in this matter is incapable of fulfilment (Ab.R.N. 8.22). It has been suggested that the verse also lies behind 1 QS 9.3–5 but if so the reference is an extremely oblique one. Moreover, the Covenanters, for all their rejection of the official cult in Jerusalem, had every intention of resuming sacrifice after the Temple had been purified. Cf. 1 QSb. II – V, 19; 1 QM 2.1–6 *et al.*

formula צא למד that it was intended as a christian halakha.[1]
Here there is recognition of one distinctive feature of the
Matthaean, as opposed to contemporary Jewish, usage, i.e., the
metaphorical rather than literal meaning of θυσία. However,
both persist in understanding the saying as primarily directed
to the Pharisees and as possessing the character of a command.
Whereas in the present pericope it is not difficult to find an
object to which ἔλεος and θυσία can refer e.g., Jesus' relationship with sinners and the Pharisees' imprisonment within petty
regulations, it is less easy to find such an object for Matthew's
other use of the quotation in 12.7. Also to be noted is the
presence in the latter of a different formula to introduce the
saying, underlining the fact that it is the content, not form, that
is important so that the introduction to 9.13 is merely a
polemical device.

Realising the inadequacy of these interpretations, G. Barth
has argued that the quotation from Hosea is less a commandment than a statement about the true will of God. Its content is
the love-commandment and this forms the hermeneutical principle with which Matthew approaches the Law and determines
its validity.[2] This approach to Matthew is, as we shall see, open
to serious objections. Here it is sufficient to point to the 'I' form
of the saying and the well-documented interest Matthew displays in highlighting the christological orientation of the
tradition. Thus the really distinctive aspect of Matthew's use of
the quotation is still lacking. There occurs in this passage less a
command concerning ethical behaviour or a statement about
the fundamental will of God, although that may also be
present, than 'the summons to the christological knowledge that
Jesus acts in accordance with Scripture'.[3] The quotation, therefore, is not primarily intended as an evaluation of the Law, or
as a definition of the character of God, but as a christological
affirmation. Even the criticism of the Pharisees' over-scrupulous

---

[1] The first is maintained by H. Braun, *Radikalismus*, II, 3 n. 7; the second by
R. Hummel, *Auseinandersetzung*, pp. 38–9.

[2] G. Barth, 'Law', p. 83.

[3] H. J. Held, 'Matthew as Interpreter of the Miracle Stories', in G. Bornkamm, G. Barth and H. J. Held, *Tradition and Interpretation in Matthew*
(ET 1963), p. 258. The christological purpose of the quotation is also
recognised by E. Lohmeyer, *Matthäus*, p. 174; P. Bonnard, *Matthieu*, p.
131, and R. Guelich, 'Law', pp. 45–6.

concern for obedience and neglect of mercy has less to do with their failure to associate with publicans and sinners than their inability to discern the ἔλεος of God at work in the ministry of Jesus. Thus, in Matthew, Jesus' transgression of the rabbinic regulations is not justified through abrogation of the Mosaic provisions from which they were derived nor through objection to the validity of their deduction from that Law, but by the simple statement that Jesus has come and that his mission, as the Old Testament anticipated, would be one of mercy to sinners. His response, therefore, moves in a different realm altogether to that of the Law. The consequence of this for the Law, however, cannot as yet be determined.

An orientation towards the Law has recently been advocated even for the Marcan account. According to S. Schulz, the action of Jesus in eating with publicans and sinners is 'eine offenbare Demonstration gegen Moses'.[1] For all its insistence upon the rules concerning cleanliness and the payment of tithes, however, the Law never intimates that these are transgressed if one eats with another who has not observed these regulations. Mark's narrative certainly betrays no hint that its author interpreted the Law in this fashion. This implication was first drawn by Pharisaic casuistry and it is that alone which Christ disregards when he sits at table with such people.[2] The climax of the Marcan account is Jesus' statement concerning his mission to sinners rather than to the righteous. In his gospel the emphasis seems to lie on the content of this affirmation rather than on the authority or character of the one who is making it. The Lucan version parallels the Marcan account

---

[1] S. Schulz, *ZTK*, 58 (1961), 190. Cf. E. Stauffer, 'Neue Wege', p. 171. See also, though more moderately, B. H. Branscomb, *Law*, p. 137; J. Parkes, *Jesus*, p. 39, and E. Lohmeyer, *Temple*, p. 28.

[2] It is reading too much into the narrative to suggest that the Pharisees' criticism was motivated less by Jesus' unconcern for their discriminatory regulations than by his extension of the grace and forgiveness of God to unwarranted recipients. This is rather the thrust of his reply to them. Cf. E. Linneman, *Parables*, pp. 69–70 against O. Hofius, *Tischgemeinschaft*, p. 22. That Jesus understood the meal as an anticipation of the eschatological meal in the Kingdom of God, as maintained by O. Hofius, p. 19; J. Jeremias, *Jesus*, pp. 74–7; E. Lohmeyer, *Temple*, p. 28, and H. Riesenfeld, *Jésus Transfiguré* (1947), pp. 318ff., is too theological an interpretation of the evidence. See rather T. A. Burkill, 'Anti-Semitism in St. Mark's Gospel', *NT*, 3 (1959), 47 n.2.

closely. His narration of the vision to Peter in Acts 11.3ff. seems to indicate that he drew no radical implications for the Law from the practice of Jesus in this matter, at least so far as its relevance for the Gentiles was concerned. Meanwhile, the addition εἰς μετάνοιαν, which rounds off Jesus' saying relating to his mission, lays stress upon the nature of the mission itself rather than upon the principle Jesus is enunciating, as in Mark, or the person of Jesus himself, as in Matthew. In all three accounts, therefore, though in characteristically different ways, the narrative culminates in an utterance which is nothing less than a self-attestation of Jesus. As we have noted, Matthew's insertion of the quotation in 9.13a merely relates the reply of Jesus more closely to the query of the Pharisees with its basis in the Law and simultaneously heightens the christological thrust of the pericope. But in so doing he has only amplified two elements that were already present in the Marcan tradition, though in less explicit form.

What basis does that tradition have in the actual ministry of Jesus? Bultmann objects to the presence of the two final statements of Jesus in their present context. He claims that the point of the story, as expressed in these two sayings, does not possess a sufficiently close connection with the situation described at the beginning of the pericope. He also maintains that the address of the criticism to the disciples rather than Jesus indicates that the origin of this pericope lay in the debates of the early church. While he endorses the authenticity of the parable relating to the physician, in another context, he refuses to accept the genuineness of either the Hosea quotation in Matthew or the 'I came' saying in the Marcan tradition.[1] The association of Jesus with Jewish outcasts, however, is quite what one would expect as an aspect of his ministry and can scarcely be a later innovation.[2] The likelihood of this issuing in Pharisaic condemnation is also strong, and on such an occasion the parabolic reference to the physician and the sick would be entirely

---

[1] R. Bultmann, *Tradition*, p. 18. See also P. Bonnard, *Matthieu*, p. 130.

[2] On this see especially the remarks of J. Schniewind, *Das Evangelium nach Markus* (1958⁸), pp. 27–8, and W. Beilner, *Christus*, p. 15. Cf. also W. R. Farmer, 'An Historical Essay on the Humility of Jesus Christ', *Christian History and Interpretation: Studies Presented to John Knox* (1967, ed. W. R. Farmer, C. F. D. Moule and R. R. Niebuhr), pp. 103ff.

appropriate. I have also argued that the final saying concerning Jesus' mission to sinners provides a fitting climax to the encounter. Less certainty attaches to the authenticity of the quotation from Hosea in Matthew's account, but the possibility of this being an independent utterance of Christ should not be overlooked.[1] While the singling out of the disciples as the object of attack is not psychologically impossible in the context of Jesus' ministry, it could be that the form of the narrative has here been affected by later circumstances.

2 SABBATH-CONTROVERSIES

The first of the sabbath-controversies, that concerning the eating of grain in the field, occurs in all three gospels (Matt. 12.1–8; Mark 2.23–8; Luke 6.1–5). Only in Matthew is it specifically linked with the preceding pericope through the temporal reference ἐν ἐκείνῳ τῷ καιρῷ. However, neither chronological nor purely stylistic considerations lie behind this redaction but rather the desire to form a thematic bridge between the two passages.[2] It is no accident, then, that immediately after Jesus' declaration concerning the 'light yoke' which he lays upon his disciples, this conflict with the creators of the 'heavy burdens', the Pharisees, should follow. His further addition, ἐπείνασαν, like Luke's ψώχοντες ταῖς χερσίν, is merely formal in character and serves only to clarify the actual situation which is presupposed in the Marcan account.[3] Bultmann, again noting that Jesus' reply is preceded by a questioning of the disciples' behaviour rather than his own practice,

[1] Cf. W. C. Allen, *Matthew*, p. 90; A. H. McNeile, *Matthew*, p. 119; M.-J. Lagrange, *Matthieu*, p. 182; J. Schmid, *Matthäus*, p. 170. Some support for this may be found in the slight agreement of the quotation with the Hebrew over against the LXX (καὶ οὐ for μή). At the very least, since the evangelist regularly uses the LXX rather than the Hebrew, this suggests the quotation was earlier than Matthew. Cf. G. D. Kilpatrick, *Origins*, p. 90.

[2] Cf. D. Hill, *The Gospel of Matthew* (1972), pp. 209–10.

[3] It is not, therefore, as has occasionally been suggested, of any theological significance. G. Barth, 'Law', p. 81, is quite unjustified in his claim that 'the freer sense of the Marcan text, in which the absolute binding force of the law is no longer recognised, cannot be upheld by him: the disciples did not wantonly break the Sabbath. From this it follows that in Matthew's congregation the Sabbath was still kept, but not in the same strict sense as the Rabbinate.' Similarly, G. D. Kilpatrick, *Origins*, p. 116; G. Bornkamm,

suggests that the later church is endeavouring to involve him in the justification of its sabbath customs. It would appear, however, that the Pharisees directed their attention to the disciples because Jesus was not engaged in the activity himself. As elsewhere, he then assumes full responsibility for his disciples' action.[1] What exactly was it to which the Pharisees took exception? It cannot have been the journey undertaken, since presumably they had not exceeded the sabbatical limit. Nor could it have been the plucking and eating of standing corn, for permission to do this was given in the Law provided no instrument was used (Deut. 23.24–5; cf. Lev. 19.9–10; 23.22; Deut. 24.19ff.). It would seem, then, that it was not the act itself but the time of its performance that was at issue.[2]

In reply, Jesus refers to the action of David and his followers in eating the shewbread in the Temple (1 Sam. 21.1–6). This breach of the Law had been the subject of considerable rabbinic discussion, David's action being justified by reference to the actual danger to his life which hunger had brought about

'End-Expectation', p. 31 n.2; E. Stauffer, 'Neue Wege', p. 167. Mark does, in fact, use ἐπείνασεν in v.25 with reference to the incident with the shewbread, and it is just possible that Matthew's addition was an attempt to assimilate the sabbath-encounter more fully with it. So W. Rordorf, *Sunday*, p. 60.

[1] Thus L. Goppelt, *Jesus*, p. 63, *contra* R. Bultmann, *Tradition*, p. 16; E. Lohse, *TWNT*, VII, 22 n.172. On this practice generally see the valuable study of D. Daube, 'Responsibilities of Master and Disciples in the Gospels', *NTS* 19 (1972), 1ff.

[2] According to Shabb. 7.2 the third of the 39 activities forbidden on the sabbath was reaping. The Law, of course, forbade work on the sabbath altogether (Ex. 31.14–15; 34.21; 35.2; Num. 15.32–6). According to K. Bornhäuser, 'Zur Pericope vom Bruch des Sabbats', *NKZ*, 33 (1922), 326, this merited stoning (Num. 15.32ff. cf. Sanh. 7.4; Deut. 17.10ff. cf. Sif.Deut. 17.10) and since this had to be preceded by a warning it explains the Pharisaic criticism here. D. Flusser, *Jesus* (1969), p. 46 (following S. Pinès, 'The Jewish Christians of the Early Centuries of Christianity according to a New Source', *The Israel Academy of Sciences and Humanities Proceedings*, II [1966], 63), suggests that all that was at issue here was Pharisaic criticism of a Galilean practice, according to which it was permissible not only to pick up grain and rub it between the fingers but to rub it in one's hand as well. However, in order to maintain this, he has to insist, without other support, that the clear reference to 'plucking' in all three gospels – an act which unquestionably violated all current practice of the sabbath laws – is secondary.

(Bill., 1, 618ff.). The point of the analogy is contested. It has
been regarded as providing a precedent for the violation of
ritual laws when moral factors predominate, a distinction that
is unlikely for Jesus and misses the heart of the comparison. So
does the suggestion that, since Scripture does not condemn
David for his behaviour, the rigidity with which the Pharisees
interpreted the ritual laws was based on a misunderstanding of
their legitimate sphere of application. More is involved in the
quotation than that.[1] Other approaches have sought to bring
the contexts of the two incidents, or the figures that dominate
them, into closer connection. It has been suggested that there
are good grounds for thinking that David's action took place
on a sabbath. However, unlike the additional precedent cited
in Matt. 12.5–6, there is no reference to the sabbath in the
illustration.[2] Alternatively, Jesus has been regarded as making
a veiled messianic claim, the idea of his being the 'Son of David'
lying implicit in his use of the analogy. This has the merit of
exposing the inadequacy of the previous suggestions, for the
comparison is not between the conduct of David and his
followers on the one hand, and Jesus and his disciples on the
other, but between Jesus and David themselves. However,
nowhere else in the gospels does Jesus portray himself as David's
successor, and here the emphasis is upon the authority exercised
rather than status possessed.[3] Only for Matthew may it have
had this significance (cf. Matt. 1.1ff.; 12.23; 21.9, 15), but

[1] Against W. G. Kümmel, 'Traditionsgedanke', p. 28; E. Lohmeyer,
Markus, pp. 64–5; B. H. Branscomb, *Law*, p. 146; R. Bultmann, *Tradition*,
p. 16 and, more recently, G. Strecker, *Gerechtigkeit*, pp. 32ff. E. E. Ellis,
Luke, p. 109, for the first, and A. Schlatter, *Matthäus*, pp. 394–5; C. E. B.
Cranfield, *Mark*, p. 115, for the second.

[2] See M. Hooker, *The Son of Man in Mark* (1967), p. 97 n.3. It is true that the
Old Testament material indirectly suggests that the incident took place
on a sabbath (cf. 1 Sam. 21.2–6 with Lev. 24.8–9) and that in some
rabbinic traditions this aspect of the story was further developed (b.Men.
95.6; Yalkut on 1 Sam. 21.5; cf. B. Murmelstein, 'Jesu Gang durch die
Saatfelder', *Ang.*, 3 [1930], 111ff.). However, there is no reference to this
sabbath-context in the present passage, and the rabbinic evidence is
unlikely to be early.

[3] Relevant here is Jesus' question to the Pharisees in Matt. 22.41–5: how
can David's Lord be David's son? See further V. Taylor, *Mark*, p. 216,
against the messianic interpretations of J. Schniewind, *Matthäus*, p. 156,
and L. Goppelt, *Jesus*, p. 63: also the rejection by H. Braun, *Qumran*, 1,

even then in association with the other and secondary to it. In Mark, the weight probably lies on the principle implicit in David's action which Jesus is shortly to develop in a unique way (cf. Mark 2.27). Luke, in accordance with his interest in the ministry of Jesus, is more concerned with the model provided by David's behaviour as anticipatory of Christ's own activity (cf. Luke 5.32). It must be stressed, however, that in all three accounts there is no intention to justify the disciples by means of an Old Testament precedent. In different ways in each gospel it is the authority of Jesus which is paramount, whether this is conceived in personal (Matthew), didactic (Mark) or practical (Luke) terms. The ground is thereby removed from two objections raised against the authenticity of the quotation. Some have hesitated in this connection because they did not feel the illustration was sufficient to justify the conduct of the disciples but, as we have seen, it is not as a precedent that it is cited. Others have dismissed it because of the rabbinic mode of argumentation employed whereas what we have here is a novel use of the Old Testament, christological in character, so striking that it must stem from Jesus himself.[1]

This approach to the question is further developed in the two Matthaean additions which follow (Matt. 12.5–7). The service of the priests in the Temple was a recognised exception to the sabbath law in Pharisaic casuistry, based as it was on the provisions in Lev. 24.8f. and Num. 28.9f. (cf. Bill., 1, 620–2). No more than the previous illustration, however, does this yield

---

25, of the attempt by G. Friedrich, 'Messianische Hohepriestererwartung in den Synoptikern', *ZTK*, 53 (1956), 289, to view David here in terms that the Qumran community would have found recognisable, i.e., as the Messianic High Priest.

[1] For the first, see G. Barth, 'Law', p. 82 and W. Rordorf, *Sunday*, p. 60; for the second, E. Schweizer, *Das Evangelium nach Markus* (1967), p. 39. It also overcomes the objection of D. Daube, *Rabbinic Judaism*, p. 68, that the illustration, since it was drawn from haggadic material, was anything but conclusive from a scholarly, legal, point of view, for it was not intended to produce a valid halakha. (However, J. W. Doeve, *Jewish Hermeneutics in the Synoptic Gospels and Acts* [1954], pp. 106–7, finds the illustration to be in full accord with the first interpretative rule, *gezerah shawah*, of Hillel. See also S. Cohon, *JBL*, 48 [1929], 97.) A. J. Hultgren, 'The Formation of the Sabbath Pericope in Mk. 2.23–28', *JBL*, 91 (1972), 38–43 rightly recognises the christological emphasis but attributes this to the early church, as also the setting provided in the opening verses.

a suitable precedent for the disciples' conduct, since their activity and that of the priests are scarcely parallel.[1] Nor is it intended to add a more technically astute halakhic proof though, from a formal point of view, the example would have carried more weight with rabbinic hearers.[2] The key to the citation lies in the following words: ὅτι τοῦ ἱεροῦ μεῖζόν ἐστιν ὧδε which, as the similar sayings in 12.41 and 42 demonstrate, are to be understood as referring to Jesus himself. Just as the priests could 'profane' the sabbath in the service of the Temple yet remain innocent, so could Jesus' disciples in the service of one who was greater than the Temple (v.7b). Thus as in vv.3ff. it is a question of authority rather than legality as such which is at stake.[3] The introductory λέγω δὲ ὑμῖν, as its omission in 12.41-2, and addition by Matthew elsewhere (e.g., 5.39; 19.9), indicates, is probably redactional, sharpening the emphasis upon authority already embedded in the saying.

As we have seen, a similar christological concern informed Matthew's use of the quotation from Hos. 6.6 in 9.13 and this is also present in his citation of it in the following verse. A moral law/ritual law antithesis can scarcely be intended since, even if Matthew recognised the distinction, plucking ears of corn could scarcely be justified in terms of obedience to the moral law. It is also unlikely that Jesus is requesting the Pharisees to have mercy on the disciples, as that not only implies sin on their part but is too limited an interpretation of ἔλεος. A wider reference is indeed found for it if it is understood in terms of the priority of the 'love-commandment' over sabbath regulations. As in 9.13, however, the statement is in the context of others in which the christological element is dominant. The ἔλεος of which Jesus spoke in the earlier passage was primarily his fellowship with outcasts; in this instance it is his provision for disciples who are engaged in ministry with him. Thus he is insisting that if only the Pharisees had understood something of the nature

---

[1] This had already been pointed out by J. Wellhausen, *Das Evangelium Matthaei* (1904), p. 59.

[2] *Contra* R. Hummel, *Auseinandersetzung*, p. 42, and E. Lohse, *TWNT*, VII, 23 n.180.

[3] We have here, then, an idiomatic use of the neuter. See further J. Schniewind, *Matthäus*, p. 156; L. Goppelt, *Typos* (1939), p. 102. Most commentators apply the saying to Jesus.

of his mission they would not have condemned his disciples for their action.[1] In the previous passage the quotation appeared to be at least pre-Matthaean, if not originally from Jesus himself. Through the addition in v.7b, with its reference to τοὺς ἀναιτίους, it is inseparably linked with vv.5–6. Most probably, then, the whole block is derived from earlier tradition, and though it may echo the early church's apologetic struggles with Jewish opponents over the Law, it is not at all improbable that it had its original basis in an encounter between Jesus and the Pharisees. This could have possessed a different context to that in which it is set here though, if this is the case, the controversy which produced this response cannot have been all that dissimilar to the present incident.[2]

With an introductory καὶ ἔλεγεν αὐτοῖς Mark's account moves directly from the illustration concerning David to the declaration that the sabbath was made for man and not man for the sabbath. This saying has frequently been treated as an expression of Jesus' radicalism with regard to the Law, as a discarding of the entire sabbath theology of post-exilic Judaism.[3] In order to contest this, attention has been drawn to the principle enunciated in Mek.Ex. 13.14 and b.Yom. 85b to the effect that 'the sabbath is delivered to you and not you to the sabbath'. At first glance this rabbinic statement appears to have broad application, but in its context 'diese Grundsatze... besagt nur,

---

[1] In this connection, the suggestion of E. E. Ellis, *Luke*, p. 109, that the disciples' meal took place during an interval in a preaching tour, is quite credible. On the above interpretation of v.7 see further B. Gärtner, *The Temple and the Community in Qumran and the New Testament* (1965), p. 115. See also R. Walker, *Heilsgeschichte*, p. 139 and n.82, who claims, however, that v.7 is a hellenistic argument from the pre-Matthaean debates over the Law and that the whole passage, since for Matthew the question of Law is no longer relevant, has only a *heilsgeschichtlich*, and therefore aetiological, significance.

[2] For the authenticity of these verses, but in another context, see W. C. Allen, *Matthew*, p. 128; T. W. Manson, *The Sayings of Jesus* (1954), pp. 187–8; J. Schmid, *Matthäus*, p. 206. R. Bultmann, *Tradition*, p. 16, and G. Barth, 'Law', p. 82, acknowledge their pre-Matthaean origin. The attempt by J. W. Doeve, *Jewish Hermeneutics*, pp. 165–7, to defend the authenticity of vv.5–7 by reference to Jewish methods of argumentation and allusion is interesting but, in some details at least, rather tenuous.

[3] So, for example, W. Rordorf, *Sunday*, pp. 62–3; E. Stauffer, 'Neue Wege', p. 167; S. Schulz, *Botschaft*, p. 85; E. Schweizer, *Markus*, p. 40.

dass der sabbat lediglich zur Rettung eines Menschenlebens entweiht werden dürfte' (Bill., II., 5).[1] The Marcan statement is clearly more sweeping in character but care must be exercised in deciding its precise field of reference. Certainly Mark, with his Gentile christian audience in mind, intended it to be understood in as comprehensive a way as possible and no doubt regarded it as setting to one side the relevant Mosaic regulations. For him it expressed a principle of far-reaching ethical significance for all men, one that would find ready appreciation in the minds of his readers. It is much less certain, however, that either Jesus or his disciples drew this conclusion from the saying. The practice of the early christian communities in tolerating observance of the sabbath does not suggest that the radical implications of Jesus' statement were everywhere evident (cf. Rom. 14.5ff.; Gal. 4.10; Col. 2.16ff.). Without doubt such implications are latent within it, but Jesus does not explicitly draw attention to them. His silence at this point renders the dual behaviour in the early church quite explicable, for as long as the principle being enunciated was clearly understood, continued observance of the sabbath, though not perhaps the ideal, was permissible.[2] Mark himself may well have allowed this possibility for non-Gentile christians.

[1] Cf. H. Braun, *Radikalismus*, II, 70 n.2; E. Lohse, 'Sabbat', p. 85. The attempt by T. W. Manson, 'Mark 2.27', *Coniecitanea Neotestamentica*, XI (1947), 138–46 to link this rabbinic saying, which he regards as an affirmation of the sabbath as Israel's unique possession, with 2.27 by positing an original 'Son of Man' i.e., Jesus and his disciples, reference behind ἄνθρωπος has been cogently criticised by V. Taylor, *Mark*, p. 219, who points out, *inter alia*, that Jesus took a wider view of the sabbath than the Jewish claim that it was made for Israel alone and that there is no evidence to suggest that he taught it was made for the Elect Community. These same objections may be directed against the similar interpretation of M. Hooker, *Son of Man*, pp. 95ff., who argues from an older Jewish tradition behind Jub. 2.31 *et al.*, according to which Israel is spoken of as 'Man'. For other criticisms see F. W. Beare, 'The Sabbath was made for Man', *JBL*, 79 (1960), 130–6, and A. J. B. Higgins, *Jesus and the Son of Man* (1964), p. 29. F. W. Borsch, *The Christian and Gnostic Son of Man* (1970), p. 28 n.98, also postulates an original 'Son of Man' saying here.

[2] The authenticity of v.27, though not necessarily in its present context, has recently been defended against strong critical attacks by E. Käsemann, 'The Problem of the Historical Jesus', *Essays on New Testament Themes* (ET 1964), p. 38; H. Braun, *Radikalismus*, II, 70 n.1; E. Lohse, 'Sabbat', p. 85; W. Rordorf. *Sunday*, pp. 63–5 and E. Schweizer, *Markus*, p. 39.

The omission of v.27 in the Matthaean and Lucan accounts is well accounted for by Matthew's substitution of an argument that is more relevant to his Jewish audience and Luke's satisfaction with the original scriptural illustration as a prelude to his interpretation of v.28 in terms of the character of Jesus' sabbath ministry. Neither Luke nor Matthew, therefore, should be accused of seeking to avoid the saying on account of its radical position with regard to the Law for, as has already been indicated, Matthew's version tends in a similar direction, as does Luke's citation of the David illustration.[1] Furthermore, Matthew's interest in the authority of Jesus and Luke's concern with his ministry rendered the presence of v.27 less appropriate in their accounts.[2] Most probably, then, vv.27–8 were already bound together in Mark's tradition and while the words καὶ ἔλεγεν αὐτοῖς introducing v.27 may indicate that the original context of these verses lay in another *Streitgespräch*, it is more likely that the formula merely marks a new stage in the argument (cf. 7.14; 10.11) so that Mark has preserved its rightful position. In this controversy, then, as elsewhere in Jesus' encounters with the Pharisees, polemical utterances lead to a gnomic declaration of considerable significance (cf. Mark 7.15; 10.9; 12.17).[3]

All three gospels record as the climax of their narrative the statement that the Son of man is lord of the sabbath. Matthew clearly regards this final saying as both the goal and ground of the various christological assertions that have preceded it. The

---

[1] *Contra* G. D. Kilpatrick, *Origins*, p. 116; V. E. Hasler, 'Gesetz', p. 19; E. Lohse, 'Sabbat', p. 89; G. Barth, 'Law', p. 81; J. Schreiber, *Theologie des Vertrauens* (1967), pp. 87–8, and many of the commentators. For a criticism of their viewpoint from a different perspective see R. Walker, *Heilsgeschichte*, pp. 138–9.

[2] J. W. Leitch, 'Lord also of the Sabbath', *SJT*, 19 (1966), 427–8, and A. Suhl, *Funktion*, p. 83, are quite correct in suggesting that Matthew and Luke omitted it in order to pursue their particular christological emphases, but fail to realise that a similar motif is present in Mark, if in a different fashion to the other two accounts.

[3] This overcomes several of the difficulties noted by V. Taylor, *Mark*, p. 218, with respect to the present position of vv.27–8. His remaining objection also falls away if behind v.28 lies a statement of Jesus that is more in accord with vv.25f. and v.27. This, as we shall now see, is precisely the case. The not dissimilar objections of H. E. Tödt, *The Son of Man in the Synoptic Tradition* (ET 1965), pp. 130–1, may also be countered in this way.

Son of man is the counterpart of David and the Temple and superior to them. It is he who authorises the kind of behaviour that is legitimate on the sabbath. This is the import of the particle γάρ with which the transition is made from the previous verses to the concluding saying. In his account, then, the emphasis throughout is placed upon the personal authority of Jesus. Mark's inclusion of the saying indicates that his account is also ultimately dominated by a christological concern. As his use of ὥστε demonstrates, however, it is rather in the expression of the principle outlined in v.27, earlier foreshadowed in David's conduct, that the superiority of Christ expresses itself. This, as has already been mentioned, is a perspective that would have considerable appeal to his Gentile readers.[1] Luke's introduction of the final declaration with καὶ ἔλεγεν αὐτοῖς is probably an echo of the opening words in Mark 2.27. His account moves directly from the David illustration to Jesus' concluding utterance, so that at first sight these do not appear to be linked in any specific way, as they are, for example, through Mark's inclusion of the general principle in v.27 of his narrative, and Matthew's insertion of further illustrative material. Does this mean that the parallel with 1 Sam. 21.1–6 is regarded by him solely as a justification of the disciples' action to which the saying concerning the Son of man's lordship over the sabbath has been loosely appended? It could do so, but in view of his interest, already noted, in the ministry of Jesus and his emphasis, soon to be observed, on the sabbath as the day of ministry *par excellence*, the saying in Luke 6.5 is probably related to the scriptural reference as conclusion to premise.[2] For Luke, how-

---

[1] See further J. Dupont, *Gnosis* (1949), p. 196 n.2 and F. Gils, 'Le Sabbat a été fait pour homme et non l'homme pour le Sabbat', *RB*, 69 (1962), 518, who also provides a detailed survey of the many alternative solutions that have been proposed to account for the link between vv.27 and 28.

[2] Cf. W. Grundmann, *Lukas*, pp. 135–6; J. Schmid, *Lukas*, p. 127, and J. W. Doeve, *Hermeneutics*, p. 165. So far as the addition in Luke 6.5D is concerned, with its narration of an encounter between Jesus and a man working on the sabbath, since it is clearly not part of the original synoptic tradition it would be out of place to discuss it here. Its authenticity is, of course, a matter of debate, especially since J. Jeremias' detailed arguments in its favour in his *Unknown Sayings*, pp. 49–54. The most thorough recent treatment is that of W. Käser, 'Exegetische Erwägungen zur Seligpreisungen des Sabbatarbeiters Lk. 6.5D', *ZTK*, 65 (1968), 414–30.

ever, it is the action of David, rather than the principle implicit within it or the authority it exhibits, which is decisive just as in 6.5 it is Jesus' sabbath ministry which is understood by him to express his lordship over it rather than, as in Mark, the principle of behaviour enunciated by him or, as for Matthew, the personal authority of Jesus himself. Thus whereas for Matthew the emphasis is placed upon who Jesus is and for Mark upon what he says, for Luke it is upon what he does. In different ways, therefore, all these accounts possess a christological orientation through which the issue of the legality or illegality of the disciples' action is set in a different context to that of the Law.

It only remains to ask whether this concluding saying is authentic in its present form. Without entering into a full-scale discussion of the disputed term ὁ υἱός τοῦ ἀνθρώπου this is not easy to decide, but almost certainly there lies behind it a saying in which simply 'man' was intended as the subject of κύριος.[1] This means that the verse originally advanced an argument similar to that in v.27, and that the transition to its present meaning took place through a mistranslation of the Aramaic *bar-nasa*. While this term can hardly be interpreted as a direct reference to Jesus himself, there can be little doubt that he regarded himself as one to whom it was especially applicable. Therefore the saying does not merely involve the reiteration of a 'creation ordinance', for quite apart from its being more specific than the Genesis narrative on man's relationship with the sabbath, the christological point, though considerably more muted than in the gospel accounts, is by no means absent. The authority of Jesus is latent in the permission granted his disciples so to act on the sabbath and on his corresponding exegesis and teaching to that effect. According to this, it is not a question of his affirming the sabbath or merely enlarging its scope. Nor is it a case of his express abrogation of it or his sanction of its occasional infringement. He takes rather a position above it so that it is incorporated into an entirely new

---

[1] This approach to v.28 has most recently been advocated by J. Jeremias, 'Die alteste Schicht der Menschensohnlogien', *ZNW* (1967), n.9 (cf. *New Testament Theology*, I [ET 1971], 261), who also rightly criticises its equation with 'I' in G. Vermès, 'The Use of בר נשא/בר נש in Jewish Aramaic' in M. Black, *Aramaic*, pp. 310–28.

framework and viewed from a quite different perspective. As a result, what is acceptable or unacceptable in the way of conduct upon it is defined in relation to an altogether new reference point i.e., Christ's estimate of the situation. Though this may have implications so far as the validity of legal regulations is concerned, they are not elaborated upon here. Rather than leading in that direction, Jesus' teaching raises the question of the identity of the one who stands behind it. It leads to a consideration of his own authority, and of the response that is appropriate to it, rather than to reflection on the status of Law.[1]

This interpretation of Jesus' attitude towards the sabbath, and of the contributions of the evangelists, is confirmed by an examination of the sabbath-healing narratives. In the opening verse of the following pericope (Matt. 12.9ff.; Mark 3.1ff.; Luke 6.6ff.) both Matthew and Luke reveal their redactional tendencies. Thus to εἰς τὴν συναγωγὴν Matthew adds αὐτῶν, again highlighting the Pharisaic opposition, and Luke καὶ διδάσκειν, further emphasising the nature of Jesus' sabbath-ministry. According to Matthew, the Pharisees also challenge him with a direct question, whereas in Mark and Luke they merely observe him with this query in their minds, Jesus meanwhile reading their thoughts. By prefacing the question with the words εἰ ἔξεστιν Matthew also moves the question of the

---

[1] There is a further interpretation of this controversy which, while acknowledging that it deals with far more than the issue of Law, views it in terms of the coming in the ministry of Jesus of the eschatological sabbath rest towards which Jewish thought was orientated. This subtle and highly theological understanding of the incident, which has obvious associations with the teaching on the sabbath in Hebrews, has, in different ways, been advanced by such notable scholars as E. C. Hoskyns, 'Jesus the Messiah', *Mysterium Christi* (ed. G. K. A. Bell and A. Deissman, 1930), pp. 74–8; H. Riesenfeld, *Jésus Transfiguré*, pp. 318–22; G. Hebert, *The Throne of David* (1941), pp. 154–9; J. M. Robinson, *The Problem of History in Mark* (1957), p. 47, and R. H. Fuller, *The Foundations of New Testament Christology* (1965), pp. 149ff. This view has also been advanced by F. W. Borsch, *The Son of Man in Myth and History* (ET 1967), pp. 322ff., in association with his emphasis upon the reiteration of its original purpose as laid down in the creation narratives. At the centre of this controversy, however, stands neither the creation nor eschatological sabbath but the redefinition of it implied by the presence of Christ and expressed in his teaching and ministry.

Law more explicitly into the foreground. It is important to note that both Pharisaic opposition and the issue of legality are already latent in Mark's ἵνα κατηγορήσωσιν αὐτοῦ (Mark 3.26 cf. Luke 6.7b).

In the Marcan account Jesus brings the man forward into the centre of the crowd and asks whether on the sabbath it is lawful to do good or evil, to save life or destroy it.[1] According to rabbinic practice, the sick or injured were to be treated on the sabbath day only if life were in danger, and it was presumably this attitude which lay behind the Pharisees' outlook here.[2] By substituting ἀγαθοποιεῖν for θεραπεύειν, however, Jesus brings all kinds of benevolent activity under consideration, and rabbinic parallels to this question are completely lacking. So broad is the application of his question that it is frequently interpreted as explicitly abrogating the Mosaic commandment.[3] If the saying is dealing with the question of Law, however, it is strange that it has no relevance to the man around whom the story centres, for his life is not saved if his hand is healed, nor is his life lost if it is not. W. Rordorf concludes from this that 'we can solve the difficulty only by assuming that these words of Jesus originally had no connection with the sabbath healings or that for Jesus this sort of "proof" was after all conclusive'.[4] There is, however, a third alternative and it is the

---

[1] The deliberate action of Jesus, together with the later command to the paralysed man to stretch out his arm (Matt. 12.9; Mark 3.5; Luke 6.10) has been interpreted as a direct provocation of the Pharisees who have already warned him once of a breach of sabbath regulations. So K. Bornhäuser, NKZ, 33 (1933), 327. This would necessitate the opponents being the same in each case, and it is suggested that this is indicated by the article in εἰς τὴν συναγωγὴν (Matt. 12.9; Luke 6.11). Mark, however, omits the article and it is probably secondary. Moreover, while this would explain their determination to kill him (Matt. 12.14; Mark 3.6), it is difficult to see why they do not seek to stone him immediately and why collusion, according to Mark, occurs with the Herodians.

[2] For the evidence see Bill., I, 623–9 and I. Abrahams, Studies, I, 129–35.

[3] So S. Schulz, ZTK, 58 (1961), 193; G. Barth, 'Law', p. 79; R. Hummel, Auseinandersetzung, p. 45.

[4] W. Rordorf, Sunday, pp. 69–70. He decides for the latter, interpreting Jesus' words in terms of the urgency and decisiveness of his mission. Cf. T. W. Manson, Sayings, p. 90; D. E. Nineham, Mark, pp. 109–10; E. Earle Ellis, Luke, p. 109. That v.4 cannot be regarded as an isolated saying but is an integral part of the tradition is affirmed by R. Bultmann, Tradition, p. 12.

twofold reaction of the Pharisees which provides the clue to its presence. Not only do they refuse to answer the question (v.4b), but in Mark it is also stated that they hardened their hearts. If the question had been directed to the issue of Law they could easily have replied to it in terms of their oral tradition and demonstrated that, on their premises, it was irrelevant to the present situation. Furthermore, L. Cerfaux has convincingly shown that their reaction is identical to that of Israel with regard to the prophetic message, and signifies a closing of the heart to the messenger of God himself, not merely a rejection of his ethical demands.[1] The question therefore has rather a christological thrust. This would be again understood by Mark in terms of the extraordinary new principle that Christ was outlining.[2] It was neither intended by Jesus as a casuistic justification for healing on the sabbath, nor as a programmatic setting aside of the sabbath law, but as a further call to decision with respect to his own person and work. The authenticity of the saying, generally unquestioned as a result of its radical character, is guaranteed rather by its christological intention. It could hardly have been created by the primitive church as a weapon in the conflict over the Law with its Jewish opponents. This also helps to explain why Jesus was not at his trial deemed ἔνοχος θανάτου by reason of his sabbath infringements, and the Pharisees more concerned with his claims for himself than his attitude to the Law or tradition.[3]

---

[1] '"L'aveuglement d'esprit" dans l'évangile de saint Marc', *Recueil Lucien Cerfaux* (1954), p. 8.

[2] *Contra* H. B. Swete, *Mark*, p. 52; E. Lohmeyer, *Markus*, p. 69, and V. Taylor, *Mark*, p. 222, κακοποιεῖν and ἀποκτείνειν are more in the nature of rhetorical counterparts than veiled references to the intention of his opponents to destroy him. For Mark's understanding of the saying see further J. Dupont, *Gnosis*, p. 196, and for Luke's particular interest in the idea of salvation note his adoption of 10 of the 14 occurrences of σώζειν in Mark, his additions in 3.4ff.; 8.12, 36, 50; 13.23; 19.9; 23.39, and perhaps 7.50; 17.19; 19.10, as well as the constant occurrence of this theme in the Birth Narratives. On the whole question see esp. I. H. Marshall, *Luke: Historian and Theologian* (1970).

[3] Cf. J. Blinzler, *The Trial of Jesus* (1959), pp. 127ff., 291ff.; P. Winter, *On the Trial of Jesus* (1961), p. 130. It is in the late Gospel of Nicodemus 1-2 that the charge of 'sabbath-transgression' first seems to occur. R. A. Guelich, 'Law', p. 55, rightly observes for the Marcan account therefore, that 'even from the standpoint of form one must be cautious in assigning its

In the Matthaean account the material has undergone considerable modification and assumes the form of a *Streitgespräch*. Instead of focussing attention upon the healing and Jesus' radical query, we find the illustration: if one can help a sheep which has fallen into a pit on the sabbath, how much more a man? (vv.11–12a) and concludes with a general approval of well doing on the sabbath (v.12b). It has been customary to understand this in terms of an appeal to oral tradition as justification for the healing. However, there was no fixed rabbinic rule in such cases at this time (cf. Bill., 1, 629–30), while the form of the question suggests that Jesus is not appealing to rule but to the actual custom of his hearers (cf. Matt. 7.9ff.).[1] Even so, Jesus' suggestion that one would κρατήσει αὐτὸ καὶ ἐγειρεῖ goes beyond not only the stricter rabbinic view, according to which only feeding and watering of the animal was allowed and not its removal, but also the milder opinion which allowed the lowering of articles which might enable the beast to escape from the pit *of its own accord*. Matthew's alteration has been frequently interpreted as the substitution of either a christian regulation or principle which, while it results in a freer attitude to the sabbath than that found in Judaism, nevertheless restricts the radical nature of Mark 3.4.[2] It should be noted, however, that v.12b is not so much a piece of legislation for the christian community as the response to the question which Matthew has placed into the mouths of the Pharisees in v.10b. Stylistic considerations, therefore, not theological, have

Sitz-im-Leben to the debates of the Palestinian church', while V. Taylor, *Mark*, p. 220, who describes it as 'an original narrative which. . .is on its way to become a Pronouncement-story', considers it 'a tradition based on reminiscence'.

[1] Cf. T. W. Manson, *Sayings*, pp. 188–9; B. H. Branscomb, *Law*, p. 222; W. G. Kümmel, 'Rabbinen', p. 10; G. Barth, 'Law', p. 79 n.3, and R. Hummel, *Auseinandersetzung*, p. 45, are therefore at fault in arguing for Jesus' quotation and/or approval of a rabbinic prescription here. An even stricter view was, of course, current in Qumran, as CDC 11.13 demonstrates.

[2] G. D. Kilpatrick, *Origins*, p. 116, and W. Rordorf, *Sunday*, p. 68 n.3, regard it as a casuistic justification of a sabbath infringement; G. Barth, 'Law', p. 79, and R. Hummel, *Auseinandersetzung*, p. 45, view it in terms of the priority of the love-commandment over sabbath legislation; G. Strecker, *Gerechtigkeit*, p. 33, considers it a placing of the moral law over against ceremonial requirements.

determined the form of the saying. Furthermore, the second stage of the argument in v.11a, when it is taken together with 12b, is in reality nothing other than the 'radical' argument of Mark 2.27 in illustrative form. Its force, then, cannot be any less than that of Mark 3.4 which itself is similar in character to Mark 2.27.[1] We must conclude, therefore, that in seeking to integrate a tradition from another sabbath context into the framework provided by the Marcan account, in order to provide his Jewish audience with a more relevant demonstration of the superiority of Jesus' demands, Matthew has retained the radical nature of the attitude of Jesus. The unsuitability of the argument from a scribal point of view (the jump from 11b to 12a) indicates that its creation as a weapon in the Jewish-christian defence of the Law appears unlikely. Matthew, through highlighting the Pharisaic opposition (cf. also the omission of the Herodians in 12.14) and recasting the pericope in the form of a controversy, again places the person of Jesus in stronger relief than in Mark.[2] Luke, for the most part, parallels the Marcan account. Some of the dramatic details are lacking, and the reaction of the Pharisees is presented in a more moderate light. This occurs through the omission of Mark's reference to their 'hardness of heart' and the removal of any explicit statement of their intention to kill Jesus (v.11). The question in v.9 almost certainly possessed for Luke a christological

---

[1] Cf. A. Schlatter, *Matthäus*, p. 400. This is also recognised by S. Schulz, *Botschaft*, pp. 178–9, and R. Walker, *Heilsgeschichte*, 138, both of whom, however, speak of an abrogation of the cultic law being implicit in v.12b. This, as we shall see, is to misunderstand the nature of Jesus' statement.

[2] The sabbath healing in Mark 1.21–8 = Luke 4.31–7 is omitted by Matthew, and although he narrates the healing of Peter's mother-in-law only Mark and Luke indicate that it took place on the same day (Mark 1.29–31; Luke 4.38–9), Matthew moving it to a quite different context (Matt. 8.14–15). Certainly this cannot have been intended to relieve Jesus of an apparent violation of the sabbath, as the present controversies indicate. *Contra* G. Bornkamm, 'End-Expectation', p. 31 n.2, cf. G. D. Kilpatrick, *Origins*, p. 116; G. Barth, 'Law', p. 91 n.1, and G. Strecker, *Gerechtigkeit*, p. 32. Perhaps it is best explained as arising from formal considerations alone. By concentrating the early miracles into a grouping of ten (Matt. 8.2 – 9.34) Matthew found both that one of the Marcan accounts had to be omitted, and that an emphasis upon the sabbath context of the other was inappropriate. Theological criteria, therefore, were absent.

significance, though again this would have been understood by him more in terms of the character of Christ's mission in bringing salvation to men than, as in Mark, in terms of his authoritative teaching or, in Matthew, of his personal status. It is interesting to note, however, that though it was again quite open to Luke to interpret the question in this particular way, he has not sought to import this understanding into the text itself by means of redactional activity. This is at once a reminder of his tendency at times to preserve the tradition more or less intact as it came to him, and a caution against attributing this in all cases to a lack of theological evaluation of the passage concerned.

Further evidence of Luke's understanding of Jesus' attitude to the Law is provided in the additional sabbath-healings recorded in 13.10–17 (the woman with an infirmity), and 14.1–6 (the man suffering from dropsy). The second, which it is more convenient to examine first, takes place in the house of a ruler of the Pharisees, in the context of a meal. With his question to the Pharisees (v.3) and his singling out of the man (v.4), it is once again Jesus who takes the initiative. After the healing Jesus' justification of his action is almost identical with that in Matt. 12.11–12b with the exception that here it is an υἱὸς ἢ βοῦς that has fallen into a well whom εὐθέως, he contends, his opponents would rescue (v.5).[1] In that rabbinic teaching allowed for action to be taken with regard to the first but not, even as we have seen on the lax-ruling, the second, and that no appeal is made to their tradition as such, once again this must be interpreted as directing itself to common practice rather than scribal regulation.[2] Again, however, the conclusion that Jesus draws from the illustration with regard to the

---

[1] The attempt to escape from the presence of υἱὸς is as early as the earliest MSS. Thus D substitutes πρόβατον, S et al. ὄνος; θ: ὄνος υἱὸς, etc. Despite these endeavours, and those of modern commentators, the more difficult reading is to be accepted. Note, however, the different solution from the Aramaic original advanced by M. Black, Aramaic, pp. 168–9. The possibility of ἢ βοῦς being an addition influenced by Luke 13.15, as G. Strecker, Gerechtigkeit, p. 19 n.3, suggests, is more real, but if so it must have taken place at an extremely early stage since the MSS. evidence for its inclusion is unanimous.

[2] Not only the rabbis (Bill., 1, 625) but also the Covenanters, with certain qualifications, allowed the freeing of a man on the sabbath (CDC 11.38).

validity of healing on the sabbath exceeds rabbinic deductions, and no argument is offered by the Pharisees in reply. Luke, therefore, draws no christological implications from the saying of Jesus at all, and does not depict the Pharisees as being offended by the implicit or explicit claims in his action. Here instead is a simple justification for his practice upon which Luke has not intruded his interpretative interests. This reflects that faithful reproduction of the tradition which he elsewhere exhibits in the gospel and Acts.[1] Certainly it is difficult to conceive his composing the incident solely as a framework for the saying in v.5 when he has already recorded the force of a similar argument of Jesus in 6.5. Since it has been demonstrated that the differences between the Matthaean and Lucan versions of the saying can largely be resolved in terms of redactional activity, it is possible that the story is the original context of the logion in Matt. 12.11.[2] It is important to note, however, that although Luke does not make interpretative changes within the pericope, by setting it at the head of two parables dealing with the need for renunciation and the seeking of the lost (14.6-24) it is subordinated to two of his characteristic themes.

The other healing occurs in the context of a synagogue-service at which Jesus is teaching. His initiative in healing the woman calls forth a denunciation from the ruler of the synagogue in which the Pharisaic position is succinctly stated (v.14). Jesus counters with the accusation ὑποκριταί signifying that their real thoughts were inconsistent with their pretended zeal and that their sincere choice of one action rather than another was completely misplaced. An illustration similar to that in Matt. 12.11 follows: does not each one of you loose his ox or ass on the sabbath and lead it to drink (v.15)? The lack of any reference to their tradition, which in fact did allow such an

---

[1] See, for example, the comments of C. F. D. Moule, 'The Christology of Acts', *Studies in Luke-Acts* (ed. L. E. Keck and J. L. Martyn, 1966), pp. 181-2, but most fully, I. H. Marshall, *Luke*, pp. 216ff.

[2] Cf. G. D. Kilpatrick, *Origins*, p. 27. For the strongest defence of its authenticity see K. H. Rengstorf, *Lucas*, p. 176. For the view that it stems from an attempt within the early community to create a setting for an isolated word of Jesus see R. Bultmann, *Tradition*, p. 12, and E. Lohse, *TWNT*, VII, 26ff.; v.1 they regard as redactional (cf. 7.36; 11.37).

action (Bill., 1,629ff., 11, 199ff.) indicates that as in Matt. 12.11 Christ is appealing to the naturalness of the act rather than to its legality.[1] To this he adds an argument *a fortiori*, similar to Matt. 12.12a: if an animal, how much more a daughter of Abraham; if one whom you have bound for a few hours, how much more one whom Satan has bound for eighteen years; if on the sabbath as well as the other days of the week, οὐκ ἔδει λυθῆναι ἀπὸ τοῦ δεσμοῦ τούτου τῇ ἡμέρᾳ τοῦ σαββάτου (v.16)?

Artificial and forced though the argument may be from a rabbinic viewpoint, it gives an invaluable insight into Jesus' attitude towards the sabbath. For him it is not only a day upon which it is appropriate to heal, it is the day on which one *must* do so. This explains why it is from the beginning of his ministry this is what he does, and why, as in the present instance, he so often takes the initiative in the matter. His practice is a direct consequence of his understanding of his mission, not, in the first instance, an attempt to provoke Pharisaic opposition by transgressing either the oral or written Law.[2] Inasmuch as it may run counter to the Mosaic Law it is indicative again of his position above it, not of any explicit stand against it. The illustration in v.15 has occasionally been regarded as a variant of Matt. 12.11–12a and of a secondary nature. However, it is inseparably tied by verbal links to the conclusion that is drawn from it, and it is extremely difficult to accept the insight this provides into the consciousness of Jesus as stemming from the early church in its debates with the Jews. Form-critically, Bultmann finds the incident displaying the least skill in composition of all three sabbath-healings. Rather than being an indication of the ineptness of those who put it together, this indicates that even from a formal standpoint its *Sitz-im-Leben* is unlikely to be found in the debates of the Palestinian church.[3] The incident is particularly significant for Luke's understanding

---

[1] B. S. Easton, *The Gospel According to St. Luke* (1926), p. 215.

[2] This has been brought out particularly forcefully by J. Kallas, *The Significance of the Synoptic Miracles* (1961), pp. 63–4. The ἔδει of Jesus is, of course, a direct verbal counter to δεῖ in the speech of the synagogue ruler. Its choice cannot be explained, however, in terms of a mere rhetorical device.

[3] For further arguments against the view of R. Bultmann, *Tradition*, p. 12, see W. Rordorf, *Sunday*, p. 66, n.3.

of Jesus' attitude to the Law, for his emphasis on the sabbath stems less from an interest in the ordinance itself or the authority with which Jesus treated it, than from a desire to highlight those works of Jesus which bring salvation and healing to men, which as v.16 makes clear, especially occur on that day. The question of Law, then, is subordinate to this wider concern.[1]

As with the plucking of the ears of grain, then, so with the healings on the sabbath, Jesus' own attitude cannot be restricted to a mere castigation of rabbinic interpretations. Nor can it be interpreted as an affirmation of the essential character of the Mosaic sabbath, allowing only its temporary features to fall away. On the other hand, there is nothing to support the view that abrogation of the sabbath was at the heart of his teaching, nor even that he was approving occasional breaches of the sabbath law in the face of some special need. More adequate is the claim that his authority over it was employed to bring to realisation its original and fundamental purpose.[2] What Jesus, in fact, takes up, however, is not a particular orientation towards the sabbath-law, but the demand that the sabbath be orientated towards, interpreted by, and obeyed in accordance with, his own person and work.[3] This is far more than a return to the original purpose of the sabbath in creation, for it is linked with the re-creation of man that is taking place through his own ministry. The real issue that is constantly brought forward in his teaching is not so much that of his keeping or not keeping the Law, or of the relationship of his teaching to it. It is the failure of his opponents to realise that his presence has inaugurated a new situation with respect to the things of God, and that it is no longer the Law but his own teaching that is decisive. It is to this that men must respond and it is by this that both belief and behaviour are to be defined.

---

[1] J. Jervell, 'The Law in Luke-Acts', *HTR*, 64 (1971), 29, therefore misinterprets Luke's outlook when he suggests that, in these sabbath-stories, no conflict with the Law is intended and that Jewish leaders do not object to his practice. Certainly Luke's faithful recording of the tradition means that the relationship of Jesus' actions to the Law is played down, as is the Pharisaic opposition, but this is mainly due to Luke's primary interest in the ministry of Jesus and does not stem from any particular concern for the preservation of the Law.

[2] As. W. G. Kümmel, 'Traditionsgedanke', p. 28.

[3] This has been clearly recognised by P. Verweijs, *Evangelium*, p. 23.

3 RITUAL UNCLEANNESS

Only Matthew and Mark record the extended debate with the Pharisees and scribes over the meaning of defilement (Matt. 15.1–20; Mark 7.1–23). Apart from Mark 7.2–4, Matt. 15.12–14 and some minor additions, omissions and alterations, both accounts contain the same material, though there are considerable differences in the way in which it has been arranged. Mark presents us with two originally separate units of tradition which, by means of his additions, he has integrated into a single argument with a field of application that is far wider than the original controversy. Matthew has compressed this material and, by his rearrangements and additions, welded it into an impressive unit centred about the problem on which the controversy is based.[1]

Both narratives commence with a complaint by the Pharisees and scribes to the effect that the disciples have defiled themselves by not observing the ritual washings before taking food. Mark alone precedes their question with a brief explanation of the tradition involved (vv. 2–4), which is usually put down to the unfamiliarity of his Gentile audience with Jewish customs. It has recently been argued, however, that a deeper reason lay behind its inclusion: it is necessary in view of the following citation which otherwise quite abruptly widens the reference of the issue that has been raised, and it therefore prepares the way for the statement in v.8. It has also been pointed out that its significance penetrates to the second Marcan section as well: for καὶ ἄλλα πολλά ἐστιν ἃ παρέλαβον κρατεῖν in 4b prepares the way for the general conclusion inserted by Mark in v.13b.[2] We must, however, go a step further, for the reference in 2b: ὅτι κοιναῖς χερσίν... ἐσθίουσιν τοὺς ἄρτους sets the scene for the comprehensive application from the words of Jesus drawn by Mark in v.19b. The insertion, therefore, has a

---

[1] The basic units are: (a) 1, 5–8, 15–20 (21–3); (b) 9–13. This analysis, for which reasons will be given in the text, stands midway between that of C. E. B. Cranfield, *Mark*, p. 230, who regards the passage as a unity, and V. Taylor, *Mark*, pp. 334, 339, 342, who understands it to be formed from three separate traditions (1–8, 9–13, 15–23), and is an extension of that put forward by A. J. Rawlinson, *Mark*, p. 93, according to which 1–2, 5, 15 is the basic unit.

[2] A. Suhl, *Funktion*, p. 80; K. Berger, *Gesetzesauslegung* (1972), p. 464.

deliberate theological intention and prepares the way for a generalising of the specific issue raised by the Pharisees. At the same time this results in a skilful unifying of the traditions which underlie the passage.[1] Concerning the historical accuracy of the reference, a difficulty arises from the contention of Büchler that such washings were in the time of Jesus applicable to the priesthood only, and that their association with οἱ Φαρισαῖοι καὶ πάντες οἱ 'Ιουδαῖοι only came about during the second century.[2] However, the widespread observance of a custom and its codification are often preceded by adherence to it among particular groups of religious people with a more rigorous attitude, and this may well have been the case here.[3] This possibility has received additional support from the Qumran literature, though knowledge of the Essene view of ritual purity had of course been known for some time. As for πᾶς it is used elsewhere by Mark in a general way as equivalent

---

[1] There is still no certainty as to what is meant by the enigmatic phrase ἐὰν μὴ πυγμῇ (v.3). It is generally interpreted either with reference to washing with the 'fist' or with the 'hands' in contrast to washing up to the elbows. Despite the suggestions of Pallis, Torrey, Black and others, however, the judgment of Wellhausen still stands: 'Was πυγμῇ heissen soll, weiss man nicht' (*Das Evangelium Marci* [1903], p. 57; cf. M/M, p. 559). Whatever their precise character, these ritual-washings were motivated by a desire to remove defilement from those partaking of the food, not in order to protect the food itself from defilement (Bill., I, 695, against W. Brandt, *Die jüdischen Baptismen* [1910], pp. 38ff.). A useful survey of the various interpretations that have been placed upon this phrase has now been provided by M. Hengel, 'Mc. 7.3 pygmē: Die Geschichte einer exegetischen Aporie und der Versuch ihrer Lösung', *ZNW*, 60 (1969), 182–98. He suggests it is a Latinism meaning 'handful' and attributes its presence in Mark to the Roman provenance of the gospel. This interpretation, however, has since been criticised by S. M. Reynolds, 'A Note on Dr. Hengel's Interpretation of pygmē in Mark 7.3', *ZNW*, 3–4 (1971), 295–6, who regards it instead as a dative of respect meaning 'with cupped hand' so that it refers to the hand upon which water is poured from a utensil. The debate goes on.

[2] A. Büchler, 'The Law of Purification in Mark vii. 1–23', *ET*, 21 (1909–10). Cf. I. Abrahams, *Studies*, II, 199–200. C. G. Montefiore, *Gospels*, I, 133–44, and E. Lohmeyer, *Markus*, p. 139, suggest a *Sitz-im-Leben* in the Diaspora where a more general practice of the washings perhaps occurred.

[3] G. Margoliouth, 'The Traditions of the Elders', *ET*, 22 (1910–11), 261–3; F. C. Burkitt, 'Jesus and the "Pharisees"', *JTS*, 28 (1927), 396. Cf. also W. Brandt, *Jüdische Reinheitslehre und ihre Beschreibung in den Evangelien* (1910), p. 33.

to 'many' (cf. 1.5, 32f.; 6.33; 11.11) and should not be pressed here.

Both gospels commence their narrative proper with the question asked by the scribes and Pharisees, and the differences in the two versions reflect the particular understanding of the controversy adopted by each evangelist. Mark places the accusation of the disciples' failure to live according to the tradition before specifying the infringement of the rules concerning ritual ablutions. This is the force of his οὐ περιπατοῦσιν and ἀλλά...ἐσθίουσιν (v.5). With his substitution of περιπατεῖν with παραβαίνειν and ἀλλά with διά Matthew has interpreted the question in a more limited sense, so that only the infringement of the tradition associated with their refusal to comply with ritual washings is in view. This need not indicate an alleviation of the sharpness of the Pharisaic attack, merely its concentration on the particular issue at hand.[1]

At this point Mark records Jesus' reply to the accusation in terms of the quotation from Isa. 29.13. This is based on the LXX which in the main follows the MT with the exception of the closing line. Even so, the LXX reading 'in vain do they worship me, teaching precepts and teachings of men' (MT, 'and their fear toward me is taught by the precept of men') is further brought into line with the situation in the narrative with the alteration to 'teaching as precepts the commandments of men'. The emphasis therefore falls upon their false teaching rather than their false worship and it is in this sense that ὑποκριταί (v.6), which occurs only here in Mark, is to be understood. Once again it refers to their error in pursuing a certain course of action rather than any deliberate dissimulation before God. Authenticity has frequently been denied to this citation on the grounds of its similarity with the LXX. While this is probably true so far as its form is concerned, it does not necessarily apply to its content.[2] The point of the quotation is

---

[1] V. E. Hasler, 'Gesetz', p. 238, thus goes beyond the evidence when he claims that this implies the disciples generally held to the tradition.

[2] Thus V. Taylor, *Mark*, pp. 337–8 against most recently S. E. Johnson, *Mark*, p. 132, and E. Schweizer, *Mark*, pp. 81–2. For while it is true, as B. H. Branscomb, *Law*, p. 162, observes, that it is just the deviation from the MT which is the main point of the quotation, Taylor, followed by C. E. B. Cranfield, *Mark*, pp. 235–6, is probably correct in maintaining

reinforced in v.8 by the words: ἀφέντες τὴν ἐντολὴν τοῦ θεοῦ κρατεῖτε τὴν παράδοσιν τῶν ἀνθρώπων.. The choice of ἐντολή over νόμος is not arbitrary, for with it he draws a strong contrast between the ἐντάλματα of the scribes (v.7b), with their multiplicity of detail and absence of integrating principle, and the unified ἐντολή of God.[1] The use of ἀφέντες... κρατεῖτε continues the emphasis upon the following out of one particular way of life rather than another, as περιπατεῖν (v.5a) before it, and indicates again that he is not thinking merely in terms of specific legal requirements.

In the following verse, however, he goes on to present a particular illustration of their disobedience i.e., their failure to observe the fifth commandment (v.9). Its origin in a context other than this is shown less in the introductory καὶ ἔλεγεν αὐτοῖς than in the prefacing of the passage with a saying almost identical with that in v.8. The reference to Corban follows (vv. 10–12). As with πυγμῇ it is not certain to what this formula precisely refers though there is little doubt as to the general nature of what is criticised.[2] If it does refer to a vow in which there is no question of the actual transfer of certain things to

that the Hebrew could also have served as the basis for the same change. The correspondence of Mark's version of the quotation with that of Paul in Col. 2.22 does not necessarily indicate Pauline influence, for most probably both were dependent upon a form of the Greek text which differed in some respects from the LXX. On this see further B. W. Bacon, *The Gospel of Mark* (1925), p. 267. The objection of E. Stauffer, 'Neue Wege', p. 171, that it was only the early church, never Jesus, who made use of such a *Schriftbeweis*, has already been set to one side. Q. Quesnell, *The Mind of Mark: Interpretation and Method through the Exegesis of Mark 6.52* (1969), p. 95, points out the frequency with which selections from Isa. 29.10–16 are quoted in the New Testament (cf. Rom. 11.8 = Isa. 29.10; Col. 2.22 = Isa. 29.13; 1 Cor. 1.19 = Isa. 29.14; Rom. 9.20 = Isa. 29.16) but does not entertain the possibility that Jesus may have been the first to bring this into the forefront.

[1] Cf. M.-J. Lagrange, *Marc*, p. 184.
[2] A convenient summary of earlier suggestions is to be found in A. J. Rawlinson, *Mark*, p. 95, though for fuller discussions see Bill., i, 711–17, and K. H. Rengstorf, *TDNT*, iii, 865–6. Further recent suggestions have come from J. A. Fitzmeyer, *JBL*, 78 (1959), 60–5; S. Zeitlin, *JQR*, 53 (1962), 160–1; G. W. Buchanan, *HTR*, 58 (1965), 319–26, and Z. W. Falk, *HTR*, 59 (1966), 309–12. The expression Δῶρον is unfortunately of little help, since it was also quite possibly a technical term in the time of Jesus.

God but only of their withdrawal from certain persons (Ned. 1.3 *et al.*), rabbinic evidence for a partial alleviation of parents in the direction outlined by Jesus does occur (Ned. 5.6; 9.1). Nevertheless, while the problem of annulling incautious vows was engaging the attention of the Rabbis as early as the time of R. Zadok (*c.* A.D. 70) and R. Eliezer (*c.* A.D. 90), it is uncertain whether this took place earlier, and on this issue, 'Mark, as an almost contemporary record, deserves greater attention than inference based on the Mishnah.'[1] In any case the rabbinic modifications do not provide close parallels to the position of Jesus, for they do not question the fundamental validity of such oaths in certain contexts, and require the initiative and co-operation of the offender before any action can be taken.[2]

It has been suggested that it is not primarily the oral tradition that Jesus attacks here, but the failure of the scribes to give priority to one written law – honouring parents (Ex. 20.12) – over another – performance of vows (Deut. 23.21ff.).[3] A vow of this kind however was very different to that contemplated in the OT.[4] In any case it is certain Mark understood it as a direct attack on the tradition, for in the concluding verse of this section his use of the technical term for 'abrogation' (ἀκυροῦντες τὸν λόγον τοῦ θεοῦ cf. 1 Esd. 6.31; Gal. 3.17) and his description of the scribes not just as passive recipients but as active participants in the tradition (τῇ παραδόσει ὑμῶν ᾗ παρεδώκατε), could not be clearer. With the homiletical expansion in v.13b (καὶ παρόμοια τοιαῦτα πολλὰ ποιεῖτε), Mark demonstrates that the Corban practice is no isolated example, but that the whole Pharisaic tradition is in doubt.[5]

It is instructive to see the way in which Matthew has handled

---

[1] V. Taylor, *Mark*, p. 339. Cf. W. G. Kümmel, 'Traditionsgedanke', p. 30.
[2] Cf. H. Braun, *Radikalismus*, II, 96 n.1; E. Percy, *Botschaft*, p. 118, against C. G. Montefiore, *Gospels*, I, 148ff.; R. T. Herford, *Pharisees*, pp. 205–6; J. Klausner, *Jesus*, pp. 289–90.
[3] So C. G. Montefiore, *Gospels*, I, 149; B. H. Branscomb, *Law*, p. 269; W. G. Kümmel, 'Traditionsgedanke', p. 30, and E. Percy, *Botschaft*, p. 117.
[4] Cf. T. W. Manson, *The Teaching of Jesus* (1963[2]), p. 317.
[5] Stylistically the presence of τοιοῦτος points to a Marcan redaction here. In 9.37 and 10.14 he shares it with Matthew and Luke in a saying of Christ but in 4.33; 6.2; 13.19 (cf. 7.13 here), it forms part of an addition to the tradition which Matthew (who parallels each narrative) does not reproduce.

the tradition to this point. In place of the Isaianic quotation, Jesus replies to the Pharisees with an accusation that is almost identical in wording to that which it counters (v.3). Over against μαθηταί he places ὑμεῖς and τὴν παράδοσιν τῶν πρεσβυτέρων sets τὴν ἐντολὴν τοῦ θεοῦ, thus producing a stylish antithetical construction. The verse corresponds to the introduction to the Corban illustration in Mark's account (v.9), but by replacing ἀθετεῖτε with παραβαίνεσε Matthew makes it clearer that it is with a specific infringement that he is concerned. Reversing the order of the Marcan narrative, he first of all introduces the Corban illustration before proceeding with the citation from Isaiah. It has been suggested that in so doing Matthew has restricted the radical nature of the Marcan attack, and is no longer attacking Pharisaic piety as a whole but only condemning the Corban practice. Cited in support is his omission of v.8 with its emphasis upon the tradition as being τὴν παράδοσιν τῶν ἀνθρώπων and of Mark's comprehensive conclusion in v.13b.[1] In view of his concentration on the disciples' action as a single transgression of the tradition it is possible that the Isaiah quotation, despite the plurals in the concluding line, applies only to this single transgression of the Pharisees. This would further explain the omission of v.13b. However, since elsewhere in his gospel the Pharisaic tradition as a whole comes under attack (cf. 16.11), it should not be inferred that Matthew or his church still observes scribal regulations in any consistent way.[2]

It has been claimed that it is Matthew who heightens the teaching of this passage.[3] The carefully-drawn distinction between παράδοσις and ἐντολή in v.3, the immediate counter-accusation of Jesus at the beginning of the controversy, the

---

[1] Cf. J. Schmid, *Matthäus*, p. 237; V. E. Hasler, 'Gesetz', p. 20, and R. Hummel, *Auseinandersetzung*, p. 47, all of whom conclude that the scribal tradition still had general authority for Matthew and his church.

[2] R. Walker, *Heilsgeschichte*, pp. 140–1, agrees that no fundamental difference exists between the Matthaean and Marcan accounts, but claims that it is Jewry as a whole that Matthew's aetiological construction of an original *Gesetzesdebatte* wishes to condemn. Hummel's application of Isa. 29.13 solely to the conscious dissimulation of the Pharisees, on the basis of Matthew's characteristic alteration of Mark 7.6b to ὑποκριταί, ignores the emphasis in 15.9b.

[3] Cf. S. Schulz, *Botschaft*, p. 175.

substitution of θεός for Μωϋσῆς as the author of the law that is transgressed (v.4), could point in this direction. However, the distinction in v.3 is clearly drawn in Mark 7.8–9. Mark also counters with an immediate attack on the Pharisees even if its import is not fully clear till v.8, and his language in vv.8, 9 and 12 no less equally implies that the commandment of Moses is the commandment of God. The fact of the matter is that both accounts view the Pharisaic tradition from a similar theological perspective, but bear witness to it in a thoroughly distinctive way. In Mark it is through the widening of an attack upon a specific issue into a general critique both by the Pharisees of the disciples of Jesus and by Jesus of their tradition. In Matthew it is through setting in bolder relief the distance between a single scribal regulation and the demand of God and *vice versa*, an example that is nevertheless for him a paradigm of Jesus' attitude to the whole tradition. That Jesus himself called into question both the practice of Corban and the tradition as a whole cannot be doubted.[1]

With v.14 Mark introduces the final section of his narrative, and in so doing returns to the subject raised at the beginning of his account. Matthew takes over the verse with only minor alterations (v.10).[2] The solemnity of the words with which Christ demands the attention of the crowd here indicates that a principle of far-reaching importance is to be enunciated. The originality of the following verse (v.15), or at least of its present formulation, has occasionally been questioned but on the whole

---

[1] Against B. H. Branscomb, *Law*, pp. 170ff. A Merx, *Das Evangelium Matthäus* (1902), pp. 239–40, and I. Abrahams, *Studies*, II, 200, claimed that the distinction between the oral and written Torah was not sufficiently distinct for such words to have been uttered by Jesus. B. Gerhardsson, *Memory and Manuscript* (1961), p. 21 n.5, claims, however, that we have here a simple and practical distinction between written and oral Torah, even though the technical term for the distinction is not used.

[2] This verse has frequently been regarded as an editorial link by means of which material that is only thematically related to the question in v.5 is attached to the controversy. Cf. V. Taylor, *Mark*, p. 342, who compares 2.21f., 27f.; 3.27ff.; 4.21ff., and 7.17. 2.21f. and 3.27ff. are introduced, however, without any editorial activity whatsoever, while 2.27ff. and 4.21ff. are simply prefixed with καὶ ἔλεγεν αὐτοῖς. The closest analogy to the form of v.14 is provided three verses later in 7.17, but Taylor himself allows that this 'may rest on a tradition that private instruction was given to the disciples'. We would claim the same for v.14 with regard to the crowd.

its authenticity is strongly attested.[1] Opinions do vary, however, as to which evangelist has recorded the more primitive form of the saying. In Mark it runs: οὐδέν ἐστιν ἔξωθεν τοῦ ἀνθρώπου εἰς πορευόμενον εἰς αὐτὸν ὃ δύναται κοινῶσαι αὐτόν. ἀλλὰ τὰ ἐκ τοῦ ἀνθρώπου ἐκπορευόμενά ἐστιν τὰ κοινοῦντα τὸν ἄνθρωπον. It is suggested that Matthew, by substituting εἰς τὸ στόμα for εἰς αὐτὸν and ἐκ τοῦ στόματος for ἐκ τοῦ ἀνθρώπου has not only rendered superfluous the later request for an explanation (v.15b), but together with his omission of Mark's οὐδέν, has also restricted the comprehensive character of the Marcan version.[2] The alteration, however, is primarily an endeavour to link the saying more firmly to the accusation with which the controversy began (οὐ γὰρ νίπτονται τὰς χεῖρας ὅταν ἄρτον ἐσθίωσιν: [v.2b]) and is a further example of the way in which Matthew has so carefully integrated the material around the initial issue. That Mark also understood the first part of the saying as primarily concerned with food is clear from his expansion of it in vv.18b–19a. Moreover, there is every indication that Matthew understood his alteration in v.11b in the widest possible fashion. Word, feeling and thought stood for the Jewish mind in the closest relationship, a fact to which Matthew elsewhere bears clear testimony (Matt. 12.34b; cf. Luke 6.45b; James 3.14) and in his elaboration of the saying in v.18 he demonstrates beyond doubt that this was the intention behind v.11b. Matthew's alteration in v.11b is therefore not to be interpreted any less comprehensively than its Marcan counterpart, and was no doubt chiefly introduced to complete the parallel with the first part of his saying.[3] While it is probably

[1] See, most recently, N. Perrin, *Rediscovering the Teaching of Jesus* (1967), p. 70.
[2] So, for example, G. Barth, 'Law', pp. 89ff., and E. P. Blair, *Jesus in the Gospel of Matthew* (1960), pp. 114ff. Matthaean originality has only been occasionally suggested, but see M.-J. Lagrange, *Matthieu*, p. 304; E. Lohmeyer, *Markus*, p. 142; and C. E. B. Cranfield, *Mark*, p. 230. A simpler form of the saying also occurs in the Gospel of Thomas 83.24–7: 'For that which goes into your mouth will not defile you; but that which goes out of your mouth that will defile you.' Its relation to and dependence upon the synoptic tradition are explored in W. Schrage, *Das Verhältnis des Thomas-Evangeliums zur synoptischen Tradition* (1964), pp. 55–7.
[3] To see a reflection of the struggles within the early church over the defilement issue in the Matthaean (Petrine) and Marcan (Pauline) versions, as B. W. Bacon, *Studies*, pp. 351–2, and W. D. Davies, *Setting*, pp. 338–9, suggest is, therefore, quite unjustified.

Matthew who has preserved the saying in its most genuine form, both versions retain a measure of ambiguity as to the application of the saying and therefore justify the following request for clarification as well as the description παραβολή (Mark 7.17; Matt. 15.15).

Two further questions must therefore be addressed to this saying. How successfully does it provide an answer to the Pharisaic criticism of the disciples' behaviour? What implications does it have for the Old Testament laws concerning defilement? At first sight it appears to be related to the original question only in the most general terms, for here it is the eating of food, not the washing of hands, that is at issue. In the controversies that have so far been considered, however, we have noted Jesus' refusal to debate within the terms of his opponents. Rather has he tended to answer in such a way as to lift the discussion to a higher level, a fact that has been insufficiently related to the issue defined at the beginning of the controversy.[1] As to its bearing upon the question of Law, not only is the Marcan form generally interpreted as directly undermining the Mosaic regulations as to clean and unclean, but for some this is true of the Matthaean version as well.[2] Leaving the Matthaean and Marcan understanding to one side until the

---

[1] This is so again, recently, in the analysis of Q. Quesnell, *Mark*, pp. 93ff., who feels it to be true for vv.6–8 and 9–13 as well. He concludes from this that Mark is not primarily writing an historical account, but giving 'a dramatic presentation of Christian doctrine about Pharisaic tradition and about true and false defilement' (p. 95). An exception is W. Beilner, *Christus*, pp. 81–2, who does take account of Jesus' earlier procedure, but feels that this is not sufficient to validate the link between the saying and the context that is provided for it here.

[2] So A. H. McNeile, *Matthew*, p. 226, and R. Walker, *Heilsgeschichte*, p. 142. More radical implications are occasionally drawn from this saying: (a) that Jesus deliberately focussed his attention on the Law here, turning altogether from the halakhic controversy with which the narrative began (E. Stauffer, 'Neue Wege', p. 172); (b) that in so doing he carries the distinction between the word of God and the word of man within Scripture itself (E. Lohmeyer, *Matthäus*, p. 247); (c) that, in fact, he abrogates not only laws distinguishing between clean and unclean but also the distinction that was fundamental to the whole ancient world, between the sacred and the profane (E. Käsemann, *Essays*, p. 101). A full discussion of the OT laws on clean and unclean themselves has now been provided by W. Paschen, *Rein und Unrein. Untersuchung zur biblischen Wortgeschichte* (1970).

remainder of the passage has been examined, it should be noted that such a repudiation by Jesus of, for example, the food laws contained in Lev. 11 and Deut. 14 (cf. Judith 10.5; Dan. 1.5, 8.16; Tobit 1.10–11; Esth. 14.17; 2 Macc. 6.7) renders inexplicable the hesitations of the primitive church on the issue (Acts 10.14–15; 15.28ff., Rom. 14.14; Gal. 2.11ff.). This is not to suggest that originally the saying was nothing more than an instance of semitic hyperbole reiterating the prophetic conviction that 'pollutions from within are more serious than pollutions from without' (cf. Hos. 6.6), for if the explanatory teaching in the following verses is at least true to his intention, this explanation is quite inadequate.[1] As with our previous findings with regard to sabbath, we must conclude that the principle outlined in this saying neither attacks nor, even in a qualified sense, affirms the Law. It moves in a different realm altogether, for it expresses an entirely new understanding of what does and does not constitute defilement. Beyond that, however, 'keineswegs folgt aus den Worte Jesu direkt, dass es verboten sei, die Reinheitsgebote weiter zu bewahren, noch, dass er nun mit diesen Worten die verpflichtende Kraft aufgehoben hätte'.[2] The latter is undoubtedly latent within the

[1] So C. E. B. Cranfield, *Mark*, pp. 239–40, against A. J. Rawlinson, *Mark*, p. 96; H. J. Schoeps, 'Gesetz', p. 218; J. Parkes, *Jesus*, p. 83, and Q. Quesnell, *Mark*, p. 98. The difference between the prophetic emphasis and that present in the saying is well defined by A. G. Hebert, *Throne*, pp. 100–1, and E. Lohmeyer, *Matthäus*, pp. 247–8. The saying of Johanan ben Zakkai in Pesik. 40b which is often quoted as a parallel to that of Jesus is in some respects similar to the prophetic position. It rather strikingly declares that 'Death does not defile, nor water cleanse', but then immediately adds that obedience to the rules of purification is necessary 'because it is an ordinance of the King of Kings'. E. Percy, *Botschaft*, p. 118 n.2, has therefore rightly described the first part of the saying as merely 'theoretisch'. It is precisely the lack of such an addition as ben Zakkai makes, and upon which, contrary even to prophetic teaching, the emphasis falls, that distinguishes the utterance of Jesus, a point that B. H. Branscomb, *Law*, pp. 181–2, recognises but does not sufficiently stress.

[2] W. Beilner, *Christus*, p. 85. That the abrogation of such laws is only implicit in the saying is the opinion of H. B. Swete, *Mark*, p. 150; E. Klostermann, *Das Markusevangelium* (1936), pp. 69–70; M.-J. Lagrange, *Marc*, p. 189; B. H. Branscomb, *Mark*, pp. 125–6; P. Verweijs, *Evangelium*, p. 22, and P. Bonnard, *Matthieu*, p. 226. G. Barth, 'Law', p. 89, points out for Matthew that any contravention of the Mosaic legislation is extremely unlikely since he has just argued from that same law to the invalidity of

saying, but no more than that. Do we have here, then, a reply of Jesus to his critics that lacks all christological undertones? Certainly there is no explicit reference to his own authority, nor any to the special character of his mission. What we do have, however, is a word that by its sheer originality cannot but call attention to the one who has uttered it. The christological factor is present in the content of the word itself.

At this point Matthew inserts a short passage attacking the Pharisees which has no parallel in the Marcan account (vv. 12–14). In it Jesus is approached by the disciples, who explain to him that the Pharisees were offended at his saying (v.12b). In reply Jesus passes two judgments upon them (vv.13–14), the second of which occurs in slightly different form in Luke 6.39 (cf. Rom. 2.19). In the first they are pictured as a φυτεία which, not having been planted by God, will be rooted up; in the second as τυφλοί...ὁδηγοί who will fall into a pit.[1] G. D. Kilpatrick regards this section as pivotal in Matthew's account and interprets it as making his whole narrative more an attack on the Pharisees themselves than on their tradition.[2] This can hardly be the case, for within this section itself there are two indications that the latter is included within the condemnation. With τὸν λόγον in 12b Matthew relates the insertion to v.11 and not to the whole preceding argument as has sometimes been alleged.[3] Moreover, in v.14 he specifies that it is precisely in their capacity as interpreters of the Law that they are being attacked here. The section may be regarded as a composition of Matthew, vv.13 and 14 being isolated sayings from the tradition which are redactionally linked to this narrative through v.12. Its effect is to highlight, as elsewhere in the first gospel, the

the traditions. He overlooks the fact that the same is true for Mark as well. Q. Quesnell, *Mark*, pp. 93–4, acknowledges this, but concludes that a contradiction exists between vv.6–8 and 15.

[1] Against B. W. Bacon, *Studies*, p. 351, φυτεία must refer to the Pharisees themselves and not to their traditions; the metaphor is a familiar picture of the community of God, e.g., CDC 1.7; 1 QS 8.5; 11.8; Cf. H. Braun, *Radikalismus*, II, 124 n.1. For its use in apocryphal and rabbinic literature consult Bill., I, 720ff.

[2] G. D. Kilpatrick, *Origins*, p. 108. Cf. also V. E. Hasler, 'Gesetz', p. 21.

[3] Cf. the similar use of the phrase to refer to a preceding statement in 19.11, 22; 26.44; 28.15, in contrast to the wider use of τοὺς λόγους in 7.28; 19.1 and 26.1.

distance between Jesus and the Pharisees, and incidentally to throw into greater relief the authority of Jesus. One cannot leave the passage without bringing it into comparison with Matt. 17.24–7 where the possibility of causing offence to the Jews is also in the foreground. Why did Jesus on that occasion comply with custom, yet here refuse to observe it? This could be explained in terms of one practice being more at variance with his own convictions than the other, but it is more likely that it was not the practice itself but the attitude of the people involved which determined his action. In the one instance it was the Pharisees' unnecessarily taking offence at his breach of their tradition, in the other certain Jews' seeking genuine information concerning his attitude to their customary practice.[1]

It has already been suggested that through their respective elaborations in 7.18–20 and 15.17–18, Mark and Matthew demonstrate a not dissimilar understanding of the saying. This is confirmed by the lists of things causing defilement which follow (7.21–2; 15.19), despite Matthew's redaction of Mark. Thus G. D. Kilpatrick wrongly refuses to give διαλογισμοὶ πονηροί, which is at the head of Matthew's list, its rightful significance, for it negates his claim that with his list in contrast to Mark 'a principle of morals is thus converted into a precept of law'. Nor, in view of his inclusion of πορνεῖαι and βλασφημίαι, should his list be too closely identified with the second table of the commandments.[2] The greater prominence accorded to the Decalogue commandments probably springs from the tradition rather than Matthew himself. It has been suggested, however, that both explanation of the saying and corresponding list come from the early church, or Mark himself, and not Jesus. Certainly redactional activity is noticeable in Matthew's ascribing the question to Peter, and Mark's location of it εἰς οἶκον, but D. Daube has shown that the general pattern of this section of the narrative is quite frequent in Jewish controversies (cf. also

---

[1] We perhaps have here, then, precedent in the ministry of Jesus for Paul's later discrimination between weaker brethren and legalistic christians, with the modification of his conduct out of concern for the one yet not for the other.

[2] See G. D. Kilpatrick, *Origins*, p. 38, and, on the latter point, E. Lohmeyer, *Matthäus*, p. 250; G. Kretschmar, 'Ein Beitrag zur Frage nach dem Ursprung frühchristlicher Askese', *ZTK*, 61 (1964), 57, and, in part, K. Berger, *Gesetzesauslegung* (1972), pp. 391–2.

Mark 10.1ff.; 19.1ff.).[1] The Marcan list has been traced to Hellenistic, Jewish and Pauline sources. However, the influence of Hellenistic lists is unlikely, since similar Jewish lists lay closer to hand in the composition of such a series, the evidence for Pauline vocabulary is, on closer inspection, not impressive, while even the parallels with Jewish literature can, with one exception, be traced back to the LXX version of the Old Testament. Most probably, then, catechetical interests have elaborated upon an original saying of Jesus (vv.18, 19a, 20) in a Jewish-christian, though not legalistic, direction in Matthew, and in a Hellenistic-christian direction in Mark.[2]

It remains only to examine the additions peculiar to Mark in v.19b and Matthew in v.20b. Mark's conclusion from Jesus' saying in v.18 is expressed in the abrupt phrase καθαρίζων πάντα τὰ βρώματα.[3] The awkward masculine καθαρίζων is to be interpreted as a participle of manner agreeing with the subject of λέγει in v.18a, and the whole phrase as a typical Marcan parenthesis which draws out the implications of what has been stated.[4] Just what those implications are, however, has generally been misunderstood. Contrary to the widespread view that Mark is here primarily concerned with the consequences of Jesus' teaching for the OT food-laws, it is far more likely that he is clarifying

---

[1] D. Daube, *Rabbinic Judaism*, pp. 142–3.

[2] C. E. B. Cranfield, *Mark*, pp. 242–3, goes so far as to suggest that the vocabulary allows for the whole list to go back to Jesus. To the objection that such lists are not found elsewhere in the sayings-tradition he points to the list of commandments in 10.19, a parallel that is interesting but not fully apposite.

[3] Despite J. Wellhausen, *Marci*, p. 55, ὀχετον (bowel), the reading in D, is not to be accepted. Its alteration of καθαρίζων to καθαρίζει is also due to an attempt to overcome the grammatical difficulty of Mark's construction. The emendations of A. Pallis, *Notes on the Gospels According to St. Mark and St. Matthew* (1903), pp. 14–15, and M. Black, *Aramaic*, pp. 217–18, not only lack all textual warrant but are far from being the simplest answer to the irregularity.

[4] Cf. esp. F. Field, *Notes on the Origin of the New Testament*, pp. 31–2, and C. H. Turner, 'Parenthetical Clauses in Mark', *JTS*, 26 (1925), 149. This interpretation goes back to many of the Greek Fathers and is the most widely accepted among modern commentators. In view of Turner's investigation there is no need to regard it as a later gloss. The other alternative, to take the words as they stand so that καθαρίζων refers to ἀφεδρῶνα as a further description of the natural process, founders on the awkwardness of the construction.

the situation with respect to foods involved in idol-worship for his Gentile-christian readers. In other words, he has in mind a similar problem to that dealt with by Paul in Rom. 14.1ff. and 1 Cor. 8.1ff. Though he also undoubtedly regarded the Mosaic regulations as no longer binding upon those to whom his gospel was addressed, as in Rom. 14 this may not necessarily have involved his repudiation of the food-laws so far as Jewish-christians were concerned. So long as it is recognised that all foods are 'clean' (Mark 7.19b), that the 'Kingdom of God' (Rom. 14.17) does not especially involve adherence or non-adherence to them, it remains open for laws to be observed if the individual so desires. Mark's comment, therefore, is not necessarily to be regarded as a radical attack upon the Mosaic prescriptions. Matthew's omission of it, therefore, does not, as is frequently asserted, result from any disagreement with Mark's supposedly anti-Law conclusion but from his retouching the whole story from a stylistic and thematic standpoint in accord with the more Jewish situation of his hearers and from his postponement of comment on Jesus' words to v.20b: τὸ δὲ ἀνίπτοις χερσὶν φαγεῖν οὐ κοινοῖ τὸν ἄνθρωπον. Against all attempts to see in this addition of Matthew a restriction of criticism to the custom of ritual hand-washing, indicative of his congregations' continued observance of much of the rabbinic tradition, the addition in v.20b merely concludes Matthew's thematic co-ordination of the material around the initial issue that we have observed in practice throughout.[1]

We conclude, therefore, that both Matthew and Mark reflect the central elements of Jesus' response to his opponents, particularly the position he adopted directly *against* the scribal regulations, yet in some sense to one side of, if also above, the Old Testament commandments. It is precisely because he does not take up a definite position *vis-à-vis* the Mosaic regulations that their observance by the early christians, which is not necessarily incompatible with their recognition of the principle outlined here, becomes quite understandable. Beyond that, Mark has added interpretative material in such a way as to draw the widest possible conclusions for his Gentile audience concerning Jesus' repudiation of Pharisaic tradition and creation of a new

[1] *Contra* E. Stauffer, 'Neue Wege', p. 172; G. Barth, 'Law', pp. 87-8, and R. Hummel, *Auseinandersetzung*, pp. 48-9.

situation with respect to the eating of food offered to idols. Matthew, on the other hand, has again highlighted Jesus' antagonism to the Pharisees, with special reference to their teaching and, aware of the interests of his more limited circle of Jewish-christian readers, concentrated attention on the particular tradition involved in the controversy. In both accounts the presence of a christological element, more subdued than in previous encounters, was noted.

4 DIVORCE NARRATIVES

It is the Pharisees who initiate the discussion with Jesus on divorce and in both Matthew and Mark, who alone record the debate, their intention is to 'test' him (Mark 10.2b; Matt. 19.3a).[1] According to the latter they ask simply εἰ ἔξεστιν ἀνδρί γυναῖκα ἀπολῦσαι, challenging him to deny the very idea of divorce and so bring himself into contradiction with the Mosaic law (Deut. 24.1ff.). Matthew, however, has the additional phrase κατὰ πᾶσαν αἰτίαν and is frequently interpreted as modifying the radical nature of the question in Mark.[2] If the Pharisees were merely seeking to draw him into the rabbinic disputes of the day and to have him pronounce upon the validity and invalidity of grounds for divorce, however, the element of testing is all but removed, for there would be no guarantee that the answer would at the same time necessarily provoke both of the major parties.[3] More probably the addition, while intended to set the controversy within the context of the discussions current in the time of Jesus and later, was, for Matthew, made by the Pharisees in the full realisation that

---

[1] Despite the tentative suggestions of R. Bultmann, *Tradition*, p. 52, *et al.*, that the omission of προσελθόντες Φαρισαῖοι in D is correct, it is, with the majority of MSS and commentators, probably to be accepted. This is confirmed by the presence of πειράζειν for in the only other two places in Mark where this occurs with reference to questioners, it is descriptive of the Pharisees (Mark 8.11; 12.15).

[2] Among others by B. H. Branscomb, *Law*, p. 150; W. Kümmel, 'Traditionsgedanke', p. 30; G. D. Kilpatrick, *Origins*, p. 106; T. W. Manson, *Sayings*, p. 292; G. Barth, 'Law', p. 95, *et al.*

[3] There is little likelihood of its being a Pharisaic attempt to discredit him in the eyes of Herod Antipas by encouraging him to express an opinion, as did John, on the tetrarch's recent marriage. See however J. Bowman, *The Gospel of Mark* (1965), p. 208.

Jesus' reply would question the whole practice of divorce, and so was not an attempt to reduce the debate to the level on which their thinking proceeded.[1]

The two narratives diverge in the following verses. In Mark, Jesus asks them what Moses commanded in this matter, to which they reply that ἐπέτρεψεν them to divorce the person concerned so long as she was given a document to that effect (v.4). The use of the term ἐπιτρέπειν is interesting, for it tallies with the later rabbinic attitude to Deut. 24.1–4, according to which divorce was regarded as sanctioned only for Israelites and not others. This indicates that the Pharisaic error lay not, as many have asserted, in their failure to distinguish between a command and a permission, but in their lack of awareness that a situation had now arrived which clarified the purpose for which the regulation had been allowed and in so doing put that legislation in an entirely new light. This becomes more apparent when it is recognised that σκληροκαρδία has reference primarily to their disobedience of God's will and is not descriptive of their attitude to their wives, nor of the primitive character of their ethical understanding.[2] It has, therefore, the same force as εἰς μαρτύριον αὐτοῖς in Mark 1.44.

The Mosaic provision is now contrasted with that which was ἀπὸ δὲ ἀρχῆς κτίσεως (v.6a). There follows an amalgam of Gen. 1.27 and 2.24, the quotation being based on the LXX. D. Daube claims that the rabbinic device of quoting an example followed by a precept is to be found here, though he regards only the first, the argument from Gen. 1.27, as being authentic, 2.24 having been added prior to the writing of the gospel or possibly by Mark himself. The argument is based upon the rabbinic interpretation of 1.27 in terms of the creation of the

---

[1] A different interpretation is provided by N. Turner, *Grammatical Insights into the New Testament* (1965), p. 61 (cf. A. Isaakson, *Marriage and Ministry in the New Temple* [1965], p. 122), who argues that though, before an anarthrous noun πᾶς usually means 'every', nevertheless in biblical Greek (perhaps under semitic influence) occasionally it carries the sense 'any', so that here the question has the same intention as the parallel in Mark. While this is grammatically possible, Matthew's purpose in making such additions in similar contexts is clearly to point to the regulations which the following teaching will affect (cf. 15.20b; 22.36b).

[2] Cf. H. Greeven, 'Zu den Aussagen des N.T⁵. über die Ehe', *ZEE*, 1 (1957), 114; J. Behm, *TDNT*, iii, 614 and E. Schweizer, *Markus*, p. 115.

ideal androgynous figure, an original unity man has no authority to destroy. In his treatment Daube also makes mention of the quotation of 1.27 in CDC 4.20–1 and interprets it in similar fashion. There the verse is linked with Gen. 7.9, which he likewise regards as a later addition, and is cited as an argument against polygamy.[1] However, one may rightly question the plausibility of such a conception in the mind of Jesus as well as point to the awkward dismissal of 2.24 and 7.9 as secondary additions because of their incompatibility with it. Rather than 2.24 being an independent argument for monogamy it is placed in the service of a right understanding of 1.27: i.e. marriage is indissoluble because of the linking together of man and woman by God (1.27) and particularly in view of the unity thereby created (2.24).[2] To this understanding of the verses there is no parallel in either the rabbinic or sectarian literature while the conclusion in v.9 to the effect that man must not separate what

---

[1] D. Daube, *Rabbinic Judaism*, pp. 72–3. Cf. Mek.Ex. 12.40; Gen.R. 8.9; Philo, *De Opif. Mun.* 24.76. On this whole question see further K. Berger, 'Hartherzigkeit und Gottes Gesetz: Die Vorgeschichte des antijüdischen Vorwurfs in Mc. 10.5', *ZNW*, 61 (1970), pp. 1–47. For the Qumran material see especially P. Winter, 'Sadoqite Fragments IV, 20–21, and the Exegesis of Gen. 1.27 in late Judaism', *ZAW*, 68 (1956), 71–84, and 'Gen. 1.27 and Jesus' Saying on Divorce', *ZAW*, 70 (1958), 260–1. Three interpretations of this verse are, in fact, possible. It has been held to refer to: (a) a prohibition against re-marriage after divorce so long as the first wife is living; (b) the forbidding of polygamy; (c) the permission for a man to marry once only during his lifetime.

[2] Cf. H. Baltensweiler, *Die Ehe im Neuen Testament* (1967), pp. 57–9. A. Isaakson, *Marriage and Ministry in the New Temple*, pp. 144–5, raises additional objections against Daube's views: (a) the idea of an androgynous Adam is late; (b) he would hardly have been regarded as the ideal human being; (c) the idea does not strengthen the argument for indissolubility since two sexes emerged anyway. Along with G. Delling, 'Das Logion Mark 10.11 (und seine abwandlungen) im NT', *NT*, 1 (1956), 272, and most of the commentators, however, he places great emphasis on μία σάρξ as expressing the idea of sexual union and therefore does regard 2.24 as an independent argument for indissolubility. Cf., however, J. Schniewind, *Matthäus*, p. 204, who takes it to mean, in accordance with Gen. 1.27, 'one person'. The theory is also rejected by M. R. Lehmann, 'Gen. 2.24 as the Basis for Divorce in Halakah and NT', *ZAW*, 72 (1960), 263–7, who regards the citation as referring to the 'pre-Sinai Noachite legal status of the Jews' which, according to j.Kidd I. 1; Gen.R. 18.5 *et al.*, did not include the right of divorce. The evidence on which this view is based, however, is again late.

God has joined together goes beyond even the Genesis conception itself. Gen. 1.27 did not especially sanction monogamy or polygamy and 2.24f. originally referred to woman's origin from man's flesh rather than to the nature of the union between them.

What is the significance of this appeal to Genesis over against Deuteronomy? In the first place, it should be noted that the appeal is made to the situation recorded in Genesis and that Christ is not merely placing an earlier statement of 'Moses' in contrast to a later one.[1] There is, however, no explicit rejection of the Deuteronomic provision. In v.5 it is described by Christ as 'a commandment' given for a special purpose (πρὸς τὴν σκληροκαρδίαν). To interpret Μωϋσῆς in v.4 in the sense of its authority originating in 'Moses, not God', is quite unwarranted since the following change of subject from Moses to God is not made sufficiently clear if an explicit contrast is intended.[2] This is far from asserting, however, that Deut. 24.1 is quite compatible with the teaching in Genesis in that, strictly speaking, it does not command divorce but only seeks to minimise its gross abuse by granting some protection to the woman. The description of the provision as an ἐντολή indicates that it is not so understood here and that Jesus is doing far more than bringing out the true meaning of Deut. 24.1.[3] In fact, the

[1] So rightly J. Jeremias, *Weltvollender*, pp. 64ff.; C. H. Dodd, 'Natural Law in the NT', *New Testament Studies* (1953), pp. 135–6, against E. Klostermann, *Markus*, p. 99; W. Grundmann, *Markus*, p. 204; D. E. Nineham, *Mark*, p. 261.

[2] Cf. B. S. Easton, *Christ in the Gospels* (1930), pp. 113–14; H. Greeven, *ZEE*, I (1957), 114–15; R. Hummel, *Auseinandersetzung*, pp. 49–50; W. Beilner, *Christus*, pp. 128–9. It is therefore incorrect to characterise Moses' action as 'Menschenwerk', as J. Jeremias, *TDNT*, IV, 864; A. Suhl, *Funktion*, p. 75; K. Berger, *Gesetzesauslegung* (1972), p. 540, or as being 'abrogated' as B. H. Branscomb, *Law*, pp. 152–4; W. G. Kümmel, 'Traditionsgedanke', pp. 30–3; E. Stauffer, 'Neue Wege', p. 173; H. Merkel, 'Jesus und die Pharisäer', *NTS*, 14 (1967), 207; A. Isaakson, *Marriage*, p. 27, and S. Schulz, *Botschaft*, p. 89.

[3] *Contra* C. E. B. Cranfield, *Mark*, p. 319, and earlier A. Ott, *Die Ehescheidung im Matthäusevangelium* (1939), pp. 9ff.; R. C. H. Lenski, *Matthew*, p. 711; N. B. Stonehouse, *Witness*, p. 204. J. Murray, 'Divorce', *WTJ*, 9 (1946), 31ff., goes considerably further than this, claiming that Deut. 24.1 merely forbids a man to re-marry his divorced wife after she has been married to another man. He finds the reason for this prohibition to be the sacred quality which was attached to the original marriage bond and therefore

Deuteronomic provision is thus neither abrogated nor expounded but set in a context in which it now no longer applies, except as a condemnation of those who refuse to accept the new state of affairs which has now come into existence. As in Mark 3.5, therefore, though less explicitly, the saying contains an indirect reference to the Pharisees' refusal to acknowledge the ministry of Jesus.[1] H. J. Schoeps has made a close examination of the possible parallels to the argument from the creation will of God, and concluded that in the Apocryphal and Pseudepigraphal writings, and in the literature of Hellenistic Judaism, such a procedure is never used as a critical principle with regard to the Law, while for rabbinic theology, despite some formal parallels, it was an impossibility. He concludes that 'if Jesus propounded such a norm, its authority stemmed exclusively from his person. There was no accepted Jewish tradition upon this point.'[2] We are once again therefore,

finds a direct link between the teaching of this passage and that of Gen. 2. So also A. Isaakson, *Marriage*, pp. 21ff. Agreeing with this assessment of Deut. 24.1 are G. von Rad, *Deuteronomy*, p. 150; P. Buis and J. Leclérq, *Le Deutéronome* (1963), p. 159, and J. Rennes, *Le Deutéronome* (1967), p. 108, all of whom regard vv.1–3 as the protasis, and the apodosis in v.4 alone. Earlier, G. R. Driver, *A Critical and Exegetical Commentary on the Book of Deuteronomy* (1895), p. 269, provided the same formal analysis though, unlike these three, still regarded the right of divorce as taken for granted. It must be emphasised again, however, that whatever may be the case in the Old Testament, Jesus indicates *he* regarded divorce as commanded by God for a certain purpose.

[1] The clearest comment on Jesus' attitude to this regulation is provided by Paul in Gal. 3.19: τί οὖν ὁ νόμος; τῶν παραβάσεων χάριν προσετέθη, if as E. de W. Burton, *The Epistle to the Galatians* (1921), pp. 187–8, asserts χάριν is given a telic force. Where, however, Paul sets the law in *heilsgeschtliche* perspective against the prior covenant with Abraham which still remains valid, Jesus sees it in relation to God's will in creation which also continues in force.

[2] H. J. Schoeps, 'Restitutio Principii as the Basis for the Nova Lex Jesu', *JBL*, 66 (1947), esp. 453–5. He explains that pre-Mosaic Torah, like the Noachian precepts, was never regarded as lessening the authority of Mosaic legislation. Rather was the latter understood as a progressive enlarging and completion of the first. A partial analogy provided by R. Eliezer ben Hyrkanos, who argues for the special authority of circumcision from its chronological priority to the Decalogue (Tanch. לך לך 20b), is not really parallel for there is not even the setting of one law over *against* another here. The pre-eminence given by the rabbis to quotations from the Law over the prophets also provides a partial analogy but, as

both through this method of argument and the conclusion drawn from it, brought face to face with the christological issue.

Matthew reverses the Marcan order and places the Genesis citations, and conclusion drawn from them, as Jesus' response to the initial question. The minor alterations in wording in 4b and 5a are insignificant, but is it the case that by his completion of the second quotation with the words καὶ κολληθήσεται τῇ γυναικὶ αὐτοῦ he has abandoned the Marcan emphasis on Gen. 1.27 as the basic premise of the following conclusion, with the result that Jesus' rejection of divorce is not veiled but intelligible to all? It seems far more likely, however, that the addition comes from the tradition rather than Matthew himself. As such it is merely intended to complete the quotation and so clarify the link between Gen. 1.27 and the conclusion drawn from it.[1] It is, then, the Pharisees who introduce the Mosaic provision into the discussion, an alteration which more strongly emphasises their opposition to the absolute requirement that, significantly, now precedes their argument. The use of ἐντείλατο in their question and ἐπέτρεψεν in Jesus' answer (v.8) is, however, the reverse of the Marcan order and with it Matthew has sharpened Jesus' response, portraying his expression as a deliberate correction of the Pharisaic terminology.[2] He has also

---

R. Bultmann, *Tradition*, pp. 49–50 and n.1, points out, the meaning of this procedure is not always clear and usually rabbinic interest lies in a harmonisation of 'apparently' conflicting statements. C. H. Dodd, 'Natural Law', p. 136, draws attention to the teaching of some rabbis according to which certain fundamental laws, including adultery, were given to Adam in the act of creation, but this view is not expressed earlier than the third century and the method employed is highly artificial. In any case, once again no conflict of laws is in view.

[1] Cf. G. Strecker, *Gerechtigkeit*, p. 22, against D. Daube, *Rabbinic Judaism*, p. 83, and R. Hummel, *Auseinandersetzung*, p. 50 n.87. K. Stendahl, *The School of Matthew* (1954), p. 148, plausibly suggests that it may stem from catechetical influence.

[2] Cf. J. Schniewind, *Matthäus*, p. 204; J. Schmid, 'Markus und der aramäische Matthäus', *Synoptische Studien* (1953), pp. 177ff. A Isaakson, *Marriage*, pp. 101–2, claims that Matthew has here preserved the more original form of the exchange. In view of the evidence collected by Daube concerning rabbinic attitudes to Deut. 24.1, however, it is quite possible that ἐπιτρέπειν could have been used by the Pharisees here. Isaakson takes no note of this material.

highlighted the distance between the Mosaic provision and his own declaration in the following verse by means of the antithetical framework in which the two statements are set. This is further established by the more exact differentiation (cf. 15.4) between God (ὁ κτίσας: 19.4a) and Moses (19.7–8), as well as by the repetition in v.8b: ἀπ' ἀρχῆς δὲ οὐ γέγονεν οὕτως. Thus also in Matthew, Jesus' reply cannot be interpreted as exegesis of the intention behind the Mosaic regulation nor simply as an anchoring of his marriage ethic in a creation ordinance. As before, Matthew's rearrangement and alteration of Mark places in bolder relief both the error of the Pharisees and the authority of Jesus, and though formally it may have more in common with rabbinic methods of argument this does not result in a lessening of the radical character of Jesus' response.[1]

Mark precedes the central saying of the discourse equating divorce and adultery with a change of location εἰς τὴν οἰκίαν and restricts the hearers to his disciples, while Matthew suggests that it is addressed openly to the Pharisees.[2] Whereas Mark introduces it with an impersonal καὶ λέγει αὐτοῖς Matthew, as we have noted, formulates this in antithetical relationship to the statement in v.8 with the phrase λέγω δὲ ὑμῖν. Finally, Matthew omits ἐπ' αὐτήν which follows μοιχᾶται in the second half of Mark's saying, but qualifies ἀπολύσῃ in the first part with the additional μὴ ἐπὶ πορνείᾳ. Mark's insertion in v.10a is in accord with his editorial procedure elsewhere (2.1; 7.17; 9.28) and is probably secondary, at least so far as εἰς τὴν οἰκίαν is concerned, for it is quite possible as in 7.17 (cf. Matt. 15.15ff.) that it was to the disciples alone that his further remarks were directed.[3] Matthew's omission again highlights

---

[1] *Contra* R. H. Charles, *The New Testament Teaching on Divorce* (1921), pp. 85ff.; B. H. Streeter, *Gospels*, p. 259; G. Barth, 'Law', p. 158; R. Hummel, *Auseinandersetzung*, p. 50 and A. Suhl, *Funktion*, p. 75.

[2] The main variant readings of Matt. 19.9, as well as the addition of a second sentence, are textual importations from Matt. 5.32 (cf. W. C. Allen, *Matthew*, p. 207).

[3] Cf. V. Taylor, *Mark*, p. 415. E. Lohmeyer, *Markus*, p. 201, suggests that it reflects the situation of the early church in which its leaders are being instructed with respect to future legislation. However, against A. W. Mosley, 'Jesus' Audiences in the Gospels of St. Mark and St. Luke', *NTS*, 10 (1963), 139ff., it must be contended that the redaction does not necessarily introduce post-resurrection material into the gospel nor, as R.

the distance between Jesus and the Pharisees, for in his account the saying has the character of a criticism of their practice rather than, as in Mark, the declaration of a rule of conduct. His λέγω δὲ ὑμῖν and rearrangement of vv.8–9 is significant, for it provides a clear example of the way in which an antithesis is formed from material in which it did not originally occur, a factor to which we must return when the Sermon on the Mount comes in for consideration, and gives his account a more explicit christological emphasis.

The relation of the form of the saying in these two accounts with that in Matt. 5.32 and Luke 16.18 may be left until the Antitheses are examined for, with one exception, the general drift of the sayings is quite similar. We come then to the much controverted phrase μὴ ἐπὶ πορνείᾳ in Matt. 19.9. Certainly the uniformity of the tradition in Mark 10.11; Luke 16.18 and I Cor. 7.10 makes it virtually inescapable that an addition to the original words of Jesus is present here.[1] Most frequently, however, the clause has been viewed as a casuistic modification of Jesus' demand, occasioned either by the practical needs of the early church, or as a result of rabbinic influence upon the

---

Bultmann, *Tradition*, p. 26, maintains, an independent saying of Jesus. D. Daube, *Rabbinic Judaism*, pp. 142–3, has defended the unity of this verse with the rest of the pericope on the grounds of its general rabbinic format.

[1] There are few dissenters from this conclusion, and the majority of those who do so hold to a general view of Matthaean priority. So A. Schlatter, *Matthäus*, p. 572; E. C. Butler, *The Originality of St. Matthew* (1951), p. 32; M.-J. Lagrange, *Matthieu*, p. 369, *et al.* Note also, however, E. P. Gould, *Mark*, p. 186, and H. B. Swete, *Mark*, p. 218. The most recent defence of its authenticity has been attempted by A. Isaakson, *Marriage*, pp. 75–92. His case rests upon: (a) a denial of the argument from the Marcan, Lucan and Pauline parallels, since Matthew could have had access to an independent tradition which for the other gospels was not relevant and (b) a denial that it represents a casuistic rejudaisation of an originally absolute prohibition, since Matthew's intention is to tighten up the requirements of the law, not relax them. His first suggestion would be feasible except for Matthew's similar interpretative activity elsewhere in the gospel which he has not taken into account, and which must tip the scales in favour of the clause being a secondary addition. As for his second point, it is my contention throughout that Matthew's additions, omissions and alterations are not in such instances due to a judaistic bias, but rather to a desire for a clarification of the precise way in which the teaching of Jesus affects the oral and written Torah.

primitive communities.[1] Numerous interpretations have been advanced as to its meaning,[2] in respect of which the following factors must be taken into consideration. In the first place, ἀπολύειν as the technical term for divorce cannot mean a separation *a toro et mensa* without right of re-marriage. In any case this, the classical Catholic position, ignores the context of Matt. 19.9 which centres around the question of divorce, not separation.[3] Secondly, παρεκτός in 5.32 (cf. μή ἐπί here) must be given an exclusive, not inclusive sense (cf. 2 Cor. 11.28; Acts 26.29; *Did.* 6.1; *Test. Zeb.* 1.4) and cannot mean 'not even in the case of πορνεία'. Thirdly, the word πορνεία does not signify μοιχεία and elsewhere in Matthew's gospel the two are carefully distinguished (Matt. 15.19, cf. Mark 7.22; 1 Cor. 6.9; Heb. 13.4).[4] Therefore the clause could scarcely have been inserted by Matthew with reference to Jewish christians who, as long as they were subject to Jewish law, would be compelled to divorce a wife who had committed adultery (Sot. 5.1; Yeb. 2.8).[5]

---

[1] For the first cf. E. Schweizer, 'Matth. 5.17–20', *Neotestamentica* (1963), p. 405; W. D. Davies, *Setting*, p. 388; and for the second, H. Braun, *Radikalismus*, II, 110 n.4; G. Strecker, *Gerechtigkeit*, p. 132; A. Hummel, *Auseinandersetzung*, p. 51.

[2] Surveys and critiques of the main lines of interpretation have been recently provided by B. Vawter, 'The Divorce Clauses in Mt. 5.32 and 19.9', *CBQ*, 16 (1954), 155–67; A. Isaakson, *Marriage*, pp. 127–35; E. Schillebeeckx, *Le Mariage* (1966), pp. 151ff. and D. W. Shaner, *A Christian View of Divorce according to the Teaching of the New Testament* (1969), pp. 9–30, 67–79.

[3] Against recently J. Dupont, *Mariage et Divorce dans l'Évangile Matthieu* (1959). R. Schnackenburg, *Moral Teaching*, pp. 139ff., and J. Schmid, *Matthäus*, pp. 103ff., consider this solution still to be the most tenable but are aware that it is not free from difficulty.

[4] This is also the case in the apocryphal and pseudepigraphal writings. Cf. R. H. Charles, *Divorce*, pp. 91–111, and A. Isaakson, *Marriage*, pp. 133ff., who gives special attention to the apparent exceptions in Ecclus. 23.23; Test.Jos. 3.8. It can scarcely be objected that the term was used as an alternative for μοιχεία to avoid its being employed twice in the same sentence. A double use of the latter would only have served to make the saying yet more pointed. We see, then, that it cannot be the case, as has been frequently suggested, that Jesus here agrees with the position of Shammai in allowing adultery as the only ground of divorce.

[5] Such an exception is often considered to be wholly in accord with Jesus' own intention, since it would be self-evident. Cf. K. Stendahl,

Again the term πορνεία cannot without difficulty be restricted to mean marriage within the forbidden degrees (Lev. 18), for it is normally employed to denote any unlawful intercourse, and in Acts 15.20f.; 1 Cor. 5.1 and Heb. 12.16 it is by no means certain that a restricted connotation is intended.[1] Nor can it apply merely to pre-marital sexual intercourse which, if it took place on the wife's part, should, according to the oral Law, issue in divorce (b.Ket. 5a, cf. Matt. 1.19), for such a specialised meaning of the term would not have been readily comprehended.[2] Finally, to equate πορνεία with continued infidelity, since the term refers not so much to unchastity in general as to particular instances of it, gives a precision to the word which it does not warrant. The correct term here would be rather πόρνη or πορνείαι.[3]

'Matthew', *PCB* (1962), pp. 777 *et al.* This, of course, when considered an authentic part of the original saying, has been the traditional Protestant solution.

[1] Thus Lev. 18, which Acts 15.20f. is said to echo, includes more than a list of the forbidden degrees; in 1 Cor. 5.1 because of its wide application, it is the most suitable term to describe this abnormal relationship; Esau, in Heb. 12.16, was, according to tradition, a man of generally unchaste actions (cf. C. Spicq, *L'Épître aux Hébreux* [1953], pp. 400ff.). Moreover, an incestuous marriage of the first degree, or a marriage contracted within the forbidden relationships by a proselyte, was regarded as a nullity and made divorce unnecessary (cf. J. D. Eisenstein, 'Incest', *JE*, VI, 572). The wide acceptance of this view owes most to the detailed presentations of J. Bonsirven, *Le Divorce dans le Neuf Testament* (1948), and H. Baltensweiler, *Ehe*, pp. 98ff.

[2] Against A. Isaakson, *Marriage*, pp. 135–42. Nevertheless as B. Malina, 'Does πορνεία mean Fornication?', *NTS* 14 (1972), 10–17, rightly points out, the term did not have as general a meaning as we accord it, for pre-betrothal, non-commercial and extra-cultic intercourse were not prohibited in either written or oral Torah.

[3] Contrast, however, J. Blinzler, 'Die Strafe für Ehebruch in Bibel und Halacha', *NTS*, 4 (1957), 32–47; A. M. Dubarle, 'Mariage et Divorce dans l'Évangile', *Or.Sy.* 9 (1964), 61–74, and F. J. Leenhardt, 'Les femmes aussi...à propos du billet de répudiation', *RTP*, 19 (1969), 31–40. In addition it could be urged that Jesus' teaching would therefore be less demanding than that required of the OT prophet (Hos. 2). It has occasionally been suggested that the term is used metaphorically of spiritual infidelity. Despite parallels in the OT (Jer. 3.6–9 *et al.*), NT (Rev. 17.2; 18.3; 19.2) and a certain affinity of thought with 1 Cor. 7.14ff. this runs counter to Matthew's usage in 15.19 and overlooks the fact that it is only in symbolic contexts that it has this meaning in the NT.

We move towards a more acceptable solution by taking up the suggestion of B. Vawter that the exceptive clauses in Matthew are preteritions, i.e., they are exceptions to the proposition itself, not simply to the verb ἀπολύω.[1] He insists that μή be understood simply as the negative particle nullifying ἐπί, the latter signifying a circumstance or state, one of its customary usages, so that the phrase be interpreted 'πορνεία is not involved'.[2] In 5.32 παρεκτός is to be regarded in an 'exclusive' sense, but with the more moderate meaning 'quite apart from the matter of πορνεία'. As for πορνεία itself, in keeping with its most general meaning, i.e., 'uncleanness', it should be regarded as a reference to the עָרְוַת דָּבָר of Deut. 24.1. These sayings may then be generally translated: 'I say to you, whoever dismisses his wife – the permission in Deut. 24.1 notwithstanding – and marries another, commits adultery.' This means that the emphasis upon indissolubility (already present in γαμήσῃ ἄλλην) that is the thrust of Mark and Luke is also preserved in Matthew. It has been urged that a stronger exceptive force should be given to παρεκτός, but a consideration of the other passages in which it is used in the NT and in apocalyptic literature indicates that 'apart from' is probably the more basic meaning of the term.[3] It has also been pointed out that the grammatical structure of עָרְוַת דָּבָר differs from that of λόγου πορνείας in 5.32, even more so that in 19.9, and that no instance has been found of its use as a translation phrase. However, no literal translation need be intended in 5.32 and the clause in 19.9 is probably a cryptic reference to the earlier statement, while there is some evidence that

---

[1] B. Vawter, *CBQ*, 16 (1954), 163–5. His position has been criticised by B. Leeming and R. A. Dyson, 'Except it be for Fornication', *Scr.* 8 (1956), 75–82. It can perhaps be noted here that J. D. M. Derrett, *Law in the New Testament* (1970), pp. 373ff., also tries to avoid a casuistic interpretation by understanding the clause as a command only if the husband was unable to continue in a non-sexual relationship with his wife, a view which, unconvincingly it seems to me, he feels to be plain on the reasoning of Mark alone.

[2] Not dissimilar is the Matthaean expression μὴ ἐν τῇ ἑορτῇ in Matt. 26.5 considered in relation to the whole of the preceding verse.

[3] 2 Cor. 11.28 is clearly intended in the more moderate sense, as also *Did.* 6.1 and Test.Zeb. 1.4. Even Acts 26.29 can be translated 'apart from' as well as 'except'.

πορνεία had become, at least in Matthaean circles, a technical term for the content of the Deuteronomic permission.[1] There is more point to the objection that since he had already dismissed it in the previous verses there was no need for Jesus to mention Deuteronomy further. This may well be so but it is not necessarily the case with Matthew. It is precisely at this point that Vawter's suggestion, weakened by his argument for the authenticity of the addition, has its strength. Here, in the climactic saying of the narrative, it is perfectly in accord with Matthew's redactional method that he should round the encounter off with a reference to the provision around which the controversy revolved. This was precisely his procedure in the controversy over defilement that has just been examined (15.20b). Though it may seem that it would have been more appropriate for the clause to have been placed earlier if it was meant to qualify the whole statement, its present position is the one in which a *parenthesis* is most likely to be inserted.

Matthew's omission of ἐπ᾽ αὐτήν is scarcely significant, for the phrase merely explicates the thought of μοιχᾶται. Through Jesus' use of the latter term the position of the wife is, for the first time, raised to that of the man for, in Jewish practice, adultery, whether viewed from the perspective of the wife or the third party, could only be committed against the husband.[2] In view of his addition of the following verse (10.12) it is quite possible that the words have been added by Mark, so that here,

---

[1] Matthew replaces ἀποστέλλειν in Deut. 24.1 by the more technically correct ἀπολύειν in 5.32 and 19.9. The enigmatic phrase μὴ ὑπὲρ ἃ γέγραπται in 1 Cor. 4.6 most probably also has a technical significance. The LXX renders the phrase, rather woodenly, ἄσχημον πρᾶγμα.

[2] The recent attempt by N. Turner, 'The Translation of Μοιχᾶται ἐπ᾽ Αὐτήν in Mk. 10.11', *Bib.Tr.* 7 (1956), 1–2, to refer the phrase to the second wife founders on his failure to instance any occurrence in Mark of the use of ἐπί = with. It is not sufficient to cite Ap. Const. 1, 3 and *Acts of Thomas* 56 in support, as does B. Schaller, *ET*, 83 (1972), 107–8. On the basis of his interpretation of this phrase, Schaller attempts to argue that since Mark 10.11 places the emphasis upon the re-marriage it is less stringent, and therefore less likely to be authentic, than the original teaching of Jesus whose kernel is to be found in vv.2–9. See B. Schaller, 'Die Sprüche über Ehescheidung und Wiederheirat in der synoptischen Überlieferung', *Der Ruf Jesu und die Antwort der Gemeinde* (ed. E. Lohse, 1970), pp. 237–8, 243–4. He regards it as an item of later community paranesis.

as there, the position of the wife is highlighted. In Mark 10.12[1] the right of the wife to divorce her husband is explicitly stated, a state of affairs that was impossible in Jewish circles. However, Salome (Jos., *Ant.* xv.259) and Herodias (Mark 6.17) have been cited as instances in which women in high places took this right for themselves, and it has been suggested that Jesus may have had such cases in mind in formulating this statement. But would Christ have been likely to lay down a principle with regard to so exceptional a case and, if he had done so, would it not have been of particular interest to Matthew?[2] It is far more likely to be Mark's application of the words of Jesus to the situation of his Gentile readers, of which examples may be found elsewhere in his gospel (cf. already 7.13b, 19b and see later 10.12; 12.28a, 31b).[3]

Thus, in this controversy as in the preceding, Matthew and Mark by their alterations, omissions and additions have each shaped the original encounter according to the character of their respective tendencies and audiences. Particularly noteworthy have been Matthew's desire to draw out the implications of Christ's teaching for the Mosaic commandment and Pharisaic requirement to which it is most relevant, as well as Mark's desire to give that teaching its widest possible application, while once again Matthew's tendency to focus on the

[1] The reading in D, despite the support of J. Wellhausen, *Markus*, p. 84; C. G. Montefiore, *Gospels*, I, 234, and V. Taylor, *Mark*, p. 420, is improbable. The attempt in the reading in A, and the emendation of C. C. Torrey, *Gospels*, pp. 94ff., to bring the verse more into line with the thought of 5.32, cannot be accepted.

[2] Nevertheless, this view has been maintained by F. C. Burkitt, *The Gospel History and its Transmission* (1907), pp. 98–101. To argue, as T. W. Manson, *Sayings*, p. 137, has done, that there is no evidence that Herodias divorced her husband is questionable. Cf. E. Neufeld, *Ancient Hebrew Marriage Laws* (1944), p. 184, and J. Jeremias, *Jerusalem zur Zeit Jesu* (1962³), p. 407 n.109. The upper strata of Jewish society could well have been influenced by the same eclectic pressures as the Jews at Elephantine, who also seem to have allowed this right to their wives. See further, E. Bammel, 'Markus 10.11f. und das jüdische Eherecht', *ZNW*, 61 (1970), 95–101.

[3] In addition to the objections raised above, B. Schaller, 'Die Sprüche über Ehescheidung und Wiederheirat in der synoptischen Überlieferung', *Der Ruf Jesu*, p. 229, insists that on formal grounds the secondary character of the saying in comparison with the adjoining verses is apparent, i.e., a conditional sentence with ἐάν as against conditional relative sentences.

authority of Jesus and the opposition of the Pharisees has come into view. Nevertheless, at the same time both have managed to preserve the fundamental tenor of Christ's attitude to the Law. His teaching, as we have seen, has no parallel with the contemporary Jewish position which it surpasses in its absolute prohibition of divorce, the equation of such a divorce when followed by re-marriage with adultery, and the possibility of that adultery being committed against the wife. The third-century rabbinic statements (cf. Bill., 1, 320) to the effect that 'he who separates from his first wife the Altar itself sheds tears over him...', alluding to Mal. 2.10ff., are restricted in application to the 'first' wife and do not characterise divorce as adultery, so that they cannot be considered a significant parallel.[1] This is also true of the prophetic (Mal. 2.10–16) and apocryphal (Ps.Sol. 8.10) texts that have occasionally been compared with it. Mal. 2.10–16 is the most difficult portion of the whole book and contains a considerable amount of textual corruption. In fact, originally there was no attack on mixed-marriages and divorces here but instead a sharp condemnation of apostasy to a heathen cult in Jerusalem.[2] Ps.Sol. 8.10 on the other hand is simply a re-affirmation of the prophetic criticism in Jer. 5.8.[3] While it also certainly exceeds the teaching of the Mosaic law and results in a portion of it no longer being applicable to the present situation, Jesus took a position which nevertheless did not involve talk of its abrogation or less than divine status. Indeed, in so far as the Pharisees persist in their rejection of Jesus' demands, it stands as a continuing condemnation of them.[4]

5   THE RICH YOUNG MAN

All three gospels record the encounter between Jesus and the Rich Young Man who is concerned with the quest for eternal

---

[1] Cf. W. G. Kümmel, 'Rabbinen', p. 6; B. Lanwer, 'Gesetz', p. 35; E. Percy, *Botschaft*, p. 146, and H. Braun, *Radikalismus*, p. 110.

[2] Cf. A. Isaakson, *Marriage*, p. 31; C. C. Torrey, 'The Prophecy of Malachi', *JBL*, 17 (1898), 4–11; F. F. Hvidberg, *Weeping and Laughter in the OT* (ET 1962), pp. 120–3.

[3] Cf. H. E. Ryle and M. R. James, *The Psalms of Solomon* (1891), p. 77.

[4] As such it is an anticipation of the 'Pauline' doctrine that δικαίῳ νόμος οὐ κεῖται, ἀνόμοις δέ...(1 Tim. 1.9).

life (Mark 10.17–22; Matt. 19.16–22; Luke 18.18–23). With one exception, the omission of Μὴ ἀποστερήσῃς in v.20, purely stylistic differences appear to be present in Luke. Following Mark closely in order and terminology, he omits only the vivid details of Mark 19.17a, 17b, 21b, 22a. On the other hand, Matthew contains three significant alterations: the removal of the ascription ἀγαθέ and the disclaimer τί με λέγεις ἀγαθόν; in the opening question (v.16b); the addition of Lev. 19.18 to the list of commandments in Jesus' second response (v.19f); the insertion of τέλειος in his closing challenge (v.21a). He also rearranges the Marcan Pronouncement-story into a *Schulegespräch*. Whereas Mark has only a single-question, to which Jesus gives a threefold reply, Matthew prefaces each response with a corresponding question. His explicit instruction to keep the commandments in v.17b also has a didactic effect.[1]

Matthew's first alteration is clearly an attempt to avoid the doubt Mark's account appears to cast on the person of Jesus, and thus as stemming from christological considerations.[2] A less recognised factor is also at work, however, of which an indication already occurs in Matthew's re-structuring of the pericope, i.e., a didactic emphasis which highlights the issue of Law. This may be detected in the similarity of the introductory words in 19.16a with those prefacing the query of the scribe concerning discipleship in 8.19 instead of the more urgent opening request in Mark 10.17a, as well as in the presence of the title διδάσκαλε which, in Matthew, only appears in the mouth of opponents or, as in 8.19 and here, Jews seeking information from him as a rabbi.[3] This coincides with the particularly Jewish character of Matthew's question according to which a specific good work is sought which might bring eternal life (cf. Bill., i, 808ff.) as well as the further query in v.20c, which may echo the Jewish teaching relating to 'good works' over and above the law (cf. Bill., iv, 536ff., 559ff.). In fact, one should probably see the disclaimer in Mark 10.17a not so much in terms of Jesus' self-

---

[1] On the basic authenticity of the Marcan account, rarely questioned, see V. Taylor, *Mark*, p. 424.

[2] An exception to this generally held view is E. Lohmeyer, *Matthäus*, pp. 284–5, who claims that the variations stem from differing translations of the Aramaic in the sources behind Matthew and Mark.

[3] Cf. F. Hahn, *Hoheitstitel*, pp. 76ff.; G. Strecker, *Gerechtigkeit*, p. 124.

depreciation of his own authority, as of his desire to centre attention upon the commandments that God has revealed. If this is the case, Matthew's omission of ὁ θέος, which elsewhere he introduces into Marcan contexts (15.4; 19.6), then becomes understandable. N. B. Stonehouse has suggested that this is even the emphasis of the Marcan account, so that with his reply Jesus was merely diverting attention away from himself and insisting that first concern must be with the commandments.[1] Nevertheless, in view of the question's deliberate focus upon the person of Jesus and the reply's explicit reference to God, christological tension cannot altogether be eliminated. This is even more the case if, as is probably correct, ὁ θέος is to be regarded as an interpretative Marcan addition (cf. Mark 2.7; 12.29).[2] This Matthew has avoided, not only from a desire to safeguard the authority of Christ but also to focus attention more directly upon the Law as the crucial issue which is involved in the encounter.

In the list of ἐντολαί which follows, all but one in Mark derive from the second table of the commandments (v.19). Attempts to identify Mark's insertion of μὴ ἀποστερήσῃς with either the tenth commandment or negative form of the eighth are doubtful, as is the validity of its omission from certain MSS.[3] Most probably its inclusion, together with the omission of the first-table of the commandments, and placing of the fifth commandment at the conclusion of the series, reflects the Jewish-Hellenistic 'sozialen Reihe' which were loosely based on

[1] N. B. Stonehouse, *Origins of the Synoptic Gospels* (1963), pp. 94ff. He draws attention to the use of the enclitic με in the question in Mark 10.18 (cf. Matt. 19.17).

[2] Cf. E. F. F. Bishop, 'εἰ μὴ εἷς ὁ θέος', *ET*, 49 (1937–8), 363–6. V. Taylor, *Mark*, pp. 426–7, provides a valuable critique of the different interpretations of Jesus' disclaimer that have been advanced.

[3] Most commentators support the first of these suggestions, but the usage of the term elsewhere (OT: Ex. 21.10; Deut. 24.14(A); NT: 1 Cor. 6.7–8; 7.5; 1 Tim. 6.5) argues against it. The second is ruled out by the position the term occupies after μὴ ψευδομαρτυρήσῃς. Its omission from B*KWΔ *et al.* is most probably to be explained on the grounds of its absence from the Decalogue. Other suggestions – that they reflect a specially Galilean form of the Decalogue, as E. Lohmeyer, *Galiläa und Jerusalem* (1936), pp. 84ff., or that they were directed to the situation of Jesus' hearer, as R. M. Grant, 'The Decalogue in Early Christianity', *HTR*, 40 (1947), 1ff. – are just as uncertain.

the Decalogue.[1] Luke's omission of μὴ ἀποστερήσῃς is probably due to his primary interest in the social requirements of the Decalogue which, as Luke 10.28ff. demonstrates, are for him equivalent to the love-commandment, while his inversion of the sixth and seventh commandments follows the order in the LXX and elsewhere in the NT (Luke 18.20; Rom. 13.9; James 2.11). Matthew's addition of Lev. 19.18 in v.19f is significant, for elsewhere he attaches particular importance to the 'love-commandment'. His positioning of it at the end of the series here, and its separation from the other commandments through the interpolation of καί, in view of the comprehensive character attributed to it in 7.12b and 22.40, probably indicates the special significance attached to it in comparison with the preceding commandments. The omission of μὴ ἀποστερήσῃς probably stems less from Matthew's desire to focus attention upon the importance of the Decalogue commandments than from catechetical influence in the tradition before him, as already in Matt. 19.19 over against Mark 7.21.[2] Neither Matthew, Mark, nor Luke, therefore, unduly point up the importance of the commandments, and this no doubt reflects the attitude of Jesus himself.[3]

The final addition εἰ θέλεις τέλειος εἶναι (v.22a) is often held to be indicative of a two-level ethic in the Matthaean community. G. Barth has demonstrated that on at least three grounds this is improbable: the questions in vv.17a and 21a are essentially the same; this is confirmed by the course of the following discussion in vv.23ff.; nowhere else does Matthew display evidence of a similar tendency.[4] This is not to say, however, that Jesus' instruction to sell all his goods and give the

---

[1] On this see especially K. Berger, *Gesetzesauslegung* (1972), pp. 419–20. He points out that the form in which they are stated (μη + aor.), has no parallel in the Decalogue citations of the LXX, Philo or Paul.

[2] Cf. K. Stendahl, *School*, pp. 62ff.

[3] This has been rightly recognised by H. Röthlisberger, *Kirche am Sinai* (1965), p. 40.

[4] G. Barth, 'Law', pp. 96ff. Cf. W. D. Davies, *Setting*, pp. 209ff.; G. Strecker, *Gerechtigkeit*, p. 142 n.1, and W. Trilling, *Israel*, pp. 192ff. On the historical connection between pp. 17–22 and 23–7 see C. E. B. Cranfield, *Mark*, pp. 325–6, and V. Taylor, *Mark*, pp. 424–5, against R. Bultmann, *Tradition*, pp. 21–2, and, more recently, N. Walter, 'Zur Analyse von Mc. 10.17–31', *ZNW*, 53 (1962), 206–18.

proceeds to the poor, is merely setting out the implications of obedience to the commandments.[1] Yet nor is it an adequate view, between these two extremes, to interpret Jesus' demand in terms of a 'radicalisation' of the Law.[2] It is difficult to resist the conclusion that what Jesus requires here is something altogether new, more a surpassing of the Law than its radicalisation. For not only is obedience to the commandments insufficient (Mark 10.21a: ταῦτα πάντα ἐφύλαξα. τί ἔτι ὑστερῶ) but even the selling of all one's goods for the poor for in all three accounts the really crucial demand is that of following Jesus (Mark 10.21c and pars.).[3] To be τέλειος, therefore, involves obedience to the all-embracing demands of Jesus, and should logically issue in discipleship and it is only those who pursue this path who have ζωὴν αἰώνιον. Whether this is in agreement with the meaning Matthew attaches to τέλειος in 5.48 cannot be determined until that passage itself comes under consideration.

Once again, therefore, the three evangelists have handled the tradition before them in such a way as to focus attention upon their own redactional interests. In addition to his refashioning of Mark in order to safeguard the authority of Christ and his centring the pericope more firmly around the Mosaic Law, Matthew has indicated his particular interest in the love-commandment, as well as his tendency to coin descriptive terms with which to sum up an aspect of the material he is recording. Mark, for his part, has incorporated material which widens the scope of the initial moral demands stemming from Jesus and so makes his reply more relevant to a non-Jewish audience.

[1] Against N. B. Stonehouse, *Origins*, p. 98; W. Trilling, *Matthäus*, p. 193; V. E. Hasler, *Gesetz*, p. 22.

[2] As in G. Bornkamm, 'End-Expectation', p. 29; G. Barth, 'Law', pp. 102–3 and the elaboration of this passage in the Gospel of the Nazareans (Origen, *Com. on Mt. XV.14*). Despite J. Jeremias, *Unknown Sayings*, pp. 33–6, this is unlikely to preserve independent tradition of the original incident.

[3] Cf. S. Schulz, *Botschaft*, p. 193: 'Erfüllung der Gottesforderung gibt es nur noch durch Jesu nachfolge'. His assessment of Matthew negates that of A. Suhl, *Funktion*, p. 78, who claims that 'ist bei Matthäus das Gesetz zu einer durchaus verpflichtenden Norm geworden'. The view of V. E. Hasler, 'Gesetz', p. 22, therefore, that for Matthew 'Nachfolge ist Nächstenliebe, darum Gesetzeserfüllung' (cf. also G. Bornkamm, 'End-Expectation', p. 29; G. Barth, 'Law', pp. 102–3; W. Trilling, *Israel*, p. 193, and G. Kretschmar, *ZTK*, 61 [1964], 55), is also incorrect.

Luke, with one minor alteration, has also brought the material more into line with the Hellenistic-Jewish preoccupation with social requirements. So far as Jesus' attitude to the Mosaic commandments is concerned, it is clear from this narrative that his reference to the Law is primarily intended as an endorsement of its value as a testimony to, or its forming a springboard for, the more ethically-demanding and uniquely personal claim which follows. The christological reference in this passage is therefore more emphatic than in the debates concerning defilement and divorce which preceded it.

6   THE GREATEST COMMANDMENT

The commandments to love God (Deut. 6.5) and to love one another (Lev. 19.18) are bracketed together in each of the synoptic gospels. In both Matthew and Mark they form part of one of the controversies during the last week of Christ's ministry, and are quoted by Jesus in response to a query concerning the fundamental commandment in the Law (Matt. 22.34–40; Mark 12.28–34). Luke refers to them towards the beginning of his Travel Narrative, where they form a scribe's response to his own enquiry concerning the inheritance of eternal life (Luke 10.25–8). These differences in context, speaker and application suggest that the narratives in Matthew and Mark, on the one hand, and Luke on the other, have their basis in two separate incidents, though it is not out of the question that all three derive from the one event which has come down through two, or even three, different channels of tradition.[1] With regard to originality, the Marcan narrative is generally favoured though preference for Luke's version is shown in some quarters.[2] In

---

[1] For the first: cf. T. W. Manson, *Sayings*, pp. 259ff.; K. H. Rengstorf, *Lucas*, p. 138; E. E. Ellis, *Luke*, p. 158; for the second: J. M. Creed, *Luke*, p. 151; R. Bultmann, *Tradition*, pp. 23, 51; F. W. Beare, *Records*, pp. 158–9. According to M.-J. Lagrange, *Matthieu*, p. 430; G. Bornkamm, 'Das Doppelgebot der Liebe', *Neutestamentliche Studien für Rudolf Bultmann* (1959²), pp. 87–93, and G. Barth, 'Law', p. 95 n.2, the differences between the two are such that Matthew did not have Mark before him at all, while E. Lohmeyer, *Matthäus*, p. 327 and W. Beilner, *Christus*, p. 134, have argued that each gospel had its own independent tradition.

[2] As, for example, by A. J. Rawlinson, *Mark*, p. 171; B. S. Easton, *Luke*, p. 169; B. H. Branscomb, *Mark*, p. 219; F. W. Beare, *Records*, p. 159.

the discussion that follows an attempt will be made to disentangle the complex issues involved in the relationship between, and authenticity of, these three accounts, as well as to
trace the particular significance which each evangelist has
placed upon the tradition.

The Marcan narrative is related in the form of a *Schulegespräch* in which the polemical note is completely lacking, while
in both Matthew and Luke the encounter has the nature of a
controversy. In Mark, the query is posed by a scribe who has
been impressed with Jesus' previous teaching. Matthew, however, introduces a reference to the Pharisees which, as elsewhere, is intended to highlight their opposition to Jesus (v.34a).
He specifies the questioner as a lawyer, and relates that the
purpose of his query is to 'test him'. Luke's preface speaks only
of the lawyer who is also described as 'testing him'. Despite his
preference for νομικός elsewhere (cf. 7.30; 11.46ff.), other
agreements with Matthew suggest a common source behind
their accounts, though the presence of Lucan terminology surrounding it (ἰδοῦ; τίς; ἀνιστάναι) suggests that at least part of
v.25a stems from his own redactional activity.[1]

In Mark the following enquiry concerns the ἐντολὴ πρώτη
πάντων, in Matthew the ἐντολὴ μεγάλη. However, since
μεγάλη = μεγίστη here, an instance of the positive being used
for the superlative, and πρώτη is to be interpreted in the sense of
'pre-eminent' rather than 'logically prior', both have a similar
meaning.[2] Discussions concerning the importance of various
commandments in the Law were of course much in the air in
contemporary rabbinic circles, not only in the distinguishing of
'lighter' and 'heavier' regulations, but in the specifying of
commandments that were considered to be of central importance.[3] Mark's πάντων is most probably redactional, and this

---

[1] T. Schramm, *Lukas*, pp. 47ff., also finds a common source with Matthew
(cf. also διδάσκαλε; ἐν τῷ νόμῳ; ἐν ὅλῃ τῇ διανοίᾳ), but traces Luke's other
changes to the influence of the Marcan narratives in 10.17ff. and 12.28ff.
[2] Cf. Moulton, III, 31 *et al.* This is confirmed by Matthew's equation of
μεγάλη and πρώτη in v.38. Attempts have frequently been made to
interpret ποία in its classical sense: 'what class', 'what nature', rather than
its later meaning as an equivalent to τίς. With the grammarians, however,
the weaker sense is probably to be preferred. Cf. M/M, p. 524; A/G, p.
691; Funk, p. 155.
[3] See Bill., I, 900ff.; I. Abrahams, *Studies*, I, 21ff.

results in a widening of the boundary of the original question from that of the Law to that of morality in general. The presence of this broader context is reinforced through the additions in vv.31a and 32–4 as we shall see in a moment. Matthew's replacement of πάντων with ἐν τῷ νόμῳ not only sets the discussion even more firmly in the Jewish context of the day, but quite possibly reflects the terminology of the original question. In so doing, however, he betrays the secondary nature of his insertion πειράζων in the previous verse, for there is no real temptation involved in any answer that Jesus might give. While it is true that, at a later stage at least, some sections of Judaism remained suspicious of such distinctions within the Law (b.Hag. 11b) few doubted the legitimacy of such an activity, and since different solutions to the problems were provided by the rabbis, and their answers were regarded as haggadah rather than as legal decisions, it is scarcely probable that an element of risk was involved in any answer that Jesus might give. Most probably it is from the perspective of a differentiation between Jesus and the Pharisees that Matthew formed a controversy out of this incident. This accords well with Matthew's heightening of the polemic against the Pharisees not only in respect of their persons but with regard to their teaching as well (cf. Matt. 15.14; 16.12; 19.8; 23.4).[1] This is less the case with the Lucan question, which diverges most markedly from the other accounts. This (with the exception of ἀγαθέ) is an exact replica of the query regarding eternal life addressed to Jesus in 18.18 by the Rich Young Ruler. One may compare also the similarity of the introductory words of Jesus' reply in v.26a with 18.19a concerning the content of the Law. It would appear that Luke's own hand is at work in its construction, rather than its originating in the tradition, and that he is deliberately creating a setting in terms of 18.18ff. for the quotation which follows. The further agreement with Matthew in the use of διδάσκαλε need not stem from literary dependence upon a common source, but from the redactional interests of each evangelist. Luke takes it from the parallel in 18.18; Matthew employs it in accordance with his special use of the term, i.e., on the lips of those who are

---

[1] Cf. G. Barth, 'Law', p. 78. For a contrary view see E. Lohmeyer, *Matthäus*, p. 328.

uncommitted, or opposed, to Jesus. Nor need ἐν τῷ νόμῳ (v.26b) in the question by Jesus that follows, reflect the presence of Matthew's addition in v.36c, for it occurs elsewhere in material where Lucan redaction is at work (cf. 2.23–4; 24.44). Significantly enough the other terms in the question, γράφειν and ἀναγινώσκειν, both occur together with ἀνιστά'ναι (cf. v.25a) in Luke 4.16–17, a passage which is generally admitted to be a Lucan construction.

Mark alone records the Shema as part of Jesus' answer to the scribal enquiry (v.29). This undoubtedly stems from his desire to establish a comprehensive principle which, in view of the recognition of monotheism as the chief pillar of orthopraxy, was regarded as being moral as well as doctrinal in character. In a Gentile context it was perfectly natural and, from an apologetic point of view, extremely relevant that the first commandment should insist on the uniqueness of God, to be followed by the social-ethical emphasis of Lev. 19.18 in the second.[1] That a certain hierarchy is presupposed in the differentiation between the 'first' and 'second' commandments can scarcely be avoided, and this corresponds to the emphasis upon piety as the chief virtue in both Hellenistic and Palestinian Judaism. Nevertheless, Mark's additional comment in v.31b to the effect that 'there are no other commandments greater than these' also makes it clear that a fundamental distinction exists between these two and all others. This thought is explored further in the

[1] Cf. G. Bornkamm, 'Doppelgebot', p. 86, who demonstrates that this addition lay in pre-Marcan tradition and most probably had its origin in a Hellenistic-Jewish context. See also F. Gils, *RB*, 69 (1962), 520. Thus the view of O. H. M. Lehmann, 'Religious Experience in the Gospels and in Contemporary Rabbinic Literature', *St.Ev.* 1 (1959), 558ff. (cf. D. Daube, *Judaism*, pp. 247–50), that for Jesus 'the Shema might well be taken as the foremost of the commandments' (p. 559), cannot be accepted, though as E. Neuhäusler, *Anspruch und Antwort Gottes* (1962), p. 117 n.13, rightly maintains, it stands 'als Überschrift zum folgenden Doppelgebot, das daraus wächst und sich darauf begründet'. By Jesus, however, it is presupposed, rather than stated to be such. As Bornkamm notes (pp. 88–9), the form in which the first commandment is quoted, and the scribe's response to it, are also indicative of the apologetic interests of the gospel *viz.*, the substitution of διανοίας for δυνάμεως (v.30, interpreted as συνέσεως in v.33) and the presence of the Greek formula ἐπ' ἀληθείας εἶπας in v.32. Cf. also the discussion in V. Furnish, *The Love Command in the New Testament* (1972), p. 29.

following verses (vv.32–4) which are also peculiar to Mark, in which the scribe commends the reply of Jesus and extends it by affirming the superiority of love to God and man over all burnt-offerings and sacrifices. To interpret this further statement in terms of the rejection of ritual commandments is, however, unjustified. It should be kept firmly in mind that it is found on the lips of the scribe, a firm point in favour of its authenticity, and is in fact quite in line with the prophetic emphasis (Hos. 6.6; cf. Prov. 21.3).[1] What Mark, as elsewhere (cf. Mark 2.27), has done is to incorporate material from his tradition that would by analogy be of particular interest to his Gentile readers when consideration of the sacrifices associated with pagan worship was taken into account.[2]

Apart from his omission of this pericope, no doubt occasioned by its featuring a sympathetic scribe, Matthew makes three significant alterations in his account of Jesus' reply. In the first place he omits the Shema, not so as to frame an answer that was rabbinically correct since the Shema could not, strictly speaking, be interpreted as a commandment, but again to focus the issue directly on the commandment itself.[3] Next, his quotation of the two OT provisions, by means of his additional ὁμοία αὐτῇ, brings the second into closer relationship with the first and once again illustrates the particular significance he attached to Lev. 19.18. This is further emphasised by the conclusion Matthew has given to the encounter in v.40, i.e., on these two commandments hang all the law and the prophets (cf. also

---

[1] *Contra* E. Lohmeyer, *Markus*, p. 261; V. E. Hasler, 'Gesetz', p. 24; R. Hummel, *Auseinandersetzung*, p. 52, and K. Berger, *Gesetzesauslegung* (1972), pp. 194, 197. The saying of R. Johanan in Ab.R.N, 1.4 only equates loving kindness with sacrifice as a substitute, not as something superior to it.

[2] Arguing partly from the language and partly the present-conception of the Kingdom in v.34, G. Bornkamm, 'Doppelgebot', pp. 88ff., has convincingly argued that it was not Mark who introduced this passage or its interpretation here. C. Burchard, 'Das doppelte Liebesgebot in der frühen christlichen Überlieferung', *Der Ruf Jesu*, pp. 46ff., also suggests that the terminology of 'first' and, by analogy, 'second', has its content in Hellenistic-Jewish Christianity, where it is closely related to the Shema (see esp. pp. 51–5).

[3] Against D. Daube, *Judaism*, p. 250. As we have seen, elsewhere Matthew has no hesitation in including material that would not be acceptable on Jewish presuppositions.

5.17; 7.12). The force of κρέμαται has generally been interpreted in terms of (a) the 'basic principle' of the Law, or (b), the command from which all others can be 'exegetically deduced'.[1] The first holds that by these two commandments all others are to be weighed and gauged but this scarcely tallies with Matthew's attitude to the Law, or the love-commandment, that elsewhere has been expressed. The second brings it into line with the technical rabbinic equivalent חלד' (cf. Bill., I, 907ff.), which refers to the exegetical deduction of a halakah from a given portion of Scripture, but this means Matthew would not be ascribing to Christ anything essentially different from that of Hillel (b.Shabb. 31a) and Akiba (Sif.Lev. 19.18) and leaves unexplained the emphasis upon μεγάλη and πρώτη. More probably we have here a figurative use of the term by which, as with the first interpretation, an absolute differentiation between these two and all other laws is expressed yet, in accordance with the second, a dependent relation between the two is established that does not destroy the validity of the lesser commandments.[2] Despite its more restricted application, then, this accords with the central point in the Marcan account though, as is customary in Matthew, it is expressed in more Jewish a manner and related more specifically to the Jewish Law.[3]

The conclusion of the Lucan narrative moves in as different a sphere to the other accounts as its introduction. The scribe, having replied to Jesus' counter-question by means of Deut. 6.5 and Lev. 19.18, is commanded by Jesus: 'do this and you

---

[1] For (a): H. B. Swete, *Mark*, p. 285; B. H. Branscomb, *Law*, p. 95; V. E. Hasler, 'Gesetz', pp. 23-4. (b): A. Schlatter, *Matthäus*, p. 657; F. V. Filson, *Matthew*, p. 238; B. Gerhardsson, *Manuscript*, p. 138; R. Hummel, *Auseinandersetzung*, p. 52; W. Trilling, *Israel*, p. 173.

[2] A/G, p. 451, liken the relationship to that of a door upon its hinges; G. Bertram, *TDNT*, III, 919, to objects suspended from a nail, and both provide parallels from Greek literature for this usage. G. Bornkamm, 'Doppelgebot', p. 93, and G. Barth, 'Law', p. 78, who accept this view, nevertheless do not perceive that it speaks against their contention that the 'love-commandment' is for Matthew a principle for discriminating between the OT laws.

[3] We can conclude, therefore, that the differences in the Matthaean account can all be explained in terms of his redactional activity and do not necessitate the positing of an independent source behind his narrative. Cf. R. Hummel, *Auseinandersetzung*, p. 51 n.91.

shall live'. The lawyer's attempt to make a casuistic evasion of this demand (v.29) by asking 'who is my neighbour?', and Jesus' reply in terms of the Parable of the Good Samaritan then follows (vv.30–7). In fact, the chief weight of the account falls on the parable and it is obvious that Luke is not interested in theoretical questions concerning the status of the Law. Instead, by means of the framework he has created for the *Doppelgebot* and Parable, the typical Lucan themes of salvation and compassion come to expression.[1]

It has, of course, frequently been suggested that the conjunction of the two commandments, though not as scriptural citations, had already taken place in pre-christian Judaism. Three examples are found in the Testaments of the Twelve Patriarchs, but the presence of christian interpolations elsewhere in this work necessarily casts doubt on the authenticity of these parallels (Iss. 5.2; 7.6; Dan 5.3). In any case the commandments form part of a series and are not set forward as the basic principle of moral activity.[2] A definite link between the two, to which more significance is attached, does occur in Jub. 36.7–8, but the first injunction speaks only of 'fearing' God and the application of the second is limited to 'brethren'. In several passages, Philo declares that piety and service towards God, and philanthropy and justice towards men, are the highest commandments (*De Spec.Leg.*, II, 63; *De Abr.*, 208; *Vit.Mos.*, II, 163; *et al.*), and though the term 'love' is not explicitly used he undoubtedly extended the application of the second requirement to all men, not merely, as in the OT, to Jewish citizens (Lev. 19.18), the resident-alien (Lev. 19.34) or, occasionally, the enemy (Ex. 23.4). However, neither in Palestinian nor Hellenistic Judaism did the singling out of these two commandments negate the principle of the equivalence of commandments, according to which, whatever importance was attached to individual instructions, from the point of view of obedience all had the same status. So Ab. 2.1b: 'Behave towards an easy commandment exactly as towards a difficult one, for

---

[1] The effects of Luke's redaction are further explored in H. Zimmerman, 'Das Gleichnis vom barmherzigen Samariter', *Die Zeit Jesu* (ed. G. Bornkamm, K. Rahner, 1970), pp. 58–69. His view of its original meaning – that Jesus is the point of the Parable – is, however, arguable.

[2] See also Test.Zeb. 5.1; Gal 4.2; Jos. 11.1; Benj. 3.3.

you do not know what reward will be given for the command-ments.' This is also the emphasis in the conclusion of Hillel's dictum in b.Shabb. 31a. For the same reason, the statement of Akiba in Sif.Lev. 19.18 and Matt. 22.37 and pars. have nothing in common but their structure and the use of the word 'great'. However, this term does not have the same decisive use as in Matthew, so that any attempt to consider them as equivalent cannot be sustained.[1] Such a fundamental distinction between these two and other regulations as is indicated here was therefore impossible. It has been too little recognised, however, that what Jesus says here is not his last word on what is demanded by God, nor on his own assessment of the requirements of the Law. Certainly he has answered the initial question as to which is the most important commandment in the *Law* but he has not gone beyond that, as he did in 19.16ff., to speak of the chief requirement of *God* in the new situation which his coming has inaugurated, nor of the way in which the Law as a whole is related to it. This is confirmed in the Marcan account by the closing remark of the scribe in v.34b. His willingness to accept Jesus' pronouncement only places him οὐ μακρὰν from the Kingdom of God not, however positively the phrase is interpreted, within it. However, in view of 19.19ff., attempts to view this as the central element in Matthew's understanding of the teaching of Jesus are unacceptable.[2] To this it need only be added that, in these passages, the christological issue is again muted, implicit only in the authority of one who could pronounce upon the question of the fundamental requirements of the Law in so decisive and radical a fashion.

In this examination of controversies and debates over the Law, the vague outlines that emerged from a study of incidental sayings and actions of Jesus concerning his relationship to the Law, as also that of the evangelists who recorded it, have been set in sharper relief. Further evidence has come to light of Matthew's tendency to intensify the portrait of Pharisaic opposition, to bring into clearer focus the individual Old Testament and Jewish regulations at stake in the encounters

[1] Cf. M. Smith, *Parallels*, p. 138.
[2] See further W. Trilling, *Israel*, pp. 187ff.; G. Strecker, *Gerechtigkeit*, pp. 136ff., against E. Schweizer, 'Matthäus 5.17–20', p. 405; G. Eicholz, *Bergpredigt*, p. 103, *et al.*

surveyed and, in various ways, to highlight the personal authority of Christ. Mark, who incorporates a good deal of legal material and also takes careful note of the part played by Pharisaic opposition within it, nevertheless indicates that for him it is largely on the uniqueness of the ethical principles enunciated by Jesus and the Pharisaic antagonism towards them that his christological emphasis lies. That is to say, he is more concerned with the apologetic relevance of such statements to his Gentile audience than with their consequences for the status of the Old Testament Law. In Luke, the issue of Law and Pharisaic reaction is even further in the background and he appears to incorporate material dealing with it only when it serves to point up the saving preaching and healing ministry of Christ, and the corresponding stress upon love and compassion in his teaching. For it is this which he is chiefly interested in depicting, so that the issue of the Law has no specific interest for him.

As for Jesus' own attitude to the Law, such categories as 'exposition' or 'completion' on the one hand, and 'radicalisation' or 'sharpening' on the other, were all seen to be inadequate. Nevertheless, to speak in terms of its 'abrogation' is also inappropriate. We are left with three main alternatives, each of which recognises the element of discontinuity with the Old Testament through the uniqueness that adheres to Christ's teaching, yet differs from each other in the weight they allow to rest on the continuity between the two. In them the demands of Jesus are interpreted as the expression of the direct will of God in the new situation which his coming has brought, resulting in:

(a) the 'transcendence' of all Old Testament laws, without further definition of the relationship between the two;[1]
(b) the 'legislation' of a new Mosaic or Messianic Torah which chronologically replaces the old;[2]
(c) the 'fulfilment' of the Law by means of his obedience to the Cross.[3]

For further light on the adequacy of these alternatives, as also upon Jesus' attitude to the oral Law which to this point he has consistently opposed, it now becomes necessary to turn our

---

[1] As E. Percy, *Botschaft*, pp. 164–5; P. J. Verweijs, *Evangelium*, pp. 17ff.
[2] B. W. Bacon, *Studies*, *passim*; W. D. Davies, *Setting*, pp. 14ff.
[3] H. J. Ljungmann, *Gesetz*, pp. 121ff.

attention away from the controversies and discussions over specific legal issues, to his more extended teaching in the gospels in which reference to the Law occurs.

C EXTENDED TEACHING

There are two sets of passages in the gospels in which aspects of the Old Testament Law are treated in the context of more extensive teaching by Jesus on various subjects, and in one of them the general relationship between the Law and his ethical demands comes in for special attention. To what extent the form in which these passages now present themselves is a later construction, and in what particulars it has its basis in the ministry of Jesus, is a question for discussion, for it is clear that both the evangelists themselves and the tradition before them have had a hand in their formulation. The passages are the Speeches against the Pharisees (Mark 12.37b–40; Matt. 23.1–36; Luke 11.37–52, cf. 20.45–7) and the Sermons on the Mount and Plain (Matt. 5–7; Luke 6.20–49, cf. Luke 16.16–18).

I SPEECHES AGAINST THE PHARISEES

In place of the small section in Mark in which the scribes are attacked by Jesus (Mark 12.37b–40), Matthew, drawing upon material present in other traditions, has composed an impressive critique of the Pharisaic way of life (Matt. 23.1–36). Luke parallels only the Marcan pericope here (Luke 20.45–7) but elsewhere incorporates much of the additional material that is in Matthew into an extended polemic arising from a controversy between Jesus and a Pharisee (Luke 11.37–52). Both elaborations are undoubtedly secondary, reflecting as they do the redactional interests of the evangelists (cf. Matt. 5.1ff.; 10.1ff.; Luke 7.36ff.; 14.1) but much of the material they contain is certainly original. Due to the parallels with Luke a Q basis is generally acknowledged, though additional material from a source peculiar to Matthew is also usually posited.[1]

---

[1] The most detailed attempt to trace the history of the tradition comes from E. Haenchen, 'Matthäus 23', *Gott und Mensch* (1965), pp. 29–54. The basis of the Matthaean and Lucan elaborations in some kind of extended speech

Here, however, we are only concerned with those passages in which the question of Law is involved.

In contrast to Mark's mention of τῶν γραμματέων (12.38a, cf. Luke 20.46a) and Luke's division of the woes between οἱ Φαρισαῖοι (11.42ff.) and οἱ νομικοί (11.46ff.), Matthew links the two throughout. The combination is redactional in the six woes (23.13, 15, 23, 25, 27, 29) and is probably so here (23.2).[1] Matthew's failure to distinguish between the two groups is frequently held to reflect the situation of his time, in which the scribes did in fact belong to the Pharisaic party.[2] While this may be so, this combination also occurs in Mark 7.1–5 (cf. Matt. 15.1), and already in the time of Jesus the majority of the scribes had allied themselves with the Pharisees, so that there is a partial historical basis for their conjunction. Moreover, elsewhere Matthew links together the Pharisees and Sadducees, an impossible combination after A.D. 70.[3] Luke also refers to both Pharisees and scribes at several points in his gospel where redactional activity is evident (Luke 6.7; 7.30; 11.53; 15.2)

of Jesus appears probable. As V. Taylor, *Mark*, p. 494, observes, 'when these sayings were uttered cannot be determined, but their decisiveness and the width of the opposition revealed suggest an advanced point in the ministry best associated with Jerusalem'.

[1] Apart from 15.1 where he copies Mark 7.1, Matthew always has the order 'scribes and Pharisees'; cf. 5.20; 12.38; 23.2ff.

[2] See especially G. D. Kilpatrick, *Origins*, pp. 113ff.; F. W. Beare, *Records*, pp. 214–15; H. F. Weiss, *Der Pharisäismus in Lichte Überlieferung des Neuen Testaments* (1965), pp. 108–9, and W. G. Kümmel, 'Die Weherufe über die Schriftgelehrten und Pharisäer', *Antijudaismus im Neuen Testament?* (1967, ed. W. Eckert, N. P. Levinson and M. Stohr), p. 137, and many commentators.

[3] The attempt by G. D. Kilpatrick, *Origins*, p. 120, to overcome this difficulty by arguing that Matthew referred to the non-Pharisaic Jews of his time as Sadducees fails to convince. R. Hummel, *Auseinandersetzung*, pp. 18ff., and R. Walker, *Heilsgeschichte*, pp. 11ff., both challenge Kilpatrick's thesis, but they dispute the 'historicising' solution proposed by Strecker. Hummel claims that the Pharisees are the real opposition, scribes and Sadducees only being mentioned in conjunction with them, and that this reflects the solid front of Judaism over against the church in the post-A.D. 70 period. Walker maintains that the terms Sadducees, scribes, Pharisees are merely synonyms referring to 'die eine, das (damalige) Israel des Matthäus-Evangeliums literarische repräsentierende Lehrerschaft' (p. 20). Cf. also S. van Tilborg, *The Jewish Leaders in Matthew* (1972), esp. pp. 1–6.

and his differentiation between them in 11.37ff. is certainly more in accord with their respective functions, though not entirely successful.[1] In any case, as Luke 11.45 itself makes clear, the two could not be completely distinguished.

The first Matthaean section follows in vv.2–4, commencing with the description of the scribes and Pharisees sitting ἐπὶ τῆς Μωϋσῆς καθέδρας. This appears to be a metaphorical reference to their authority with regard to the teaching and interpretation of the Mosaic Law (cf. Ab. 1. 1ff.).[2] Attempts to elicit from the tense of καθίζειν an element of presumption in their assuming this position must be rejected, for if that had been the meaning here we should have expected him to add 'therefore pay no attention to what they say'.[3] The sweeping command that follows in v.3 – πάντα οὖν ὅσα ἐὰν εἴπωσιν ὑμῶν ποίησαι καὶ τηρεῖτε, κατὰ δὲ τὰ ἔργα αὐτῶν μὴ ποιεῖτε – is commonly regarded as a creation of the Jewish-christian community or as representative of Matthew's fundamental affirmation of rabbinic teaching.[4] Between these two extremes attempts have been made to qualify the comprehensive πάντα in v.3a by linking it with the reference to Moses in the previous verse and restricting Jesus' demand for obedience to their exposition of the Law and not the interpretations added to it.[5]

Against these suggestions the following objections must be raised: (a) to ascribe it to an extremely conservative Jewish-christian milieu hardly accords with other material in Matthew associated with the Law that has come from, or been preserved in, a Jewish-christian tradition (e.g., 15.19; 17.24; 22.40).

---

[1] Cf. J. Wellhausen, *Matthaei*, p. 117, and J. Schmid, *Matthäus*, p. 319.

[2] Cf. I. Renov, 'The Seat of Moses', *IEJ*, 5 (1955), 262–7. He rejects attempts that have been made (cf. T. W. Manson, *Sayings*, p. 228, following E. L. Sukenik, *Ancient Synagogues in Palestine and Greece* [1934], pp. 58ff.) to identify it with a literal seat of office in the synagogue.

[3] Against J. Weiss, *Die Schriften des Neuen Testaments* (1907), 1, 370; A. Merx, *Matthäus*, p. 321; and Moulton, II, 458.

[4] The first is the view of E. Haenchen, 'Matthäus 23', p. 31; G. Barth, 'Law', p. 86; W. Trilling, *Israel*, pp. 203–4; G. Strecker, *Gerechtigkeit*, p. 16; S. Schulz, *Botschaft*, p. 161, and R. Walker, *Heilsgeschichte*, p. 134; the second that of R. Hummel, *Auseinandersetzung*, p. 31 and H. Merkel, *NTS*, 14 (1968), 198–9.

[5] This interpretation has been taken up again most recently by A. Wilder, *Ethics*, p. 130 n.30; N. B. Stonehouse, *Origins*, p. 32, and W. D. Davies, *Setting*, p. 106.

This, as we shall see, is also the case in certain other passages from a similar source that have yet to be considered; (b) a fundamental affirmation of rabbinic tradition would be inconsistent in the light of Matthew's explicit denial of it, not only in 16.12, but also 12.11–12a; 15.3ff.; 15.12–14; 19.8–9;[1] (c) the close connection with v.2 rather stresses the authority possessed by the scribes and Pharisees, and this cannot be artificially restricted to that teaching which was a faithful interpretation of the Law. Accordingly, v.3a must be allowed its widest sense, without being interpreted as a dogmatic affirmation of the validity of the rabbinic teaching, and two factors indicate that what we have here is only a preliminary statement which is not intended to be the last word on the matter.[2] In the first place the emphasis in the verse lies in its closing half, 'but do not perform their works', and 3a chiefly functions as a rhetorical preparation in order to point up this charge. Secondly, the insertion of v.4, which speaks of their laying burdens upon others by means of their teaching, yet doing nothing to relieve their load, serves not only to explain the closing words of the previous verse, 'for they talk but do not do anything', but to set the whole of v.3 in proper perspective.[3] This indicates that, for Matthew at least, a blanket approval

---

[1] It has been suggested by H. Merkel, 'Jesus und die Pharisäer', *NTS*, 14 (1967–8), 198–9, that Matt. 16.12, with its warning to beware of the 'leaven' of the Pharisees and Sadducees, is pre-Matthaean. He argues that διδαχή is not a favourite Matthaean term. This is unlikely, for the deliberate clarification of the disciples' understanding in the first part of the verse is certainly a Matthaean characteristic. (Cf. G. Barth, 'Law', pp. 108ff.) Moreover, elsewhere we have seen Matthew retaining tradition which speaks of the erroneous nature of the Pharisaic διδαχή (15.6ff.), introducing material from another source which contains the same emphasis (15.14; 23.16), or altering the tradition to point up the inadequacy of rabbinic teaching (19.8). As for διδαχή itself, it is redactional in one of the only two other uses of it in the gospel (22.33). While, in Mark, ζύμη is left unexplained and, in Luke, it is interpreted as ὑπόκρισις, the original metaphor, as in Matthew, is probably to be interpreted in general terms of the unfortunate pervasive influence of Pharisaic activity.

[2] As recently W. Beilner, *Christus*, p. 203; G. Strecker, *Gerechtigkeit*, p. 16, and earlier E. Klostermann, *Matthäus*, pp. 181–2, and J. Schmid, *Matthäus*, pp. 319–20.

[3] φορτία βαρέα and οὐ...κινῆσαι are usually interpreted in this way. It is not possible therefore to equate the former with the weightier demands of the Law which bring 'death' rather than the 'life' they appeared to

of the scribal teaching cannot have been intended by 3a (cf. also 23.16ff., 24).

It is instructive here to take note of Christ's method of argument in certain other passages at which we have looked. So, for example, in the story of the Rich Young Ruler (Matt. 19.16ff. and pars.) his reply at first appears to be an absolute endorsement of the Mosaic Law. It soon becomes clear, however, that it is only used as the first step in the discussion and that his intention is to surpass its demands and, in the end, leave it quite out of sight. This also occurs in the more primitive Marcan account of the divorce narrative (Mark 10.1ff.), in which Jesus first directs their attention to the Law only to press beyond it to a new and higher demand. So here, 3a is to be regarded as an introductory statement which cannot be separated from the context in which it is placed and interpreted as a comprehensive affirmation of the oral tradition. This understanding of πάντα ...εἴπωσιν is confirmed by the presence of an apparently similar over-statement in v.5a: πάντα...τὰ ἔργα αὐτῶν ποιοῦσιν ...which, in view of the accusation in v.3b that τὰ ἔργα αὐτῶν consist in many cases precisely in οὐ ποιοῦσιν, cannot be intended in an exhaustive sense. Since v.5a is clearly redactional it is just possible that v.3 could therefore be redactional as well. The presence of τηρεῖν (cf. 11.2, 19; 23.5) and ἔργα (cf. 19.17; 28.20), both of which are favourite Matthaean terms, would lend support to this suggestion as well as his particular use of πᾶς in such redactional passages as 3.15b; 5.18c; 28.20a.

In the remainder of the speech it is the works of the Pharisees that are chiefly criticised, their teaching only coming in for consideration in vv.16–22 (to be discussed later in connection

promise, thus anticipating the Pauline doctrine of Rom. 7.10 *et al.* (Against W. C. Allen, *Matthew*, p. 244; A. H. McNeile, *Matthew*, p. 330; J. Schniewind, *Matthäus*, p. 227; A. Schlatter, *Matthäus*, p. 667.) This can scarcely be the meaning of Luke 11.46 and it is unlikely to be the meaning here since, as we have just seen, v.3a cannot be restricted to the scribal exposition of the Mosaic commandments apart from their own casuistic interpretations. Nor, on the other hand, can κινεῖν be understood figuratively of the scribal and Pharisaic refusal to 'touch' the loads themselves. (Against Bill., I, 914; E. Klostermann, *Matthäus*, p. 182; A. Schlatter, *Matthäus*, pp. 667ff.; E. Lohmeyer, *Matthäus*, p. 337.) In view of its use elsewhere (cf. Rev. 2.5; 6.14) and again the parallel in Luke, this is extremely unlikely.

with Matt. 5.33ff.), and vv.23–4 (Luke 11.42) and even then only from the viewpoint of their 'practice' of it. The latter speaks of the Pharisaic custom of tithing, a requirement that was firmly grounded in the Mosaic Law (Lev. 27.30; Num. 18.21; Deut. 12.6; 14.22) and rightly interpreted in the Mishnaic provision in Maas. 1.1. According to scribal regulations it included τὸ ἄνηθον (Maas. 4.5) and τὸ κύμινον (Dem. 2.1) though there is no evidence that τὸ ἡδύοσμον was also liable. Luke differs as to the first two examples and has instead τὸ πήγανον καὶ πᾶν λάχανον, the first of which, according to Sheb. 9.1, was not subject to tithing, and the second far too comprehensive in comparison with scribal teaching. In both, therefore, though more strongly in Luke, the tithing described exceeds later rabbinic requirements.

This concentration on minutiae leads to their neglecting τὴν κρίσιν καὶ τὸ ἔλεος καὶ τὴν πίστιν (Matthew), τὴν κρίσιν καὶ τὴν ἀγάπην τοῦ θεοῦ (Luke). E. Haenchen suggests that the counterbalancing threefold sequence in the Matthaean version is probably the more original, and this closely reflects the prophetic threesome in Mic. 6.8.[1] The description of these characteristics as τὰ βαρύτερα τοῦ νόμου, despite the interpretative additions in 7.12; 22.40, is probably to be ascribed to Matthew's tradition, for here it is not directly the love-commandment according to which the whole of the Law is to be expounded but a somewhat larger circle of basic demands,

[1] E. Haenchen, 'Matthäus 23', p. 39. The differences between the two forms of the saying are so great that it is better to put them down to different forms of the tradition than to Matthaean alteration (R. Bultmann, *Tradition*, p. 131), or the elegance of Lucan idiom (M.-J. Lagrange, *Luc*, p. 344). At first sight it is tempting to see other motives at work in the alterations (cf. G. Bornkamm, 'End-Expectation', pp. 26–7; G. Barth, 'Law', p. 115), especially in view of Matthew's particular interest in ἔλεος and πιστεύειν and Luke's emphasis upon ἀγαπᾶν. It is rather Luke, however, who shows special interest in the substantive πίστις, Matthew only employing the verbal form, while his emphasis upon ἀγαπᾶν (never ἀγάπη) is always in a manward direction. In addition one could ask why, if redactional factors were at work, Matthew did not alter κρίσις to δικαιοσύνη when the former only occurs in contexts of judgment throughout his gospel, and the latter forms a vital theme in his theological understanding. πίστις here is generally related by commentators to men rather than God, but the Mic. 6.8 background cannot be avoided. Cf. T. W. Manson, *Sayings*, p. 235; F. V. Filson, *Matthew*, p. 246.

and the terminology has no recognisable Matthaean counter-part.[1] This once again reflects the interest in the basic com-mandments of the Law, at times in the Decalogue itself, that we have noticed elsewhere in Matthew's tradition, an interest that is motivated by a feeling for scriptural rather than legalistic conviction. Nor should this evaluation be interpreted as having a normative function for Matthew's paranesis, or that of Jesus from whom it originally stems, since the scribal performance is only being measured against its own standard and not against the more demanding claims of Christ. In the context of a polemic against the Pharisees and scribes, at that chiefly against their works and not their teaching, christological considerations are not the primary concern.

Christ's closing injunction follows: ταῦτα δὲ ἔδει ποιῆσαι κἀκεῖνα μὴ ἀφεῖναι (cf. Luke 11.42c).[2] Because of its appar-ently conservative affirmation of the rabbinic regulations it is usually relegated to the Jewish-christian community, though recently it has been emphasised that despite its inclusion by Matthew it is not characteristic of his theological position, and is explicitly contradicted elsewhere.[3] Its appearance in Luke, a gospel not generally given to extreme Jewish-christian ten-dencies, should call for caution in ascribing it to such a milieu, yet to regard it as a genuine conservative approval of the tradition by Jesus, or as an ironical remark, seems inadequate.[4] The solution may again lie in the area of Christ's apologetic procedure, for the weight of the comment falls on the first part of the sentence, as the positive ἔδει. . .ποιῆσαι indicates, and this the following negative μὴ ἀφεῖναι only serves to emphasise.

[1] The phrase is regarded as an editorial insertion by G. Barth, 'Law', p. 80, and R. Hummel, *Auseinandersetzung*, p. 75, though E. Haenchen, 'Matthäus 23', p. 39, and G. Strecker, *Gerechtigkeit*, p. 136 n.4, ascribe it to pre-Matthaean tradition.

[2] The claim of J. Weiss, *Schriften*, I, 373, and E. Klostermann, *Matthäus*, p. 186, that its omission from D is correct, so that with J. Wellhausen, *Das Evangelium Lucae* (1904), p. 61; A. Harnack, *The Sayings of Jesus* (ET 1908), p. 101; W. Grundmann, *Lucas*, p. 248, and T. W. Manson, *Sayings*, p. 98, it is an interpolation from Matthew, is unacceptable.

[3] Among earlier writers see A. Harnack, *Sayings*, p. 110; B. H. Branscomb, *Law*, p. 212; R. Bultmann, *Tradition*, p. 131. A recent advocate of its unrestricted approval by Matthew is H. Merkel, *NTS*, 14 (1968), 199.

[4] For the first cf. A. H. McNeile, *Matthew*, p. 335; for the second cf. J. Schniewind, *Matthäus*, p. 233.

No more than in v.3a, then, should it be isolated from its polemical context and interpreted as a deliberate affirmation of the oral tradition. Nor need κἀκεῖνα any more than πάντα, be literally pressed, for originally it meant no more than 'the less important demands' or, in the tradition as a result of the addition in v.23b, 'the less significant requirements of the Law'. This is abundantly clear for Matthew who in the following verse with both the criticism ὁδηγοὶ τυφλοί and attached proverb concerning the gnat and the camel implicitly polemicises against the minutiae of scribal tradition.

For neither evangelist then, nor for Christ, was a recognition of the validity of the scribal teaching either intended or implied. No particular emphasis upon such teaching occurs in Luke's tradition, the Pharisees being directed to the basic norms of ethical behaviour. Matthew, rather than evidencing a nomistic tendency in this passage, has by his inclusion within and addition to this verse, only highlighted the Pharisaic failure as against the *Law* (v.23b), through a concentration upon insignificant elements in their *tradition* (v.24).[1] In addition he has through his insertion ὑποκριταί in v.23 and in the remaining Woes, made use of a term which has not only polemical but also theological significance for his gospel. The term most probably goes back to Christ himself (Mark 7.6, cf. Matt. 15.7; Luke 6.42, cf. Matt. 7.5) and refers, as we have seen, to the Pharisees' capacity for genuine self-deception.[2] Matthew gives particular weight to another aspect of the term, their playing to the audience of man rather than God (cf. Matt. 6.2, 5, 16; 22.18), an aspect which receives special considera-

---

[1] Vv.25–6 (cf. Luke 11.39ff.) have sometimes been interpreted as an attack upon the Pharisaic traditions concerning ceremonial uncleanness, or even upon the provisions concerning defilement in the Mosaic Law. (Cf. B. H. Branscomb, *Law*, pp. 202ff.; S. Schulz, *Botschaft*, p. 176.) However, although an indirect reference to the Pharisees' concern for ceremonial cleanness may be involved, the main thrust of the parable is directed against the scribes and Pharisees personally. See further T. W. Manson, *Sayings*, p. 269; E. Haenchen, 'Matthäus 23', p. 40; P. Bonnard, *Matthieu*, p. 341, and R. Hummel, *Auseinandersetzung*, p. 58.

[2] E. Haenchen, 'Matthäus 23', pp. 37ff. (followed by E. Schweizer, 'Matthäus 5.17–20', pp. 403f.), incorrectly regards the word as peculiarly Matthaean. Nevertheless, Matthew does elaborate the charge of hypocrisy extensively in his gospel. See further S. van Tilborg, *Jewish Leaders*, pp. 8–25. He also notes the link in Matthew between ὑπόκρισις and ἀνομία.

tion here in 23.5–12 (though without the term specifically being attached to it) and in vv.25–6, 27–8. Elsewhere, however, it continues to express the sincere yet misplaced direction of their religious zeal (Matt. 23.13, 15, 29) or teaching (23.16, 23). That even their desire to appear righteous before men rather than God goes unrecognised by them and is not basically due to conscious dissimulation, appears from the epithet τυφλός in v.26. For Matthew, then, the term is a comprehensive expression for Pharisaic piety and serves as the theological antithesis to the similarly comprehensive δικαιοσύνη which he uses to denote that which Jesus demands of his followers and of τέλειος which is descriptive of the character of those obedient to them.[1] In these passages, however, except in so far as the decisiveness of the attack upon the Pharisees indirectly calls into question the authority of the one who dares to speak in such a manner, christological motifs are not expressly in sight. In view of the absence of any reference to Christ's own more radical demands here, this is not entirely unexpected.

---

[1] Cf. W. Trilling, *Israel*, pp. 108ff., and W. G. Kümmel, 'Weherufe', p. 141, who consider both senses of the word to be present in the gospel. Attempts have, of course, been made to deny the authenticity of this attack upon the scribes and Pharisees in Matt. 23 and Luke 11. Hence it has been suggested that the gospel writers highlighted the opposition to them out of all proportion to the original encounter (H. F. Weiss, *Pharisäismus*, pp. 98ff.; earlier R. T. Herford, *Pharisees*, pp. 114–15; D. W. Riddle, *Jesus and the Pharisees* [1928], p. 144, *et al.*), redirected an attack that was generally against the Sadducees (G. Chwolson, *Das letzte Passamahl Christi und der Tag seines Todes* (1892), pp. 118ff.), misunderstood a critique of the Shammaites as a criticism of the whole (W. O. E. Oesterley and G. H. Box, *Synagogue*[2], p. 123; I. Abrahams, *Studies*, 1, 15ff.), failed to see that Jesus' statement was a defence of Pharisaism against hypocrisy (A. Geiger, *Judentum und Christentum* [1903], pp. 17ff.; G. Lindeskog, *Die Jesusfrage im neuzeitlichen Judentum* [1938], pp. 274ff.; M. Friedländer, *Bewegungen*, pp. 87ff., *et al.*; cf. Ab. 1.17; Sot. 3.4; b.Sot. 22b, *et al.*). Our examination has shown, however, that while Matthew undoubtedly heightens the polemic against the Pharisees in comparison with Mark (cf. further T. F. Glasson, 'Anti-Pharisaism in St Matthew's Gospel', *JQR*, 51 [1961], 316–20), this is nonetheless firmly grounded in the tradition itself and only sharpens or (in some instances) extends the original polemic of Jesus. Moreover, the gospels themselves indicate that not all Pharisees and scribes were opposed to the message of Jesus, so that such attacks as Matt. 23 are directed more to the vices which generally characterise their behaviour than to every individual within their community.

2 THE SERMONS ON THE MOUNT AND PLAIN

Both Matthew and Luke incorporate extended sermons of Jesus at a comparatively early stage in their gospel narratives (Matt. 5–7; Luke 6.20–49) and both contain material relevant to the issue of Law (Matt. 5.17–48; 7.12; Luke 6.27–36). Only in Matthew, however, is an explicit link between the two present. A small segment of the Matthaean teaching, this time more closely related to the question of the Law, does occur later in Luke's gospel (Matt. 5.18, 32; Luke 16.16–18), as well as one other isolated parallel (Luke 12.58–9). The preface to this has a parallel in Matthew divorced from the Sermon (Luke 16.16; Matt. 11.13).[1] It is preferable to examine first the individual injunctions of Christ (Matt. 5.21–48; 7.12; Luke 6.27–36; 16.18), before turning to his more general statements (Matt. 5.17–20; 11.13; Luke 16.16–17) and the wider context in which these occur. In the first place, however, certain significant conclusions may be gathered from a general consideration of the origin of the antithetical framework in Matt. 5.21–48 through which the teaching of Christ is directly related to the Mosaic Law.

Antitheses

The question at issue is whether these are to be regarded as part of the original instruction of Jesus, or whether they owe their presence to the tradition stemming from the early christian community, or to the hand of Matthew himself.

A firm starting point is gained by recalling Matthew's redaction of Mark 10.1ff., especially his addition of the introductory formula λέγω δὲ ὑμῖν in 19.9a and his rearrangement of v.8 to form an antithetical framework not present in the Marcan narrative. In so proceeding Matthew was not introducing an alien element into the pericope, but merely sharpening the antithesis that already existed in a loose form in the earlier account, as well as intensifying the polemic against the Pharisees and the authority of Jesus. With regard to a similar

---

[1] L. Vaganay in 'L'absence du Sermon sur la Montagne chez Marc', *RB*, 58 (1951), 5–46, and 'Existent-il chez Marc quelques traces du Sermon sur la Montagne?', *NT*, 1 [1955], 150–62, has sought to discover traces of the sermon in Mark's gospel, but the evidence he adduces is not at all convincing.

saying over divorce we find the same phenomenon here, for in 5.31–2a over against Luke 16.18, Matthew has again prefaced the statement with an introductory formula and set it in antithetical relationship to the same Mosaic provision as in 19.8. The presence of ἐγώ as part of this formula only occurs in Matthew's gospel and must be regarded as a further attempt at heightening the significance of Christ. Outside 5.21–48 it only occurs in the declaration to Peter in 16.18. Two further antitheses have material for comparison in Luke. A parallel to Matt. 5.39bff. occurs in Luke 6.29ff., but again the introductory formula and antithetical context are lacking in the latter account. The following passage is even more instructive, for here Matthew actually provides a legal context in which to set the declaration in 5.44bff. Elsewhere he assigns special significance to Lev. 19.18 (Matt. 7.12; 22.39) and in one instance introduces it to form part of just such a framework for a saying of Jesus as this (19.19b).[1] What is particularly of interest here is the presence in Luke of an introductory formula: ἀλλὰ ὑμῖν λεγω τοῖς ἀκούουσιν (6.27a). In his gospel, however, it serves only as a preface to the collection of sayings which follow rather than, as in Matthew, both here and elsewhere, of an individual logion. When Matthew uses this formula then, as with the antithetical framework itself, in both instances he is not innovating but taking up and extending the application of a feature already firmly embedded in the tradition.

For the remaining three antitheses there is no comparative material on which an analysis of Matthaean redaction can be based, and it has been generally concluded that they stem from Jesus.[2] Quite apart from the evidence already supplied

[1] The limitation of Matthew's provision of the antithetical form to the third antithesis alone, while the remainder stem from the tradition cannot, therefore, be sustained. Against B. W. Bacon, Studies, p. 181; B. H. Streeter, Studies, pp. 248ff.; B. H. Branscomb, Law, pp. 234ff.; B. Lanwer, 'Gesetz', p. 23; G. D. Kilpatrick, Origins, pp. 26, 85; E. Percy, Botschaft, p. 150, and W. D. Davies, Setting, pp. 387ff.

[2] So already M. Albertz, Die synoptischen Streitgespräche (1921), pp. 146ff., and since then R. Bultmann, Tradition, pp. 134–6; W. G. Kümmel, 'Rabbinen', pp. 4, 6; H. Braun, Radikalismus, II, 5 n.2; G. Bornkamm, RGG³, I, 1048; G. Barth, 'Law', p. 94; R. Hummel, Auseinandersetzung, p. 72; K. Niederwimmer, Freiheit, p. 155 n.7; S. Schulz, Botschaft, p. 186, and many others. Most recently see E. Lohse, 'Ich aber sage euch', Der Ruf Jesu, pp. 189–90 and 200–1.

concerning the secondary nature of the third, fifth and sixth antitheses, it has been suggested that there are other grounds on which a distinction can be made between these and the first, second and fourth. It is argued that while the sayings paralleled in Luke (3, 5, 6) are, formally speaking, wisdom sayings which Matthew has artificially formulated into legal pronouncements, the first group of sayings (1, 2, 4) were never divorced from their antithetical structure since the radical statements they contain are only intelligible in relation to that with which they are set in contrast. Furthermore, whereas in the original antitheses the premise takes the form of a prohibition which is radicalised, in the secondary formulations it is an instruction which is not only surpassed, but overthrown. While the second of these arguments is quite correct,[1] it is difficult to agree that in 1, 2 and 4 we have sayings that are only intelligible in relation to the thesis, while in 3, 5 and 6 this is not the case. Further evidence that even in these formulations the antithetical framework might have a secondary character comes from a tendency in Matthew's tradition that has already been noted. In 15.19 it was observed that the list of things causing defilement was more accurately rendered in terms of the Decalogue, with 'murder' and 'adultery' (after 'evil thoughts') being placed at the head of the list. Since no decisive importance was attached to this alteration by Matthew himself, it was regarded as most probably stemming from prior catechetical influence. More significantly in 19.18–19 the list of commands set over against the more radical demand of Jesus was also fashioned into greater conformity with the Decalogue, commencing with the prohibitions against 'murder' and 'committing adultery'. We seem to detect, then, in the tradition prior to Matthew, a desire to set the positive demands of Christ in more direct relationship with the Decalogue commandments. Moreover, in both instances these commandments, although surpassed, are not

---

[1] The attempt therefore by H. Marriott, *The Sermon on the Mount* (1925), pp. 250–1; E. von Dobschutz, *ZNW*, 27 (1928), 342; A. Descamps, *Les Justes et La Justice dans Les Évangiles* (1950), pp. 120ff., and J. Dupont, *Les Béatitudes* (1958), p. 157, to find not only a 'radicalising' present in the fourth antithesis, but also an 'abrogation' is to be rejected, as is the similar endeavour by B. Lanwer, 'Gesetz', p. 26 and N. B. Stonehouse, *Witness*, p. 199, with respect to the last antithesis.

explicitly abrogated. In the first case this occurs through their juxtaposition with their more radical neighbours, i.e., 'murder' – 'evil thoughts'; 'adulteries' – 'fornications', and in the second through the more demanding call to discipleship, i.e., 'sell all and give'.

It is therefore at least possible that for the first two antitheses dealing with murder and adultery, as well as the fourth, since its interest in oaths is elsewhere a matter of concern in Matthew's tradition (Matt. 23.16–22), the formulation is not authentic, but rather a framework into which originally isolated words of Christ have been set.[1] Innovation in part this may have been but not in essence, since such an activity is merely drawing out the implications of that OT background against which Christ's ministry was framed and which he himself, on several occasions, brought into direct relation with his own teaching (Matt. 12.1ff.; 19.1ff.; 19.16ff.). It is by no means improbable that similar discussions originally lay behind these statements that have since dropped away in the handing on of the tradition.

[1] E. von Dobschutz, ZNW, 27 (1928), 342, therefore, cannot be followed when he claims that the first two antitheses were original formulations on the analogy of which the remaining four were composed, a view that has recently been revived by H. T. Wrege, *Bergpredigt*, p. 58. E. Percy, *Botschaft*, pp. 143ff., on the other hand, has argued that the second antithesis was a later insertion into the gospel resulting from a catechetical desire to include a reference to the seventh commandment. Such a desire however, as we have seen, pre-dates the composition of Matthew. He reasons further from the presence of similar teaching within rabbinic Judaism, yet, as we shall see, substantial differences between the antithesis and its Jewish parallels are discernible. As to the different manner of argument here – it is the only antithesis in which a redefinition of the thesis occurs – surely this counters any idea of its creation on the 'analogy' of the earlier models. It should also be noted that while the distinction between 1, 2, 4 and 3, 5, 6 occurs from the material point of view, stylistically Matthew has veiled it by imposing a formal division between the first three and last three antitheses: thus (a) only the first and fourth antitheses commence with the formula Ἠκούσατε ὅτι ἐρρέθη τοῖς ἀρχαίοις (b) there is the presence of πάλιν at the beginning of the fourth antithesis: (c) in 1, 2, 3 the antithesis has a conditional form, while in 4, 5, 6 it is an affirmative or negative imperative. That the shortened formula which introduces the third antithesis is indicative of its merely being an extension of the second, or of its pre-Matthaean formulation is, against J. Schmid, *Matthäus*, p. 102; F. W. Beare, *Records*, pp. 59, *et al.*, to be rejected. Only 1 and 4 have the full formula, 2, 5, 6 omitting ἀρχαίοις, and 3 both ἀρχαίοις and ἠκούσατε, so that there is no strict uniformity throughout.

Furthermore, we know from Mark 7.10, with its quotation of
Ex. 20.12 followed by 21.7, that the basis for the antithetical
construction, even the formulation of the thesis in two sections
in Matt. 5.21, 33, 43, is also grounded in the teaching of Jesus.
Thus even if, with H. Conzelmann, we agree that it is at least
questionable whether the antithetical character of these particular sayings goes back to Jesus himself, we must insist that it
condensed the impression which the teaching and attitude of
Jesus conveyed, and that formally it was not altogether without
foundation in the manner in which his own message was at
times presented.[1]

However, for the present, we must leave to one side the consideration of the precise significance of the introductory formulas to both thesis and antithesis, since the special intent with
which they are used can only be understood in light of the statements they introduce.

First Antithesis (Matt. 5.21–6). In this passage the thesis contains
a prohibition – οὐ φονεύσεις – based on the Decalogue (Ex.
20.13; Deut. 5.18), together with a legal pronouncement –
ὃς δ' ἂν φονεύσῃ ἔνοχος ἔσται τῇ κρίσει – in conditional form,
whose source is uncertain.[2] It has frequently been regarded as a
reflection of scribal casuistry and the following antithesis therefore interpreted as a direct attack upon the oral tradition.[3]
κρίσις could relate to the judicial tribunals which dealt with
such cases, but these were set up to administer the Law and
should not be considered in contradiction to it (Bill., 1, 257ff.).
Furthermore, the antithesis that follows is a counter to the first
part of the thesis – the Decalogue commandment – not the so-
called 'scribal amendment'. It has been suggested, therefore,
that the whole of the thesis is grounded in the OT and that the
addition in 21b is only a reflection of those passages prescribing
the death-sentence for one who has murdered (Ex. 21.12; Lev.

[1] H. Conzelmann, *Grundriss der Theologie des Neuen Testaments* (1967), p. 140.
[2] The insertion of εἰκῇ in DWΘλφ *et al.* is less a 'probable' part of the original
text qualifying the antithesis (T. W. Manson, *Sayings*, p. 155), or a genuine
semitic idiom (cf. CDC 7.8), reinforcing the saying rather than limiting it
(P. Wernberg-Møller, *NTS*, 3 [1956–7], 71–3), than a later gloss added,
perhaps, in defence of Christ's use of μωρός in Matt. 23.17.
[3] Cf. A. H. McNeile, *Matthew*, p. 61; M.-J. Lagrange, *Matthieu*, p. 97;
N. B. Stonehouse, *Witness*, p. 201.

24.17; Num. 35.30–1; Deut. 19.11–12).[1] However, it is reasonable to ask why κρίσις rather than θάνατος was used if this were the case (cf. Mark 7.10b). The solution is to be found in other Old Testament passages such as Deut. 17.8–13 which speak explicitly of the activity of 'judgment' lying behind such a sentence.[2] It is this rather than the later scribal procedure that the thesis had in view, and the whole of v.21 must be considered an expression of the Old Testament position.

The counter-statement of Jesus then sets side-by-side three radical statements which assert the equivalence of anger, insult and contempt with murder and therefore go far beyond the Jewish requirement in v.21.[3] Certainly, the rabbis, as the OT (Prov. 14.17; 15.1; 16.32; 29.11, 22; Eccles. 7.9), Apocrypha and Pseudepigrapha (Ecclus. 1.22; 10.6; 27.30; 28.3, 7;

[1] As W. C. Allen, *Matthew*, p. 47; A. Schlatter, *Matthäus*, p. 166; B. Lanwer, 'Gesetz', p. 23; W. Michaelis, *Das Evangelium nach Matthäus*, i (1948), 254; T. W. Manson, *Sayings*, p. 155; E. Lohmeyer, *Matthäus*, p. 120. It has sometimes been suggested that it is a combination of both Old Testament law and scribal tradition that is involved here. So C. Votaw, *DB*, Ext. Vol., 25ff.; R. Hummel, *Auseinandersetzung*, p. 72; G. Barth, 'Law', p. 94, and G. Strecker, *Gerechtigkeit*, p. 146.

[2] This is to be preferred to the other solutions that have been offered: (a) M. McNamara, *The New Testament and the Palestinian Targum to the Pentateuch* (1966), pp. 127–9, who claims that it is a reference to a current Jewish paraphrasis, not of the law-texts which speak of 'death' for the murderer rather than 'judgment', but of Gen. 9.6. This he regards as the basis from which the Jewish law of murder developed; (b) R. A. Guelich, 'Law', pp. 76ff., who rightly interprets κρίσις as 'judicial process' but argues that the 'judicial practice' in the time of Jesus was chiefly in view. This is possible for 22a, but less likely for 21b; (c) E. Percy, *Botschaft*, pp. 125ff., who refers it to the 'local court' through which such judicial process was channelled in the first century. This usage however is lexically foreign to both classical and NT Greek (L/S, i, 997); (d) W. C. Allen, *Matthew*, p. 47, who understands it as 'judicial sentence', ἔνοχος being followed by a dative of penalty. In 22b, however, where the dative is present a penalty is lacking, and in 22c where the idea of penalty is explicit, the dative is lacking. This also speaks against its being interpreted in the sense of 'divine sentence' as has occasionally been suggested.

[3] It can scarcely be maintained, therefore, that the teaching in v.22a relating to anger is 'thoroughly Jewish' and a 'rabbinic commonplace' as is the case with B. H. Branscomb, *Law*, p. 240, and C. G. Montefiore, *Gospels*, ii, 60. See also H. Huber, *Die Bergpredigt* (1932), p. 80; H. M. Teeple, *Prophet*, p. 79; A. Finkel, *Pharisees*, p. 162. ἀδελφός should, of course, in v.22a, be referred to the 'fellow-Israelite'. Cf. H. F. von Soden, *TDNT*, i, 145.

30.24; Ps.Sol. 16.10) before them, often spoke out against anger (Ab. 2.10; 5.11; b.Ber. 29b) and for gentleness (b.Ned. 28a; b.Pes. 113b; b.Kidd. 71a). The only apocryphal or pseudepigraphal statement to approach Matt. 5.22a is 2 Enoch 44.2 which asserts that 'he who vents anger on any man without injury, the Lord's great anger will cut him down'. In contrast to Jesus' statement, however, this specifies a concrete application of the emotion (cf. Prov. 19.11), contains the modifying clause 'without injury', and is probably to be reckoned later than the saying of Jesus.[1] The rabbis certainly adjudged it to be a particularly heinous sin (b.Shabb. 105a; Tos.Bab.Kamm. 9.31), but this relates to 'gewaltsame Zornes-ausbruch' not, as in Matt. 5.22, 'um irgendwelche Zornesauf-wallung überhaupt als Äusserung des Unwillens'.[2] The un-fortunate consequences for the person himself are spelled out in such passages as b.Pes. 66b; Tanch.Huqq. 29ff.; j.Ber. 4.2, 7d, and though the element of 'judgment' does appear, nowhere is the warning formulated either as a deliberate rule or in the context of the sixth commandment. Therefore, the form in which they are uttered, and the judgment of which they speak, is substantially milder than the corresponding statement of Jesus. Closer to 5.22a is the saying in b.Ned.11a that 'He who loses his temper is exposed to all the torments of Gehenna', but both this and b.Ned. 22b are only speaking of the period over which the anger lasts, while that of R. Eliezer in Der.Er. 10 that 'he who hates his neighbour, lo he belongs to the shedders of blood' goes far beyond the 'momentary anger' of which Jesus speaks, and refers to something that was already condemned in the Law (Lev. 19.17).

In general we may conclude that the saying of Jesus (a) deals with 'anger' of a much less concrete variety; (b) heightens the emphasis on judgment by associating it with the punishment for

---

[1] K. Berger, 'Gesetzesauslegung' (1968), pp. 154–5, does not give sufficient weight to these differences. His desire to place 5.22a firmly in the context of late-Jewish exegesis of the sixth commandment in light of Gen. 9.6 must therefore be questioned, the more so in view of the way in which the saying is formulated. Jesus leaves mere exegesis far behind. He 'legislates', and the content of his 'legislation' is set over against the sixth command-ment. On this see further comments of W. G. Kümmel, 'Rabbinen', p. 4.

[2] Cf. E. Percy, *Botschaft*, p. 134.

transgression of the sixth commandment; (c) formally gives the impression of being more than ethical advice; (d) is almost certainly earlier than all the rabbinic utterances which have been examined. Against general opinion to the contrary, this is also most likely the case with 22b and c, for the various rabbinic parallels contain stronger *Schimpfwörter*, prescribe more lenient punishment, and are not usually stated in as strong terms. No real parallel therefore occurs.[1] His teaching is thus something new which speaks on an altogether different level to the OT law that preceded it. It does not merely affirm it nor does it explicitly abrogate it. Yet it certainly surpasses it. This is confirmed by the two illustrations in vv.23ff. (cf. Mark 11.25) and vv.25ff. (Luke 12.57-9) which either by Matthew or, more probably, already in the tradition were appended to this antithesis. Rather than any incompatibility lying between these examples and the material that precedes, a real continuation of thought occurs, for here the positive side of the negative demand in v.22 is set out in terms of reconciliation.[2]

[1] Cf. J. Leipoldt, *Rabbinen*, pp. 34ff.; B. Lanwer, 'Gesetz', p. 33; E. Percy, *Botschaft*, p. 141. This is also true for Qumran. See H. Braun, *Qumran*, I, 16 against H. M. Teeple, *Prophet*, p. 179. On 22b, c, see further H. Huber, *Bergpredigt*, p. 85; E. Percy, *Botschaft*, pp. 137-43. This removes a frequent barrier to their acceptance as an authentic part of Jesus' reply. Objections upon lexical grounds are considered and dismissed by R. A. Guelich, 'Law' Exc. I, pp. 271-82. He also rejects attempts to distinguish between intention (22a) and deed (22b, c) so that the latter are regarded as secondary additions diminishing the cutting power of the antithesis, for throughout 5.21-48 it is not the dichotomy between thought and deed that is involved. (Against E. Klostermann, *Matthäus*, p. 43; T. W. Manson, *Sayings*, pp. 155ff.; J. Schmid, *Matthäus*, p. 98.) It should also be noted that interpretation of 22b, c, as christian halakoth of a practical nature scarcely does justice to the utterly 'impractical' nature of legislating with respect to such common and mild epithets as ῥακά and μῶρος, not to speak of the disproportionate punitive consequences that we have associated with them. (Against R. Bultmann, *Tradition*, p. 134, n.1; H. Braun, *Radikalismus*, II, 24 n.9, and V. E. Hasler, 'Das Herzstück der Bergpredigt', *TZ*, 15 [1959], 92ff.) In any case, what likelihood is there of the early church's creating the saying concerning Μωρέ when it was aware that Jesus himself had hurled this epithet at the Pharisees (Matt. 23.17)?
[2] J. Jeremias, 'Lass allda deine Gabe', *ABBA* (1966), pp. 103-7; E. Lohmeyer, *Matthäus*, pp. 124-5; H. T. Wrege, *Bergpredigt*, p. 61. Their significance has, however, been rather over-interpreted by H. J. Ljungmann, *Gesetz*, p. 77.

Second Antithesis (Matt. 5.27–30). The thesis is formulated as a
straightforward citation of the seventh commandment (Ex.
20.14; Deut. 5.18) and there is no question of scribal interpretation being involved. The antithesis with its equation of
the lustful glance with adultery has been commonly interpreted
as in complete agreement with rabbinic teaching and as offering
no advance upon it. Already in the OT self-enticement towards
another woman, whether by means of 'coveting' (Ex. 20.17;
Deut. 5.21; Prov. 6.25) or 'seeing' (Job 31.1ff.) was condemned. This same line of thought was continued in the
Apocryphal and Pseudepigraphal literature, where both 'heart'
and 'eyes' were warned against dwelling upon a woman (Eccles.
9.5, 8; 42.12) or even considered to be equivalent to fornication
(Ecclus. 26.9; Jub. 20.4; Test.Reu. 4.8, 11; 5.6, 14.1; Benj.
8.2). This is also the substance of several rabbinic passages, e.g.,
'He who looks at a woman with desire is as one who has criminal
intercourse' (Tr. Kalla, cf. Bill., I, 299ff.). However, these
concern more 'das lüsterne Beschauen entblösster Körperteile'
than 'die innere Begierde nach einer bestimmten Frau', of
which 5.28 speaks.[1] Moreover, in rabbinic thought adultery
could not be committed by a minor, with the wife of a minor,
or with the wife of a non-Jew (b.Sanh. 52b), so that this must be
considered as a restriction upon those utterances in which
adultery is traced back to desire.[2] Again, whereas the Jewish
parallels use 'heart' like 'eye', as an instrument through which
adultery is committed, in 5.28 it is referred to as the basis of the

---

[1] Cf. E. Bischoff, *Rabbinen*, p. 42, on Ab.Zar. 20a; b.Erub. 18b and b.Ber. 61a.
G. F. Moore, *Judaism*, II, 267ff.; C. G. Montefiore, *Gospels*, II, 63; B. H.
Branscomb, *Law*, p. 242; T. W. Manson, *Sayings*, p. 157, and H. Braun,
Radikalismus, II, 5 n.2, are therefore mistaken in identifying Jesus' position
with rabbinic teaching here. The attempt by P. Bonnard, *Matthieu*, p. 66,
to define the action in Matt. 5.28 as a 'regard-geste concret', and that of
A. Pallis, *Notes*, pp. 30–1, to interpret βλέπειν by means of the modern
Greek expression κοιτάζειν 'he who pays attention to', are both uncon-
vincing, as is the suggestion of V. E. Hasler, *TZ*, 15 (1959), 94, who finds
evidence of christian casuistry at work in the different steps of adultery
that are indicated – thought in the heart, covetous look, use of the hand,
actual deed. Certainly, however, 'lust' includes not only the emotion but
the will for possession of what does not belong to one. Cf. F. Büchsel,
TDNT, III, 171.
[2] Certainly no equation with Qumran can be defended (see H. Braun,
Qumran, I, 16, against H. M. Teeple, *Prophet*, p. 79; R. A. Murphy, *The*

action and, in any case, is regarded here and elsewhere as 'der Mittelpunkt des inneren Lebens des Menschen'.[1] Finally, what are uttered by the rabbis as occasional ethical pronouncements is here more strictly formulated and not one of these sayings comes from a rabbi who preceded, or was contemporary with, Christ. This was not simply an exposition or radicalisation of the seventh commandment, for by equating the covert desire with the overt act Jesus was demanding a new relationship which actually transcended the requirements of the Law. The seriousness of the demand is underlined by the appended sayings in vv.29–30 (cf. Matt. 18.8–9; Mark 9.43ff.) which rather than being inapplicable here are, in view of the frequent warnings against 'hand' and 'eye' in rabbinic sayings against adultery, extremely pertinent.[2]

Third Antithesis (Matt. 5.31–2). Instead of being grounded in a Decalogue commandment the premise of the following antithesis is based on the divorce regulations in Deut. 24.1ff.[3] It has already been noted that this antithesis is to be treated as a separate unit to that which precedes it. Clearly Matthew introduced it at this point because of the related substance of the two sayings, but it would be unjustified to regard it as

---

DSS and the Bible [1957], p. 85), while the oft-quoted saying in Mek.Ex. 15.37 refers to the OT regulation in Num. 15.37ff. which speaks of 'whoring' only in a metaphorical sense, and therefore cannot be considered a real parallel. E. Percy, *Botschaft*, pp. 143–4, does not notice this.

[1] J. Behm, *TWNT*, III, p. 614. Cf. more fully C. Edlund, *Das Auge der Einfalt* (1952), pp. 23ff.

[2] G. D. Kilpatrick, *Origins*, pp. 18–19, has located several specifically Matthaean characteristics in the sayings, thus arguing against the suggestion of E. Lohmeyer, *Matthäus*, p. 126, that their link with the antithesis is pre-Matthaean.

[3] *Contra* E. Lohmeyer, *Matthäus*, p. 127; J. Schmid, *Matthäus*, p. 104, *et al.* The attempt by K. Berger, 'Gesetzesauslegung' (1968), p. 159, to explain Jesus' approach in vv.27ff. and vv.31f., as also the following antithesis in vv.33ff. in terms of the late Jewish exegesis of the Decalogue commandments, which was controlled by the thought of preventing impurity, cannot be admitted because (a) it is a surpassing, not exposition, of the commandment that is here involved; (b) other motives are involved than that of impurity, i.e., here the 'oneness' and 'indissolubility' of marriage; (c) for this antithesis, at least, exegesis of a Decalogue commandment is not involved.

merely an extension of the previous pericope and as basically linked, not with the provision in Deut. 24.1ff., but with the seventh commandment. Here we need to look briefly at the relationship of Matt. 5.32 and Luke 16.18 to the Marcan and Matthaean parallels already examined. The exceptive clause and introductory formula apart, both of which are peculiar to Matthew, Mark 10.11, Luke 16.18a and Matt. 19.9 are in agreement that (a) anyone who divorces his wife (b) and marries another (c) commits adultery, to which Mark 10.11c adds 'against her'. This, it was suggested, was an addition demonstrating Mark's particular interest in the wide application of the saying (cf. also v.12). It is therefore Luke 16.18a which emerges as the most original formulation of the first part of the saying. Matt. 5.32a, although it stylistically parallels Luke 16.18a, nevertheless stands to one side from all three versions of the logion for it omits (b) and instead of (c) has 'makes her an adulteress', so that the divorce is located not in the further marriage of the divorcing partner, but in the further marriage of the divorced wife, thus bringing the whole saying more in line with the Jewish understanding of adultery.[1]

This last point is made more explicit by 5.32b which speaks of the adultery committed by the person marrying the divorced wife. It is only Luke 16.18b which parallels this second part of the Matthaean saying, Matt. 19.9 restricting itself to the first clause only, and Mark 10.12 providing a different turn of the argument altogether. Is it possible to discover a deliberate 'Jewish' modification in 5.32? It is rather the case that since the question of adultery has already been dealt with in the previous pericope it is Matthew's concentration on the theme of divorce which has resulted in the more limited nature of 5.32 over against its parallel formulations, including his own re-definition of adultery in 19.9. This also results in a more pointed antithesis:

---

[1] R. C. H. Lenski, *Matthew*, p. 226, seeks to avoid this conclusion by attaching great significance to the passive character of the verb, and claims that rightly interpreted it means: 'he brings it about that she is stigmatised as an adultress' (i.e., at the time of the divorce). In view of the significance attached to re-marriage as a component in the committing of adultery in Matt. 19.9, Mark 10.11, Luke 16.18 and Matt. 5.32b here, this is scarcely probable. Cf. G. Strecker, *Gerechtigkeit*, p. 132.

ὃς ἂν ἀπολύσῃ τὴν γυναῖκα αὐτοῦ/δότω αὐτῇ ἀποστάσιον
πᾶς ὁ ἀπολύων τὴν γυναῖκα αὐτοῦ . . ./ποιεῖ αὐτὴν μοιχευθῆναι

The exceptive clause, as we have already seen, is also geared directly to the Deuteronomic provision. Thus the theme of adultery is introduced only in a subordinate way to emphasise the newness of the teaching on *divorce*.[1] However, it would not be true to say that while Luke represents a 'new' teaching regarding both divorce and adultery, Matthew has a 'new' teaching regarding divorce only. The emphasis in Matthew is certainly upon the latter, but the new definition of divorce necessarily brings with it, if only as a consequence, a new situation with regard to adultery as well. No rabbi would have regarded a re-marriage of the divorced wife as adultery, though certainly he would have objected less to that idea than the ascription of adultery to the man when he re-married. It is only in the concentration on the wife that the more Jewish atmosphere of Matt. 5.32 consists. We conclude, then, that it is the Lucan formulation in 16.18 that is probably the most original form of the saying.[2]

It has already been noted that this saying of Jesus cannot be considered an 'exposition' of the sixth commandment, even less a declaration of the true 'intention' behind Deut. 24.1. Though, as is generally maintained, an 'abrogation' of Deut. 24.1 appears to be involved, even this is not strictly the case. Certainly the teaching of Jesus altogether transcends the Mosaic regulation but, as we have seen, that regulation continues to bear witness against the Pharisees concerning their 'hardness of heart' and indirectly testifies to their refusal to accept the new situation, and the demands appropriate to it, inaugurated by the presence of Jesus. Rabbinic or other parallels were entirely lacking.

Fourth Antithesis (Matt. 5.33–7). No exact parallel exists to either part of the thesis in v.33: οὐκ ἐπιορκήσεις/ἀποδώσεις δὲ τῷ κυρίῳ τοὺς ὅρκους σου. It is possible that the third Decalogue commandment lies behind its formation, but as v.33 deals with only a particular application of that commandment, it is

---

[1] Cf. further G. Strecker, *Gerechtigkeit*, pp. 133ff.

[2] In agreement here are R. Bultmann, *Tradition*, p. 132; T. W. Manson, *Sayings*, pp. 136ff.; G. Strecker, *Gerechtigkeit*, p. 131, and, most recently, H. Baltensweiler, *Ehe*, pp. 59ff.

unlikely that any direct relationship exists between the two. Nearest to v.33a is Lev. 19.12, while behind 33b lie such passages as Num. 30.2ff.; Deut. 23.21ff., and Ps. 50.14 (LXX 49.14).[1] Elsewhere in the Mosaic legislation oaths in God's name are explicitly enjoined. As with the addition in v.21b, the second clause of the thesis has the nature of a summary of the OT position.

In the antithesis not only 'false oaths' and 'unfulfilled oaths' are excluded, but all oaths. ὅλως is quite emphatic and any attempt to weaken its force by reference to the distinction between public and private life, its limitation to a prohibition of false swearing, or the restriction of its application to the casuistic examples of oaths that follow in vv.34b–36, must be rejected.[2] Neither should Matt. 23.16ff. (vv.18–20, probably stemming from the community) be regarded as contrasting with the radical demand of 5.34a, for as in 23.3a and 23.23b the teaching is not to be construed as a positive command for the disciples, but is rather an attack upon the Pharisees at the level of their own teaching by proving to them the real and binding character of their spurious oaths.[3] The first two sugges-

---

[1] The latter provides the closest formal parallel, but it is concerned with 'vows' rather than 'oaths'. The attempt by W. C. Allen, *Matthew*, p. 53; T. W. Manson, *Sayings*, p. 158, and W. D. Davies, *Setting*, p. 240, to understand v.33b in terms of 'vows' cannot be accepted, for it not only introduces confusion into the use of the term ὅρκος in v.33b over against ἐπιορκεῖν in v.33a, but also an alien element into the context of the whole pericope, difficulties that can only be overcome by regarding the whole of v.33 (Allen), or v.33b (Manson, Davies) as secondary. Earlier, S. Liebermann, *Greek in Jewish Palestine* (1942), pp. 115ff., had argued for an interchange of the two terms in Jewish circles, while P. Fiebig, *Jesu Bergpredigt* (1924), p. 66 n.171, had pointed out that in the Mishnah (Ned. 2.1) the two were often placed in conjunction with one another. H. Danby, *Mishnah*, p. 204 n.1, has nevertheless maintained that in rabbinic teaching a distinction between the two continued to exist for 'a vow forbids a certain thing to be used. . .while an oath forbids the swearer to do a certain thing although it is not a thing forbidden in itself'.

[2] In agreement are A. Schlatter, *Matthäus*, pp. 181ff.; J. Schneider, *TWNT*, v, 178–9, and G. Stählin, 'Zum Gebrauch von Beteuerungsformeln im NT', *NT*, 5 (1962), 117.

[3] It is thus unnecessary to regard it as pre-redactional material that is not in agreement with Matthew's thought, as G. Strecker, *Gerechtigkeit*, p. 16 n.6; R. Hummel, *Auseinandersetzung*, pp. 79–80, and S. Schulz, *Botschaft*, p. 161, attempt to do.

tions have no basis whatever in the text and even if vv.34b–36 are, as is generally suggested, regarded as an expansion from the christian community, it is not necessary to interpret them in a casuistic manner, for μήτε...μήτε should be understood in the sense of μηδέ...μηδέ (cf. Bill., I, 328).[1] Nor should the expression in v.37 be regarded as a new 'substitute' oath for those excluded by Jesus. Rather does the prohibition against swearing assert the binding character of all words.

Warnings against the taking of oaths and vows lightly already occur throughout the OT (Jer. 7.9; Hos. 4.15; Zech. 5.3; 8.7; Eccles. 5.4–5; 9.2) and Apocrypha (Wisd. 14.30–1; Ecclus. 23.9ff.), as also the Rabbis (Bill., I, 328ff.), but these never lead to a prohibition of all oaths as we find in this saying of Jesus. Comparison has frequently been made with b.Shab. 36a in which the double 'yes' and 'no' are interpreted as an oath. However the evidence of this rabbinic text is extremely late (c. A.D. 350), wherever else the expression occurs in the rabbinic sources it is always in a non-formulaic sense, and repetition is a common semitic usage to emphasise the character of what is being said.[2] The occurrence of the expression in 2 Enoch 49.1ff. that is also commonly mentioned in this connection is probably a later interpolation, since only one MSS. tradition contains it.[3] Again therefore, both in regard to contemporary

---

[1] P. Minear, 'Yes and No: The Demand for Honesty in the Early Church', *NT*, 13 (1971), 1–13, regards vv.34b–35 as illustrating only the negative prohibition, and as obscuring the thrust of the positive command for honesty, but R. A. Guelich, 'Law', Exc. II, pp. 283–93, rightly points out that 'the meaning and intent of vv.34b–36 was neither to counter simply the scribal practice of using substitute formulas for the divine name, nor was it aimed merely at the common asseverative phrases of the day, but rather these clauses elaborate the implications of 5.34a and in doing so block any casuistic attempt to sidestep its thrust' (pp. 286–7).

[2] See J. Mann, 'Oaths and Vows in the Synoptic Gospels', *AJT*, 21 (1917), 362; A. Schlatter, *Matthäus*, p. 183; K. Bornhäuser, *Bergpredigt*, p. 88; J. Staudinger, *Die Bergpredigt* (1957), p. 105.

[3] Cf. A. Vaillant, *Le Livre des Secrets d'Hénoch* (1952), p. 109 n.7. Against the suggestion of V. E. Hasler, 'Gesetz', p. 14, that the addition is illustrative of Matthew's casuistic tendency, G. Strecker, *Gerechtigkeit*, p. 133, notes that v.37b, due to the presence of the typical Matthaean terms περισσός and πονηρός is probably redactional and this explicitly prevents any casuistic misunderstanding of v.37a. Resort therefore to (a) the priority of James 5.12 (M. Dibelius, *Der Brief der Jakobus* [1964⁴], p. 268, et al.);

Jewish teaching and Old Testament requirements, we have a pronouncement of Jesus that moves in a different realm to anything that can be brought into relation with it.

Fifth Antithesis (Matt. 5.38–42). A number of OT passages contain the thesis of v.38 with its reference to 'an eye for an eye and a tooth for a tooth' (Ex. 21.24; Deut. 19.21; Lev. 24.20). In each case other applications of the principle involved are present and these differ in each context in which the passages occur. Thus again we appear to have a summary of the Law's demands on a particular point.[1] The opening words of the antithesis in v.39 – μὴ ἀνιστῆναι τῷ πονηρῷ – have been subject to two main lines of interpretation, its traditional understanding in terms of 'non-resistance' and the more recent view of its signifying the 'foregoing of legal rights'. In favour of the latter it is argued that (a) the following illustration in v.39b which speaks of a slap on the cheek is, according to rabbinic parallels, a case of insult rather than damage (cf. Tos.Bab.Kamm. 8.4; Bill., I, 341ff.; IV, 1, 18ff.); (b) the second and third examples in vv. 40–1 do not deal with mutilation but also have a judicial context, the first through Matthew's addition τῷ θέλοντί σοι κριθῆναι...λαβεῖν which alters a robbery setting in the Lucan parallel (Luke 6.29), and the second being an insertion by Matthew into the text;[2] (c) the omission of the phrase 'life for life' from the biblical maxim quoted; (d) the OT legal back-

(b) a mis-translation of the Aramaic (T. W. Manson, *Sayings*, p. 159, *et al.*); or (c) remote parallels (E. Kutsch, *Ev.Th.* [1960], pp. 206ff.), in an attempt to safeguard the radical nature of the saying, all become unnecessary. B. H. Branscomb, *Law*, p. 243, is therefore quite wrong when he asserts that 'here again the teaching is quite in line with many rabbinic utterances'. See rather G. Stählin, *NT*, 5 (1962), 116; E. Percy, *Botschaft*, pp. 147–8. Also in error are K. Schubert, *Scrolls*, p. 126, and R. E. Murphy, *Bible*, p. 85, who regard Jesus' attitude as 'Essene'. Certainly the sectarians placed great restrictions upon the use of oaths, but they did allow them in certain circumstances (CDC 15.1ff.; 16.2ff.; Jos., War II.135; Philo, *Quod Omnis Probus*, 84). Cf. Philo, *De Spec.Leg.* IV, 40 *et al.*

[1] It is now unnecessary to continue to insist on its being a principle of *justice* rather than being a demand for savage *retribution*. Cf. Deut. 22.35 *et al.*, where the spirit of revenge is strongly condemned, and *inter alia* R. de Vaux, *Ancient Israel* (ET 1961), pp. 10–12.

[2] F. Filson, 'Broken Patterns in the Gospel of Matthew', *JBL*, 75 (1956), 227–31.

ground in such passages as Deut. 19.15–21, where both ἀνιστάναι and πονηρός occur.[1]

This interpretation however is not without difficulty. While the 'insult' character of the action in v.39b, and possibly the judicial context of vv.40–1 may be accepted, is it possible to restrict v.39a to so limited a sphere? In other antitheses the examples following are merely illustrative of the more general principle which precedes them (v.22bff.; 34bff.), while the two final illustrations in Matthew (cf. Luke 6.30) are related to daily life and the judicial background does not appear at all.[2] Further, it is not only the phrase 'life for life' that is omitted from the thesis but several other applications of the principle as well (Ex. 21.24–5; Deut. 19.21), while Lev. 24.20 does not contain the expression at all. The particular words quoted in the premise are therefore probably to be regarded as representative of the principle that is involved throughout all these expressions. Again, whereas Deut. 19.15ff. may lie behind the idea contained in v.39b, it is such passages as Ex. 21.24ff. which are linked with v.39a and there a wider principle is involved.[3] Finally, πονηρός, as in 5.37; 6.13; 13.19, 38, must refer to

---

[1] On this interpretation see esp. D. Daube, *Rabbinic Judaism*, pp. 254–65, and S. D. Currie, 'Matthew 5.39a – Resistance or Protest', *HTR*, 57 (1964), 140ff. Cf. also W. C. Allen, *Matthew*, p. 54; H. Marriott, *Sermon*, p. 189; A. Schlatter, *Matthäus*, pp. 186ff.; H. Huber, *Bergpredigt*, p. 99; G. D. Kilpatrick, *Origins*, p. 20; E. Percy, *Botschaft*, p. 152.

[2] Such illustrations have been helpfully designated as 'focal instances' which by their very specificity and extremeness force the hearer to start thinking in a definite direction. Cf. R. C. Tannehill, 'The "Focal Instance" as a Form of New Testament Speech: A Study of Matthew 5.39b–42', *JR*, 50 (1970), 372–85. If the statement to which they are linked is regarded as a basic principle rather than legal ruling, it could then be argued that they seek to bring the hearer to a similar point, but by a different route, to that which he will reach by application of that principle to actual circumstances.

[3] The same may be said for Deut. 25.11, the passage which Daube, *Rabbinic Judaism*, pp. 254–65, claims lies behind the Mishnaic elaboration of the teaching on 'insult', also of the view of K. Bornhäuser, *Bergpredigt*, pp. 96ff. and H. J. Ljungmann, *Gesetz*, p. 84, that the presence of ῥαπίζειν and στρέφειν in Matthew's version of the saying recalls Isa. 50.6, which elsewhere he introduces into the Marcan account in 26.67. Daube explains the citation of Ex. 21.24ff. here instead of Deut. 25.11 by suggesting that either the Deuteronomic basis was not yet settled, or that Jesus was ignorant of technical rabbinic usage (p. 264).

Satan and, so understood, is more compatible with the traditional explanation. It is important to note however that μὴ ἀναστῆναι 'n'est donc pas simple conciliation, encore moins complaisance en face de l'insulter. S'il est la negation d'une hostilité déclarée c'est qu'il est animé positivement par un esprit nouveau.'[1] In Luke, all four examples are quite removed from a Jewish setting and form general illustrations of the principle that love for an enemy should extend to the point of not being conscious of one's own rights. The context of both sets of illustrations is possibly redactional.[2]

Anticipations of the teaching of Jesus occur in the OT (Job 31.29; Prov. 20.22; 25.21-2), Apocryphal (Ecclus. 28.1ff.) and Pseudepigraphal (2 Enoch 50.3-4) writings, though in each case the principle of retribution is maintained by affirming that God would ultimately honour it. The rabbis also praise the spirit of forbearance and the renunciation of right as virtuous (Sif.Deut. 19.19; b.Meg. 28a; b.Taan. 25b; b.Pes. 113b *et al.*), but there are also statements which indicate that it was exercised only in certain circumstances (b.Yom. 87b) while others manifest a quite contradictory spirit (b.Yom. 22b). Closer parallels are found in b.Shabb. 88b; b.Ber. 17a and Ab.R.N. 26.11, but in Matthew the principle outlined in 5.39a is more comprehensive in scope, while in v.39bff. not only is patient bearing of evil required, but the giving to the opponent what is demanded. Moreover, the first gospel does not contain ethical advice so much as an incisive ethical command.[3] It is uncertain whether there was any literal application of the lex talionis in

---

[1] H. Clavier, 'Matthieu 5.39 et la non-résistance', *RHPR*, 37 (1957), 52-3. Too positive an interpretation is given the phrase, however, by H. E. Bryant, 'Mt. 5.38-39', *ET*, 48 (1936-7), 236-7, who comparing the teaching in Rom. 12.17; 1 Thess. 5.15 and 1 Pet. 3.9 translates it as 'do not retaliate'. The verb ἀνιστάναι is never used in this sense. See A/G, p. 66; L/S, 1, 140.

[2] According to E. Lohmeyer, *Matthäus*, p. 135, and H.-W. Bartsch, 'Feldrede und Bergpredigt', *TZ*, 16 (1960), 11ff., different traditions lie behind the two accounts, but R. A. Guelich, 'Law', pp. 123-35, for both this and the following antithesis, has convincingly argued that the differences are all explainable in terms of redactional activity. The present Lucan form is probably the most original, as R. Bultmann, *Tradition*, p. 135, maintains.

[3] See, however, B. H. Branscomb, *Law*, p. 247, and A. Finkel, *Pharisees*, p. 165. H. Braun, *Radikalismus*, 1, 92 n.1, contests the claim of R. Murphy, *Bible*, p. 85 and V. E. Hasler, *TZ*, 15 (1959), 100-2, that the Qumran

this period, though there is some evidence that corporal punishment had been or was being replaced by financial adjustments (cf. Bill., 1, 341ff.). It is generally agreed however that the principle of retribution itself still remained a basic tenet in rabbinic teaching.[1] We may conclude, then, that here once again Jesus brings a new norm which altogether transcends that embedded in the Law and reiterated, in however qualified a manner, by its interpreters.

Sixth Antithesis (Matt. 5.43–8). The quotation from Lev. 19.18 enjoining love of one's neighbour which forms the first half of the premise is followed by an additional clause – καὶ μισήσεις τὸν ἐχθρόν σου – which has no direct parallel in the OT. It has been frequently suggested that it is Jewish teaching on the subject that is being summarised, but since this has not been the case in any of the other theses it is unlikely to be so here. Moreover, C. G. Montefiore has rightly complained that the Jewish evidence is ransacked in vain for such an explicitly drawn conclusion as this.[2] One passage that does speak strongly in similar terms to 5.43b is Ab.R.N. 16 which appears to command hatred for one whose conduct did not befit a Jew. However, the date of the passage is uncertain and it stands virtually alone in the literature. A background in Essene attitudes has recently been advocated but this is also unlikely since nowhere else has an Essene context been in view. Moreover, on the whole the sectarians at Qumran seem to have preserved the OT attitude towards enemies and reserved their anger until the

---

literature provides a parallel in 1 QS 10.17ff. For an attempt to equate Matt. 5.39ff. with the teaching in 2 Enoch 50.3–4, see K. Berger, 'Gesetzesauslegung' (1968), p. 171.

[1] See, for example, the admission of C. G. Montefiore, *Rabbinic Literature and Gospel Teachings* (1930), p. 52. Passages in which a literal approach appears to be present may be found in Jos., *Ant.* iv.8.35 which Daube, *Rabbinic Judaism*, p. 255, claims may have been influenced by Roman law. It has also been suggested that Philo in *De Spec.Leg.* iii, 3 may have been affected by Hellenistic thought. Stricter views were also held by the Boethuseans and R. Eliezer, but these he regards as survivals of the older doctrine and not characteristic of contemporary practice.

[2] C. G. Montefiore, *Gospels*, ii, 80, against, most recently, V. E. Hasler, *TZ*, 15 (1959), 103ff. and G. Barth, 'Law', p. 94. In addition, M. Smith, 'Hate Thine Enemy', *HTR*, 45 (1952), 71–3 and M. McNamara, *Targum*, p. 127, suggest that it stems from a Targum interpretation.

eschatological day of vengeance. Their behaviour towards those outside was characterised by openness and a willingness to receive recruits and seems to have been greeted with a favourable reception (1 QS 1.9; 9.21ff.).[1] Since additions to the theses in v.21b and v.33b were summaries of the OT position, it is more than probable that the same is the case here, but there is still the difficulty encountered by the presence of the word 'hate', which seems too strong for some of the evidence (e.g., Ex. 23.4–5), though certainly some passages approach it in spirit (Deut. 7.5; 20.16–18). As elsewhere in the gospels, however, most probably it possesses a comparative rather than antithetical significance and therefore its meaning should not be too literally pressed (cf. Matt. 6.24; 10.37; cf. Rom. 9.13).[2]

The reply is to be viewed as an antithesis to the whole of v.43 and not merely to the additional clause. Its sense then is not 'love your neighbour' and 'love your enemy also', for in the command 'love your enemies' the distinction between enemy and neighbour is completely annulled.[3] In vv.44b–47 various illustrations of this principle, together with the ground and motive for their observance (v.45), are appended, and these with minor changes and two additional examples are paralleled in Luke (vv.27b–28; 32–5).[4] A general background to the teaching is provided by those places in the OT where some form of kindness to the enemy or stranger is enjoined (Ex. 23.4; Lev. 19.34; Job 31.29; Prov. 24.17; 25.21). Similar sayings occur in the rabbinic writings (Lev.R. 19.17; Tos.Bab.Mes. 2.26ff.), but these do not attain to the comprehensive principle

---

[1] E. F. Sutcliffe, 'Hatred at Qumran', *RQ*, 2 (1959–60), 345–56. See also Philo, *Quod Omnis Probus* 95.89–91; Josephus, *War* II. 8, 2.

[2] Cf. H. Huber, *Bergpredigt*, p. 100; E. Percy, *Botschaft*, p. 156; O. Linton, 'St Matthew 5.43', *St.Th.*, 18 (1964), 66ff.

[3] Contrast, however, G. Friedrich, 'Der Christ und die Moral', *ZEE*, 11 (1967), 289. In view of the examples that follow the widest possible sense should be attributed to ἐχθρός. S. G. Brandon, *Jesus and the Zealots* (1967), p. 310, rather extremely regards this reply as unauthentic, claiming that Matthew here makes Christ speak in 'pacific' terms due to danger which threatened the church at Alexandria during his time.

[4] Luke probably echoes the more original tradition since (a) *Did.* 1.3ff., which stems from a similar background to Matthew and was probably acquainted with the Matthaean text, includes in part elements of all sections of Luke; (b) Luke is not known for constructing such parallelism as is characteristic of these sayings. See further E. Percy, *Botschaft*, pp. 149–50.

outlined in v.44. Several other passages which recommend the return of evil with good (Midr.Ps. 41.8; Gen.R. 38.3 *et al.*) or intercession for those who inflict damage (b.Ber. 10a; b.Sanh. 37a *et al.*) fall short in the same way. A closer parallel in Tos.Bab.Kamm. 9.29 is similar in spirit but speaks only of an occasional, not continuing, hostility and, as is evident from its omission in the parallel passage Bab.Kamm. 8.7, must be late. Meanwhile other passages juxtapose sympathetic and un-sympathetic attitudes (b.Yom. 22b–23a). R. Bultmann is there-fore correct when he claims of this and the related sayings that they 'contain something characteristic, new, reaching out beyond popular wisdom and piety and yet are in no sense scribal or rabbinic nor Jewish apocalyptic'.[1]

It is now time to return to the introductory formulas and antithetical construction which are characteristic of each of these six pericopes. In the formula: ἠκούσατε ὅτι ἐρρέθη τοῖς ἀρχαίοις each word needs careful examination. τοῖς ἀρχαίοις has been read as both an ablative and dative construction. Stylistically it is unlikely to be the first since, though used often in Matthew in the passive, it is accompanied by a propo-sition (usually ὑπό or διά) when the parties by whom things are spoken are mentioned. Elsewhere in the New Testament the dative is clearly intended. Further, if such emphasis were being placed upon οἱ ἀρχαίοι it is strange that the order of the phrase was not reversed and that reference to them was omitted from three of the six antitheses. ἀκούειν occurs in the rabbinic writings in a twofold sense: (a) 'you have heard such-and-such a tradition'; (b) 'you have understood such-and-such a law in a particular way'. Both connotations have been suggested for Matt. 5.21ff.[2] Our discussion of the antitheses, however, rules

---

[1] R. Bultmann, *Tradition*, p. 105. Cf. H. Haas, *Idee und Ideal der Feindesliebe in der ausserchristlichen Welt* (1927), p. 23; W. G. Kümmel, 'Rabbinen', pp. 7ff., and the extended discussions in E. Bischoff, *Rabbinen*, pp. 63ff., E. Percy, *Botschaft*, pp. 156ff., and N. Perrin, *Teaching*, pp. 148ff.

[2] For (a) Bill., I, 253; E. Klostermann, *Matthäus*, p. 42; G. Dalman, *Jesus-Jeshua*, pp. 65ff.; G. Barth, 'Law', p. 93; for (b) S. Schechter, 'Some Rabbinic Parallels to the NT', *JQR*, 12 (1900), 427ff.; C. G. Montefiore, *Gospels*, I, 56; I. Abrahams, *Studies*, p. 16; B. H. Branscomb, *Law*, p. 240; D. Daube, *Rabbinic Judaism*, pp. 55ff.; W. D. Davies, *Setting*, pp. 101ff.; M. Smith, *Parallels*, p. 154; H. T. Wrege, *Bergpredigt*, p. 58.

out these possibilities and it is far more likely that the verb is being used in a non-technical sense to describe the hearing of the Law by the listeners in the synagogue.[1] ἐρρέθη is also employed in the rabbinic writings in a technical sense to mean 'it has been taught as tradition', while elsewhere it is an employment of the passive to avoid mention of the divine name. Grammatically the former runs into difficulty on the following dative of indirect object, while materially it would conflict with the premises of the six antitheses, all of which quote the Law in direct or summary form. In view of Matthew's deliberate ascription of Mosaic commandments to God elsewhere in the gospel (Matt. 15.4), it is unlikely to be a reference to the Law being received as part of the tradition and must rather be regarded as an oblique reference to God himself.[2]

Each word of the introductory formula is countered in the preface to the antitheses:

$$\text{ἠκούσατε ὅτι ἐρρέθη τοῖς ἀρχαίοις}$$
$$\text{ἐγὼ δὲ λέγω ὑμῖν}$$

In itself the latter expression is not particularly distinctive since it can be paralleled elsewhere, both within the New Testament and outside it, e.g., it occurs on the lips of John the Baptist (Matt. 3.9) and Paul (Gal. 5.2), and elsewhere in Jub. 36.11; 1 Enoch 92.18; 94.1, 3; 102.9; Test.Reu. 4.5; 6.5; 2 Enoch 2.2. In its present context, however, it gains a new significance through its association with the unique instructions which it introduces, and raises the question of the identity of the one who has uttered them. We have also drawn attention to the use of the phrase ואני עדמר among the rabbis in the intro-

---

[1] So T. W. Manson, *Sayings*, pp. 153ff., and E. Lohmeyer, *Matthäus*, p. 117. W. C. Allen, *Matthew*, p. 47, suggests that it was the presence of the crowd which partly explains the use of this term rather than ἀναγινώσκειν which Jesus employed in his discussions with the scribes. Against (b) it may further be urged that such an interpretation puts the weight in the formula upon ἠκούσατε when it is ἐρρέθη that is particularly emphasised. R. A. Guelich, 'Law', p. 208, points out that both the contrast intended by ἐρρέθη and λέγω, and the presence of ἐρρέθη alone in the introduction to the third antithesis, demonstrate that this is so.

[2] Cf. J. Jeremias, *Parables*, p. 203 n.57; E. Percy, *Botschaft*, p. 124 and J. Schmid, *Matthäus*, p. 97, against W. G. Kümmel, 'Traditionsgedanke', p. 31; G. Barth, 'Law', p. 94, and G. Strecker, *Gerechtigkeit*, p. 146.

duction of a contrary halakhic opinion, to a received interpretation, and while allowing a heightened awareness of personal authority to Jesus here, M. Smith claims that it is not
possible to find evidence of this in the use of an expression
customary in Jewish legal argumentation.[1] In view of the non-
technical use of the other introductory formula this is, however,
extremely unlikely, while from the viewpoint of content much
more than a new or contrary halakhic opinion is involved in
Jesus' demands and, consequently, much more than rabbinic
authority in his use of this expression.

As for the relationship between Jesus' authoritative utterances and the Old Testament words with which they are introduced, we have noted once again that it is a surpassing or
transcending of the Law that is the keynote throughout. His
teaching cannot be regarded merely in terms of the 'exposition'
or 'completion' of the Law, its 'radicalisation' or 'sharpening',
or the 'abrogation' of some or all its commandments. He neither
moves out from the Law in expounding his demands nor relates
these, whether positively or negatively, back to it. This suggests
that it is the first of the possible solutions mentioned at the end
of the previous section which, to this point at least, most
correctly interprets Jesus' relationship to the Law. For more
light on this, as on Matthew's presentation of it, we must turn
to the introductory section in Matt. 5.17–20 with which the
antitheses are prefaced and which is the central text in our
study. Here the final clue to the answer is to be found.

Preface, Epilogue and Context

Preface (Matt. 5.17–20). This passage has long been considered
of fundamental importance for an understanding of Jesus'
attitude to the Law. In the first stage of historico-critical enquiry
it was almost unanimously accepted as an authentic utterance
of Jesus. However, with the arrival of form-critical methodology

---

[1] M. Smith, *Parallels*, p. 30. Note, however, that the passages he cites do not
contain a real parallel to the first half of the antithesis. His argument,
therefore, begins from a point of disadvantage greater than he is willing
to allow. E. Lohse, 'Ich aber sage euch', pp. 194–200, recognises a greater
element of authority implicit in the content of the antithesis introduced
by these words, but still regards Jesus' use of them in the light of the
formula and interprets his treatment of the Law by means of the idea of
'radicalisation'.

it was, for the most part, relegated to a conservative Jewish-christian milieu. Since the advent of *redaktionsgeschichtliche* analysis more emphasis has been placed on the rôle of the evangelist in re-working the tradition. Nevertheless, where investigation of its genuineness has been undertaken, the passage generally continues to be viewed as a creation of the later church rather than as an original utterance of Jesus, though this has been less true of v.17 than of the succeeding verses. On the whole, however, there has been a marked reluctance in recent treatments of the passage to press through to a discussion of its authenticity.

Matthew 5.17.

Μὴ νομίσητε ὅτι ἦλθον καταλῦσαι τὸν νόμου ἢ τοὺς προφήτας. οὐκ ἦλθον καταλῦσαι ἀλλὰ πληρῶσαι.

Although this verse has no parallel in the other synoptic gospels, it is helpful to bring it into comparison with Matt. 10.34 (cf. Luke 12.51) with which structurally it has much in common. There, the opening words μή νομίσητε are employed as a rhetorical device to strengthen the positive aspect of the following statement and the same may be assumed to be the case in 5.17.[1] Since other occurrences of Luke's use of δοκεῖν (cf. 12.51: δοκεῖτε;) stem from his special material rather than from Q or his redactional activity (cf. Luke 13.2f., 4f.) it is difficult to know whether Matthaean redaction is present in the use of νομίζειν in 10.34. Although in a few places δοκεῖν occurs in the tradition (cf. 3.9; 6.7; 24.44; 26.53), Matthew often uses it in other contexts where νομίζειν would have been appropriate (cf. 17.25; 18.12; 21.28; 22.17, 42; 26.66). This suggests that the presence of the latter in 10.34 stems from his tradition, and that the same may be true in 5.17. So slight is

[1] Cf. W. Trilling, *Israel*, p. 171; S. Légasse, 'Jésus: Juif ou non?', *NRT*, 86 (1964), 692. Thus they are not intended to reflect a misunderstanding of Jesus' actions on the part of his disciples or opponents, nor, as others have maintained, a reflection of the debates between the more conservative Palestinian and radical Hellenistic congregations. For the latter see R. Bultmann, *Tradition*, p. 138; H. Braun, *Radikalismus*, ii, 7 n.2; E. Percy, *Botschaft*, pp. 120–1; G. Barth, 'Law', p. 66, and G. Harder, 'Jesus und das Gesetz', *Antijudäismus im Neuen Testament* (ed. W. Eckert, N. P. Levinson and M. Stöhr, 1967), p. 108.

the material for comparison, however, that it is difficult to be certain.

These two sayings, 5.17 and 10.34, also share the term ἦλθον which elsewhere in Matthew occurs in sayings which have particular christological significance. Although three of the five occasions on which it occurs in Matthew are paralleled in the tradition (9.13; 11.19; 20.28) it is probably redactional in 10.34. The Lucan version of 10.34 has instead παραγίνεσθαι and since this does not appear to be a particularly Lucan term, it is more likely to have been in the Q form of the saying.[1] Furthermore, Matthew has quite clearly added ἦλθον in the following saying (10.35, cf. Luke 12.53). Most probably, then, ἦλθον in 10.34 is redactional also, Matthew having been influenced in his choice of words by the other logia in which the word appears, and by his general tendency to heighten the christological import of Christ's sayings. This means that its presence in 5.17 may be redactional as well and that a similar motive may lie behind its insertion.

The literary character of the second part of the saying in v.17 – a negative statement followed by its positive counterpart – again parallels the construction in 10.34. Of thirteen similar formulations in Mark's gospel, Matthew adopts eleven (as against Luke, who retains only six) and in addition creates ten others. Of these ten, nine clearly have a basis in Matthew's tradition.[2] This suggests that Matt. 5.17b is unlikely to have been a purely Matthaean creation.[3] In six of the other nine

---

[1] Six of the seven remaining uses of παραγίνεσθαι in Luke occur in passages where Luke seems to have had traditional material before him: so Luke 7.4; 7.20; 11.16; 14.21; 19.16; 22.52. It occurs twenty times in Acts, about half of which fall into the latter section of the book, but only once in the 'we-sections' of the work (21.18). As for Matthew, two ἦλθον sayings are paralleled in Luke (Matt. 11.19/Luke 7.34; Matt. 18.11/Luke 19.10), one in Mark (Matt. 20.28/Mark 10.45) and one in both Luke and Mark (Matt. 9.13/Mark 2.17/Luke 5.32).

[2] From Mark cf. Matt. 9.12/Mark 2.17; 9.13/2.17; 9.17/2.22; 9.24/5.39; 15.11/17.15; 16.23/8.33; 19.6/10.8; 20.23/10.40; 20.28/10.45; 22.32/12.27; 26.39/14.36. Also Matt. 4.4/Luke 4.4 (Deut. 8.3); (5.17); 5.39/Luke 6.29; 6.13/11.4; 7.21/6.46; 10.20/12.12; 10.34/12.51; 16.12 (from 16.11); 16.17(M); 17.12/Mark 9.13.

[3] In certain of the sayings which owe their construction to Matthew it is the positive element which is added (4.4; 6.13; 7.21), in others the nega-

constructions, material for the additions is already present in the parallel text. As for the remainder, 4.4b is filled out from material in Deut. 8.3; 5.39a appears to be a firm element in the tradition, and 6.13 is most probably an addition from a liturgical context. We can reasonably infer, then, that both elements of 5.17 were also located in the tradition upon which the evangelist worked.

In view of Matthew's general interest in the fulfilment of prophecy, the phrase ἢ οἱ προφῆται in v.17b has frequently been regarded as an addition either from his own hand or that of a later interpolator.[1] The exclusive concentration upon the Law in the following verses (vv.18ff.) strengthens this suggestion, but is there anything of a stylistic nature to confirm it? The use of the disjunctive ἤ in place of the correlative conjunction in this sentence is commonly explained by the negative form of the sentence.[2] However, this is not strictly a negative clause. Moreover, of the thirteen remaining occurrences of ἤ, far more than either of the other gospels, nine are probably due to Matthew's editorial activity and eight of these are similar in construction to the phrase in 5.17, i.e., a conjunction followed by a noun.[3] An analysis of these various additional phrases, however, indicates that in every instance a non-theological motive is at work and that more often than not it is merely an unconscious association of ideas that lies behind its insertion. A further consideration strengthens the likelihood of this also being the case here. Elsewhere in the gospel where the whole phrase 'the Law and the prophets' is a redactional addition (7.12; 22.40), it is the imperative, not predictive, aspect of

---

tive (5.39; 10.20; 17.12), while in 16.12 it is both. 10.34 only formulates the positive and negative elements of Luke 12.51 into this particular stylistic framework. 16.17 comes from M, so we have no means of knowing to what extent Matthew has rearranged the saying.

[1] So (a): A. H. McNeile, *Matthew*, p. 58; A. Merx, *Matthäus*, I, 77; G. Dalman, *Jesus*, p. 62; H. Weinel, *Die Bergpredigt* (1920), pp. 38–9; J. Schmid, *Matthäus*, p. 87; (b): W. C. Allen, *Matthew*, p. 46; C. G. Montefiore, *Gospels*, II, 47.

[2] Funk, p. 231.

[3] From Mark: 15.4ff./Mark 7.10ff. (3); 13.21/Mark 4.17. Editorial in Marcan passages, cf. 12.25/Mark 3.25; 16.14/8.28; 18.8/9.43. In Q material, 5.18/Luke 16.17; 6.25/12.22. Without parallel, 10.11, 14; 17.25.

the prophetic message that is stressed. As I shall demonstrate later this is most probably its meaning in 5.17 as well. The addition of οἱ προφῆται, therefore, does not spring from a desire to introduce a reference to Christ's fulfilment of Old Testament prophecy that would tie in with Matthew's development of this theme throughout the gospel, but is rather a simple expansion resulting from an association of two frequently combined ideas.

We must now look more closely at the content of the negative and positive clauses, and this particularly concerns the terms καταλύειν ('to abolish') and πληροῦν ('to fulfil'). A. Merx sought to explain the first of these terms by means of the rabbinic practice of 'loosing' or 'relaxing' the commandments but the context will scarcely allow the verb to be interpreted in so moderate a sense here.[1] H. J. Ljungmann, in accordance with its usage elsewhere in the NT, orientates the term rather to οἰκοδομεῖν and interprets it in terms of 'tearing down'.[2] In the passages to which he refers, however, it would seem to be the context which enables this meaning to be given to the verb rather than its being inherent in the term itself, and elsewhere καταλύειν approaches more nearly to the sense of 'destroying' (Acts 5.38; Rom. 14.20). Only in Gal. 2.18 does the Law come into view but there Paul is referring to isolated provisions with which the ideas of 'building up' and 'tearing down' can be associated, not to the Law as a whole as in 5.17. In pre-christian passages where νόμος is explicitly in view, the meaning given to καταλύειν is clearly 'abolish' or 'annul' (2 Macc. 2.22; 4 Macc. 5.33), and this sense of the verb with νόμος is attested in classical Greek from Herodotus onwards.[3]

---

[1] A. Merx, *Matthäus*, pp. 73ff.

[2] H. Ljungmann, *Gesetz*, pp. 17, 59ff. Cf. earlier, A. Plummer, *Matthew*, p. 76. It is used of the stones in the Temple: Matt. 24.2/Mark 13.2/Luke 21.6; of the Temple itself: Matt. 26.61/Mark 14.5–8; Matt. 27.40/Mark 15.29; Acts 6.14; and of the church considered as a 'building': Gal. 2.18; 2 Cor. 5.13.

[3] In 4 Macc. 5.33 the translation 'break' in R. H. Charles' edition (p. 673) fits uneasily into the context and makes better sense when rendered 'abolish' or 'annul'. See also Philo, *De Spec.Leg.* III, 182, and Josephus, *Ant.* XIII.296; XIII.408. For examples from classical and Hellenistic literature, consult L/S, 1, 899–900.

We come to the disputed term πληροῦν. The most widespread interpretation of this word has been in terms of setting out the 'true meaning', 'spirit', 'intention' or 'basic principles' of the Law so as to 'complete', 'perfect', 'express' its full significance.[1] However, this understanding of the term (as well as ignoring the LXX usage documented below) relies upon an 'inner-outer' dichotomy which cannot be upheld for the time in which the gospels were written. A second line of interpretation, which has also been extremely influential, concerned itself with the possibility of the Aramaic term קוּם underlying the Greek term, and rendered it accordingly as 'validate', 'establish', 'confirm'.[2] An examination of the LXX usage, however, reveals that πληροῦν never translates קום, use being made rather of such terms as ἱστάναι and βεβαιοῦν, while it is used, or one of the group of words associated with it, to translate מלא. While the OT מלא is rendered in the Targums by a form of קיים, the consistent testimony of the LXX usage casts considerable doubt on the presence of the latter as an Aramaic background to πληροῦν here. An occasional attempt has also been made to solve the issue by reference to the statement of R. Gamaliel in b.Shabb. 116a–b, alluding to Deut. 4.2: 'wherein it is written, I came not to destroy the Law of Moses nor to add to the Law of Moses'. It has been suggested that this utterance preserves the words actually uttered by Jesus, Matthew's version being a mistranslation of the original saying. However, this not only demands an improbable confusion on the part of Matthew but also entails his bypassing the usual LXX rendering προστιθέναι, which only a few verses later he employs in exactly this sense (Matt. 6.27, 33).[3]

We do better to turn our attention to such occurrences of מלא = πληροῦν as occur in the literature prior to and con-

---

[1] So, excluding earlier liberal scholars who all but unanimously adopted this view: Klostermann, Kümmel, Dibelius, Lanwer, Windisch, Michaelis, Lagrange, Dupont, Johnson, Filson, Blair, Staudinger, Eicholz, et al.

[2] As Bächer, Fiebig, Schrenk, Branscomb, Schlatter, Jocz, Percy, et al.

[3] Cf. H. T. Wrege, Bergpredigt, p. 37 n.3, against H. J. Schoeps, 'Jésus et la loi juive', RHPR, 33 (1953), 15ff., and J. Jeremias, TDNT, IV, 868 n.221. According to W. D. Davies, 'Matthew 5.17, 18', Christian Origins, p. 38, to go behind Matt. 5.17 to a late corrupt Talmudic text for the meaning of Jesus is to employ 'Procrustean' methods.

temporary with the NT.[1] In some cases, it simply refers to the 'filling up' of some actual or metaphorical volume or to the 'termination' of a stated period of time. Other passages speak of the 'fulfilment' of a prediction, promise, threat, undertaking or obligation. G. Barth has recently interpreted πληροῦν in such passages as indicating the actual 'realisation' of that which is referred to. H. J. Ljungmann wishes to place the emphasis upon the state which such actualisation brings, i.e., upon the fact of its full 'completion'.[2] Since the idea of realisation alone could have been expressed by other terms than מלא/πληροῦν, it is justifiable to look for some extra significance in the term. However, it is debatable whether Ljungmann's emphasis on completion can be located in all the passages mentioned. More light is thrown on this question, however, by the specifically christian use of the term.

The NT uses of the word concur with that of the LXX, but what is especially striking is the large number of passages given over to the idea of fulfilment of OT prophecies as well as its explicit relation to the idea of Law. Again G. Barth has interpreted its sense in terms of the 'active realisation' of the prophecies and Law, and H. J. Ljungmann in the sense of bringing to a 'full completion' all that the Law stood for.[3] A. Descamps, though he agrees with Barth that realisation is the basic meaning,

---

[1] For detailed references to these other uses of the term in both OT and NT, see esp. A. Descamps, *Les Justes et la Justice dans les Évangiles* (1950), pp. 124ff. A survey of terms other than the מלא = πληροῦν complex which bear on the theme of fulfilment is provided by C. F. D. Moule, 'Fulfilment-Words in the New Testament: Use and Abuse', *NTS*, 14 (1968), 302–8. The non-biblical material which he also discusses adds little to the discussion (see pp. 311–12).

[2] G. Barth, 'Law', pp. 68–9; H. J. Ljungmann, *Gesetz*, p. 60. See further 1 Kings 2.27; 8.15, 24; 2 Chron. 6.4, 15; 36.21–2; Ps. 20.5–7 (LXX 19.5–7); Ps. (LXX) 126.5; Isa. (LXX) 13.3; Jer. 44.25 (LXX 51.25); 1 Macc. 2.55.

[3] For the first, see also E. Schweizer, 'Matthäus 5.17–20', p. 400; G. Strecker, *Gerechtigkeit*, p. 147. For the second: W. D. Davies, 'Matthew 5.17, 18', pp. 31ff., and C. F. D. Moule, *NTS*, 14 (1968), 314–17. For the use of πληροῦν in connection with prophecy see Matt. 1.22; 2.15; 2.23; 4.14; 8.17; 12.17; 13.14, 35; 21.4; 26.54, 56; 27.9; Mark 14.49; Luke 4.21; 22.16; John 12.38; 13.18; 15.25; 17.12; 18.9, 32; 19.24, 36; Acts 1.16; 3.18; 13.27; James 2.23. For its use in connection with the Law, see Matt. 5.17; Rom. 13.10 and Gal. 5.14.

nevertheless insists that such realisation involves something qualitatively new, thus arguing for a more specifically christian content in the term.[1] All three, however, doubt that Jesus ever spoke in such terms. It seems to me that Descamps has placed his finger on a central aspect of the term, the quality of newness, or superiority that attaches to the fulfilment. The distinctive quality of Jesus' instructions in 5.21ff. make that very apparent, as Matthew himself recognises by setting them within an anti-thetical framework. What Descamps does not see, however, is that this transcendence of the Law also involves reference to the Law's function in pointing forward to that which has now arrived in its place. This aspect of the Law's operations is explicitly insisted upon by Matthew in 11.13, which speaks not only of the Prophets but also the Law as *prophesying* (see further below), but it is nevertheless implicit in the use of the term here. What I would argue then, and it is this possibility that seems to have been constantly overlooked, is that precisely the same meaning should be given to the term πληροῦν when it is used of the Law as that which it has when it is used of the Prophets. The prophetic teachings point forward (principally) to the actions of Christ and have been realised in them in an incomparably greater way. The Mosaic laws point forward (principally) to the teachings of Christ and have also been realised in them in a more profound manner. The word 'fulfil' in 5.17, then, includes not only an element of discontinuity (that which has now been realised *transcends* the Law) but an element of continuity as well (that which transcends the Law is nevertheless something to which the Law itself *pointed forward*).

Is it possible that the use of the term 'fulfil' here stems not merely from Matthew's tradition but directly from Jesus' own understanding?[2] C. F. D. Moule has recently suggested that

---

[1] A. Descamps, *Justice*, pp. 127–32.

[2] I should perhaps make it clear at this point that in all this I am assuming that Jesus probably spoke in Aramaic. Despite renewed interest in the possibility of his having spoken Greek (as in N. Turner, *Grammatical Insights into the New Testament* [1965], pp. 174–88), the former seems more likely though (note J. A. Fitzmeyer, 'The Problem of Vernacular Hebrew in the First Century A.D. and the Language of Jesus', *JTS*, 24 [1973], 1–23) it could be that Jesus occasionally spoke in Hebrew. On this issue generally see also J. Barr, 'Which Language did Jesus Speak? – Some Remarks of a Semitist', *BJRL*, 53 (1970), 9–29.

this is possible. He points to certain other sayings of Jesus, whose authenticity he feels should not be seriously doubted, where a unique sense of the term πληροῦν comes into view.[1] In such passages as Mark 1.15; Matt. 26.54; Luke 4.21 and 22.16, a new quality attaches to the term through the uniqueness that belongs to the ministry of Jesus or the Kingdom associated with him. This is quite clear in the saying concerning the fulfilment of the Passover in the Kingdom of Heaven, for when that takes place the earthly shadow will have become the reality. Jesus could also invest this term (or, to be more precise, its Aramaic equivalent) with a heightened meaning when speaking of the time in which his ministry was occurring, for that time had not only arrived but was the consummation, in a qualitatively new way, of all the earlier καιροί. He could also use it of those OT prophecies which in it were being realised in a way the prophets themselves could only dimly foresee. That being the case, could not the Law also have been regarded in this manner, especially when it too only imperfectly gave utterance to that full expression of the will of God contained in Jesus' teaching?[2]

This possibility is strengthened by the fact that Matthew, for whom this term has vital theological significance, nowhere else displays the same comprehensive and distinctive use of it as

[1] See C. F. D. Moule, *NTS* 14 (1968), 317–18 (drawing on R. N. Longenecker, *Paul*, pp. 139–40), though he does not accord to πληροῦν the same meaning that is being argued for it here. One who does insist on its authenticity and whose interpretation comes closer to that set out here is A. Feuillet, 'Morale Ancienne et Morale Chrétienne d'aprés Mt 5.17–20: Comparaison avec la Doctrine de l'Epître aux Romains', *NTS* 17 (1971), 124. He regards its meaning as being that of 'conserving through perfecting and surpassing', but relates it to the whole content of the OT rather than to the legal element alone.

[2] In 5.18–19 this fulfilment of the Law seems to take place in Jesus' teaching. However, the import of ἦλθον in 5.17 and ποιήσῃ in 5.19, and the stress on obedience throughout the Sermon (esp. in 7.15–27), indicate that his practice is also in view. To define this primarily in terms of the redemptive aspect of Christ's ministry is unduly restrictive. While this is undoubtedly the ultimate outcome of his obedience, it is not the aspect of it which is being emphasised here. Contrast, however, H. J. Ljungmann, *Gesetz*, pp. 61ff.; B. Gerhardsson, *Manuscript*, p. 327; V. E. Hasler, 'Gesetz', pp. 9ff.; R. Schnackenburg, *Moral Teaching*, pp. 57–8, and J. M. Gibbs, 'The Son of God as the Torah Incarnate in Matthew', *St.Ev.*, IV (1968), 42.

Jesus does in Mark 1.15; Matt. 26.54; Luke 4.21; 22.16 and which I am proposing for Matt. 5.17. This means that it is scarcely probable, as has so often been asserted, that the word 'fulfil' in 5.17 comes from his own hand.[1] It is also unlikely to have been added in transmission of the tradition, for the only use of it which stems from that source (Matt. 26.56, cf. Mark 14.49) almost certainly comes from Jesus' own lips. The present structure of the verse, of course, is partly Matthaean in character. It is formulated precisely in the same way as Matthew has constructed 10.34. Comparison of 10.34 with Luke 12.51 reveals that Matthew has essentially preserved the structure of the first, or negative, section of the saying. However, the second has been given a greater symmetry through his repetition of the last phrase of the first section before concluding with its positive counterpart. Thus behind the repetition of οὐκ ἦλθον καταλῦσαι in 5.17 probably lay a simple οὐχί (cf. Luke 12.51) followed by ἀλλὰ πληρῶσαι. Since there is every reason to think that the structure reflected in Luke 12.51 has its basis in a genuine utterance of Jesus, there are no formal grounds on which the authenticity of the original Aramaic saying behind 5.17 should be contested.

All this suggests that rather than being a Matthaean construction,[2] or a creation of the early Palestinian church, the saying is substantially authentic. While Matthew's use of ἦλθον, addition of οἱ προφῆται and understanding of πληροῦν demonstrate traces of his own particular interests, the basic thrust of the saying has not been significantly altered. He has simply

---

[1] Cf. C. F. D. Moule, *NTS* 14 (1968), 316. One may ask, however, whether Matthew always understood his formulations 'in the shallower sense of "prediction-fulfilment"', as he suggests. Although his use of the word may be less striking than in the above passages, in some instances it is not a 'prediction' as such to which he turns, but a statement occurring in a particular *heilsgeschichtlich* context which is typologically related to its uniquely new counterpart in the new age that has dawned (e.g. Matt. 2.15; 2.18; 13.14; 27.9). On these passages see further R. Gundry, *The Old Testament Quotations in St. Matthew's Gospel* (1967), who, however, makes little use of form- and redaction-critical perspectives; R. S. McConnell, *Law and Prophecy in Matthew's Gospel* (1969), who tends to pay insufficient attention to the context of the citations, and, most helpfully, W. Rothfuchs, *Die Erfüllungszitate des Matthäus-Evangeliums* (1969).

[2] As, for example, G. Strecker, *Gerechtigkeit*, p. 144; R. Hummel, *Auseinandersetzung*, p. 66; K. Niederwimmer, *Freiheit*, p. 154 n.6.

heightened the christological element within it, noted in passing that what is true for the Law is also true for the Prophets, and, in view of his interest in the prophetic aspect of the Law, probably interpreted πληροῦν in a slightly more specialised way than Jesus intended it. Since Matthew alone preserves the saying, however, some account must be given for its omission from the other two gospels. Relevant here is the fact that of other sayings containing references to the character of Jesus' ministry, two come from Mark (Matt. 9.13; 20.28), and two come from Q (Matt. 10.34; 11.19). Its omission from Mark, therefore, could well be explained by its transmission in Q or, as is more likely, in special Matthaean tradition. In any case, its concentration upon the status of the Law would not have been particularly relevant to Mark's audience. Luke already omits one of these sayings which lay in his Marcan source (Mark 10.45, cf. Matt. 20.28). To this may be added his general lack of interest in the issue of Jesus' relationship to the Law. However, on occasions he does incorporate 'legal' material from Q into his gospel without commenting upon it (Luke 16.16ff.). While its omission from Luke may possibly be explained on redactional grounds, this saying of Jesus is far more likely to have been preserved in M and was not therefore available to either of the other evangelists.

5.18.

ἀμὴν γὰρ λέγω ὑμῖν, ἕως ἂν παρέλθῃ ὁ οὐρανὸς καὶ ἡ γῆ, ἰῶτα ἓν ἢ μία κεραία οὐ μὴ παρέλθῃ ἀπὸ τοῦ νόμου, ἕως ἂν πάντα γένηται.

To begin with, the redactional nature of ἀμὴν γάρ λέγω ὑμῖν in 5.18, in view of the parallel statement in Luke 16.17, is evident.[1] We have then, doubly so through the presence of

---

[1] Matthew is the only New Testament writer to use the formula ἀμὴν λέγω ὑμῖν together with this conjunction (Matt. 10.23; 17.20/Luke 17.6; Matt. 13.17/Luke 10.24). Its redactional nature has been opposed by J. Jeremias, 'Kennzeichnen der ipsissima vox Jesu', *ABBA* (1966), pp. 145ff., but his objections are dealt with by W. Trilling, *Israel*, p. 169 n.12, in some detail. Considerable discussion has lately centred on the prehistory and significance of the 'Amen-formulas' in the gospels. According to V. Hasler, *Amen* (1969), they have their background in the Greek version of prophetic formulas characteristic of the Hellenistic synagogues and early Hellenistic-christian churches, and were used to lend authority

ἀμην and the introductory formula, a further example of Matthew's deliberate heightening of the christological factor in a saying related to the Law. There is also through the presence of γάρ a binding together of sayings which were originally uttered in separate contexts.

The central clause in v.18 affirms the continuing validity of the Law and is not dissimilar to various rabbinic passages where the same theme is developed (Bill., 1, 247ff.). In view of the reference to ἰῶτα ἓν ἢ μία κεραία in which the emphasis particularly rests upon the repetition of the numeral,[1] any attempt to circumvent the emphasis placed upon even the most insignificant elements in the Law must be resisted.[2] In Matthew,

to the instructions of the exalted Christ relating to specific situations. K. Berger, *Die Amen-Worte Jesu* (1970) (see also 'Zur Geschichte der Einleitungsformel "Amen, Ich sage Euch"', *ZNW*, 63 (1972), 45–75), maintains that they must be seen principally against the apocalyptic Amen-sayings in such texts as the Testaments of the Twelve Patriarchs and were a product of Greek-speaking Jewish Christianity in which Jesus was viewed as an apocalpytic teacher-mediator of eschatological revelation. What we may have here, however, as is the case with other traditional expressions and modes of argumentation in Matthew's gospel, is the adoption of a particular form, perhaps stemming from his interest in apocalyptic ideas (see further G. Barth, 'Law', pp. 58–62) which is nevertheless invested with a quite new meaning on the basis of his general christological outlook.

[1] Cf. Funk, p. 250. Matthew's ἢ μία κεραία is sufficiently accounted for by his inclusion of ἰῶτα ἕν. The form of the first phrase is, as we have seen, typical of Matthaean redaction. Further indication of an addition comes from a comparison of the rabbinic parallels where one or other of these items appears but never both together, as well as the unlikelihood of Luke's omitting reference to ἰῶτα which also represented the smallest Greek letter.

[2] It cannot therefore be reduced to (a) the 'moral' law only as R. Mackintosh, *Law*, p. 28; J. Hänel, *Schriftbegriff*, p. 163; M.-J. Lagrange, *Luc*, p. 440; or (b) the 'Decalogue' and 'love-commandments' on which so much emphasis was placed in Hellenistic Judaism, as S. Schulz, *Botschaft*, p. 183. Nor should it be (c) expanded into a reference to the 'OT Scriptures', as A. Schlatter, *Matthäus*, p. 156; (d) interpreted in such a way that the emphasis falls upon the 'wholeness' rather than the 'detailed items' of the law, as H. J. Ljungmann, *Gesetz*, pp. 39ff.; P. J. Verweijs, *Evangelium*, pp. 17–18; (e) evaded by regarding it as a misunderstood ironical statement addressed to the Pharisaic conception of Torah, as T. W. Manson, *Sayings*, p. 135, or (f) passed over by viewing it merely as another way of emphasising the 'unverganglichkeit', not the 'verbindlichkeit' of the Law, as K. Benz, *Gesetz*, p. 42. Similar attempts to overcome the force of the

however, this admission of the Law's continued validity appears to be qualified by the two clauses which precede and follow the central element of the saying. This has been contested for the first of these statements ἕως ἂν παρέλθῃ ὁ οὐρανὸς καὶ ἡ γῆ which some have regarded as merely a vivid and idiomatic way of saying 'never'.[1] Others have viewed it as a *terminus ad quem* restricting the validity of the Law to the duration of the present Age.[2] However, the words should not be literally pressed in either direction so that as in Luke, which probably has the more original form of the saying, we have a rhetorical figure which merely emphasises how hard it is for the Law to pass away.[3]

A qualifying clause does appear, however, in the final words of the Matthaean saying, ἕως ἂν πάντα γένηται.[4] Three main meanings have been suggested for this clause: (a) the eschatological events at the end of the Age;[5] (b) the accomplishment

saying in Luke are to be as strongly rejected. Against all these attempts see esp. W. G. Kümmel, 'Traditionsgedanke', p. 33; J. Staudinger, *Bergpredigt*, p. 76, *et al.*; G. Barth, 'Law', p. 65.

[1] So W. C. Allen, *Matthew*, p. 46; C. G. Montefiore, *Gospels*, II, 51; E. Klostermann, *Matthäus*, p. 41; J. Dupont, *Béatitudes*, p. 116 n.2, and A. Feuillet, *NTS*, 17 (1971), 125.

[2] E.g., A. Schlatter, *Matthäus*, p. 156; E. Lohmeyer, *Matthäus*, p. 109; J. Schniewind, *Matthäus*, p. 54; F. V. Filson, *Matthew*, p. 83; H. T. Wrege, *Bergpredigt*, pp. 39–40.

[3] W. Trilling, *Israel*, pp. 167ff. The redactional nature of Matthew's introductory formula and insertion ἰῶτα ἓν has already been noted, as well as his addition ἕως ἂν πάντα γένηται at the conclusion of the verse. εὔκοπος is not a Lucan term, for in the only other two occasions in which it is found in his gospel it is taken over from Mark (Luke 5.23/2.9; 18.25/10.25) and never occurs in Acts. Only a few scholars have in fact contested Lucan originality as, for example, A. Harnack, *Sayings*, p. 56; B. C. Butler, *Originality*, p. 43.

[4] So stylistically and materially awkward is it often considered to be that it has not infrequently been regarded as a late gloss. Cf. E. Wendland, 'Zu Matthäus 5.18, 19', *ZNW*, 5 (1904), 253ff.; A. H. McNeile, *Matthew*, p. 59; C. G. Montefiore, *Gospels*, II, 52. W. D. Davies, 'Matthew 5.17, 18', p. 61, brusquely replies that 'there is no obvious support for this view, however, apart from the difficulty the phrase presents to the interpreter'.

[5] Of Christ's death and surrounding events: J. Jeremias, *The Sermon on the Mount* (1965), p. 24, and esp. W. D. Davies, 'Matthew 5.17, 18', pp. 60ff.; of the fall of Jerusalem: A. Feuillet, *RB*, 56 (1949), 85; of the eschatological events in the last days: J. Wellhausen, *Matthaei*, p. 18; W. C. Allen, *Matthew*, p. 47; A. H. McNeile, *Matthew*, p. 59; E. Klostermann, *Matthäus*, p. 41; J. Schmid, *Matthäus*, pp. 87–8; F. V. Filson, *Matthew*, p. 84.

of the Law,[1] or of the will of God;[2] (c) the fulfilment of the OT Scriptures in the person and work of Christ.[3] γίνεσθαι is used frequently throughout Matthew's gospel, mostly in the active mood, in the sense of 'happen'. On a number of these occasions it is found in the context of 'the coming to pass' of events predicted beforehand (1.22; 21.4; 26.54, 56). On the other hand, the most direct parallel to 5.18d is, of course, 24.34, where ἕως ἂν πάντα ταῦτα γένηται clearly refers to the 'taking place' of the final eschatological events. Only in Matt. 6.10 and 26.42 is it used of certain things being 'done', but in both these verses, in contrast to 5.18d, γίνεσθαι occurs in the imperative Linguistically, therefore, its application to either (a) or (c) appears more probable and since in the majority of passages the emphasis is upon the 'happening' of something announced previously, it is the latter interpretation which is given the most support. In addition, while the parallel in 24.34 appears to stress the 'eschatological' events and hence favour (a), with his addition ταῦτα Matthew explicitly relates it to the prior list of predictions in 24.4ff.[4]

---

[1] In its entirety: B. Lanwer, 'Gesetz', p. 18; A. M. Honeyman, NTS, 1 (1954–5), 142; H. J. Ljungmann, Gesetz, p. 40; G. Strecker, Gerechtigkeit, p. 144; H. T. Wrege, Bergpredigt, p. 38; in the Cross: Th. Soiron, Die Bergpredigt Jesu (1941), p. 237; J. Staudinger, Bergpredigt, p. 78; in the love-commandment: E. Schweizer, 'Matthäus 5.17–20', p. 402; R. Hummel, Auseinandersetzung, p. 68.

[2] B. Weiss, Das Matthäus-Evangelium (1898⁹), p. 104; G. Barth, 'Law', p. 66.

[3] R. C. H. Lenski, Matthew, p. 204; R. A. Guelich, 'Law', pp. 242ff. In O. Hanssen, 'Zum Verständnis der Bergpredigt. Eine missionstheologische Studie zu Mt. 5.17–18', Der Ruf Jesu, pp. 107–8, the emphasis is placed on the realisation of the Law in the reality of the christian community.

[4] In agreement with this is A. Feuillet, NTS, 17 (1971), 126. The detailed attempt by W. D. Davies, 'Matthew 5.17, 18', pp. 60ff., under (a) to relate both the term and the first ἕως clause to the death of Christ runs into several other difficulties: (i) the figurative use of 'heaven and earth' which, though possible, is scarcely probable; (ii) the supposition that Jesus' death terminated the 'old age'; (iii) his reliance upon the concept of the 'new age' as 'anticipating' itself in the radical teaching of Jesus in 5.21ff.; (iv) the drawing of a distinction between the annulment of the Law 'in principle' though not 'in fact', which occurs as the result of such teaching. The recent attempt by E. Schweizer, 'Matthäus 5.17–20', pp. 402ff., under (b) to equate γίνεσθαι with the declaration of the love-commandment in 7.12 and 22.40 quite apart from the linguistic improbability, also fails to convince for: (a) it is extremely doubtful whether

When we turn to a consideration of (c), however, we are immediately faced with difficulty. Not only is ὁ νόμος in 5.18 a reference to the demands of the Law and not the OT Scriptures as has been commonly asserted, but even the reference to οἱ προφῆται in 5.17b was to their imperative, not predictive, element. How then is it possible to explain the phrase ἕως ἂν πάντα γένηται along the lines suggested by the linguistic usage? The clue has already been provided by our study of πληροῦν in v.17. The conjunction of that term with the prophetic predictions would have been quite customary, but its predication of the Law provided a striking and unexpected juxtaposition of ideas. Nevertheless, it was recognised that the Law could also be viewed as a 'pointing forward' to that ideal which was becoming reality in the teaching of Jesus. Thus πάντα here refers to the demands of the Law, in their detail as well as in their totality, understood, however, not as mere imperatives but as signs which look forward to that which is now appearing in the teaching of Jesus. In it they are now about to 'come to pass' (v.18d) and consequently to find 'fulfilment' (v.17b). Have we, apart from 5.17, any other indication that such could have been the thought of Matthew with this addition in v.18d?

We do, and find it in Matthew's version of a Q logion that has already been given brief mention (11.13). Interestingly enough, this is paralleled in Luke in 16.16, that is in the saying which prefaces Luke's version of Matt. 5.18. Whereas Luke 16.16 simply states that 'the Law and the prophets were until John', Matthew inverts the order of prophets and Law, and inserts a reference to the fact of their 'prophesying'.[1] Both versions of the saying, whose basic authenticity has never been really in dispute, declare that with John a decisive change has taken place from the point of view of God's revelation to man.

the 'love-commandment' can be considered the focal point of the new teaching Jesus brought, and therefore as the uniquely 'new commandment' which Schweizer claims to have replaced the old; (b) γίνεσθαι cannot be equated with πληροῦν. The second point has already been demonstrated. The first will be amplified towards the conclusion of the consideration of this verse.

[1] It is Luke therefore who preserves the more original form of the saying. Cf. T. W. Manson, *Sayings*, p. 134; E. Bammel, 'Is Luke 16.16–18 of Baptist's Provenance?', *HTR*, 51 (1958), 101; G. Barth, 'Law', p. 64.

The period of the Law and the prophets has now given way to the proclamation of the Kingdom of God. However, neither infers that the Law has been abrogated, for this is as specifically guarded against in Luke (see the following verse, 16.17) as it is here in Matthew (5.18). In both, however, it is in the demands of the Kingdom, not in its own continued existence, that the Law is validated (Luke 16.16b/Matt. 11.12; Luke 16.18/ Matt. 5.21ff.).[1] Matthew's addition ἐπροφήτευσαν is less an attempt to guard against an antinomian misunderstanding of the Q form of the saying, than a clarification of its meaning in light of his own theological appreciation of both Law and prophets as pointing forward to that which has now come in Christ.[2]

We see, then, that Matthew's addition in 5.18d has a not dissimilar effect to that in 11.13a, and that in both instances he has not imposed upon the tradition an interpretation that is alien to it, but merely clarified that which was already implied in it. Thus the original form of Matt. 5.18/Luke 16.17 did not contain an assertion of the eternal duration of the Law in Jewish or Jewish-christian terms, but rather a rhetorical statement emphasising how difficult it was for the Law to perish. In the contexts in which the saying is set, it is clear that it is in the Law's transformation and 'fulfilment' in the teaching of Jesus that its validity continues.

In his detailed analysis of the passage, H. Schürmann has persuasively argued for the pre-Lucan character of 16.16–18. While he does not enter into a full discussion of the authenticity of this tradition, he does find hints in Luke 16.14f., 19ff. of a

---

[1] It is therefore incorrect to infer from Matthew's alteration that his saying continues to assert the validity of the Law along strict Jewish-christian lines as W. G. Kümmel, 'Traditionsgedanke', pp. 33ff., and G. Barth, 'Law', p. 64, *et al.* seem to do. It is also an error to argue that in Luke the Law continues to possess its validity alongside and in conjunction with the preaching of Jesus. Cf. H. Flender, *Luke*, p. 124; W. Wink, *John the Baptist in the Gospel Tradition* (1968), pp. 51–7, against H. Conzelmann, *Luke*, pp. 160–1, who places so much emphasis upon this verse. The basic authenticity of the saying has never really been in dispute.

[2] G. Strecker, *Gerechtigkeit*, p. 144, therefore unnecessarily considers it to be *vor-redaktionnell* on the basis of its dealings with the Law merely from a predictive and not ethical point of view. See rather S. Schulz, *Botschaft*, p. 189, though he restricts the fulfilment of ὁ νόμος in this context to the setting forth of the 'love-commandment'.

polemical context in the ministry of Jesus which could have formed the original setting for such utterances over the Law.[1] Jesus' apparent endorsement of the Law in polemical or apologetic contexts elsewhere (cf. Matt. 19.18f.; 23.2f.; 23.23f.) indicates that, on more than one occasion, he pronounced upon the value of the Law in a general way. Certainly, in view of the interpretation that has been proposed, this saying need no longer be viewed as a creation of the legalistic Jewish-christian element in the church which both Matthew and Luke have modified through their redactional activity.[2] Nor is it likely that Matthew understood it in terms of the 'love-commandment' that is elsewhere stressed in his gospel. It is true that in Matt. 7.12 and 22.40 this is presented as a definitive summary of the Law and the prophets but in both these passages it is only *their* significance that is under consideration and Jesus does not set out *his own* more radical demands. So, for example, in Matt. 19.16ff., where the love-commandment occupies a prominent place, Jesus' demand to 'sell all and give to the poor' and his call to personal discipleship indicate that his own requirements go far beyond obedience to it. The same is true in Matt. 5.43ff., while the remaining antitheses show that there are other norms upon which Jesus' ethic is predicated than the 'love-commandment' alone.[3]

As for the Lucan section itself (Luke 16.16–18), it appears at first sight to be an anomaly in the gospel, for nowhere else have we found Lucan interest in the Law itself, as seems to be the

---

[1] H. Schürmann, 'Sprachliche Reminiszenzen an abgeänderte oder ausgelassene Bestandteile der Spruchsammlung im Lukas- und Matthäus-Evangelium', *NTS*, 6 (1960), 193ff. He has even suggested that the tradition behind the Matthaean construction in Matt. 5.17–20 comes from the same source. This has already been shown to be unlikely for v.17 while the link between vv.17–18 is clearly Matthaean. It is also improbable for vv.19–20, as shall be demonstrated shortly. More speculative attempts to prove the pre-Lucan character of 16.16–18 from rabbinic methods of argument and ideas are found in J. D. M. Derrett, 'Fresh Light on St Luke XVI', *Law*, pp. 78–99, and D. Daube, *Rabbinic Judaism*, pp. 292ff. The pre-Lucan structure of Luke 16.16–18 had already been affirmed by E. Hirsch, *Frühgeschichte*, II, 65.

[2] *Contra* B. H. Branscomb, *Law*, pp. 225–6; E. Schweizer, 'Matthäus 5.17–20', pp. 399–403; G. Strecker, *Gerechtigkeit*, pp. 143–4; R. Hummel, *Auseinandersetzung*, p. 68; R. Walker, *Heilsgeschichte*, p. 135.

[3] *Contra* E. Schweizer, 'Matthäus 5.17–20', pp. 402–6.

case here. According to Schürmann, vv.16–17 were merely retained as an introductory piece to v.18, the subject of which would be of interest in Gentile-christian circles. Alternatively it has been viewed as a subordinate element in the critique against the Pharisees with which the whole of the chapter deals, challenging them with the fact that it is no longer the Law to which they should pay attention, but the preaching of the Kingdom (v.16).[1] While this satisfactorily explains Luke's addition in v.16b as well as the parable which follows (vv.19ff.), and accords with his emphasis on the ministry of Christ elsewhere in legal sections, the retention of vv.17–18 probably results from his faithfulness in preserving the tradition (cf. 14.2ff.) even when it does not yield to his particular concerns.

5.19.

ὃς ἐὰν οὖν λύσῃ μίαν τῶν ἐντολῶν τούτων τῶν ἐλαχίστων, καὶ διδάξῃ οὕτω τοὺς ἀνθρώπους, ἐλάχιστος κληθήσεται ἐν τῇ βασιλείᾳ τῶν οὐρανῶν. ὃς δ' ἂν ποιήσῃ καὶ διδάξῃ, οὗτος μέγας κληθήσεται ἐν τῇ βασιλείᾳ τῶν οὐρανῶν.

This verse is linked with v.18 through the conjunction οὖν, a Matthaean insertion which is almost certainly inferential.[2] There follows a warning against those who 'loose', i.e., refuse to observe,[3] μίαν τῶν ἐντολῶν τούτων τῶν ἐλαχίστων for they shall be least in the Kingdom. The word τούτων has been frequently related to ἰῶτα ἓν ἢ μία κεραία in v.18, in which case the two verses were probably transmitted together in Q and stem from a Jewish-christian wing of the church. On the other hand, it has also been suggested that since the words in v.18, because of their figurative character, cannot function as a

---

[1] So F. W. Danker, 'Luke 16.16 – An Opposition Logion?', *JBL*, 77 (1958), 231–43.

[2] E. Lohmeyer, *Matthäus*, p. 110, and W. Trilling, *Israel*, p. 180, concur as to Matthaean redaction but deny an inferential intention.

[3] λύειν, therefore, is not to be interpreted as 'abrogate' (A. Lukyn-Williams, *Matthew*, I, 157) nor seen in light of the rabbinic practice of 'forbidding and allowing' (A. Merx, *Matthäus*, pp. 85ff.). Even less should it be understood with H. J. Ljungmann, *Gesetz*, p. 50, in terms of the 'loosing' of a commandment from that to which it is bound, preserving his emphasis upon 'wholeness' in 5.17–18. The term is merely intended as a negative counterpart to ποιεῖν.

true grammatical antecedent, it was an isolated logion inserted here by Matthew to emphasise the continuing validity of the Mosaic commandments.[1] The opposition against which this verse is directed has then been variously described as Hellenistic-christian (Bultmann, Käsemann, Barth), Pauline (Manson, Beare, Brandon) or, as is more likely, Jewish-christian (charismatic?) antinomianism (Schweizer, Davies, Hummel). However, much of the debate on this issue has been rather misplaced. While the ἀνομία of the scribes and Pharisees that is attacked in Matt. 23.28 appears to be based on a careless attitude to the basic moral standards of the Mosaic Law, in 7.23; 13.41 and 24.11ff. it is a lax approach to the commands of Christ which is in view. Most probably, Matthew regarded the teaching of these passages as applicable to certain one-sidedly charismatic sections of the Jewish-christian congregations to whom he was writing. There is a strong possibility, then, that Matthew both interpreted and applied the saying in 5.19 in a similar manner. Before pursuing that further, however, two other ways of understanding τούτων should be considered.

As an alternative to relating it to the least significant commandments in the Mosaic legislation, it has been proposed that a reference to the Decalogue, or to the rabbinic distinction between 'light' and 'heavy' commandments is in mind.[2] A reflection of rabbinic discussion is unlikely, however, for though the rabbis did grade the commandments, the descriptions 'great' and 'small' are not present in such contexts and it was

---

[1] For the former, cf. E. Klostermann, *Matthäus*, pp. 40–1; G. Schrenk, *TDNT*, II, 548–9; H. J. Ljungmann, *Gesetz*, pp. 48ff.; W. Trilling, *Israel*, p. 181 n.82 and H. Schürmann, 'Wer daher eines dieser geringsten Gebote auflöst...', *BZ*, 4 (1960), 241; H. T. Wrege, *Bergpredigt*, pp. 40–1. For the latter, cf. E. Lohmeyer, *Matthäus*, p. 110; Th. Soiron, *Bergpredigt*, p. 239; R. Hummel, *Auseinandersetzung*, p. 67.

[2] For the former cf. F. Dibelius, 'Zwei Worte Jesu', *ZNW*, 11 (1910), 188ff.; A. Schlatter, *Matthäus*, pp. 157f. J. Hänel, *Schriftbegriff*, p. 163, and A. Wilder, *Eschatology*, p. 130, refer it to the weightier matters of the Law and S. Schulz, *Botschaft*, p. 184, to the Hellenistic-Jewish concentration on the Decalogue and love-commandment. For the latter see T. W. Manson, *Sayings*, p. 154; K. Bornhäuser, *Die Bergpredigt* (1923), p. 57, *et al.* Thus the saying has often been directed against the scribes and Pharisees. Cf. H. Huber, *Bergpredigt*, pp. 68–9; J. Staudinger, *Bergpredigt*, pp. 78–9, *et al.* Against both of these views see especially the detailed discussion by H. Röthlisberger, *Kirche*, pp. 38–9.

not only the 'lesser' commandments that were relaxed. Reference to the Decalogue or weightier matters of the law is ruled out by the presence of ἐλαχίστος, as well as by the consistent usage of νόμος throughout this passage, and the gospel, of the Torah as a whole.

Most suitable is its interpretation as a demonstrative with adjectival character, referring not in a general way to the commandments of which v.18b metaphorically speaks, but rather to those associated with v.18d, i.e., in Christ's own teaching. In view of other sayings in the gospel that stem from Matthew's tradition, or are typical of Matthaean understanding, this suggestion has considerable force.[1] So far as Matthew itself is concerned, while the noun ἐντολή refers to Old Testament commandments, elsewhere the cognate verb is also used of Jesus' own demands (cf. 28.20).[2] (As we have already seen, ἀνομία is more frequently used of disobedience to such demands than rejection of the Law.) However, there are some grounds for thinking that Jesus himself could have used the noun in this more specialised sense. This is borne out by the fact that elsewhere in tradition that has good claims to being authentic, interest is expressed in similar terminology to that utilised here. So, for example, in Matt. 18.6/Mark 9.42 Jesus speaks of ἕνα τῶν μικρῶν τούτων τῶν πιστευοντῶν εἰς ἐμέ. Matthew alone reiterates this in vv.10, 14, though without the personal reference to Christ. Peculiar to Matthew, but also originating with Jesus, is Matt. 25.40, with its reference to ἑνὶ τούτων τῶν ἀδελφῶν μου τῶν ἐλαχίστων. This is repeated, minus the reference to Jesus himself, in v.45. In these contexts the ideas 'one', 'small' and 'these' are brought into conjunction, in the first instance with 'children', in the second with 'brethren'. These, through their being linked with Christ, exchange their literal sense for a 'christian' meaning. However, this explicit christological reference is omitted in the reiterations (cf. 18.10, 14;

[1] It has only been rarely advanced, and never with the strength it deserves. See, however, E. Lohmeyer, *Matthäus*, pp. 111–12, and C. A. Carlston, *NTS*, 15 (1968), 78 n.2, 79 n.7, who are convinced that Matthew at least interpreted it in this way, and J. M. Gibbs, *St.Ev.*, iv (1968), 43, who considers it to have been Jesus' understanding as well.

[2] This passage also picks up three other themes found in Matt. 5.19 and its immediate context, represented by the terms διδάσκοντες, τῆρειν (here ποιεῖν) and πάντα.

25.45). Is it too much to suggest that something similar has occurred in relation to 'the commandments' in 5.19? If so, the expression would refer not to the Mosaic legislation but to Christ's own instructions. Quite possibly, then, the original context of the saying behind 5.19, 5.19 itself being Matthew's reiteration of it, was also in the ministry of Jesus. It now becomes explicable why the verse goes on to insist that one who disobeys the least of these teachings, as a disciple, remains within the Kingdom (cf. 18.20; 25.40), whereas in v.20 (cf. 18.6ff.; 25.45) the scribes and Pharisees who do keep many of the least significant OT requirements (cf. 23.23) are excluded from it.

Matthaean redaction is possibly present in the use of διδάσκειν and οὕτως in the remaining section of the verse, for both are Matthaean terms, and the same is true of ἐν τῇ βασιλείᾳ τῶν οὐρανῶν, though behind it a similar expression no doubt occurred.[1] With this saying, then, it is not only by means of his redactional activity but by his insertion of it at this point, so that τούτων refers back to v.18d, that Matthew has continued to develop the theme of the previous two verses. In so doing he has not violated the sense of the original logion that lay behind it, but as with v.18, has succeeded in integrating it more theologically into a framework of ideas which already formed, in a general way, its wider context.[2]

---

[1] For a discussion of Matthew's understanding of this term see A. Kretzer, *Die Herrschaft der Himmel und die Söhne des Reiches* (1971).

[2] E. Käsemann, 'Die Anfänge christlicher Theologie', *Exegetische Versuche und Besinnungen* (1964), II, 83, commenting on the 'legal-ruling and retributory-consequence' character of the saying, regards 5.19 as an example of the 'Sätze heiligen Rechtes' formulated in the christian community. K. Berger, 'Zu den sogenannten Sätzen heiligen Rechts', *NTS*, 17 (1970), 10–40 (see also 'Die sog. "Sätze heiligen Rechts" im NT', *TZ*, 5 [1972], 305–30), on the contrary, regards such statements as conditional relative clauses of wisdom, rather than legal, character with definite apocalyptic overtones whose *Sitz-im-leben* is the instruction of new converts in a Gentile setting. It is by no means certain, however, that all such statements should be relegated to a milieu in the early church and we have produced sufficient grounds for presuming that behind 5.19 an authentic saying is to be found. Nor, as we have seen, was the original saying a strong Jewish-christian legalistic utterance which Matthew has transformed through his redactional work in and around the logion. Against E. Lohmeyer, *Matthäus*, pp. 109–10; E. Schweizer, 'Matthäus 5.17–20', pp. 400–1; G. Barth, 'Law', p. 66; G. Strecker, *Gerechtigkeit*, pp. 145ff.; W. Trilling, *Israel*, pp. 179ff.; S. Schulz, *Botschaft*, p. 184.

5.20.

λέγω γὰρ ὑμῖν, ὅτι μὴ περισσεύσῃ ἡ δικαιοσύνη ὑμῶν πλεῖον τῶν γραμματέων καὶ φαρισαίων, οὐ μὴ εἰσέλθητε εὐ τὴν βασιλείαν τῶν οὐρανῶν.

Matthaean redaction has also taken place in the final saying in this sequence. Like v.18, it is through γάρ linked inferentially with the verse that precedes it. Once again, however, the conjunction indicates that a saying is being introduced here from another context. The form of the saying is also quite possibly Matthaean. The construction with ἐὰν μὴ is paralleled in 18.3, whereas Jesus himself seems to have favoured the more impersonal formulation lying behind the ὃς ἄν of Mark 10.15 (cf. Luke 18.17). The term περισσεύειν is almost certainly redactional as well. Matthew elsewhere adds it, in an explanatory manner, to the sayings in 13.12 and 25.29 and alters περισσεύματα to the verbal form in 15.37 (cf. Mark 8.8). (The cognate term περισσός is redactional in its only two occurrences (5.37b; 5.47) both in the Sermon on the Mount.) Most probably, the reference to δικαιοσύνη is redactional as well (cf. 3.15; 5.6, 10; 6.33 and perhaps 6.1 and 21.32). It is a favourite Matthaean term and behind it a less theologically charged expression may have originally stood. ἡ βασιλεία τῶν οὐρανῶν is also typically Matthaean; it is ἡ βασιλεία τοῦ θεοῦ which is customarily referred to elsewhere.

It might be argued that since more than half the other 'entrance-sayings' in Matthew appear only in his gospel, that quite possibly the whole of v.20 is a Matthaean construction. However, the traditional character, indeed authenticity, of each of these additional sayings is quite capable of being defended (see, for example, 7.21; 18.3 and 23.13). This suggests that a traditional, if not authentic, utterance probably underlies v.20 as well. Most probably it stated that 'Whoever does not do more than the scribes and the Pharisees, will not enter into the Kingdom of God.' Its insertion here is in line with Matthew's tendency elsewhere in passages dealing with the Law, to introduce material from other sources in which Jesus criticises the conduct of his religious opponents (cf. esp. 12.11–12; 15.13–14; 23.6ff.). The precise origin of the saying behind v.20 in the tradition, however, is difficult to determine. Both M and Q have been proposed, while others have been content to suggest that it comes from an isolated piece of tradition.[1]

In this saying, then, the disciples are warned that their obedience must exceed that of the scribes and the Pharisees if they wish to be guaranteed an entrance into the Kingdom of Heaven. So far as Matthew's reference to δικαιοσύνη is concerned, the word must be understood in terms of 'conduct' and the comparative construction in which it occurs can lexically best be understood in a quantitative, not qualitative, sense. Certainly, in Matthew's usage elsewhere it is conduct alone which is in view, and this is also the emphasis in the preceding (v.19) and succeeding (vv.21–48) verses, as well as the general thrust of the whole Sermon (7.24–7).[2] In that such conduct, as the following antitheses demonstrate, transcends the demands of the Law, we can also speak of a new quality attaching to it.

Since *righteousness* is for Matthew a comprehensive term signifying the character of the instructions Jesus sets before his followers and, as such, the positive counterpart to the *hypocrisy* of the Pharisees, one can rightly view it as forming the theme of the material that follows. It is scarcely correct, however despite the frequency with which it has been asserted, that v.20 should be viewed as the introduction to 5.21–48. The antitheses themselves are primarily directed at the Mosaic Law rather than at the oral tradition. This means that it is rather 5.17–20 as a whole that should be regarded as a preface to that which follows. Nevertheless, in so far as criticism of Pharisaic tradition and behaviour is not altogether absent from 5.21–8, Matthew's insertion of this verse in this context is far from inappropriate.

[1] For the first see B. H. Streeter, *Gospels*, p. 256; G. D. Kilpatrick, *Origins*, pp. 25f., T. W. Manson, *Sayings*, p. 153. The second has been contended by H. Schürmann, *BZ*, 4 (1960), 243. On the third see J. Schniewind, *Matthäus*, p. 53; Th. Soiron, *Bergpredigt*, pp. 243f., and W. Trilling, *Israel*, p. 183. In view of the analysis I have suggested, the attempt by H. T. Wrege, *Bergpredigt*, pp. 42f., to locate pre-Matthaean tradition behind the saying on the ground of a supposedly Semitic construction underlying περισσεύειν. . .πλεῖον with δικαιοσύνη having exclusive rather than (as here) comparative force, cannot be sustained.
[2] On this see especially the detailed examination of G. Strecker, *Gerechtigkeit*, pp. 150ff.

If it focusses attention on an aspect of Jesus' attitude to the Law that has particular significance for him, it is nevertheless in accord with inferences that may be drawn from particular disputes over the Law between Jesus and the religious teachers of his time.

In each of these verses, then, Matthew is not so much imposing upon the tradition of Jesus' words a weight that it cannot bear, or pointing it in a direction substantially at variance with Jesus' original intention. On the contrary, he attempts to draw out some of the theological implications and practical consequences of the attitude Jesus adopts. This leads him to emphasise the prophetic and so provisional function of the Mosaic legislation and underline its realisation and fulfilment in Christ's ministry, to highlight the authoritative character of Jesus' utterances and indicate the polemical ramifications of his position for contemporary Jewish approaches to the Law, and to stress the need for obedience to Jesus' teachings and find an adequate ethical terminology to describe the character or the conduct which Jesus demands. It therefore becomes apparent that it is not so much *Jesus'* stance towards the Law that he is concerned to depict: it is how the *Law* stands with regard to him, as the one who brings it to fulfilment and to whom all attention must now be directed. As this analysis has sought to demonstrate, however, such a way of posing the issue stems from the authentic words of Jesus which Matthew's account enshrines.

Epilogue (Matt. 5.48/Luke 6.36; Matt. 7.12/Luke 6.31). These verses have commonly beeen interpreted as 'summing up' the respective viewpoints of the evangelists on the question with which we have been concerned. Thus the call to 'perfection' in imitation of God in 5.48 is rightly regarded as gathering up all that has so far been said into a single term which, for Matthew, has a comprehensive 'theological' significance.[1] The detailed treatment of P. J. du Plessis indicates that the Hebrew words תמים, שלם and the LXX translation τέλειος refer to the

---

[1] Cf. recently A. Descamps, *Justice*, pp. 197ff.; W. Trilling, *Israel*, p. 195; E. Neuhäusler, *Anspruch*, p. 51. The Matthaean character of the term has only occasionally been denied. See W. C. Allen, *Matthew*, p. 55; F. W. Beare, *Records*, p. 60; P. Bonnard, *Matthieu*, p. 76.

'wholeness' of the individual in his ongoing life before God, which by its nature involved a moral aspect as well. In the Essene writings the idea occurs with special reference to observance of the totality of the demands of the Law.[1] Matthew,however, gives a new content to the term for he sets it over against the Law (5.21ff.; 19.20), though in aligning it with the new demands that Jesus makes does relate it to the fulfilment of the Law through his teaching. Consequently there are no strict parallels in either the OT or Essene writings, while in rabbinic parallels where imitation of God is the theme, the idea of imitating his perfection is not expressly found.[2] For Matthew then, where δικαιοσύνη is present in the obedient disciple through his acceptance and practice of Jesus' demands, he may be characterised, in his whole relationship to God, as τέλειος. This is in accord with the interpretation given it in the passage dealing with the encounter between Jesus and the Rich Young Man.[3]

Matthaean redaction is also evident in the citation of the Golden Rule in 7.12 and in the addition, over against Luke 6.31, of πάντα, οὖν and οὕτως, all favourite Matthaean terms which we have encountered before. This verse has also frequently been held to close that section of the Sermon which commences in 5.17ff. and, in so doing, to sum up the essence of

---

[1] P. J. du Plessis, 'ΤΕΛΕΙΟΣ: The Idea of Perfection in the NT' (Diss. 1959), pp. 94–115.

[2] Cf. E. Percy, *Botschaft*, p. 163; E. Neuhäusler, *Anspruch*, pp. 49–50. The distinctiveness of Matthew's usage makes a dependence upon Essene (G. Barth, 'Law', pp. 98ff.; J. Gnilka, 'Die Kirche des Matthäus und die Gemeinde von Qumran', *BZ*, 7 [1963], 59ff.; W. D. Davies, *Setting*, pp. 208–15), or even OT (A. H. McNeile, *Matthew*, p. 73; A. Schlatter, *Matthäus*, p. 197; J. Schniewind, *Matthäus*, p. 73; H. J. Ljungmann, *Gesetz*, pp. 89ff.; A. Descamps, *Justice*, p. 196; W. Trilling, *Israel*, p. 194; K. Stendahl, *Matthew*, p. 137) ideas most unlikely, though it does of course share a common substratum with both.

[3] As in Matt. 19.22a, then, the term cannot embody an idea of conduct that is defined as a radical interpretation of the Law (as G. Bornkamm, 'End-Expectation', p. 29; G. Barth, 'Law', pp. 102ff.) nor a new understanding of the Law (as V. E. Hasler, 'Gesetz', p. 22, and W. Trilling, *Israel*, pp. 193ff.) but only a transcending or fulfilling of the same. On the other hand the 'existential' definition of E. Fuchs, 'Die vollkommene Gewissheit', *Neutestamentlichen Studien für R. Bultmann* (1954), pp. 130ff. in terms of a 'situation ethic' goes too far in the other direction.

Jesus' demands. Matthew's interest in the 'love-commandment' has already been noted in 19.19 and particularly in 22.34ff. where, as here, a reference to 'the Law and the prophets' is appended (22.40). Two factors combine to make it unlikely that such a comprehensive understanding of the verse was intended by the evangelist. In the first place, the conjunction οὖν rather than possessing a general resumptive function is most probably a loose connecting link with that which precedes, for which parallels can be found elsewhere in the gospel.[1] Secondly, while the 'love-commandment' possessed decisive significance for the content of the Law, it was not set forward as the central norm of his own demands. Even when the 'love-commandment' is re-defined in terms of his own teaching (as in 5.43ff.) it forms only one component within it. Furthermore, there can now be no doubt that Jesus' positive formulation of this principle had been anticipated in earlier Jewish thought, though its application to people outside the immediate religious and national circle and its elevation to a position above the other commandments does give it a special, if still not definitive, position in his teaching.[2] Thus the view that in this declaration of the 'love-commandment' the Law and the prophets had their 'fulfilment' cannot be sustained.[3]

In Luke these two sayings occur in quite different forms and in quite different contexts, the first as the preface to the section on 'judging' in Luke 6.37ff., the second as the centrepiece of the Lucan formulation of the material paralleled in Matt. 5.39ff. (Luke 6.27–35). Their positioning indicates that for Luke also they have considerable significance attached to them. In fact they provide the key to Luke's interest in, and understanding of, this section of his tradition. It is clear that Luke has not orientated this part of his sermon around the Law but rather around ideas of 'love' and 'mercy', and the unity of structure that is characteristic of these sections indicates the

---

[1] See further E. Lohmeyer, *Matthäus*, p. 110; W. Trilling, *Israel*, p. 180.

[2] On the first point, see the detailed investigation of A. Dihle, *Die Goldene Regel* (1962), as also the more recent essay of H. Hruby, 'L'amour du prochain dans la pensée juive', *NRT*, 91 (1969), 493–516. However, the discussion in I. Abrahams, *Studies*, I, 21–2, suggests that, on the question of the boundaries within which the principle applied, their conclusions may have to be somewhat tempered.

[3] *Contra* E. Schweizer, 'Matthäus, 5.17–20', pp. 402ff.

presence of redactional activity here no less than in Matthew.[1] This of course corresponds to what we have discovered for Luke elsewhere in 'legal' material where the emphasis is less upon the relationship to the Law inherent in Jesus' actions, than upon the compassionate nature of his preaching ministry or teaching involved therein. Here, however, the 'legal' framework has been dropped altogether and Luke's intentions are clearly exposed. That his formulation of the sermon was as decisively moulded by the Gentile audience he was addressing, as Matthew's was by his Jewish-christian circle of readers is quite evident. In the same way that Matthew conditioned his material by reference to the commandments which lay at the base of daily Jewish practice, so Luke, clothing the words of Jesus in Greek dress, emphasises the concrete and active character of love in everyday life precisely against the commonly accepted principle of reciprocity which lay at the root of relationships in the ancient world.[2] Both evangelists, therefore, have taken the original words of Jesus and, by isolating one aspect of their application, directed them to the particular situation they are addressing.

Context. One final aspect of the Sermon requires examination. This has to do with the contention that its wider context in the first gospel suggests that the teaching of Jesus is represented as a New Law promulgated by a second Moses or as a New Torah decreed by the Messiah. It is not possible to examine all the passages in which the conception of Jesus as a New Moses or as a Messianic *Torahlehrer* has been said to occur. However, since it is reasonable to assume that if these ideas were developed, they would be especially discernible in those passages in which

---

[1] Cf. C. Spicq, *Agapé dans le Nouveau Testament* (1958), 1, 98ff.; W. Grundmann, 'Die Bergpredigt nach der Lukasfassung', *St.Ev.*, 1 (1959), 180–9; H.-W. Bartsch, 'Feldrede und Bergpredigt: Redaktionsarbeit in Lk. 6', *TZ*, 16 (1960), 17ff. A heightened eschatological interest has been suggested by the latter for the Lucan account, but although he recognises the eschatological interest in Matt. 7.15ff., he does not give sufficient weight to such verses as Matt. 5.19, 20, 22, 29, 30, 45.

[2] Cf. esp. the illuminating discussion in W. C. van Unnik, 'Die Motivierung der Feindesliebe in Lukas vi.32–5', *NT*, 8 (1966), 284–300. The Hellenistic character of many of Luke's terms had already frequently received notice.

ethical instruction is given by Jesus, we can restrict ourselves to those pericopes in which such has been claimed to occur, as well as to the broader context in which the Sermon on the Mount itself is set. Our examination of the contemporary Jewish literature produced no evidence for the belief in either conception during the time of Jesus. Here we seek to discover whether Jesus, or particularly Matthew, was the first to develop such a category of explanation.

Revitalising a very early tradition which depicted Matthew's gospel as containing Five Books of Teaching parallel to the Five Books of Moses, B. W. Bacon, separating off the Prologue (Matt. 1–2) and Epilogue (Matt. 26–8), isolated the Sermon (5–7), Missionary Charge (9.36 – 10.42); Parables (13.1–52); Ecclesiastical Material (17.22 – 18.35) and Eschatological Discourse (23.1–25, 46), each preceded by narrative (and sometimes debate) material, and followed by a closing formula (7.28–9; 11.1; 13.53; 19.1; 26.1). Since he announced it, his view has won considerable support.[1] However, most probably, the formulas are 'opening' and not 'closing' formulas at all;[2] the books of the Pentateuch do not each consist of lists of commandments prefaced by narrative material, and the so-called 'Five Books' of Matthew cannot be said to correspond in content in any way to the individual Pentateuchal books to which each is related;[3] the ascription 'legal' to such passages as the parabolic and eschatological discourses is scarcely justifiable, while

---

[1] See B. W. Bacon, 'Jesus and the Law: A Study of the First "Book" of Matthew', *JBL*, 47 (1928), 203ff., expanded in *Studies in Matthew* (1930). W. D. Davies, *Setting*, pp. 16f., at the beginning of his exhaustive study of the idea provides a comprehensive list of commentators favouring or bypassing the hypothesis. To the former one may add the names of Sahlin, Dabeck, Thieme, McArthur, Bornkamm and Hahn; to the latter, Chapman, Goodspeed, Filson, Kümmel, Michaelis, Moule, Blair, Trilling, Strecker and Walker.

[2] Cf. H. B. Green, 'The Structure of St Matthew's Gospel', *St.Ev.*, IV (1968), I, 48–9.

[3] Cf. esp. P. Nepper-Christensen, *Das Matthäusevangelium – ein judenchristliches Evangelium?* (1958), p. 173 n.52, against K. Thieme, 'Matthäus, der schriftgelehrte Evangelist', *Jud.* 5 (1949), p. 144, who is led to absurd conclusions in his attempt to relate the two sets of material. See also A. Farrer, 'On Dispensing with Q', *Studies in the Gospels and Epistles* (ed. D. E. Nineham, 1955), pp. 75–6, whose own suggestions along this line soon run into difficulty.

outside the second 'half' of the 'Five Books' some of the main sections of 'legal' material occur (12.1ff.; 15.1ff.; 19.1ff.); the structure neglects Matt. 23, which is one of the most important groupings in the book, yet 18.1ff., with little teaching material in comparison, is included because of the formula in 19.1.[1] This structure, as its appearance in Psalms, Proverbs and Ecclesiasticus as well as in Megilloth and Pirke Aboth demonstrates, is an extremely widespread literary genre and not necessarily a reflection of the Pentateuch. The greatest weakness of the theory, however, is its exclusion of the Prologue and Epilogue, especially the latter which, with its treatment of the Cross and Resurrection, for Matthew overshadows the 'teaching' element of the ministry entirely.[2] It should be noted, however, that this broader view of Jesus' ministry and function is not drawn together around the idea of Messiahship. Though Jesus admits the appropriateness of this description, in Matthew's gospel in particular he does so with the greatest reluctance, intimating that this is not an altogether suitable definition (Matt. 26.63-4) while elsewhere he demonstrates the inadequacy of the traditional conception of his status (Matt. 22.41ff.). This undoubtedly reflects the practice of Jesus himself.[3]

It has often been assumed that the mention of the 'mountain' in 5.1 is a deliberate parallel to Sinai. However, the phrase ἀνέβη εἰς τὸ ὄρος probably stems from Mark 3.13[4] and explicit indications of such a parallelism are absent (cf. Heb. 12.18ff.), while the association of an 'anonymous' mountain with the main aspects of Jesus' ministry in Matthew – temptation, calling of disciples, transfiguration, last commission – indicates rather its function as the place of 'revelation'.[5] Moreover, even if it

[1] Cf. E. J. Goodspeed, *Matthew, Apostle and Evangelist* (1959), pp. 26–7; J. Chapman, *Matthew, Mark and Luke* (1937), p. 211.

[2] Cf. G. Strecker, *Gerechtigkeit*, p. 147 n.2, and E. P. Blair, *Jesus*, p. 135, *et al.*

[3] See, most recently, D. Catchpole, 'The Answer of Jesus to Caiaphas (Mt 26.64)', *NTS*, 16 (1970).

[4] See further, O. J. Seitz, 'Love Your Enemies', *NTS*, 16 (1969), 39–40.

[5] This has been most fully worked out by J. Jeremias, *Der Gottesberg* (1919), pp. 143ff. Stressing its purely geographical significance are W. C. Allen, *Matthew*, p. 38; N. B. Stonehouse, *Witness*, p. 134; A. Schlatter, *Matthäus*, p. 128; P. Nepper-Christensen, *Matthäus*, pp. 175ff., and W. Förster, *TDNT*, v, 484.

existed, such an identification would not necessitate the concept of a New Moses or New Law, since in Cant.R. on 1.3 where there is such a parallelism, an inference to the teacher concerned as being a New Moses or delivering a New Torah would be impossible.[1] Nevertheless, the presence of a New Torah promulgated by a New Moses, or of a Messianic Torah within 5.17–48 has frequently been assumed. We have seen, however, that neither the form nor content of the Sermon justify such a description, for while it is true that the demands are formulated in a legal style, this is merely to deliver them in the most forceful possible way and not to imply anything as to their character. So far as their content is concerned, they quite transcend the Law, and such is their character that any legal terminology is entirely inadequate to describe them. Though they are ultimately christological rather than paranetic in character the person to whom they draw attention is not depicted at any point in the narrative in specifically Messianic colours. Ideas of a New, or Messianic, Torah and of a New Moses or Messianic Lawgiver, therefore, are entirely absent in this section of Matthew's gospel and there is nothing to suggest that they were an element in the original teaching or approach of Christ which form their nucleus.

Nowhere else in the passages that have been examined is there any hint of the presence of such notions. Elsewhere the only possibilities for the occurrence of these ideas in a teaching context are in the Transfiguration narrative, where the disciples are commanded 'Listen to him' (Matt. 17.5, cf. Deut. 18.15), and in the Resurrection account, where Jesus himself commands his disciples to instruct others in his teaching (Matt. 28.20). In the first, however, it is the teaching of the way of the Cross that is intended, scarcely a subject relevant to a New Moses–New Torah schema,[2] and in the second, it is the glorified

---

[1] A further parallel is provided by M. Bacher, *Die Agada die babylonischen Amoräer* (1913), p. 101.

[2] See esp. J. Blinzler, *Die neutestamentliche Berichte über die Verklärung Jesu* (1937), p. 144, and F. Gils, *Prophète*, pp. 36–7 as well as M. E. Thrall, 'Elijah and Moses in Mark's account of the Transfiguration', *NTS*, 16 (1970), 314. In this connection it is worth noting the questionable nature of the argument for the return of Moses from his appearance on the mount in the Transfiguration narrative. The decisive factor is the description of the two figures as appearing (Luke 9.31) and while this occurs only in the

Lord who speaks of his own unique instruction, the figure of Moses or the issue of Law being far from sight.[1] It is no more possible to find evidence of any specific Messianic categories being employed in these passages. The reason for this stems from the fact that the experience of Jesus in the first and authority of Jesus in the second cannot be contained within them.

It is rather a teaching that transcends the Law, and a Lord who transcends the figures of Moses and the Messiah in Jewish expectation, that is found throughout the gospel. For this reason, the further suggestion that Jesus is the Torah Incarnate rather than the giver of a *Nova Lex* is also unacceptable, for in such a conception too much emphasis is still placed upon the

Lucan account, the incidence of the word elsewhere, as well as the situation reflected in the parallel narratives, suggests an 'unveiling' of the present *status* of Moses and Elijah, rather than a coming of either again. The silence with respect to Moses when the coming of Elijah is referred to in the following passage (Mark 9.9–13 and pars.) is also extremely significant. Nevertheless, E. Lohmeyer, 'Die Verklärung Jesu nach dem Markusevangelium', *ZNW*, 21 (1922), 185–215, and G. H. Boobyer, 'St Mark and the Transfiguration', *JTS*, 41 (1940), 118–40, have argued that the story is an anticipation of the coming of Moses and Elijah with the Messiah in the Parousia. The latter maintains that, Luke 2.9 apart, all the other occurrences of the word in the Synoptists appear in a Parousia context, and that Luke 9.31 should be so regarded here. True, Matt. 16.27–8 and pars. refer to the Parousia, but the δόξα spoken of is that which is permanently associated with God. It is similar with Matt. 24.30 and pars. (cf. 'glorious throne' in Matt. 19.28; 25.31). In Luke 24.26 the term refers to his ascension (cf. 1 Pet. 1.11; 1 Tim. 3.16, as also those passages which speak of his present glory: Acts 7.55; 1 Cor. 2.8; 2 Cor. 3.18; James 2.1) and this is quite possibly in view in Mark 10.37 (cf. Matt. 20.21 'kingdom'). It is extremely unlikely, therefore, that the idea of a return of Moses is at all present in the passage, quite apart from the lack of any indication of the granting of a new Law.

[1] Cf. esp. O. Michel, 'Der Abschluss des Matthäusevangelium', *Ev.Th.*, 10 (1950–1), 21ff.; H. Kosmala, 'The Conclusion of Matthew', *ASTI*, 4 (1965), 142ff. The attempt by B. H. Branscomb, *Law*, pp. 91–2, to find a germ of the idea in Jesus' 'abrogation' of food laws, divorce and sabbath is also misplaced. There is nothing in the controversies over defilement and divorce to suggest such a conclusion. I have not felt it necessary to consider Mark 2.23ff. and pars. here, for not only does use of the expression 'Son of Man' in the synoptic accounts spring from a misunderstanding of the Aramaic, but it is most unlikely that the term 'Son of Man' was a Messianic title at all. See further D. S. Russell, *Apocalyptic*, pp. 331–4.

Law. Instead, the Torah has been fulfilled in his teaching and life in such a way that it no longer possesses its Torah-quality and no longer justifies a Torah-ascription.[1]

We commenced this examination of references to the Law in Jesus' more extended teaching with several remaining categories by which the relationship of Jesus to the Law, and Matthew's presentation of it, might be explained. It is now possible to review these in the light of the further information that has been obtained. In the first place, to define it solely in terms of 'transcendence' of his teaching over the Law placed too much emphasis upon the statement in Matt. 11.13/Luke 16.16 and neglected the positive content of 5.17–18. Moreover, this, though theologically more developed by Matthew, had its basis in the words of Jesus. However, this did not mean that his demands were to be viewed in terms of a new Mosaic or Messianic Torah. In the first place, this expectation appears to be absent in contemporary Judaism as well as those passages in the gospel where such a concept could easily have been developed. Furthermore, such an interpretation laid too much emphasis on the 'form' of the antitheses at the expense of their content. Thus it was in the idea of 'fulfilment' that the answer, both for Jesus and for Matthew, was found. It was not possible to equate this with the declaration of the love-commandment for this ran counter to the emphasis upon teaching and obedience that formed the context of 5.17. Again, any direct association of such obedience with the death of Christ lacked exegetical support. The true solution lay in understanding 'fulfilment' in terms of an affirmation of the whole of the Law, yet only through its transformation into the teaching of Christ which was something new and unique in comparison with it.

This 'fulfilment' was to be reflected in the life of the disciple. 'Righteousness' consisted in obedience to the instructions of Christ, and the life which was set in this direction was described

---

[1] See, however, J. M. Gibbs, *St.Ev.*, IV (1968), I, 38ff., and M. J. Suggs, *Wisdom, Christology and Law in Matthew* (1970), pp. 106ff. The idea of a new Law does, of course, appear later in Hermas, *Sim.* 5:6:3; 8:3:2; Barnabas 2.6; Justin, *Dial.* 11.4; 14.3; 18.3. Paul also speaks of the 'law of Christ' (cf. Gal. 6.2; 1 Cor. 9.21) but it would be a mistake to interpret this in a literal fashion. See rather the significance attached to it by C. H. Dodd, 'ΕΝΝΟΜΟΣ ΧΡΙΣΤΟΥ', *Studia Paulina* (ed. W. C. van Unnik and G. Sevenster, 1953), p. 107, and R. N. Longenecker, *Paul*, pp. 184ff.

as 'perfect'. Such 'fulfilment' was also related ultimately to Christ's wider ministry, particularly his death on the Cross. Its announcement and realisation further demonstrated that there was something distinctive about the one by whom it came. Despite the prominence given to this authority in Matthew's gospel, it was not depicted by means of such categories as the 'New Moses' or the 'Messianic Lawgiver', any more than the teaching that went with it possessed the character of a new Mosaic or Messianic Torah. Indeed, apart from the secondary and still somewhat enigmatic identification of Jesus with the Son of Man in all three synoptic accounts of the Sabbath controversies, the status and rôle of Jesus are not the object of description by any of the evangelists, while at no point in the material pertaining to Law are they the occasion of self-conscious reflection on the part of Jesus himself. Yet however indirectly they may be present, they are not only unmistakably but pre-eminently there.

CONCLUSIONS

We are now in a position to draw together the various conclusions that have been reached in the course of this examination of the synoptic accounts of Jesus' relationship to the Law
and to relate them more directly to their Old Testament, inter-
testamentary and Jewish background.

A.   At an early stage of the enquiry a certain ambivalence was
noted in his attitude towards the customs of his people. On
some occasions these were complied with, at other times not.
Nevertheless a single thread runs through all these instances and
demonstrates that a consistent purpose underlies the apparent
variations in his approach, i.e., it was the claims of his mission
which dictated the course of action that should be adopted in
any particular set of circumstances. Thus synagogue-attendance
is only associated with preaching and/or healing, observance of
the Passover is transformed through its link with his coming
death, and payment of the Temple-tax is made so as not to
offend those who were still open to his message. Similarly,
omission of fasting results from the special situation that arises
through his presence with the disciples, and release of the
would-be disciple from the performance of burial-rites stems
from the priority of discipleship over all other responsibilities.
In short, his observation or non-observation of customary
practices did not arise from an attitude of reverence or lack of
reverence to the practices themselves. It derives from the com-
patibility or incompatibility of such with the purpose of his
ministry. It would have been surprising if in this centring of
activity around his own person, teaching and ministry there
had not been found a principle relevant for his attitude to Law
as well.

With regard to the oral tradition, therefore, theoretically one
could expect his occasional compliance when circumstances
indicated that for the sake of the Kingdom such an action was
justified. However, if at any time such was the case we have no
record of it in the synoptic accounts. The picture that emerges

there is one of unrelieved opposition, and we must conclude that it was the nature of Pharisaic legalism and casuistry that rendered such an attitude necessary. Observance of such practices as blessings before and during meals, the singing of the Passover Hallel, the wearing of the customary Jewish robe, had nothing to do with prescriptions in the oral tradition. On the other hand, it would be a mistake to interpret his ignoring of such scribal regulations as those concerning the sabbath and relating to defilement as primarily a deliberate provocation of the Pharisees. It was rather in the routine fulfilment of his mission that such incidents took place and some, sabbath-healings in particular, appear to have been characteristic of his practice from the beginning of his ministry.

It is a similar picture that emerges from his teaching, despite the suggestion that Jesus occasionally argued along rabbinic lines to justify his position. Where rabbinic methods do appear to be present only formal similarities can be detected, for such are invariably used in a non-rabbinic, in some instances christological, manner. Elsewhere, he gives a veiled warning against Pharisaic influence (Mark 8.15) and in the controversy over defilement openly and comprehensively denounces the oral tradition. Denunciation of scribal casuistry also occurs in the Sermon on the Mount and in the speech against the Pharisees. The apparent validation of the oral tradition and of the rabbinic practice of tithing in the latter were seen to be statements occurring in polemical contexts in which the emphasis is laid upon quite other concerns, and which these serve as primarily rhetorical introductions. Certain other alleged affirmations of the tradition such as the prohibition of certain activities in the Temple, acquiescence in sacrificial regulations and warning against flight on the sabbath, were found on closer inspection to have no substance whatever. Our conclusion, then, is in direct contrast to that of Branscomb who claimed that 'Jesus was not opposed to the oral law as such nor did he repudiate it as a whole'.[1] Both in his actions and teaching he takes up a position over against the traditions of the Pharisees. However, it is not anti-Pharisaism as such that is the dominant motive

[1] B. H. Branscomb, *Law*, p. 173. Similar views are expressed, among others, by R. Mackintosh, *Law*, pp. 41–2; S. Cohon, *JBL*, 48 (1929), 98ff.; H. Windisch, *Sermon*, p. 147; S. Légasse, *NRT*, 86 (1964), 673ff.

behind his attitude. Rather is this a corollary of obedience to the mission he had been called to fulfil. That is his primary concern, and a negative attitude to the oral tradition is merely a by-product of it.

When we turn to the question of Jesus' relationship to the Law itself we immediately have to reckon with the apparently contradictory statements which the gospels contain. Even when community creations and evangelists' redactions have been sub-tracted, however, this divergence remains.[1] It was for this reason, in the last century, that the idea of a development in the attitude of Jesus was introduced into the discussion. How-ever, some of the most revolutionary utterances of Jesus are recorded as having taken place during the early days of his ministry (Mark 2.28; 7.15), while other seemingly con-servative statements are recounted in the closing stages of the gospel narratives (Matt. 22.40; 23.3ff.). In any case, the gospel chronologies are too insecure a foundation on which to build any substantial theory of this nature.[2] It is no more possible to draw a consistent distinction between the radical private and conservative public expression of Jesus' teachings. Although, according to the synoptic accounts, on some occa-sions he appears to have directed his most challenging remarks to his disciples alone (cf. Mark 10.11) or primarily to his

---

[1] B. Gerhardsson, *Manuscript*, p. 325 n.1, has rightly complained of E. Stauffer's radical application of this principle so as to eliminate all 'con-servative' or 'Jewish' traces from Jesus' teaching and methods of argument that 'this way of isolating Jesus from his historical milieu, and from the tradition in which he stands, is impossible to accept from the point of view of the historian, and the theologian notes here a kind of docetism'.

[2] Advocates of this view included H. J. Holtzmann, *Theologie*, I, 203ff.; L. Jacob, 'Gesetz', pp. 24ff., and F. A. M. Spencer, *The Theory of Christ's Ethics* (1929), p. 69. For earlier criticisms of this theory see A. Harnack, 'Gesetz', p. 232; F. Barth, *Hauptprobleme*, p. 105, and J. Denney, *HDB*, III, 73, who rightly observes that 'when we consider the shortness of his ministry, it seems extremely improbable that we should be able to trace within its narrow limits any "evolution" or progressive change in his attitude to the Law'. The attempt by W. L. Knox, *The Sources of the Synoptic Gospels*, I (1953), 8–16, followed by W. D. Davies, 'Matthew 5.17, 18', pp. 47ff., to discover a parallel development within the Pharisaic attitude to Jesus is just as indefensible. While an increase in the degree of opposition may be confidently assumed it was, in principle, the same throughout.

disciples though in the presence of others (Matt. 5.1ff./Luke 6.17ff.), at least one of his most controversial statements is explicitly addressed to the crowd (Matt. 15.10/Mark 7.15), another to the Pharisees (Matt. 12.8 and pars.), and yet a further insistent demand to an outsider (Matt. 19.22 and pars.).[1] More cogent is the attempt to explain the various differences in the accounts by reference to the specific audiences addressed. However, not all suggestions in this direction are equally compelling, e.g., the view that behind such apparently conservative utterances as 5.17ff. lay the fear of antinomianism among the Am-Ha-Areṣ who were listening.[2] Nevertheless, in the course of this investigation it has more than once been noticed that Jesus adapts his teaching to the audience he has been addressing. So, for example, in his condemnations of ἀνομία, he measures the general conduct of the antinomians against the standards of the Law, not against the requirements of his own teaching (Matt. 7.15ff.; 13.41; 24.11ff.). Elsewhere, in his critique of Pharisaic religiosity, he merely sets before them those basic requirements of the Law which for all their scrupulous attention to detail they failed to observe (Matt. 23.3ff., 23ff., 27ff.). On another occasion, he was content to place before them the central commands of the Law without going on to press upon them his own more radical demands (Matt. 22.36ff. and pars.).[3] At other times, after addressing the Pharisees or the crowds, he primarily explains to his disciples the implications of the epigrammatic teaching he has given (Matt. 15.15ff. and pars., Mark 10.10ff.). The value of these various attempts to account for the differences in emphasis in Jesus' teaching lies in their determination to take into consideration all the synoptic statements of Jesus, and in their isolation of one basic principle which must be admitted as a

---

[1] See further F. Barth, *Hauptprobleme*, p. 108, against J. Ph. Glock, *Gesetzesfrage*, pp. 7ff.

[2] Against H. Huber, *Bergpredigt*, p. 70.

[3] In his general investigation of the effect of an opponent audience upon the temper of Jesus' words J. A. Baird, *Audience Criticism and the Historical Jesus* (1969), has also noted that 'this emphasis on more traditional religious matters shows a pattern of adaptation to this most sensitively Jewish audience' (p. 132). As the tenor of my own investigation suggests, I am in full agreement with his insistence that more attention be paid to the audience-factor in gospel criticism.

valid contribution to the final solution of the problem. Jesus' teaching was addressed to different groups of people, in different circumstances, at different points throughout his ministry, and this cannot but have influenced the *form* his teaching would take in any given context nor could the *content* remain totally unaffected. A recognition of this principle can at least go part of the way in explaining the different emphases in his teaching that we find throughout the gospels.

Other scholars have endeavoured to solve the dilemma by reference to the overlapping of the old and new ages in the ministry of Jesus, so that during this transitional period his ethical demands could be formulated now in terms of what the two had in common, and now in terms of the new alone. However, recent studies have been concerned to demonstrate the 'presence' of the Kingdom as a reality that embraces every aspect of Jesus' ministry and not merely as something which intervenes at various points in a manner 'anticipatory' of its future consummation.[1] Earlier it had been suggested that it was impossible to find any single formula as a key of explanation to the various statements contained in the gospels, and that the principle of integration was locked in the mind of Christ and inaccessible to definition. This, however, is to admit to a theological defeatism which is quite unnecessary for, as we have seen, Jesus does declare himself explicitly on this point.[2] Nevertheless, the chief value of these two attempts at a solution lies in the dissatisfaction they express with the search for a

---

[1] Here I am thinking especially of the recent contributions by W. G. Kümmel, J. Jeremias, R. Schnackenburg and G. E. Ladd. Among those who suggested this way out of the problem were F. J. A. Hort, *Judaistic Christianity* (1898), pp. 37–8; N. B. Stonehouse, *Witness*, p. 249; W. D. Davies, 'Matthew 5.17, 18', pp. 53ff., and J. Stiassny, 'Jésus accomplit la Promesse', *BVC*, 59 (1964), 30–7.

[2] Against J. M. Creed, *Luke*, p. 207; C. J. Cadoux, 'Judaism and Universalism in the Gospels', *ET*, 38 (1926–7), 140, and earlier L. Jacob, 'Gesetz', p. 11. With particular reference to the Law this view has been most recently advocated by A. S. Dunstone, 'Ipsissima Verba Christi', *St.Ev.*, II (1964), 62, who concludes that 'many of the truths taught by the Lord are by human logic irreconcilable'. This objection also applies against those who argue that Jesus expressed no fundamental solution to the problem and that we can only deduce such from a study of his practice in individual cases. See B. H. Branscomb, *Law*, pp. 128ff.; Ch. Guignebert, 'Jesus' (ET 1935), p. 299; H. Braun, *Radikalismus*, II, 10 n.1.

purely external category of explanation and their demand that the solution be found in the person of Christ or in the character of the Kingdom, thus stressing the need for a more 'dogmatic' approach to the question.

In the course of this investigation, the various suggestions that have been made as to the nature of the principle by which Jesus' teaching may be integrated have all been assessed. With the exceptions just mentioned, that teaching was found at every point to transcend and surpass the demands of the Law. This was clearly the case in the controversies over the sabbath, defilement and divorce, in the encounter with the Rich Young Ruler, and throughout the Antitheses in the Sermon on the Mount. This indicates that such categories of explanation as 'exposition', as in traditional Catholic and Protestant thinking, or 'setting out the true meaning', as in liberal evaluations, are seen to be misplaced. More recent conceptions such as 'Tora-vershärfung' or 'radicalisation' of the Law are also unsatis-factory. With respect to all these approaches it must be insisted that Jesus neither moves out from the Law in making his own demands nor relates these requirements back to it. Even if the Law does form a general background to his own teaching, the latter is on an entirely new level above it, so that comparisons of this nature become inadequate. On the other hand, to speak of Jesus' 'rejection' or 'abrogation' of the Law is also inaccurate, for this is not necessarily a consequence to be drawn from his teaching. This means that to attach either a 'conservative' or 'radical' label to his attitude towards the Law can only be mis-leading. However, it must also be added that to interpret his demands purely in terms of 'transcending' the Mosaic Law is also insufficient, for this is to disregard the evidence in his teaching for the positive relationship to it defined by the term 'fulfilment' (Matt. 5.17). This 'fulfilment' takes place not in the first instance through his suffering and death as some have sought to maintain, but in his teaching and practice, though these, of course, ultimately culminated in the Cross. It is *to* that ministry that the Law 'prophetically' pointed, and it is only in so far as it has been taken up *into* that teaching and com-pletely transformed that it lives on.

It should be clear that if this analysis is correct, the traditional distinction between the way in which the moral and ceremonial laws are viewed by Jesus cannot be maintained. We have observed on a number of occasions that in Old Testament, inter-testamentary and Jewish thought no fundamental demarcation was made between these two aspects of the Law, and there is nothing in the gospels to suggest that Jesus demurred from this position. In the teaching and ministry of Jesus the whole Law found its fulfilment and no part of it remains unchanged. It is also significant that in his instruction there is no encouragement of the disciples to study the Law, i.e., as an end in itself. In such passages as Luke 24.27 and 22.44–5, it is for the light they throw upon him that reference to it occurs. Where reference to observance of the Law is made it is either in evangelistic (Mark 1.44f.) or polemical (Matt. 23.3) contexts or introduced as an initial standard against which those addressed might measure their conduct (Matt. 15.4ff.; 19.16ff.; 23.23). Thus, even the highest demands of the Law (e.g., Decalogue commandments) do not remain in force as an 'eternal moral law' within his teaching, but are, as Matt. 5.21ff.; 12.1ff. and 19.16ff. demonstrate, also transcended and fulfilled in his demands.[1] It has already been noted that the Ten Commandments were not viewed as the ultimate norm of conduct even by Israel herself. In one place in the gospels where a number of its provisions are in view they occur in association with other requirements and are soon left to one side in the controversy (Mark 10.17ff.), while on the two other occasions where they come into prominence this is due to the influence of the early church upon the tradition and does not stem from Jesus' original teaching (Matt. 5.21ff.; 15.19).

However, nor should too prominent a position be given to the love-commandment in the teaching of Jesus. It is true that in Matt. 7.12 and 22.40 it is presented as a summary of the

[1] See further H. Röthlisberger, *Kirche*, pp. 35–42, and F. E. Vokes, *St.Ev.*, v (1968), 142, against A. Wilder, 'Equivalents of Natural Law in the Teaching of Jesus', *JR*, 26 (1946), 134–5, and C. L. Mitton, 'The Will of God in the Synoptic Tradition of the Words of Jesus', *ET*, 72 (1960), 69. Also unsatisfactory is the distinction between the 'Ten Commandments' and the 'Eternal Moral Law' enshrined in them (R. L. Aldrich, 'The Mosaic Ten Commandments...', *BS*, 118 [1961], 251–8) and that between the Mosaic code which is abolished and those individual commands taken up unaltered into the teaching of Christ (C. C. Ryrie, 'The End of the Law', *BS*, 124 [1967], 246–7).

demands of the Law, but in both these places it is the essence of the teaching of Law and prophets which is under consideration, and Jesus does not press on to put forward his own more radical demands. This he does do in Matt. 19.16ff., where he outlines the love-commandment but then with his demand to 'sell all and give to the poor' evidently passes beyond that which was understood as required by it. This is even clearer in Matt. 5.43ff., where the OT love-commandment is not only surpassed by the new instruction Jesus gives, but is only one among several other antitheses some of which would be extremely difficult to subsume under the heading of 'love'. The re-definition of what causes defilement, for example, would appear to be derived more from some such concept as the 'purity' of God than from the principle of 'love', and the prohibition against swearing from some such notion as his 'truthfulness' or 'integrity'. In brief, there are other norms upon which the ethic of Jesus is predicated than 'love' alone.[1]

It would appear, therefore, that the central position given to the Decalogue in much Catholic and Protestant thinking is open to question, though this is not to deny that in the teaching of Jesus certain of its requirements reappear as imperatives for his disciples (Matt. 15.19). Where they do occur, however, it is alongside other ethical injunctions and in such a way that they cannot be regarded as the most central or most significant demands. On the other hand, the sole position accorded the requirement to 'love' in much, though not all, that is referred to as 'situation-ethics' is also at fault in excluding other norms as the ground of some of Jesus' demands. Thus even when the new teaching on love is given (as Matt. 5.43ff.), it forms only one component in that teaching. Nor is Jesus afraid to specify what 'love' generally means in certain concrete instances (Matt. 5.21ff.), though it must be added immediately that his teachings cannot be regarded as a 'new law'. Jesus himself

[1] See also C. S. Rodd, 'Are the ethics of Jesus situation-ethics?', *ET*, 79 (1968), 370. It could be added here that contemporary attempts to interpret this aspect of Jesus' teaching almost exclusively in terms of *mitmenschlichkeit* displace the priority accorded by Jesus to the 'first' of the two great commandments. See the conclusive study by R. Schnackenburg, 'Mitmenschlichkeit im Horizont des Neuen Testaments', *Die Zeit Jesu* (1970), pp. 70–92, which deals in particular with such passages as Matt. 5.23f., 38ff.; 23.23; Mark 7.1ff.; 12.28ff. and Luke 10.29ff.

breaks his own 'commandments' (e.g., Mark 3.5; Matt. 23.17), and thereby indicates that his teachings are more in the nature of principles whose particular application, or lack of it, depends upon the circumstances in which they come into play.[1]

We must, however, go even further than this, for as it has been remarked of the Sermon on the Mount 'we are here confronted not primarily with the question, who can perform these commandments or are they practicable or sound...rather it compels us, in the first place, to ask who he is who utters these words: they are themselves "kerygmatic"'.[2] This fact is already anticipated in the way in which Jesus' observance of such Jewish institutions as the Passover results in its being changed into something entirely new, centred upon himself, his convictions and his work (Matt. 26.17ff.). It is also hinted at in the way in which he encourages obedience to the Law as a pretext for drawing the attention of the Jewish leaders to the effects of his ministry (Mark 1.40ff. and pars.). Also significant in this respect is the way in which his encounter with the Rich Young Ruler leads on from a recognition of the value of the Law as a preliminary standard, through the demand for obedience to the 'love-commandment', to his own more radical insistence upon renunciation and the call for discipleship in his service (Matt. 19.16ff. and pars.). This is even more explicit in the controversy over fasting (cf. Matt. 9.9ff. and pars.) where Christ places his own person even more firmly, if somewhat parabolically, into the foreground. The whole question of Law, therefore, must be placed in a wider context, for the central point in these encounters, as the charges at the Trial bear out, was not the issue of law but the authority of Jesus himself.[3] Even in those passages which define his attitude to it, it is not so much a question of 'what is his relation to it?' that is at issue as 'what is its relation to him?'[4]

---

[1] For suggestions as to a basis for Christian ethics more in accord with the NT emphasis see C. F. D. Moule, 'The NT and Moral Decisions', *ET*, 74 (1963), 370ff.

[2] W. D. Davies, *Setting*, p. 435. The various estimates of its practicability that christians have advanced are discussed in J. Knox, *The Ethic of Jesus in the Teaching of the Church* (1962).

[3] Cf. W. Kümmel, 'Rabbinen', p. 13; J. Jocz, *Jewish People*, p. 27.

[4] The teaching of Jesus is therefore quite clearly the presupposition for Paul's teaching on the Law. In each, though its God-given nature is

Each of the synoptic gospels, with varying degrees of interest, and differing points of emphasis, remains faithful to the general tenor of Jesus' attitude to the Law. Least concerned with the question is Luke, who subordinates material relevant to the issue to other matters with which his gospel is particularly engaged. Thus apart from an isolated saying referring to the debate (Luke 16.18) he omits the dispute over divorce, and has no reference to the controversy over defilement at all. He turns the question regarding the Great Commandment (Luke 10. 25ff.) into a query concerning eternal life which introduces a parable on the merciful conduct demanded of one who desires it. The small section of 'legal' material (Luke 16.16–17) is subordinated to the motif of the considerate behaviour appropriate to life in the Kingdom. The tradition paralleled in Matthew's sermon (Luke 6.27ff.) is directed away from its orientation towards the Law and correlated around the twin themes of 'love' and 'mercy' which befit those who desire the reward of sonship

affirmed (Matt. 15.6, cf. Rom. 7.12, 22; Gal. 3.21), it does not form part of the primary will of God (Matt. 19.8, cf. Gal. 3.17ff.); the 'love-commandment' is the 'essence' of the Law (Matt. 22.40, cf. Rom. 13.9–10) and the principle of the 'weaker brother' is an element in the observance or non-observance of its requirements (Matt. 17.24–7, cf. Rom. 14.1ff.); it stands as a condemnation of those who are disobedient to God (Matt. 19.8, cf. 1 Tim. 1.9ff.) yet it cannot bring eternal life (Matt. 19.21, cf. Rom. 3.20ff.; Gal. 2.16ff.) nor even sanctification (Matt. 5.21ff., cf. Gal. 3.1ff.; Col. 2.16ff.); it is a testimony against men to his ministry (Matt. 8.4, cf. Gal. 3.24) and ultimately it finds its end in him (Matt. 5.17, cf. Rom. 10.4). Certainly Paul's use of πλήρωμα (Rom. 13.10) and πληροῦν (Gal. 5.14) of the relationship between the 'love-commandment' and the Law is more restricted than Matt. 5.17. However, while Paul clearly regarded love as being especially pre-eminent (1 Cor. 13.1ff.), the wider context of Gal. 5.14, as also that of Rom. 13.10, indicates that there were other fundamental norms of behaviour alongside it to which it was not reducible (cf. Rom. 14.17; Gal. 5.22–3) and these themselves are subordinate to the basic orientation of christian behaviour in the direction of the 'imitation of Christ' (Eph. 4.11ff.; Col. 3.1ff.). The differences that remain between the teaching of Paul and Jesus with regard to the Law result only from the different historical situation arising from the death and resurrection of Jesus himself. It is the latter which allows Paul to draw out the implications of Christ's teaching upon the Law to an even richer and profounder degree. Cf. W. G. Kümmel, 'Jesus und Paulus', *Heilsgeschehen und Geschichte*, pp. 105, 456. See also H. McArthur, *Sermon*, pp. 58–79; E. Jüngel, *Paulus und Jesus* (1967³), pp. 268–73, and A. Feuillet, *NTS*, 17 (1971), 135.

with the Father. In his sabbath-presentations and multiplication of sabbath-healings (Luke 6.6ff.; 13.10ff.) he demonstrates less interest in the transgression of legal or scribal
regulations than in the saving character of Jesus' ministry to
the deprived which is particularly appropriate on such a day.
While, as we have seen, he does include a fragment of tradition
dealing with the question of Law (Luke 16.16–17) he does not
in any way endeavour to develop a 'theological' answer to the
problem raised by Jesus' attitude towards it.[1]

These omissions and re-orientations of material dealing with
the Law, together with the apparently Jewish-christian stance
of the statements in Luke 16.16ff. and the removal of any suggestion of criticism of Jesus in the sabbath-stories, has been
interpreted either as indicative of Luke's fundamentally conservative attitude to the Law or as evidence of his rather dis-
interested preservation of different attitudes towards it.[2] While
it is true that Luke frequently transmits legal material without
any apparent comment (cf. Luke 6.1ff.; 14.1ff.; 16.16ff.),
nevertheless this material itself is far from being Jewish-christian
in essence. This has already been demonstrated with regard to
Luke 16.16–18, and it has also been noted that the sabbath-

[1] In Q, from which this and other passages are drawn, we find affirmations
of the continuing significance of the Law (Luke 11.42; 16.17) alongside
other passages implying that it has been superseded (Luke 16.16) and
transcended (Luke 16.18) and that it is now Jesus' words that are central
and decisive (Luke 6.47–9). There is also a critical response to the teaching
and practices of the Jewish leaders (Luke 11.39–52). Thus while there is
in Q no real reflection on the relationship between Jesus' teaching and the
Mosaic Law, the material faithfully preserves the different aspects of
Jesus' attitude. Such an assessment, of course, differs widely from that of
S. Schulz, *Q. Die Spruchquelle der Evangelisten* (1972), on these various
passages.

[2] Against H. J. Jervell, *HTR*, 64 (1971), 21–36, who considers Luke to have
'the most conservative outlook within the New Testament' and S. E.
Johnson, *Theology of the Gospels* (1966), p. 40, *et al.*, who mistakes a lack of
interest in the question of Law for the lack of a definite attitude towards it.
On Luke's tendency to preserve material other than that directly reflecting
his own interest, see, for example, G. W. H. Lampe, 'The Lucan Portrait
of Christ', *NTS*, 2 (1955–6), 160. I am fully aware that if this account of
Luke's attitude is correct, then some explanation must be found for, what
is at first sight, the conservative position outlined in Acts. A beginning in
the right direction here has been made by R. N. Longenecker, *Paul*, pp.
245ff.

story in 6.1ff. by no means reflects a conservative attitude to the Law but clearly subordinates the latter to the activity of Christ. This must also be taken into account in the interpretation of Luke 14.1ff. as the succeeding parables demonstrate. In any case, over all the sabbath accounts stands the principle enunciated in Luke 13.16 concerning the subjection of that day to the demands of Christ's mission. Luke's less substantial interest in the issue of Law, therefore, does not mean that the teaching of Jesus is so obscured that it is impossible to gain any clear idea of where he or Jesus stood on the matter, nor that his narratives reflect a conservative Jewish-christian stance towards it. Indeed, in so far as he constantly brings into the foreground one aspect of the christological issue, i.e., Jesus' preaching, teaching and healing ministry which calls men to accept and testify to their salvation, this must be regarded as theologically dominating the whole of his presentation. Though he does not explicitly state that it is in this that the Law is fulfilled, this is clearly implied in his account. The theme of his gospel that is announced at Nazareth in 4.16ff. and is reiterated during the Resurrection appearances in 24.44ff. thus also fashions the material related to the Law. In these passages the saving ministry of Jesus is presented as the 'fulfilment' of all that was promised to Israel and this is the thrust of the 'legal' material in Luke as well.

Despite his lack of reference to the material included in the Matthaean and Lucan Sermons and only a passing reference to the content of the speeches against the Pharisees, Mark has full accounts of the controversies over table-fellowship, the sabbath, defilement and divorce, and of debates concerning the way to eternal life and the nature of the Great Commandment. However, examination of his narratives shows that he is not primarily interested in the implications of Jesus' teaching for the Law or the oral tradition, but rather with its relevance and application to his Gentile audience. This explains the 'universalising' tendency in his gospel. This can be observed in the generalising of questions put to Jesus (Mark 7.5; 10.2, 28) but is especially evident in the inclusion of such statements as the sabbath being made for man in Mark 2.27, ethical interpretation of sabbath behaviour in Mark 3.4, widening of the scope of the controversy over defilement in Mark 7.3ff. and 13b, as of its application in vv.15 and 19b, extensions of the declaration on divorce with regard to the woman in Mark 10.11c and 12 and reference to monotheism as the chief commandment combined with the inclusion of comment on the inferiority of sacrifices in Mark 12.28ff.

These findings support recent investigations of Mark's gospel which have stressed the presence of a didactic as well as narrative element in his account. Unlike Matthew, this does not take the form of systematic instruction but rather 'a succession of single authoritative sentences, each bringing to an end a dispute over some issue raised by opponents with hostile intent'.[1] Thus in comparison with the other gospels the christological element is focussed less upon the ministry (Luke) or person (Matthew) of Jesus than on the unique ethical principles which he utters. While these statements primarily draw out the moral implications of Christ's teaching in the most comprehensive way for the benefit of Mark's Gentile readers, additional comments in his account point up the consequences of his teaching for the Mosaic Law (cf. esp. Mark 17.19b) and the oral tradition (cf. esp. Mark 7.13b) as well as the reasons for its rejection by the leaders of the Jewish people i.e., their hardness of heart (cf. esp. Mark 3.5).[2] Such a procedure in no way runs counter to the original teaching of Jesus for its supplanting of the Old

---

[1] C. F. Evans, *The Beginning of the Gospel* (1968), p. 54. See further E. Schweizer, 'Anmerkungen zur Theologie des Markus', *Neotestamentica* (1963), pp. 95ff.; 'Die theologische Leistung des Markus', *Ev.Th.*, 24 (1964), 340ff.; E. Grässer, 'Jesus in Nazareth: Mk. 6.1–6a: Notes on the Redaction and Theology of St Mark', *NTS*, 16 (1969), 1–23; R. P. Martin, *Mark: Evangelist and Theologian* (1972), pp. 113f., and Q. Quesnell, *Mark*, pp. 134ff., despite the latter's doubtful distinction between the character of such pronouncements before and after 8.27. This approach to Mark challenges B. H. Branscomb's conclusion that the gospel is 'matter-of-fact' and 'without much attempt at interpretation and comment' (*Law*, p. 111), as well as H. G. Wood's contention (*ET*, 51 [1939–1940], 329) that his moulding of the tradition is less sophisticated than in the other three gospels. On the other hand, K. G. Reploh, *Markus – Lehrer der Gemeinde* (1969), while he rightly emphasises Mark's concern to be a teacher of the community to whom he was writing, overestimates the degree of interpretative as opposed to factual content in the gospel.

[2] According to K. Berger, *ZNW*, 61 (1970), 1–47 (cf. *Gesetzesauslegung* [1972], pp. 537–42), behind Mark's criticism of the 'hard-heartedness' of the Jews lies a Hellenistic-Jewish tradition of pronouncements condemning

Testament Law is already latent within Jesus' teaching on specific legal matters (Matt. 15.1ff./Mark 7.1ff.) as well as in his wider instruction (Matt. 5.17ff.). Certainly he draws attention to it in a more specific and general way than either of the other two gospels, but even Luke contains hints in this direction (cf. Luke 16.17–18) while Matthew states quite plainly that individual Old Testament regulations are affected in this way (cf. Matt. 12.5–7; 19.8) and would consider it an aspect of his concept of 'fulfilment' (Matt. 5.17).[1]

With Matthew we come to the most detailed treatment of the question. Throughout the material dealing with Law there occurs a heightening of scribal and Pharisaic opposition (Matt. 12.9, 14; 15.12; 19.7; 22.34a) and a corresponding intensification of Jesus' criticisms (Matt. 9.13a; 12.5–7, 11–12; 15.3, 13–14; 16.12; 23.1ff.) against both their teaching and practice (Matt. 5.20; 9.13a; 15.13–14; 16.12; 23.1ff.). Such a tendency may well have reflected the post-Jamnia Jewish opposition encountered by his own congregations. Most significant is his explicit relation of the teaching of Jesus both to the scribal traditions which it rejected and the Mosaic regulations which it surpassed. In each of the major controversies, debates and speeches we see Matthew by his rearrangement of the material, additions, omissions and alterations, pin-point for his readers the various written or oral legal issues that Jesus' teaching has brought into dispute – sabbath restrictions (Matt. 12.11–12a; 24.20), washing of hands (Matt. 15.2b), permission to divorce (Matt. 19.8), Decalogue and love-commandment (Matt.

---

the Jews for disobedience to the Law and apostasy from their calling. T. L. Budesheim, *ZAW*, 62 (1971), 190–209, also regards Mark, especially in 1.16 – 3.19, as setting himself explicitly against the Jewish tradition. H. W. Kuhn, in *Tradition und Glaube*, pp. 209–309, however, rightly points out that Mark does not engage in a general anti-Jewish polemic so much as in an attack on the way in which the Jewish authorities have falsified the Israelite-Jewish tradition and unlawfully persecuted Jesus. Among other things, he draws attention to the way in which the controversy-stories in Mark are bracketed by Mark 1.40ff. and Mark 12.28ff. in which both the Mosaic Law and Jewish interpretation, while not regarded as definitive, are nevertheless represented in positive terms.

[1] Cf. the general conclusions of H. Anderson, 'The OT in Mark's Gospel', *The Use of the Old Testament in the New and Other Essays* (ed. J. M. Efird, 1972), esp. pp. 304–6.

19.18ff.), Mosaic regulations behind three of the Antitheses (Matt. 5.21–48) as well as the Law as a whole (Matt. 7.12; 22.36–40). These are the additions which are frequently misunderstood as being either regulatory or casuistic in character. In doing this, however, Matthew is not imposing upon the tradition a weight that it cannot bear, but merely drawing out the specific consequences of that which is present in it.[1]

In addition, considerable effort is spent by Matthew in clarifying the nature of the relationship between Jesus' teaching and the Law. This is expounded in terms of the 'fulfilment' he brought to it (Matt. 5.17). Other 'theological' conceptions can also be detected in his gospel: a special emphasis upon the 'love-commandment' as the norm of the Law (Matt. 7.12; 22.36ff.), 'righteousness' as a comprehensive term for the obedience required by Christ to his teaching (Matt. 5.20) together with 'hypocrisy' as its counterpart (Matt. 15.7; 23.23), 'perfection' as a description of the way of life that is in accord with the demands of the Kingdom (Matt. 5.48; 19.21). Clearest of all, however, is the christological emphasis throughout the passages we have considered, for at almost every point a moving into the foreground of the personal authority of Christ is discernible. This takes place in various ways e.g., through the insertion of pericopes at a particular point in his narrative (Matt. 8.1ff.; 12.1ff.), the introduction of Old Testament quotations (Matt. 9.13; 12.7) or allusions to Old Testament occurrences (Matt. 12.3–4) and realities (Matt. 12.5) which have reference to Jesus himself, the insertion of introductory formulas highlighting the authoritative character of Christ's utterances (Matt. 5.18ff.; 12.6; 19.9), the rearrangement of pericopes in order to throw into greater relief the authority of Jesus (Matt. 12.9ff.), and even the direct alteration of the words of Jesus so as to minimise misinterpretation of his status (Matt. 19.17). As a result it is not so much his relationship to the Law that he is concerned to depict (and not at all that to Moses), as how the Law now stands in relationship to Jesus as the one whose teaching and practice

[1] A. W. Argyle, 'M and the Pauline Epistles', *ET*, 11 (1970), 340–2 has rightly drawn attention to the affinity of such passages in Matthew's special source as 5.17; 5.48 and 22.40 with others in the Pauline letters e.g., Rom. 3.31; 1 Cor. 2.6 and Gal. 5.14.

transcend it and fulfil it and to whom all attention must now be directed.[1]

We conclude therefore that in their treatment of Jesus and the Law each of the gospels is primarily kerygmatic. Though presenting the material in different ways, with different emphases and different audiences in view, in each it is the figure of Christ that dominates. With varying degrees of clarity the problem raised by his attitude to the Law comes into view, and though the implications of that attitude are developed in distinctive ways, in each his fundamental position with regard to it is accurately reflected.[2] We can now ask whether this is also the case with respect to those significant alterations or elaborations we have been able to trace with any certainty as stemming from the creative activity of the early christian communities. Many of these alterations and/or elaborations were seen to be in the nature of simple expansions of the words of Jesus so as to apply his teaching to new situations which had arisen (cf. Matt. 5.34b–36; 17.24, 27; 23.20–2). Others appeared to stem from the desire for clarification of certain aspects of his teaching and were developed further by the evangelists in the composition of their gospels. In Matthew's tradition, chief among these were a realignment of aspects of Jesus' teaching with the Decalogue, especially by way of providing background for it, an approach that seems to have been motivated chiefly by catechetical interests with a view to the needs of predominantly Jewish christians rather than from any legalistic concern (cf. Matt. 5.21a, 27a; 15.19b; 19.18;

---

[1] It is also possible, via the idea of establishing the true will of God, to trace a line from Matthew's teaching on the Law to the death of Christ. Thus even in his gospel, the indirect character of the relationship between the two is preserved. See the discussion in G. Barth, 'Law', pp. 125–53.

[2] Even though Luke and Mark do not contain the logion concerning 'fulfilment' a consideration of the Lucan complex in 16.16–18 would lead one in the direction of such an idea, while the statement concerning the 'lordship' of the Son of Man over the 'sabbath' (Mark 2.28) if taken as a paradigm of his attitude to the Law, contains the doctrine *in nuce*. What M. Werner, *Einfluss*, pp. 79ff., long ago demonstrated for Mark is therefore applicable to all three accounts: in each, though under different forms, the presupposition of the Pauline understanding of the Law may be found. On Luke and Paul in this connection generally see E. Ellis, *Luke*, pp. 40–52; P. Borgen, 'From Paul to Luke', *CBQ*, 31 (1969), 168–82, and I. H. Marshall, *Luke*, pp. 219–20.

23.23b). Additions in Mark's tradition took their rise from the Gentile context to which his gospel was directed, and endeavoured to give Jesus' teaching a particular relevance to their ethical (Mark 10.19c), liturgical (Matt. 12.32–4) and (possibly) doctrinal (Mark 12.29) convictions. Lucan passages, already scarce so far as material dealing with the Law was concerned, present little by way of elaboration. However, with respect to the first and third gospels, in a number of cases what have frequently been understood as 'legalistic' sayings originating in the early communities were found to possess a quite other significance (Matt. 5.17–19; 5.23ff.; 22.40; 23.3ff.; 23.23a; Luke 16.17; 11.42).

B. How then does Jesus' attitude relate to the different stances that were taken up towards the Law in the traditions represented in the Old Testament, inter-testamentary and later Jewish writings?

1. In the earlier literature, the events which are most consistently remembered for the gracious activity of God within them are those surrounding the exodus. This being the case, it is quite striking that nowhere in the recorded words of Jesus do we have any reference to them. Luke alone uses the term ἔξοδος and that is with reference to the death of Christ. Here we have a further indication of his concern to depict the saving ministry of Jesus as the fulfilment of Judaism (Luke 9.31). This is not to say that Jesus' instruction is dissociated from the preceding grace of God. It is just that Jesus sees this at work in the preaching of the gospel and in the call for repentance (cf. Mark 1.14–15; Luke 16.16, *et al.*). The presupposition of the teaching of Jesus is thus the Rule of God that is being exercised through his ministry.[1] However, as also in the Old Testament,

---

[1] That the whole of Jesus' teaching bears an eschatological stamp is affirmed by M. Dibelius, 'Die Bergpredigt', *Botschaft und Geschichte* (1953), I, 79ff.; H. Preisker, *Das Ethos des Urchristentums* (1949), pp. 49ff.; P. Ramsey, *Ethics*, pp. 31ff.; P. J. Verweijs, *Evangelium*, pp. 8ff.; H. McArthur, *Sermon*, pp. 80–104; E. Neuhäusler, *Anspruch*, pp. 37ff. Since Schweizer's demolition of the liberal view, the non-eschatological character of Jesus' ethics has been affirmed in part by H. Windisch, *The Meaning of the Sermon on the Mount* (ET 1941), pp. 30ff.; A. Wilder, *Eschatology*, pp. 117ff., and H. Conzelmann, *Grundriss*, pp. 138ff. For criticism of this view see G. E. Ladd, *Jesus and the Kingdom* (1966), pp. 281ff.

the indicative of grace not only stands before the teaching empowering obedience to its commandments but is also present in the gift of the teaching itself (cf. Matt. 11.28ff.).[1] Furthermore, just as an element of judgment was latent within the instruction of the Law so also, though in a more penetrating fashion, a recognition of the imperative force and 'absolute' character of Christ's commandments draws attention to the seriousness of disobedience to them (Matt. 7.21ff.; 19.10) or, in the case of their rejection, to the awareness of failure (cf. Mark 1.44; 3.5; 10.22; Luke 13.17; 14.4). Though the latter is not, as in the Old Testament, associated with the giving of sacrifice, it is finally through the 'blood' of Christ that it becomes available. Thus ultimately the demands of Christ are associated with the new 'covenant' that is inaugurated through his death (Luke 22.20 and pars.), but this conception also, through the nature of the act by which it is ratified, is altogether transcended, transformed and 'fulfilled'.[2] It is once again striking that it is only here, in a passage which is only indirectly related to his teaching on the Law, that the term 'covenant' is specifically used by Jesus, and then specifically in connection with his death. There is no parallel to this anywhere in the earlier literature except, on the surface, in some of the pre-exilic prophets and in 1 Enoch. In those books, however, although the terminology is missing, the primitive idea of the

---

[1] Cf. G. Strecker, *Gerechtigkeit*, pp. 148ff.; S. Schulz, *Botschaft*, p. 191; E. E. Ellis, *Luke*, pp. 112–13, against F. Nägelsbach, *Der Schlüssel zum Verständnis der Bergpredigt* (1916), pp. 8ff.; J. Schniewind, 'Die Botschaft Jesu und die Theologie des Paulus', *Nachgelassene Reden und Aufsätze* (1952); T. W. Manson, *Teaching*, p. 299, and, most recently, J. Jeremias, *Sermon*, pp. 20ff. These presentations usually seek to show that Jesus' teaching in the Sermon was only directed to those who were already disciples. They seem to forget that elsewhere his radical demands are openly expressed both to the crowds (Matt. 15.10) and the Pharisees (Matt. 19.9). This aspect of the debate would therefore appear to be irrelevant. See further P. Bonnard, 'Le Sermon sur la Montagne', *RTP*, 3 (1953), 233ff. H. Windisch, *Sermon*, pp. 110ff., however, goes to the opposite extreme and places all the weight upon the imperative aspect of the teaching, regarding obedience to it as the means by which salvation is achieved.

[2] On this, see especially J. Behm, *TDNT*, II, 133ff.; P. J. Verweijs, *Evangelium*, pp. 28ff.; and F. C. Fensham, 'The Covenant as giving Expression to the Relationship between Old and New Testaments', *Tyn.B.*, 22 (1971), 82–94.

covenant is not (1 Enoch 89.2ff.). On the whole, then, and taking into account these major shifts of location for the grace and covenant of God, we find with regard to the context in which the teaching of Jesus is set, no antithesis to the position outlined in the Old Testament such as is sometimes expressed in the formula Gospel and Law, though this could be predicated with more justification of some later Jewish perspectives. Rather does there remain a general similarity between the two in respect of the relationship that exists between grace, instruction and judgment, one that is distinguished only by the new and unique character attaching to that which has come in Christ.

2. As with Torah, so with Christ's teaching, the primary intention is 'instruction'. Furthermore, though nowhere does he refer to his own teaching by means of the term νόμος, he does not hesitate to speak of it as consisting of ἐντολαί. However, the unique and radical character of the latter means that a clear differentiation does exist between his commandments and those of Torah. This is less noticeable in relation to the Decalogue than to many other passages in the Pentateuch, for it is also far removed from casuistry, though, as the content of the Sermon on the Mount demonstrates, a qualitative difference between the two sets of instruction is present. Certainly Jesus' teaching, apart from the superficially 'legal' manner in which some of his demands are formulated, has little in common with the extension of the Mosaic commandments in the historical and legal traditions in the Old Testament and inter-testamentary literature. It is nearer in character to the prophetic concentration on righteousness. However, this more comprehensive ethical outlook still incorporated the Law into the framework of its instruction. Parallels also occur with the wisdom tradition in the Old Testament. Here we found no reference to the official Law but merely an exposition of the sage's own, often demanding, requirements together with calls for understanding and discernment into their significance. Similar pleas may be found in Jesus' teaching (cf. Matt. 9.13; Mark 7.14), together with instructions that are even more insistent in character. Whereas the wise men taught in an independent fashion within the framework provided by the Law, Jesus took up a position beyond it. In some respects it is also close to the later apocalyptic

and wisdom literature, especially to the predominantly ethical emphasis of 1 Enoch, in which the 'soziale Reihe' came into prominence. The latter, however, never became a definition of the whole Law and in the teaching of Jesus the social commandments are more comprehensively defined and far from being the norm of his instruction. A more juristic understanding of Law developed among the parties within Judaism. The rigid adherence to the Law and the conservative approach to its interpretation in Sadducaean circles, as also the casuistic elaboration of its requirements found among the Sectarians, are at a considerable distance from his ethical formulations. While, on occasions, approximations to the form of his sayings were discovered in the rabbinic writings, the instructions contained within them were consistently derived from the requirements of the Law and, in so doing, moved in a different dimension to his own independent instruction.

3. With regard to the question of the duration of the Law, attention has been drawn to the position of the priestly material in the Old Testament with its stress upon the everlasting nature of Law and its extension in the post-biblical and late-Jewish writings. The Old Testament prophetic and wisdom traditions, however, spoke rather in terms of the continuing validity, though not eternal character, of their own Torah though this also embraced traditional legal material. In the inter-testamentary period only in 1 Enoch did this tendency appear to persist though bound together with an affirmation of the eternal nature of the Law. In contrast to these expectations, the demands of Jesus form the 'fulfilment' and 'end' of the Law (Matt. 5.17–18) and it is to his words alone that endurance beyond the dissolution of the present age is ascribed: 'Heaven and earth will pass away, but my words will not pass away' (Matt. 24.35). As in Matt. 5.18, the significance of this saying should not be pressed in too literal a manner, but it does indicate a distinction between the duration of the Law and that of Jesus' instruction. Any attempt to bridge this difference through definition of Jesus' teaching in terms of a New Torah was seen to be misplaced.

It remains only to set the authority which characterised Jesus' instruction on the Law alongside that demonstrated by the representatives of the various traditions that either preceded him or were contemporary with him. The small area of authority retained by the priests and law-teachers of Israel, whose task was chiefly to mediate and apply the past to the present, is of a different order to that possessed by Jesus. In the one instance where reference is made to it, it is regarded in only an anticipatory manner to that belonging to Christ (Matt. 12.5ff.). Such was the extent of their orientation to the past that, in distinction from Jesus, the personal authority of the priest was quite submerged in the teaching given. Furthermore, the character of his ethical instruction differed quite radically from even the most radical and exceptional of their procedures i.e., the creation of new laws. True, the earliest version of Christ's introductory remarks in the Sermon on the Mount – 'but I say to you who hear' (Luke 6.27) – recalls the words, according to Deuteronomy, with which Moses addressed Israel before delivering them the Decalogue – 'Hear, O Israel, the statutes and the judgments which I speak in your ears this day' (Deut. 5.1; cf. also 4.1; 11.18ff.; 12.28 *et al.*).[1] However, when the wider context in which such words are uttered is considered (e.g., Deut. 5.4ff.), the secondary character of Moses' rôle becomes apparent. In any case, as investigation of the background material indicated, this heightened re-writing of Moses' pronouncement and activity is the result of prophetic and, more particularly, wisdom rather than priestly influences. Since these failed to have any substantial impact in the historical writings of the inter-testamentary period it is to the traditions themselves that we must next turn.

Clearly Jesus has closer links with the prophets for whom the contemporary work of Yahweh was the decisive factor. Nineteenth-century liberal discussions often resorted to prophetic categories in explanations of Jesus' attitude to the Law, and in more recent times this view has not gone unsupported.[2] While it is true that Jesus employs prophetic arguments against his opponents these are either subordinate to the central thrust of his teaching (Mark 7.6, cf. Isa. 29.13), used in a polemical context where the full force of his demand is not expressed

---

[1] See O. J. F. Seitz, *NTS*, 16 (1969), 41–2.
[2] See A. J. Rawlinson, *Mark*, p. 92; B. W. Bacon, *Studies*, pp. 354–5, and note the dominance of 'prophetic' categories in R. Bultmann, *Theology*, I, 11ff., and J. Bowman, *The Religion of Maturity* (1948), pp. 131ff.

(Matt. 23.23, cf. Mic. 6.8), or invested with a christological significance (Matt. 9.13; 12.7, cf. Hos. 6.6).[1] Moreover, in this authoritative 'I say to you' a clear distinction between him and the prophetic 'Thus saith the Lord' becomes apparent. Though on rare occasions the latter do speak in more authoritative terms this is generally in passages containing pronouncements of judgment rather than in contexts in which positive ethical instruction is being given. As we have noted, the content of that instruction, while possessing some affinities with prophetic standards, in fact goes far beyond them.

Parallels have also been drawn between the authority of Jesus and that of the sages. Wisdom sayings have been located in 5.25f., 42, 44ff.; 7.12; Mark 2.17a, 21f.; 3.4b; 7.15; 10.9,[2] wisdom methods of argument in his debates with the scribes and Pharisees,[3] and the authority of a teacher who, to some extent, is independent of the Law in his instruction in the Sermon.[4] The so-called 'wisdom sayings', however, are either uttered in contexts where his unique teaching is not being advanced (Matt. 7.12), characteristically new demands stemming not from a discernment into the natural order of things but from insight into the character of the Rule of God expressed in his life and ministry (Matt. 2.17a; 2.21f.; 3.4b; 7.15; 10.9), or examples relevant to everyday experience which nevertheless have a new quality about them (Matt. 5.25f., 42, 44ff.). In those contexts where, like the wise men, the appeal is to creation it is the original intention of God, not merely the continuing order of the world, that is referred to, and there is also the addition of a new element not present in the primitive Old Testament narratives (cf. Mark 2.27–8; Matt. 19.8–9). Thus 'it is clear that Jesus believed that the divine intention as known to and stated by the writers of Gen. 1 and 2 was summed up and had now reached its *end* in himself just as the legal

---

[1] C. H. Dodd, 'Jesus as Teacher and Prophet', *Mysterium Christi*, pp. 60–1, who refers to these instances, does not give sufficient consideration to the purpose for which they were used. See rather the comments of L. Goppelt, *Typos*, p. 77.

[2] Especially by R. Bultmann, *Tradition*, pp. 102–4; H. Windisch, *Sermon*, pp. 40ff., and A. Wilder, *JR*, 26 (1946), 131ff.

[3] So J. L. Mackenzie, 'Reflections on Wisdom', *JBL*, 86 (1967), 2ff.

[4] Cf. H. Windisch, *Sermon*, p. 138; H. J. Cadbury, *Jesus: What Manner of Man?* (1947), pp. 57ff., 77ff.

precepts too had found their *end* in him'.[1] It appears, then, that not only does Jesus' teaching challenge the centrality often given to the 'moral law' or 'love-commandment' in christian ethics, but the fundamental position accorded to 'natural law' or the 'ordinances of creation' as well. Jesus thinks not in terms of a 'theology of creation' but of a 'new creation' that is taking place through the presence of the Kingdom of God in his own ministry. While both he and the wise men frequently speak on ethical issues in authoritative terms without reference to the Law and place great emphasis upon the consequences attached to obedience or disobedience of their sayings, the teaching and authority of Jesus move in a qualitatively new dimension. His teaching, as we have seen, though given independently of the Law, does not take place within the framework provided by it, but rather is the fulfilment of it. His authority extends not only to the demand that his teaching be observed (cf. Prov. 4.20ff.; Job 36.4) but to the call for personal discipleship as well (Mark 10.22).[2]

[1] G. F. Knight, *Law*, p. 103. The most detailed treatment of the relationship between the two ideas is to be found in E. Neuhäusler, *Anspruch*, pp. 37–41.

[2] Among the synoptics, only Matthew goes so far as to assert that Christ, rather than being the Wise Man, is the embodiment of Wisdom herself. According to M. J. Suggs, *Wisdom*, p. 28, Jesus appears in Q material as 'Wisdom's final prophet' (cf. Luke 7.31–4; 10.22; 11.49–51; 13.34–5). In other words, this material interprets the significance of Jesus by means of a 'Sophialogy' which at one and the same time accords him the highest importance and subordinates him to Wisdom herself. In Matthew, however, redactional alterations result in the identification of Jesus and Wisdom so that, as in other ways in his gospel, a more developed christology emerges (cf. Matt. 11.16–18; 11.25–30; 23.34–6; 23.37–9). In his discussion of Matt. 11.28–30, Suggs insists that the 'yoke' Jesus lays upon his disciples, in accord with late-wisdom tradition, can only be Torah itself, though certainly a Torah that has undergone re-interpretation (pp. 99–127). Indeed, he goes so far as to suggest that, for Matthew, Jesus is as much the embodiment of Torah as he is of Wisdom. This, as we have already seen, cannot really be sustained. Certainly Jesus' teaching stands in the place Torah stood but it is inadequate to describe it in terms of his being Torah-incarnate. Given Suggs' demonstration of Matthew's desire to set Jesus in the place of Wisdom, it may be more pertinent to speak of Jesus' subsuming the rôle assigned to Wisdom within his unique person rather than of the 'identification' or 'equation' of the two. More adequate here is the discussion in F. Christ, *Die Sophia-Christologie bei den Synoptikern* (1970), pp. 153–4, though his suggestions that Jesus himself probably spoke in similar terms and that Q already possessed a developed Wisdom

The authority accorded to the sage in the inter-testamentary wisdom material, though slightly more developed, is not substantially different to that depicted in the Old Testament writings (cf. Ecclus. 6.23ff. *et al.*). Much more significant is the apocalyptic literature where the merging of wisdom and prophetic traditions results in the passing of some of the authority exercised by both the wise man and the prophets to the seer. This is particularly evident in those passages where the formula 'I say to you', followed by an announcement of some significance occurs. Even if we leave to one side those verses in the Testaments of the Twelve Patriarchs which may have been subject to christian revision (Test.Reu. 4.5; 6.5; Naph. 4.1; Gad 5.3) others remain which were undoubtedly pre-christian in formulation (Jub. 36.11; 1 Enoch 92.18; 94.1, 3; 102.9; see also 2 Enoch 2.2). However, our analysis has already demonstrated the more radical character of Jesus' demands over against the ethical teaching of the seers.[1] Furthermore, Jesus, unlike the apocalyptic visionaries, does not hide himself under a pseudonym.[2] Thus their sayings provide only formal

christology are unlikely. (On the latter point, see rather D. Lührmann, *Die Redaktion der Logienquelle* [1969], esp. p. 99.) See also A. Feuillet, 'Jésus et la sagesse divine d'après les évangiles synoptiques', *RB*, 42 (1955), 161–96, and D. R. Hubbard, *Tyn.B.*, 17 (1966), 3–33, though their accounts are less satisfactory. For a discussion of the similarities and differences between Matt. 11.28ff. and Ecclus. 51.26 see H. D. Betz, 'The Logion of the Easy Yoke and of Rest (Mt. 11.28–30)', *JBL*, 86 (1967), 10ff., who also provides a short history of interpretation.

[1] This had already been demonstrated in the detailed examination of H. Preisker, *Apokalyptik*, pp. 50–69.

[2] Cf. W. Pannenberg, *Jesus – God and Man* (ET 1968), p. 61. S. Schulz, 'Die neue frage nach dem historischen Jesus', *Neues Testament und Geschichte*, pp. 33–42, however, views Jesus as an apocalyptic prophet and exegete of the Law, though one who through his announcement of the love-commandment, and its application to the Law, eschatologically radicalised the Law without abrogating it. U. Wilckens, 'The Understanding of Revelation within the Horizon of Primitive Christianity', *Revelation as History* (ed. W. Pannenberg, 1968), esp. pp. 69–71 also regards apocalyptic as the 'presupposition' through which Jesus must be approached. While it formally provides the basis of the way in which he expresses his personal authority and for his emphasis upon eschatological revelation rather than the Law, he considers the nature of Jesus' experience to exceed that of any apocalyptic visionary, however radicalised, and the content of his teaching on the kingdom, with its realised dimension, to mark a decisive difference between Jesus and his apocalyptic predecessors.

parallels to the terminology of Jesus and only contain anticipations of aspects of his teaching. The Law remains dominant in their outlook, and discipleship in Jesus' sense is never in view.

We can deal briefly with the view that Jesus' attitude to the Law stems from his origin among the Anawim of the Am-Ha-Areṣ. While it is not implausible to suggest that Jesus' family came from such a background, and that such circles formed the religious environment in which he was educated, the centrality of the Law in their way of life makes it difficult to see how he could have derived his attitude to it from their religious convictions.[1] Even less significance attaches to his alleged agreement with the Sadducaean position in such matters as ritual washings, the paying of the Temple-tax and general rejection of the Pharisaic tradition.[2] The preceding analysis has indicated how far Jesus was from operating upon Sadducaean premises, however much certain external similarities to his teaching may be found among them. There is little more to be said about the supposed similarity that has been said to exist between his attitude and that of the Qumran sect. So far as the status accorded to Law in general is concerned, the two have almost nothing in common, while such statements of Jesus as those concerning distinctions between clean and unclean and the character of the sabbath stand in direct contradiction to their outlook.[3] While the Teacher of Righteousness obviously occupied a position of considerable significance in the community, this was only due to his function as interpreter of the Law and there is no parallel to the type of ministry exercised by Jesus or the kind of allegiance demanded by him.

[1] On Jesus' attitude being influenced by the Anawim see S. Cohon, *JBL*, 48 (1929), 105ff.; W. Sattler, 'Anawim', pp. 8ff.; W. Bauer, 'Jesus der Galiläer', pp. 27ff., and W. Grundmann, *Jesus*, pp. 8ff. Note, however, the comments of L. Goppelt, *Jesus*, pp. 46–7. It is interesting to reflect on the possibility that 1 Enoch also stemmed from such circles. The primitive character of many of its attitudes has been commented upon several times throughout this investigation.

[2] This has been only rarely advocated, but see R. Leszynsky, *Sadduzäer*, pp. 286ff. and, partly, F. C. Burkitt, *JTS*, 28 (1927), 395. Contrast, however, J. Mann, *JQR*, 6 (1915–16), 415–22; W. G. Kümmel, 'Rabbinen', pp. 10–11, and J. Jocz, *Jewish People*, pp. 16ff.

[3] See the full discussion in H. Braun, *Qumran*, II, 85ff. Even here, however, the distinctiveness of Jesus' attitude to the Law over against that of the Qumran community is not fully appreciated.

CONCLUSIONS

Despite the many attempts among Jewish, and some christian, scholars to fit the authority of Jesus within the general
framework of Pharisaic Judaism, at almost every point we have
noted a formidable gap between them. Where rabbinic methods
or argument appeared to be present, only formal similarities
could be detected for such were inevitably used in a non-
rabbinic (Matt. 12.11f.; Luke 13.14; 14.15) and, in some
instances, even christological way (Matt. 12.2ff., 5ff.). The
attempt by G. Kittel to draw a distinction between the teaching
of Jesus, which was largely paralleled among the rabbis, and
the uniqueness of his person was shown throughout to be quite
false, for in both respects he broke through and transcended
the categories of contemporary Judaism.[1] Other endeavours to
find similarities between the form of Jesus' teaching and that of
rabbis indicated that, while verbal parallels sometimes do exist
e.g., between such phrases as ואני אמר and ἐγὼ δὲ λέγω ὑμῖν,
substantial differences occur in the instruction that is given
and the authority with which it is conveyed. Most significant
is the culmination of Jesus' instruction in the command to
follow him, a call to a life of discipleship for which no real
parallel can be found in the rabbinic writings.

His was a unique ministry expressing itself in a unique teaching and stemming from a unique authority (cf. Mark 1.27).[2]
This authority can neither be defined in terms of the Messianic,
even less 'Mosaic', expectations of Judaism nor regarded as an
extension of them, for in none of the passages we have examined
has a 'messianic' element, strictly so called, entered into the
picture. The one passage in the synoptics in material dealing
with the Law which presents Jesus as referring to his status,
i.e., the saying concerning the Son of Man, originally contained
no such specific formula (Mark 2.28 and pars.). On another
occasion, that in which he alludes to himself by means of the

[1] Cf. K. Rengstorf, *TDNT*, II, 139ff. Cf. esp. W. G. Kümmel, 'Rabbinen',
pp. 3ff., and E. C. Hoskyns in *Mysterium Christi*, pp. 70–1, against G.
Kittel, *Die Probleme des palästinischen Spätjudentums und das Urchristentum*
(1926), pp. 88ff. On the contrast between Jesus and Hillel see particularly
F. Delitzsch, *Jesus und Hillel* (1879), pp. 17ff.
[2] Compare the excellent analyses of this passage provided by E. G. Selwyn,
'The Authority of Christ in the NT', *NTS*, 3 (1956–7), 85–6; R. A. Harrisville, *JBL*, 74 (1955), 77, and especially H. Kosmala, 'In My Name',
ASTI, 5 (1967), 87–100.

parable concerning the bridegroom and his guests, only an analogy and not a title was intended (Mark 2.19). On the other hand, Jesus cannot be viewed merely as the mouthpiece of the absolute and eschatological will of God, for the call to personal discipleship indicates that something more is involved than this. In the passages with which we have had to deal, he appears as 'the man who fits no formula', whether Jewish or modern.[1] It has been the contention of this study that the same may be said of his teaching. This has no counterpart in the traditions of the Old Testament and inter-testamentary literature and has no parallel in the teaching of the Jewish parties of the time. As we have seen, it no less calls into question the emphasis that has been placed upon the Natural Law, Decalogue and love-commandment as foundations for ethics in much christian moral instruction. The teaching of Jesus is at once more radical and more complex than such presentations of it have been willing to allow. In view of this fact, it still has something to contribute to contemporary ethical discussion, including con-temporary christian ethical discussion, for the full potential of his insight into the human situation and the behaviour that should characterise it has yet to come into its own, and the basic relevance of his call to discipleship to even the most modern of modern men has still to be presented in more meaningful terms. Certainly his teaching questions the legitimacy of that polarity between law and love, order and freedom that is so widely pre-supposed in much contemporary secular and christian thought. To explore the full ramifications of Jesus' ethical discernment, however, and of the personal claims associated with it, would take us well out of the scope of this study.

[1] The phrase is that of E. Schweizer, *Jesus* (ET 1971), p. 13.

SELECT BIBLIOGRAPHY

The following references are restricted to those which deal in a substantial or significant way, whether in whole or in part, with some aspect of the question of the Law. Omitted therefore are standard sources, works of reference, introductions and commentaries, as well as literature cited with respect to specific points which otherwise do not deal with the main concern of this study. Included, however, are some works consulted in the general preparation of this book which, for various reasons, were not able to be included in the footnotes.

A ARTICLES

ALDRICH, R. L. 'Has the Mosaic Law been Abolished?', *BS*, 116 (1959), 322ff.

ALT, A. 'Die Ursprünge des israelitischen Rechts', *Kleine Schriften zur Geschichte des Volkes Israels* (München, 1953), I, 278–332.

ANDERSON, H. 'The OT in Mark's Gospel', *The Use of the Old Testament in the New and Other Essays, Studies in Honour of W. F. Stinespring* (ed. J. M. Efird, Durham N.C., 1972), pp. 280–306.

ARGYLE, A. W. 'M and the Pauline Epistles', *ET*, 11 (1970), 340–2.

BACON, B. W. 'Jesus and the Law: A Study of the First "Book" of Matthew (Mt. 3–7)', *JBL*, 47 (1928), 203–31.

BAMMEL, E. 'Is Lk. 16.16–18 of Baptist's Provenance?', *HTR*, 51 (1958), 101ff.

'Νόμος Χριστοῦ', *St.Ev.*, III (1964), 120–9.

BARTH, C. 'Theophanie, Bundschliessung und neuer Anfang am dritten Tag', *Ev.Th.*, 28 (1968), 521–33.

BARTSCH, H.-W. 'Feldrede und Bergpredigt: Redaktionsarbeit in Lk. 6', *TZ*, 16 (1960), 5–18.

BAUER, W. 'Jesus der Galiläer', *Festgabe für Adolf Jülicher* (Tübingen, 1927), pp. 16–34.

BAUMGARTNER, J. M. 'Sacrifice and Worship among the Qumran Sectaries', *HTR*, 46 (1953), 141–59.

BEARE, F. W. 'The Sabbath was made for Man?', *JBL*, 79 (1960), 130–6.

BEECHER, W. J. 'Torah: A Word Study in the OT', *JBL*, 24 (1905), 1–16.

BEGRICH, J. 'Berit', *ZAW*, 60 (1944), 2ff.

BELKIN, S. 'Dissolution of Oaths and the Problem of Antisocial Oaths in the Gospels and Contemporary Jewish Literature', *JBL*, 55 (1936), 227ff.

BERGER, K. 'Hartherzigkeit und Gottes Gesetz. Die Vorgeschichte des antijüdischen Vorwurfs in Mk. 10.5', *ZNW*, 61 (1970), 1–47.

'Zu den sogenannten Sätzen heiligen Rechts', *NTS*, 17 (1970), 10–40.

'Zur Geschichte der Einleitungsformel "Amen, Ich sage Euch"', *ZNW*, 63 (1972), 45–75.

BETZ, H. D. 'The Logion of the Easy Yoke and of Rest (Mt. 11.28–30)', *JBL*, 86 (1967), 10–24.

BETZ, O. 'The Eschatological Interpretation of the Sinai-Tradition in Qumran and the NT', *RQ*, 6 (1967), 89ff.

BLEIBEN, T. E. 'The Gospel of Luke and the Gospel of Paul', *JTS*, 45 (1944), 134–40.

BLINZLER, J. 'Die Strafe für Ehebruch in Bibel und Halacha', *NTS*, 4 (1957), 32–47.

BLOCH, R. 'Die Gestalt des Moses in der rabbinischen Tradition', *Moses in Schrift und Überlieferung* (Dusseldorf, GT 1963), pp. 95–171.

DE BOER, P. A. H. 'The Counsellor', *Wisdom in Israel and in the Ancient Near East* (ed. M. Noth and D. Winton Thomas, 1955), pp. 42–71.

BONNARD, P. 'Le Sermon sur la Montagne', *RTP*, 3 (1953), 233–46.

BONSIRVEN, J. 'Le divorce dans le NT', *Rech.SR*, 35 (1948), 442–6.

BOOBYER, G. H. 'St Mark and the Transfiguration', *JTS*, 41 (1940), 118–40.

BORGEN, P. 'From Paul to Luke', *CBQ*, 31 (1969), 168–82.

BORNHÄUSER, K. 'Zur Pericope vom Bruch des Sabbats', *NKZ*, 33 (1922), 325–34.

BORNKAMM, G. 'Das Doppelgebot der Liebe', *Neutestamentliche Studien für Rudolf Bultmann* (Berlin, 1954), pp. 87–94.
'End-expectation and Church in Matthew', *Tradition and Interpretation in Matthew* (London, ET 1963), pp. 15–51.

BRANSCOMB, B. H. 'Jesus' Attitude to the Law of Moses', *JBL* 67 (1948), 32–40.

BRYANT, H. 'Mt. 5.38–9', *ET* 48 (1936–7), 236–7.

BÜCHLER, A. 'The Law of Purification in Mark vii. 1–23', *ET*, 21 (1909–10), 34–40.

BURCHARD, C., 'Das doppelte Liebesgebot in der frühen christlichen Überlieferung', *Der Ruf Jesu und die Antwort die Gemeinde* (ed. E. Lohse *et al.* Göttingen, 1970), pp. 39ff.

BURKILL, T. A. 'Anti-Semitism in St. Mark's Gospel', *NT*, 3 (1959), 34–53.

BURKITT, F. C. 'Jesus and the "Pharisees"', *JTS* 28 (1927), 392–8.

BURTON, E. DE W. 'The Ethical Teachings of Jesus in Relation to the Ethics of the Pharisees and of the OT', *BW*, 10 (1897), 192–208.

CADBURY, H. J. 'Jesus and the Prophets', *JR*, 5 (1925), 607–22.

CADOUX, C. J. 'Judaism and Universalism in the Gospels', *ET* 38 (1926–7), 140ff.

CARLSTON, C. E. 'The Things that Defile (Mk. 7.14) and the Law in Matthew and Mark', *NTS*, 15 (1968), 75–95.

CHAVASSE, C. 'Jesus: Christ *and* Moses', *Th.* 54 (1951), 244–50, 289–96.

CLAVIER, H. 'Matthieu 5.39 et la non-résistance', *RHPR*, 37 (1957), 44–57.

COHON, S. 'The Place of Jesus in the Religious Life of His Day', *JBL*, 48 (1929), 82–108.

CURRIE, S. D. 'Matthew 5.39a – Resistance or Protest', *HTR*, 57 (1964), 140–5.

DANKER, F. W. 'Luke 16.16 – An Opposition Logion?', *JBL*, 77 (1958), 231–43.

DAUBE, D. 'Tests and Interpretation in Roman and Jewish Law', *JJSoc.*, 3 (1961), 3–28.
'Responsibilities of Master and Disciples in the Gospels', *NTS*, 19 (1972), 1–15.

DAVIES, P. E. 'Jesus and the Role of the Prophet', *JBL*, 64 (1945), 241–54.

DAVIES, W. D. 'Apocalyptic and Pharisaism', *Christian Origins and Judaism* (London, 1962), pp. 19–30.

'Matthew 5.17, 18', *Christian Origins and Judaism* (London, 1962), pp. 31–69.

'Reflections on the Tradition: Aboth Revisited', *Christian History and Interpretation* (ed. W. R. Farmer, C. F. D. Moule, R. R. Niebuhr, 1967), pp. 127–58.

'Paul and the DSS: Flesh and Spirit', *Christian Origins and Judaism* (London, 1962), pp. 145–78.

DÉAUT, R. L. 'Une citation de Lévitique 26.45 dans le Document de Damas I:4; VI:2', *RQ* 6 (1967), 289–91.

DELLING, G. 'Das Logion Mark 10.11 (und seine Abwandlungen) im NT', *NT*, 1 (1956), 263–74.

DERRETT, J. D. M. 'Fresh Light on St. Luke XVI: II Dives and Lazarus and the Preceding Sayings', *NTS*, 7 (1960–1), 364–80.

'Peter's Penny: Fresh Light on Matthew 17.24–7', *NT*, 6 (1963), 1–15.

'Law in the NT: Fresh Light on the Parable of the Good Samaritan', *NTS*, 11 (1964), 22–37.

DESCAMPS, A. 'Essai d'interprétation de Mt. 5.17–48', *St.Ev.*, 1 (1959), 156–73.

'Moses in den Evangelien und der apostolischen Tradition', *Moses in Schrift und Überlieferung* (Düsseldorf, GT 1963), pp. 185–203.

DIBELIUS, F. 'Zwei Worte Jesu', *ZNW*, 11 (1910), 188–92.

DIBELIUS, M. 'Die Bergpredigt', *Botschaft und Geschichte* (1953), 1, 79ff.

DOBSCHUTZ, E. VON 'Matthäus als Rabbi und Katechet', *ZNW*, 27 (1928), 338–48.

DODD, C. H. 'Jesus as Teacher and Prophet', *Mysterium Christi* (ed. G. K. A. Bell and A. Deissmann, London, 1930), pp. 53–66.

'Matthew and Paul', *New Testament Studies* (Manchester, 1953), pp. 53–66.

'Natural Law in the NT', *New Testament Studies* (Manchester, 1953), pp. 129–42.

DUBARLE, A. M. 'Mariage et divorce dans l'Évangile', *Or.Sy.*, 9 (1964), 61–73.

EASTON, B. S. 'The Sermon on the Mount', *JBL*, 33 (1914), 228–43.

EBELING, H. J. 'Die Fastenfrage (Mk. 2.18–22)', *TSK*, 108 (1937–8), 387–96.

EICHHOLZ, G. 'Die Aufgabe einer Auslegung der Bergpredigt', *Tradition und Hermeneutik* (Münich, 1965).

EICHRODT, W. 'Covenant and Law', *Int.*, 20 (1966), 302–21.

ELLISON, H. L. 'Jesus and the Pharisees', *JTVI*, 85 (1953), 35–46.

EVANS, C. F. 'The Central Section of St. Luke's Gospel', *Studies in the Gospels* (ed. D. E. Nineham, Oxford, 1955), pp. 37–54.

FARMER, W. R. 'An Historical Essay in the Humility of Jesus Christ', *Christian History and Interpretation* (ed. W. R. Farmer, C. F. D. Moule, R. R. Niebuhr, 1967), pp. 103ff.

FENSHAM, F. C. 'Covenant, Promise and Expectation in the Bible', *TZ*, 23 (1967), 305–22.

FENTON, J. C. 'Paul and Mark', *Studies in the Gospels* (ed. D. E. Nineham, Oxford, 1955), pp. 89–112.

FEUILLET, A. 'Jésus et la sagesse divine d'après les évangiles synoptiques', *RB*, 42 (1955), 161–96.

'La controverse sur la jeûne', *NRT*, 90 (1968), 113–36; 252–77.

'Morale Ancienne et Morale Chrétienne d'après Mt. 5.17–20', *NTS*, 17 (1971), 124ff.

FINKELSTEIN, L. 'The Book of Jubilees and the Rabbinic Halakha', *HTR*, 16 (1923), 39–61.

FLUSSER, D. 'A New Sensitivity in Judaism and the Christian Message', *HTR*, 61 (1968), 107–27.

FÖHRER, G., 'Das sogenannte apodiktisch formulierte Recht und der Dekalog', *KD*, 11 (1965), 47–74.

FORD, J. M. 'Reflections on W. D. Davies: The Setting of the Sermon on the Mount', *Bib.* 48 (1967), 623–8.

FREEDMAN, D. N. 'Divine Commitment and Human Obligation: The Covenant Theme', *Int.*, 18 (1964), 419–31.

FUCHS, E. 'Jesu Selbstzeugnis nach Matthäus 5', *ZTK*, 51 (1954), 14–34.

GEMSER, B. 'The Importance of the Motive Clause in OT Law', *VT*, Supp. 1 (1953), 50–66.

GERSTENBERGER, E. 'Covenant and Commandment', *JBL*, 84 (1965), 38–51.

GESE, H. 'Bemerkungen zur Sinaitradition', *ZAW*, 79 (1967), 137–54.

GIBBS, J. M. 'The Son of God as the Torah Incarnate in Matthew', *St.Ev.*, IV, 1 (1968), 38–46.

GIBLET, J. 'Prophétisme et attente d'un messie prophète dans l'Ancien Judaïsme', *L'Attente du Messie* (Paris, 1954), pp. 85–130.

GILS, F. 'Le Sabbat a été fair pour l'homme et non l'homme pour le Sabbat', *RB*, 69 (1962), 506–23.

GLASSON, T. F. 'Anti-Pharisaism in St. Matthew's Gospel', *JQR*, 51 (1961), 316–20.

GLATZER, N. N., 'Hillel the Elder in the Light of the Dead Sea Scrolls', *The Scrolls and the New Testament* (ed. K. Stendahl, 1957), pp. 233ff.

GOGUEL, M. 'Jésus et la tradition religieuse de son peuple', *RHPR*, 17 (1937), 154–75, 219–44.

GRANT, R. M. 'The Decalogue in Early Christianity', *HTR*, 40 (1947), 1ff.

GREEN, H. B. 'The Structure of St. Matthew's Gospel', *St.Ev.*, IV, 1 (1968), 47–59.

GRUNDMANN, W. 'Die Arbeit des ersten Evangelisten am Bilde Jesu', *Christentum und Judentum* (Leipzig, 1940).

'Die Bergpredigt nach der Lukasfassung', *St.Ev.*, 1 (1959), 180–9.

GUTBROD, W. H. 'Jesus and the Law: Some Considerations', *Th.*, 39 (1939), 123–7.

HAENCHEN, E. 'Matthäus 23', *Gott und Mensch* (1965), pp. 29–54.

HANSSEN, O. 'Zum Verständnis der Bergpredigt', *Der Ruf Jesu und die Antwort der Gemeinde* (ed. E. Lohse, C. Burchard and B. Schaller, Göttingen, 1970), pp. 94–111.

HARDER, G. 'Jesus und das Gesetz (Matt. 5.17–20)', *Antijudäismus im Neuen Testament* (ed. W. Eckert, N. P. Levinson and M. Stöhr, München, 1967), pp. 105–18.

HARMAN, G. M. 'The Judaism of the First Gospel', *JBL*, 14 (1895), 114–24.

HARNACK, A. 'Hat Jesus das alttestamentliche Gesetz abgeschafft?', *Aus Wissenschaft und Leben*, II, 227–36.

HARPER, W. R. 'What is Christ's Attitude toward the OT', *BW*, 3 (1894), 241–6.

HARRIS, J. G. 'The Covenant Concept among the Qumran Sectaries', *EQ*, 39 (1967), 86–92.

HASLER, V. 'Das Herzstück der Bergpredigt', *TZ*, 15 (1959), 90–106.

HEBERT, G. 'The Problem of the Gospel According to Matthew', *SJT*, 14 (1961), 403–13.

HEMPEL, J. 'Der synoptische Jesus und das AT.Ein Vortrag', *ZAW*, 15 (1938), 1–34.

HERFORD, R. T. 'The Law and Pharisaism', *Judaism and Christianity*, III (ed. E. I. J. Rosenthal, London, 1938), 91–121.

HERMANN, S. 'Die konstruktive Restauration', *Probleme biblischer Theologie* (ed. H. W. Wolff, Münich, 1971), pp. 155–70.

HOLTZCLAW, B. 'Matt. 5.17, 18', *Festschrift to Honour F. Wilbur Gingrich* (ed. E. H. Barth and R. E. Cocroft, Leiden, 1972), pp. 161–3.

HONEYMAN, A. M. 'Matt. 5.18 and the Validity of the Law', *NTS*, 1 (1954–5), 141–2.

HOSKYNS, E. C. 'Jesus the Messiah', *Mysterium Christi* (ed. G. K. A. Bell and A. Deissmann, London, 1930), pp. 69–90.

HRUBY, H. 'Begriff und Funktion des Gottes Volkes in der rabbinischen Tradition', *Jud.* 21 (1965), 23ff.

HUBBARD, D. A. 'The Wisdom Movement and Israel's Covenant Faith', *Tyn.B.*, 17 (1966), 3–33.

HUFFMON, H. B. 'The Exodus, Sinai and the Credo', *CBQ*, 27 (1965), 101–13.

HULTGREN, J. 'The Formation of the Sabbath-Pericope in Mk. 2.23–8', *JBL*, 91 (1972), 38–43.

HYATT, J. P. 'Torah in the Book of Jeremiah', *JBL*, 60 (1941), 381–96.

JEPSEN, A. 'Berit', *Verbannung und Heimkehr* (Tübingen, 1961), pp. 161–80.

'Beitrage zur Auslegung und Geschichte des Dekalogs', *ZAW*, 79 (1967), 277–304.

JEREMIAS, J. 'Lass allda deine Gabe', *ABBA* (Göttingen, 1966), pp. 103–7.

'Kennzeichnen der ipsissima vox Jesu', *ABBA*, pp. 145–52.

JERVELL, H. J. 'The Law in Luke-Acts', *HTR*, 64 (1971), 21–36.

JOHNSON, S. E. 'Jesus and First Century Galilee', *In Memoriam Ernst Lohmeyer* (ed. W. Schmauch, Göttingen, 1950), pp. 73ff.

KADUSHIN, M. 'Aspects of the Rabbinic Concept of Israel', *HUCA*, 19 (1945–6), 57–71.

KAPELRUD, A. S. 'Some Recent Points of View on the Time and Origin of the Decalogue', *St.Th.*, 18 (1964), 81–90.

KAPLAN, R. 'The Pharisaic Character and the Date of the Book of Enoch', *ATR*, 12 (1929–30), 531–7.

KÄSEMANN, E. 'Satze heiligen Rechtes im NT', *NTS*, 1 (1955), 248–60.

'The Problem of the Historical Jesus', *Essays on New Testament Themes* (ET 1964), pp. 1ff.

'Die Anfänge christlicher Theologie', *Exegetische Versuche und Besinnungen* (1964), II, 83ff.

KEE, H. 'The Old Coat and the New Wine', *NT*, 12 (1970), 13–21.

KIMBROUGH, S. T. 'The Concept of Sabbath at Qumran', *RQ*, 5 (1966), 483–502.

KLINE, M. E. 'Law and Covenant', *WTJ*, 27 (1964), 1–20.

KOSMALA, H. 'In My Name', *ASTI*, 5 (1967), 87–100.

'Nachfolge und Nachahmung Gottes II: Im judischen Denken', *ASTI*, 3 (1964), 54–110.

'The Conclusion of Matthew', *ASTI*, 4 (1965), 142ff.

KRETSCHMAR, G. 'Ein Beitrag zur Frage nach dem Ursprung frühchristlicher Askese', *ZTK*, 61 (1964), 27–67.

KUHN, H.-W. 'Zum Problem des Verhältnisses der markinischen Redaktion zur israelitisch-jüdischen Tradition', *Tradition und Glaube* (ed. G. Jeremias, H.-W. Kuhn and H. Stegemann, Göttingen, 1971), pp. 209–309.

KÜMMEL, W. G. 'Jesus und die Rabbinen', *Heilsgeschehen und Geschichte* (Marburg, 1965), pp. 1–14.

'Jesus und der Traditionsgedanke', *Heilsgeschehen*, pp. 15–35.

'Jesus und Paulus', *Heilsgeschehen*, pp. 81–106.

'Jesus und Paulus', *Heilsgeschehen*, pp. 439–56.

'Die Weherufe über die Schriftgelehrten und Pharisäer (Matthäus 23.1–36)', *Antijudäismus im NT* (München, 1967), pp. 135–47.

KUTSCH, E. 'Gesetz und Gnade', *ZAW*, 79 (1967), 18–35.

LAMPE, G. W. H. 'The Lucan Portrait of Christ', *NTS*, 2 (1955–6), 160–75.

LEEMING, B. 'Except it be for Fornication', *Scr.* 8 (1956), 75–82.

LEENHARDT, F. J. 'Les femmes aussi...à propos du billet de répudiation', *RTP*, 19 (1969), 31–40.

LÉGASSE, S. 'Jesus: Juif ou non?', *NRT*, 86 (1964), 673–705.

LEHMANN, M. R. 'Gen. 2.24 as the Basis for Divorce in Halakah and NT', *ZAW*, 72 (1960), 263–7.

LEITCH, J. W. 'Lord also of the Sabbath', *SJT*, 19 (1966), 426–33.

LINTON, O. 'St Matthew 5.43', *St.Th.*, 18 (1964), 66–79.

LIVER, J. 'The Half-Shekel Offering in Biblical and Post-Biblical Literature', *HTR*, 56 (1963), 173–98.

LOEWE, H. 'Pharisaism', *Judaism and Christianity*, I (ed. H. W. Robinson, London, 1932), 103–90.

LÖWY, M. 'Messiaszeit und zukünftige Welt', *MGWJ*, 5 (1897), 392–409.

LOFTHOUSE, W. 'Imitatio Christi', *ET*, 65 (1953–4), 340ff.

LOHSE, E. 'Lukas als Theologe der Heilsgeschichte', *Ev.Th.*, 14 (1954), 256–275.

'Jesu Worte über den Sabbat', *Judentum, Urchristentum und Kirche* (ed. W. Eltester, Berlin, 1960), pp. 79–89.

'Ich aber sage euch', *Der Ruf Jesu und die Antwort der Gemeinde* (Festschrift für J. Jeremias, ed. E. Lohse, C. Burchard and B. Schaller, Göttingen, 1972), pp. 189–203.

MCCARTHY, D. J. 'Covenant in the OT: The Present State of the Inquiry', *CBQ*, 27 (1965), 217–40.

'berit in OT and Theology', *Bib.*, 53 (1972), 110–21.

MCEACHERN, V. E. 'Dual Witness and Sabbath Motif in Luke', *CJT*, 12 (1966), 267–80.

MCKENZIE, J. L. 'Reflections on Wisdom', *JBL*, 86 (1967), 1–9.

MANN, J. 'Jesus and the Sadducaean Priests: Luke 10.25–37', *JQR*, 6 (1915–16), 415–22.

MANSON, T. W. 'Jesus, Paul and the Law', *Judaism and Christianity*, III (ed. E. I. J. Rosenthal, London, 1938), 125–41.

'Mark 2.27ff.', *Coniecitanea Neotestamentica*, XI (Lund, 1947), 138–46.

MARGOLIOUTH, G. 'The Traditions of the Elders (St. Mark 7.1–23)', *ET*, 22 (1910–11), 261–3.

MARTIN-ACHARD, R. 'La Nouvelle Alliance, Selon Jérémie', *RTP*, 12 (1961), 81–92.

MENDENHALL, G. E. 'Ancient Oral and Biblical Law', *BA*, 17 (1954), 26–46.

'Covenant Forms in Israelite Tradition', *BA*, 17 (1954), 50–76.

MERKEL, H. 'Jesus und die Pharisäer', *NTS*, 14 (1967–8), 194–208.

MICHEL, O. 'Der Abschluss des Matthäusevangelium', *Ev.Th.*, 10 (1950–1), 21ff.

MITTON, C. L. 'The Law and the Gospel', *ET*, 68 (1957), 312–15.

'The Will of God in the Synoptic Tradition of the Words of Jesus', *ET*, 72 (1960), 68–71.

MONTEFIORE, H. 'Thou Shalt Love Thy Neighbour as Thyself', *NT*, 5 (1962), 157–70.

'Jesus and the Temple Tax', *NTS*, 11 (1964–5), 60–71.

MOORE, G. F. 'The Am-Ha-Areṣ and the Haberim', *The Beginnings of Christianity* (ed. F. J. Foakes-Jackson and K. Lake, 1920), I, 439–47.

MOSLEY, A. W. 'Jesus' Audiences in the Gospels of St. Mark and St. Luke', *NTS*, 10 (1963), 139–49.

MOULE, C. F. D. 'The NT and Moral Decisions', *ET*, 74 (1963), 370ff.

'St. Matthew's Gospel: Some Neglected Features', *St.Ev.*, II (1964), 91–9.

'The Intention of the Evangelists', *The Phenomenon of the NT* (London, 1967), pp. 101–14.

'Fulfilment-Words in the NT: Use and Abuse', *NTS*, 14 (1968), 293–320.

MUILENBERG, J. 'The Form and Structure of the Covenantal Formulations', *Essays in Honour of Millar Burrows* (Leiden, 1959), pp. 351–7.

MURMELSTEIN, B. 'Jesu Gang durch die Saatfelder', *Ang.*, 3 (1930), 111ff.

NISSEN, A. 'Tora und Geschichte im Spätjudentum', *NT*, 9 (1967), 241–77.

NÖTSCHER, F. 'Bundesformular und "Amtshimmel" ', *BZ*, 9 (1965), 181–214.

NOTH, M. 'The Laws in the Pentateuch: Their Assumptions and Meaning', *The Laws in the Pentateuch and Other Essays* (Edinburgh, ET 1966), pp. 1–107.

O'HARA, J. 'Christian Fasting (Mk. 2.18–22)', *Scr.*, 19 (1967), 82–95.

PETERS, J. P. 'Christ's Treatment of the OT', *JBL*, 15 (1896), 87–105.

DE PINTO, B. 'The Torah and the Psalms', *JBL*, 86 (1966), 154–74.

PLOOY, D. 'The Anti-Sabbatic Dilemma in the Gospels', *Exp.*, 2 (1924), 196–207.

VON RAD, G. 'The Form-Critical Problem of the Hexateuch', *The Problem of the Hexateuch and Other Essays* (Edinburgh, ET 1966), pp. 1–78.

RAUSCH, J. 'The Principle of Non-Resistance and Love of Enemy in Mt. 5.43–48', *CBQ*, 28 (1966), 31–41.

REILLY, W. S. 'Our Lord and the Pharisees', *CBQ*, 1 (1939), 64–8.

RIGAUX, B. 'Révélation des Mystères et Perfection à Qumrân et dans le NT', *NTS*, 4 (1958), 237–62.

RIVKIN, E. 'Pharisaism and the Crisis of the Individual in the Graeco-Roman World', *JQR*, 61 (1970), 27–53.

ROBERTSON, E. 'Law and Religion amongst the Samaritans', *Judaism and Christianity*, III (ed. E. I. J. Rosenthal, London, 1938), pp. 69–88.

ROBINSON, H. W. 'Law and Religion in Israel', *ibid.* pp. 47–66.

RODD, C. S. 'Are the ethics of Jesus situation-ethics?', *ET*, 79 (1968), 168 ff.

ROWLEY, H. H. 'Moses and the Decalogue', *Men of God* (London, 1963), pp. 1ff.

'The Prophets and the Cult', *Worship in Ancient Israel* (London, 1967), pp. 144–75.

RYRIE, C. C. 'The End of the Law', *BS*, 124 (1967), 239–47.

SATTLER, W. 'Die Anawim im Zeitalter Jesu Christi', *Festgabe für Adolf Jülicher* (Tübingen, 1927), pp. 1–15.

SCHALLER, B. 'Die Sprüche über Ehescheidung und Wiederheirat in der synoptischen Überlieferung', *Der Ruf Jesu und die Antwort der Gemeinde* (ed. E. Lohse *et al.*, Göttingen, 1970), pp. 226–46.

SCHECHTER, S. 'Some Rabbinic Parallels to the NT', *JQR*, 12 (1900), 427ff.

SCHMIDT, J. M. 'Erwägungen zum Verhältnis von Auszugs- und Sinaitradition', *ZAW*, 82 (1970), 1–30.

SCHNACKENBURG, R. 'Die Erwartung des "Propheten" nach dem NT und dem Qumran-Texten', *St.Ev.*, 1 (1959), 622–39.

'Mitmenschlichkeit im Horizont des Neuen Testaments', *Die Zeit Jesu* (ed. G. Bornkamm and K. Rahner, Freiburg, 1970), pp. 70–92.

SCHNIEWIND, J. 'Die Botschaft Jesu und die Theologie des Paulus', *Nachgelassene Reden und Aufsätze* (1952).

SCHOEPS, H. J. 'Haggadisches zur Auserwählung Israels', *Aus Frühchristlicher Zeit* (1950), pp. 184–200.

'Jesus und das jüdische Gesetz', *ibid.* pp. 212–20.

'Paulus als rabbinischer Exeget 1: Χριστος τελος νομου', *ibid.* pp. 221–9.

'Restitutio Principii as the Basis for the Nova Lex Jesu', *JBL*, 66 (1947), 453ff.

SCHUBERT, K. 'The Sermon on the Mount and the Qumran Texts', *The Scrolls and the New Testament* (ed. K. Stendahl, New York, 1957), pp. 118–28.

SCHÜRMANN, H. 'Sprachliche Reminiszenzen an abgeänderte oder ausgelassene Bestandteile der Spruchsammlung im Lukas- und Matthäus-Evangelium', *NTS*, 6 (1960), 193–210.

'Wer daher eines dieser geringsten Gebote auflöst...', *BZ*, 4 (1960), 238–50.

'Die Warnung des Lukas vor der Falschlehre in der "Predigt am Berge" Lk. 6.20–49', *BZ*, 10 (1966), 57–81.

SCHULZ, S. 'Markus und das Alte Testament', *ZTK*, 58 (1961), 184–97.

SCHWEIZER, E. 'Matthäus 5.17–20 – Anmerkungen zum Gesetzesverständnis des Matthäus', *Neotestamentica* (Zürich, 1963), pp. 399–406.

'Observance of the Law and Charismatic Activity in Matthew', *NTS*, 17 (1970), 213ff.

SELWYN, E. G., 'The Authority of Christ in the NT', *NTS*, 3 (1956–7), 84–93.

SMITH, M. 'Hate Thine Enemy', *HTR*, 45 (1952), 71–3.

STÄHLIN, G. 'Zum Gebrauch von Beteuerungsformeln im NT', *NT*, 5 (1962), 115ff.

STAUFFER, E. 'Neue Wege der Jesusforschung', *Gottes ist der Orient* (Berlin, 1959), pp. 182ff.

'Jesus und seine Bibel', *Abraham unser Vater* (ed. O. Betz, M. Hengel, P. Schmidt, Leiden, 1963), pp. 440–9.

STERN, J. B. 'Jesus' Citation of Dt. 6.5 and Lev. 19.18 in the Light of Jewish Tradition', *CBQ*, 28 (1966), 312–16.

STIASSNY, J. 'Jésus accomplit la Promesse. Essai d'interprétation de Matthieu 5.17–19', *BVC*, 59 (1964), 30–7.

SUTCLIFFE, E. F. 'One Jot or Tittle', *Bib.*, 9 (1928), 458–60.

'Hatred at Qumran', *RQ*, 2 (1959–60), 345–55.

TANNEHILL, R. C. 'The "Focal Instance" as a Form of New Testament Speech', *JR*, 50 (1970), 372–85.

TERREY, M. S. 'The OT and the Christ', *AJT*, 10 (1906), 233–50.

THIEL, W. 'Erwägungen zum Alter des Heiligkeitgesetzes', *ZAW*, 81 (1969), 40–73.

THIEME, K. 'Matthäus, der schriftgelehrte Evangelist', *Jud.* 5 (1949), 130–52, 161–82.

TORRANCE, T. F. 'The Doctrine of Grace in the OT', *SJT*, 1 (1948), 55–65.

VAN UNNIK, W. C. 'Die Motivierung der Feindesliebe in Lukas vi..32–5', *NT*, 8 (1966), 284–300.

VAGANAY, L. 'L'absence du Sermon sur la Montagne chez Marc', *RB*, 58 (1951), 5–46.

'Existent-il chez Marc quelques traces du Sermon sur la Montagne?', *NT*, 1 (1955), 150–62.

VERMÈS, G. 'Die Gestalt des Moses an der Wende der beiden Testamenten', *Moses in Schrift und Überlieferung* (Düsseldorf, GT 1963), pp. 61–93.

VOKES, F. E. 'The Ten Commandments in the NT and in First Century Judaism', *St.Ev.*, V, II (1968), 146–54.

WALTER, N. 'Zur Analyse von Mc. 10.17–31', *ZNW*, 53 (1962), 206–18.

WEINFELD, M. 'Deuteronomy – The Present State of the Inquiry', *JBL*, 86 (1967), 249–62.

WEINGREEN, J. 'Oral Torah and Written Records', *Holy Book and Holy Tradition* (ed. E. G. Rupp and F. F. Bruce, Manchester, 1968), pp. 54–67.

'The Deuteronomic Lawgiver: A Proto-Rabbinic Type', *Transitions in Biblical Scholarship* (ed. J. C. Rylaarsdam, 1967), pp. 76–89.

WENDLAND, E. 'Zu Matthäus 5.18, 19', *ZNW*, 5 (1904), 253–6.

WIEDER, N. 'The "Law-Interpreter" of the Sect of the DSS: A Second Moses', *JJS*, 4 (1953), 158–75.

WILDER, A. N. 'Equivalents of Natural Law in the Teaching of Jesus', *JR*, 26 (1946), 125–35.

WINTER, E. K. 'Das Evangelium der jerusalemitischen Mutterkirche', *Jud.*, 9 (1953), 1–33.

SELECT BIBLIOGRAPHY

WINTER, P. 'Gen. 1.27 and Jesus' Saying on Divorce', *ZAW*, 70 (1958), 260–261.

WOOD, H. G. 'Mark's Gospel and Paulinism', *ET*, 51 (1939–40), 327–33.

WÜRTHWEIN, E. 'Der Sinn des Gesetzes im AT', *ZTK*, 55 (1958), 255–70.

YARNOLD, E. Τέλειος in St. Matthew's Gospel', *St.Ev.*, IV, I (1968), 269–73.

ZEITLIN, S. 'The Pharisees', *JQR*, 16 (1925–6), 383–94.

ZIMMERLI, W. 'Das Gesetz im AT', *Gottes Offenbarung* (Münich, 1963), pp. 249–76.

'The Place and Limit of Wisdom in the Framework of OT Theology', *SJT*, 17 (1964), 144–58.

B BOOKS

ABRAHAMS, I. *Studies in Pharisaism and the Gospels*, Cambridge, 1924.

ACKROYD, P. *Exile and Restoration*, London, 1968.

ALBECK, CH. *Das Buch der Jubiläen und die Halacha*, 1930.

ALBERTZ, D. M. *Die synoptischen Streitgespräche*, Berlin, 1921.

AMSLER, S. *L'Ancien Testament dans l'Église*, Neuchâtel, 1960.

BACON, B. W. *Studies in Matthew*, New York, 1930.

BAIRD, J. A. *Audience Criticism and the Historical Jesus*, Philadelphia, 1969.

BALDENSPERGER, W. *Das Selbstbewusstsein Jesu im Lichte der messianischen Hoffnungen esiner Zeit*, Strassburg, 1888.

BALTENSWEILER, H. *Die Ehe im Neuen Testament*, Zürich, 1967.

BALTZER, K. *Das Bundesformular*, Neukirchen, 1960².

BARTH, F. *Die Hauptprobleme des Lebens Jesu*, Gütersloh, 1911.

BARTH, G. 'Matthew's Understanding of the Law', *Tradition and Interpretation in Matthew*, London, ET 1963.

BAUR, F. C. *Vorlesungen über neutestamentliche Theologie*, Leipzig, 1864.

BEILNER, W. *Christus und die Pharisäer*, Vienna, 1959.

BELKIN, S. *Philo and the Oral Law*, 1940.

BENTZEN, A. *Messias – Moses Redivivus – Menschensohn*, Zürich, 1948.

BENZ, K. *Die Stellung Jesu zum alttestamentlichen Gesetz*, Freiburg, 1914.

BERGER, K. *Die Gesetzesauslegung Jesu. Teil I: Markus und Parallelen*, Neukirchen, 1972.

BETZ, O. *Offenbarung und Schriftforschung in der Qumran-sekte*, Tübingen, 1960.

BEYERLIN, W. *Origins and History of the Oldest Sinai Tradition*, Oxford, ET 1965.

BISCHOFF, E. *Jesus und die Rabbinen*, Leipzig, 1905.

BLACK, M. *The Scrolls and Christian Origins*, London, 1961.

BLAIR, E. P. *Jesus in the Gospel of Matthew*, New York, 1960.

BLOCH, J. *On the Apocalyptic in Judaism*, Philadelphia, 1952.

BONSIRVEN, J. *Palestinian Judaism in the Time of Jesus Christ*, New York, ET 1964.

BORNHÄUSER, K. *Die Bergpredigt*, Gütersloh, 1923.

BORNKAMM, G. *Jesus of Nazareth*, London, ET 1960.

BOURGEAULT, G. *Décalogue et morale chrétienne: Enquête Patristique sur l'utilisation et l'interprétation chrétienne du Décalogue de c. 60 a c. 220*, Paris, 1971.

BOUSSET, W. *Jesu Predigt in ihrem Gegensatz zum Judentum*, Göttingen, 1892.

Die Religion des Judentums im späthellenistischen Zeitalter, ed. H. Gressmann, Tübingen, 1926.

273

BRANDON, S. G. F. *Jesus and the Zealots*, Manchester, 1967.

BRANDT, W. *Jüdische Reinheitslehre und ihre Beschreibung in den Evangelien*, Giessen, 1910.

BRANSCOMB, B. H. *Jesus and the Law of Moses*, New York, 1930.

BRAUN, H. *Spätjüdisch-Häretischer und frühchristlicher Radikalismus*, Tübingen, 1957.

Qumran und das NT, Tübingen, 1966.

BUCHANAN, G. W., *The Consequences of the Covenant*, Leiden, 1970.

BULTMANN, R. *History of the Synoptic Tradition*, Oxford, ET 1963.

Theology of the NT, London, 1952.

BUNDY, W. E. *Jesus and the First Three Gospels*, Cambridge, 1955.

BURKITT, F. C. *The Gospel History and its Transmission*, Oxford, 1907.

BURROWS, M. *More Light on the Dead Sea Scrolls*, London, 1958.

BUTLER, B. C. *The Originality of St. Matthew*, Cambridge, 1951.

CADBURY, H. J. *Jesus: What Manner of Man?* London, 1947.

CAMPENHAUSEN, H. VON, *The Formation of the Christian Bible*, London, ET 1972.

CLEMENTS, R. E. *Prophecy and Covenant*, London, 1965.

COHEN, B. *Law and Tradition in Judaism*, New York, 1969.

COLE, A. *The New Temple*, London, 1950.

CONZELMANN, H. *The Theology of St. Luke*, London, 1960.

Grundriss der Theologie des Neuen Testaments, Münich, 1967.

CREMER, F. G. *Die Fastenfrage Jesu*, Bonn, 1965.

CROSS, F. M. *The Ancient Library of Qumran*, New York, 1961.

CULLMANN, O. *The Christology of the New Testament*, London, ET 1959.

DALMAN, G. *The Words of Jesus*, Edinburgh, ET 1902.

Jesus–Jeshua, London, ET 1929.

DANIÉLOU, J. *Sacramentum Futuri*, Paris, 1950.

DAUBE, D. *The New Testament and Rabbinic Judaism*, London, 1956.

Studies in Biblical Law, London, 1969.

DAVIES, W. D. *The Setting of the Sermon on the Mount*, Cambridge, 1964.

DELITZSCH, F. *Jesus und Hillel*, Erlangen, 1879³.

DENNEY, J. *Jesus and the Gospel*, London, 1908.

DERRETT, J. D. M. *Law in the New Testament*, London, 1970.

(ed.), *An Introduction to Legal Systems*, London, 1968.

DESCAMPS, A. *Les Justes et la Justice dans les Évangiles et le Christianisme Primitif hormis la Doctrine proprement Paulinienne*, Louvain, 1950.

DIBELIUS, M. *From Tradition to Gospel*, London, ET 1934.

'Die Bergpredigt', in *Botschaft und Geschichte*, I, Tübingen, 1953.

DIHLE, A. *Die Goldene Regel*, Göttingen, 1962.

DODD, C. H. *The Bible and the Greeks*, London, 1935.

Gospel and Law, Cambridge, 1951.

DOEVE, J. W. *Jewish Hermeneutics in the Synoptic Gospels and Acts*, 1954.

DRIVER, G. R. *The Judaean Scrolls*, Oxford, 1965.

DUPONT, J. *Les Béatitudes*, Louvain, 1958.

Mariage et Divorce dans l'Évangile Matthieu, Bruges, 1959.

EASTON, B. S. *Christ in the Gospels*, New York, 1930.

EDERSHEIM, A. *The Life and Times of Jesus the Messiah*, London, 1900.

EHRHARDT, E. *Der Grundcharakter der Ethik Jesu*, Freiburg, 1895.

EICHOLZ, G. *Auslegung der Bergpredigt*, Neukirchen, 1965.

EICHRODT, W. *Theology of the Old Testament*, London, ET 1961–5.

FAIRBAIRN, P. *The Revelation of Law in Scripture*, Edinburgh, 1869.

FALK, Z. M. *Hebrew Law in Biblical Times*, Jerusalem, 1964.

FARMER, W. R. *The Synoptic Problem*, London, 1964.

FASCHER, E. ΠΡΟΦΗΤΗ, Giessen, 1927.

FEINE, P. *Theologie des Neuen Testaments*, Leipzig, 1951[8].

FIEBIG, P. *Jesu Bergpredigt*, Göttingen, 1924.

FINKEL, A. *The Pharisees and the Teacher of Nazareth*, Leiden, 1964.

FINKELSTEIN, L. *The Pharisees*, Philadelphia, 1938.

FLENDER, H. *St. Luke, Theologian of Redemptive History*, London, ET 1967.

FLUSSER, D. *Jesus*, New York, 1969.

FÖRSTER, W. *Palestinian Judaism and the New Testament*, Edinburgh, 1964.

FRIEDLÄNDER, G. *The Jewish Sources of the Sermon on the Mount*, London, 1911.

FRIEDLÄNDER, M. *Die Religiösen Bewegungen innerhalb des Judentums im Zeitalter Jesu*, Berlin, 1905.

FURNISH, V. P. *The Love Command in the New Testament*, Nashville & New York, 1972.

GERHARDSSON, B. *Memory and Manuscript*, Uppsala, 1961.

GERSTENBERGER, E. *Wesen und Herkunft des 'Apodiktischen Rechts'*, Neukirchen, 1965.

GILS, F. *Jésus, Prophète d'après les Évangiles Synoptiques*, Louvain, 1957.

GLASSON, T. F. *Moses in the Fourth Gospel*, London, 1963.

GLOCK, J. PH. *Die Gesetzesfrage im Leben Jesu und in der Lehre des Paulus*, 1885.

GOODSPEED, E. J. *Matthew, Apostle and Evangelist*, Philadelphia, 1959.

GOPPELT, L. *Typos*, Gütersloh, 1939.

Jesus, Paul and Judaism, New York, ET 1964.

GRAYSTONE, G. *The Dead Sea Scrolls and the Originality of Christ*, London, 1956.

GRUNDMANN, W. *Jesus der Galiläer und das Judentum*, Leipzig, 1940.

GUIGNEBERG, CH. *Jesus*, London, ET 1935.

HÄNEL, J. *Der Schriftbegriff Jesu*, Gütersloh, 1919.

HAHN, F. *Christologische Hoheitstitel*, Göttingen, 1963.

HARNACK, A. *The Sayings of Jesus*, London, ET 1908.

HEBERT, A. G. *The Throne of David: A Study of the Fulfilment of the Old Testament in Jesus Christ and His Church*, London, 1941.

HELFGOTT, B. W. *The Doctrine of Election in Tannaitic Literature*, New York, 1954.

HENRY, C. F. H. *Christian Personal Ethics*, Grand Rapids, 1957.

HERFORD, R. T. *Christianity in Talmud and Midrash*, London, 1903.

The Pharisees, London, 1924.

HOFIUS, O. *Jesus Tischgemeinschaft mit dem Sündern*, Stuttgart, 1967.

HOLTZMANN, H. J. *Lehrbuch der neutestamentlichen Theologie*, Tübingen, 1896.

HORT, F. J. A. *Judaistic Christianity*, London, 1898.

L'HOUR, J. *La Morale de l'Alliance*, Paris, 1966.

HUBER, H. *Die Bergpredigt*, Göttingen, 1932.

HUGHES, H. M. *The Ethics of the Jewish Apocryphal Literature*, London, 1909.

HUMMEL, R. *Die Auseinandersetzung zwischen Kirche und Judentum im Matthäusevangelium*, Münich, 1963.

ISAAKSON, A. *Marriage and Ministry in the New Temple*, Lund, 1965.

JACOB, E. *Theology of the Old Testament*, London, ET 1958.

JAUBERT, A. *La Notion d'Alliance dans le Judaïsme aux abords de l'Ère Chrétienne*, Paris, 1963.

JEREMIAS, J. *Jesus als Weltvollender*, Gütersloh, 1930.
Unknown Sayings of Jesus, London, 1958.
Jerusalem zur Zeit Jesu, Göttingen, 1962³.
The Sermon on the Mount, London, 1965.

JOCZ, J. *The Jewish People and Jesus Christ*, London, 1949.
A Theology of Election, London, 1958.

JOHNSON, S. *Theology of the Gospels*, London, 1966.

JÜNGEL, E. *Paulus und Jesus*, Tübingen, 1967³.

KÄHLER, M. *Jesus und das Alte Testament*, Leipzig, 1896.

KAFTAN, J. *Jesus und Paulus*, Tübingen, 1906.

KALLAS, J. *The Significance of the Synoptic Miracles*, London, 1961.

KILPATRICK, G. D. *The Origins of the Gospel According to St. Matthew*, Oxford, 1946.

KITTEL, G. *Die Probleme des palästinischen Spätjudentums und das Urchristentum*, Stuttgart, 1926.

KLAUSNER, J. *Jesus of Nazareth*, London, ET 1925.
From Jesus to Paul, London, ET 1944.
The Messianic Idea in Israel, London, 1956.

KLOSTERMANN, E. *Jesu Stellung zum Alten Testament*, Kiel, 1904.

KNIGHT, G. A. F. *Law and Grace*, London, 1962.

KNOX, J. *The Ethic of Jesus in the Teaching of the Church*, London, 1962.

KNOX, W. L. *The Sources of the Synoptic Gospels*, Cambridge, 1953–7.

KOCH, K. *Die Priesterschrift von Exod. 25 bis Lev. 16*, Göttingen, 1959.
The Rediscovery of Apocalyptic, London, ET 1972.

KÖHLER, L. *Old Testament Theology*, London, ET 1957.

LADD, G. E. *Jesus and the Kingdom*, London, 1966.

LAGRANGE, M.-J. *Le Judaïsme avant Jésus Christ*, Paris, 1931.

LAKE, K., and JACKSON, F. J. F. (ed.) *The Beginnings of Christianity*, London, 1920–6.

LAUTERBACH, J. *Rabbinic Essays*, Cincinnati, 1951.

LAZARUS, M. *The Ethics of Judaism*, London, 1900–1.

LEIPOLDT, J. *Jesu Verhältnis zu Griechen und Juden*, Leipzig, 1941.

LESZYNSKY, R. *Die Sadduzäer*, Berlin, 1912.

LIGHTFOOT, R. H. *History and Interpretation in the Gospels*, London, 1935.

LIGHTLEY, J. W. *Jewish Sects and Parties in the Time of Jesus*, London, 1925.

LIMBECK, M. *Die Ordnung des Heils: Untersuchungen zum Gesetzesverständnis der Frühjudentums*, Dusseldorf, 1971.

LINDBLOM, J. *Prophecy in Ancient Israel*, Oxford, 1962.

LINDESKOG, G. *Die Jesusfrage im neuzeitlichen Judentum*, Leipzig, 1938.

LJUNGMANN, H. *Das Gesetz Erfüllen: Matt. 5.17ff. und 3.15 Untersucht*, Lund, 1954.

LOHMEYER, E. *Diatheke*, 1913.
Lord of the Temple, Edinburgh, ET 1961.

LONGENECKER, R. N. *Paul, Apostle of Liberty*, New York, 1964.

MCARTHUR, H. K. *Understanding the Sermon on the Mount*, London, 1961.

MCCARTHY, D. J. *Treaty and Covenant*, Rome, 1963.
Der Gottesbund im Alten Testament, Stuttgart, 1967².

MACDONALD, J. *The Theology of the Samaritans*, London, 1964.

MACKINTOSH, R. *Christ and the Jewish Law*, London, 1886.

MCNAMARA, M. *The New Testament and the Palestinian Targum to the Pentateuch*, Rome, 1966.

MALDWYN-HUGHES, H. *The Ethics of the Jewish Apocryphal Literature*, London, 1909.

MANSON, T. W. *The Sayings of Jesus*, London, 1954.
Ethics and the Gospel, London, 1960.
The Teaching of Jesus, Cambridge, 1963².

MANSON, W. *Jesus the Messiah*, London, 1943.

MARCUS, R. *Law in the Apocrypha*, New York, 1927.

MARRIOTT, H. *The Sermon on the Mount*, London, 1925.

MARSH, J. *The Fulness of Time*, London, 1952.

MARSHALL, L. H. *The Challenge of New Testament Ethics*, London, 1946.

MARTIN, R. P. *Mark: Evangelist and Theologian*, Exeter, 1972.

MAUSER, U. *Christ in the Wilderness*, London, 1963.

MEEKS, W. A. *The Prophet-King*, Leiden, 1967.

MEINHOLD, A. J. *Jesus und das Alte Testament*, Freiburg, 1896.

MEYER, E. *Ursprung und Anfänge des Christentums*, Stuttgart, 1925.

MEYER, R. *Der Prophet aus Galiläa*, Leipzig, 1940.

MOFFATT, J. *The Theology of the Gospels*, London, 1912.

MONTEFIORE, C. G. *The Synoptic Gospels*, London, 1927².
Rabbinic Literature and Gospel Teachings, London, 1930.

MORGENSTERN, J. *Some Significant Antecedents of Christianity*, Leiden, 1966.

MURPHY, R. E. *The Dead Sea Scrolls and the Bible*, Westminster, 1957.

MURRAY, J. *The Covenant of Grace*, London, 1954.
Principles of Conduct, London, 1957.

NÄGELSBACH, F. *Der Schlüssel zum Verständnis der Bergpredigt*, Gütersloh, 1916.

NEPPER-CHRISTENSEN, P. *Das Matthäusevangelium – ein judenchristliches Evangelium?*, Aarhus, 1958.

NEUHÄUSLER, E. *Anspruch und Antwort Gottes*, Düsseldorf, 1962.

NEWMAN, M. *The People of the Covenant*, New York, 1962.

NIEDERWIMMER, K. *Der Begriff die Freiheit im neuen Testament*, Berlin, 1966

NIELSEN, E. *The Ten Commandments in New Perspective*, London, 1968.

NÖTSCHER, F. *Zur theologischen Terminologie der Qumran-texten*, Bonn, 1956.

NOLL, P. *Jesus und das Gesetz*, Tübingen, 1968.

NORMANN, F. *Christos Didaskalos*, Münster, 1966.

NORTH, C. R. *The Old Testament Interpretation of History*, London, 1946.

ÖSTBORN, G. *Tora in the Old Testament*, Lund, 1945.

OESTERLEY, W. O. E. *The Religion and Worship of the Synagogue*, London, 1911.
The Jews and Judaism during the Greek Period, London, 1941.

OTT, A. *Die Ehescheidung im Matthäusevangelium*, Würzburg, 1939.

VAN OYEN, H. *Ethik des Alten Testaments*, Gütersloh, 1967.

PARKES, J. *Jesus, Paul and the Jews*, London, 1936.

PAUL, S. M. *Studies in the Book of the Covenant in the Light of Cuneiform and Biblical Law*, Leiden, 1970.

PERCY, E. *Die Botschaft Jesu*, Lund, 1953.

PERLITT, L. *Bundestheologie im Alten Testament*, Neukirchen, 1969.

PERRIN, N. *Rediscovering the Teaching of Jesus*, London, 1967.

PHILLIPS, A. N. *Ancient Israel's Criminal Law*, Oxford, 1970.

PREISKER, H. *Das Ethos des Urchristentums*, Gütersloh, 1949.
Die Ethik der Evangelien und die jüdischen Apokalyptik, 1915.

QUESNELL, Q. *The Mind of Mark: Interpretation and Method through the Exegesis of Mark 6.52*, Rome, 1969.

VON RAD, G. *Studies in Deuteronomy*, London, ET 1953.
Das Geschichtsbild des chronistischen Werkes, Stuttgart, 1930.
Old Testament Theology, Edinburgh, 1961–5.
Wisdom in Israel, Edinburgh, ET 1972.

RAMSEY, P. *Basic Christian Ethics*, London, 1953.

REICKE, B. *Die Zehn Worte in Geschichte und Gegenwart*, Tübingen, 1972.

REIMARUS, H. S. *Von dem Zwecke Jesu und seiner Jünger*, Brunswick, 1778.

RIDDERBOS, H. N. *Matthew's Witness to Christ*, London, 1958.

RIDDLE, D. W. *Jesus and the Pharisees*, Chicago, 1928.

RITSCHL, A. *Die Entstehung der altkatholischen Kirche*, Bonn, 1850.

ROBERTSON, A. T. *The Pharisees and Jesus*, New York, 1920.

ROBINSON, H. W. *Inspiration and Revelation in the Old Testament*, Oxford, 1946.

ROBINSON, J. M. *The Problem of History in Mark*, London, 1957.

RÖSSLER, D. *Gesetz und Geschichte: Untersuchungen zur Theologie der jüdischen Apokalyptik und der pharisäischen Orthodoxie*, Neukirchen, 1960.

RÖTHLISBERGER, H. *Kirche am Sinai*, Zürich, 1965.

ROHDE, J. *Rediscovering the Teaching of the Evangelists*, London, ET 1969.

RORDORF, W. *Sunday*, London, ET 1968.

ROWLEY, H. H. *The Biblical Theology of Election*, London, 1950.

RUSSELL, D. S. *The Method and Message of Jewish Apocalyptic*, London, 1964.

SANDER, F. *Furcht und Liebe im palästinischen Judentum*, 1935.

SANDMEL, S. *The First Christian Century in Judaism and Christianity*, New York, 1969.

SCHECHTER, S. *Some Aspects of Rabbinic Theology*, London, 1909.

SCHLATTER, A. *Die Theologie des Neuen Testaments*, Stuttgart, 1909–10.

SCHMAUCH, W. *Orte der Offenbarung und der Offenbarungsort im Neuen Testament*, Göttingen, 1956.

SCHNACKENBURG, R. *The Moral Teaching of the New Testament*, London, ET 1965.

SCHOEPS, H. J. *Theologie und Geschichte des Judenchristentums*, Tübingen, 1949.
Paul, the Theology of the Apostle in the Light of Jewish Religious History, London, ET 1961.

SCHRAMM, T. *Der Markus-Stoff bei Lukas*, Cambridge, 1971.

SCHREIBER, J. *Theologie des Vertrauens*, Hamburg, 1967.

SCHUBERT, K. *Die Religion des nachbiblischen Judentums*, Freiburg, 1955.

SCHÜRER, E. *A History of the Jewish People in the Time of Jesus Christ*, Edinburgh, ET 1896.
Das messianische Selbstbewusstsein Jesu Christi, Göttingen, 1903.

SCHULZ, S. *Die Stunde der Botschaft*, Hamburg, 1967.

SCHWEITZER, A. *The Mysticism of Paul the Apostle*, London, ET 1956².

SCHWEIZER, E. *Jesus*, London, ET 1971.

SCOTT, E. F. *The Ethical Teaching of Jesus*, New York, 1924.

SILVER, H. *A History of Messianic Speculation in Israel*, New York, 1927.

SJÖBERG, E. *Gott und die Sünder im der palästinischen Judentum*, 1939.

SMEND, R. *Die Bundesformel*, Zürich, 1963.

SMITH, M. *Tannaitic Parallels to the Gospels*, Philadelphia, 1951.

SNAITH, N. *The Distinctive Ideas of the Old Testament*, London, 1944.

SOIRON, TH. *Die Bergpredigt Jesu*, Freiburg, 1941.

SPENCER, F. A. M. *The Theory of Christ's Ethics*, London, 1929.

SPICQ, C. *Agapé dans le Nouveau Testament*, Paris, 1958.

STAERK, W. *Soter*, Gütersloh, 1933.

STAMM, J. J., and ANDREW, M. E *The Ten Commandments in Recent Research*, London, 1967.

STAUDINGER, J. *Die Bergpredigt*, Vienna, 1957.

STAUFFER, E. *Jesus and the Wilderness Community at Qumran*, Philadelphia, 1964.

STENDAHL, K. *The School of Matthew*, Lund, 1954.

STONEHOUSE, N. B. *The Witness of Luke to Christ*, London, 1951.
The Witness of Matthew and Mark to Christ, London, 1944.
Origins of the Synoptic Gospels, London, 1963.

STRAUSS, D. F. *Das Leben Jesu*, Tübingen, 1837².

STRECKER, G. *Der Weg der Gerechtigkeit*, Göttingen, 1962.

SUGGS, M. J. *Wisdom, Christology and Law in Matthew*, Cambridge, Mass., 1970.

SUHL, A. *Die Funktion der alttestamentlichen Zitate und Anspielungen im Markusevangelium*, Gütersloh, 1965.

TASKER, R. V. C. *The Old Testament in the New Testament*, London, 1946.

TAYLOR, V. *The Formation of the Gospel Tradition*, London, 1933.

TEEPLE, H. M. *The Mosaic Eschatological Prophet*, Philadelphia, 1957.

THOMPSON, J. A. *The Ancient Near Eastern Treaties and the Old Testament*, London, 1964.

THOMPSON, R. J. *Moses and the Law in a Century of Criticism since Graf*, Leiden, 1970.

THOMPSON, W. G. *Matthew's Advice to a Divided Community: Mt. 17.22 – 18.35*, Rome, 1970.

TILBORG, S. VAN. *The Jewish Leaders in Matthew*, Leiden, 1972.

TRILLING, W. *Das wahre Israel*, München, 1964³.

VERWEIJS, P. J. *Evangelium und neues Gesetz in der ältesten Christenheit bis auf Marcion*, Utrecht, 1960.

VOLZ, P. *Die Eschatologie der jüdischen Gemeinde im neutestamentlichen Zeitalter*, Hildesheim, 1966.

VRIEZEN, TH. C. *An Outline of Old Testament Theology*, Oxford, ET 1958.

WALKER, R. *Die Heilsgeschichte im ersten Evangelium*, Göttingen, 1967.

WALKER, T. *Jesus Christ and Jewish Teaching*, London, 1923.

WEINEL, H. *Die Bergpredigt*, Leipzig, 1920.

WEINFELD, M. *Deuteronomy and the Deuteronomic School*, Oxford, 1972.

WEISS, H. F. *Der Pharisäismus in lichte Überlieferung des Neuen Testaments*, Berlin, 1965.

WEISS, J. *Die Predigt Jesu vom Reich Gottes*, ed. F. Hahn, Göttingen, 1964[3].

VON WEIZÄCKER, C. *Untersuchungen über die evangelische Geschichte*, Freiburg, 1864[2].

WENHAM, J. W. *Our Lord's view of the Old Testament*, London, 1953.

WERNER, M. *Der Einfluss paulinischer Theologie im Markusevangelium*, Giessen, 1923.

WERNLE, P. *Jesus*, 1916.

WHITLEY, C. F. *The Prophetic Achievement*, London, 1963.

WIBBING, S. *Die Tugend- und Lasterkataloge im Neuen Testament*, Berlin, 1959.

WILDER, A. N. *Eschatology and Ethics in the Teaching of Jesus*, New York, 1950[2].

WINDISCH, H. *The Meaning of the Sermon on the Mount*, Philadelphia, 1941.

WREGE, H. TH. *Die Überlieferungsgeschichte der Bergpredigt*, Tübingen, 1968.

ZENGER, E. *Die Sinaitheophanie: Untersuchungen zum jahwistischen und elohistischen Geschichtswerk*, Stuttgart, 1972.

ZIMMERLI, W. *The Law and the Prophets. A Study of the Meaning of the Old Testament*, Oxford, 1965.

C DISSERTATIONS

BERGER, K. 'Die Gesetzesauslegung Jesu', München, 1968.

GUELICH, R. A. 'Not to Annul the Law Rather to Fulfil the Law and the Prophets', Hamburg, 1967.

HASLER, V. E. 'Gesetz und Evangelium in der alten Kirche bis Origenes', Zürich, 1953.

JACOB, L. 'Jesu Stellung zum mosaischen Gesetz', Göttingen, 1893.

KELLER, W. E. 'The Authority of Jesus as reflected in Mark 2.1–3.6', Cambridge, 1968.

LANWER, B. 'Jesu Stellung zum Gesetz auf dem Hintergrunde des Alten Testaments und Spätjudentums', Hilltrup, 1933.

DU PLESSIS, P. J. 'ΤΕΛΕΙΟΣ, The Idea of Perfection in the New Testament', Kampen, 1959.

PREISKER, H. 'Die Ethik der Evangelien und die jüdische Apokalyptik', Breslau, 1915.

STOTT, W. L. 'The Theology of the Christian Sunday in the Early Church', Oxford, 1966.

INDEX OF PASSAGES CITED

A. THE OLD TESTAMENT

281

B. THE APOCRYPHA AND PSEUDEPIGRAPHA OF THE OLD TESTAMENT

C. THE NEW TESTAMENT

D. THE DEAD SEA SCROLLS

E. RABBINIC LITERATURE

F. OTHER ANCIENT AND EARLY CHRISTIAN WRITINGS

INDEX OF AUTHORS